ENGLISH ACROSS THE CURRICULUM: VOICES FROM AROUND THE WORLD

INTERNATIONAL EXCHANGES ON THE STUDY OF WRITING

Series Editors: Joan Mullin, Magnus Gustafsson, Terry Myers Zawacki, and Federico Navarro

Series Associate Editors: Ana M. Cortés Lagos, Anna S. Habib, and Matthew Overstreet

The International Exchanges on the Study of Writing Series publishes books that address worldwide perspectives on writing, writers, teaching with writing, and scholarly writing practices, specifically those that draw on scholarship across national and disciplinary borders to challenge parochial understandings of all of the above. The Latin America Section of the International Exchanges on the Study of Writing book series publishes peer-reviewed books about writing, writers, teaching with writing, and scholarly writing practices from Latin American perspectives. It also offers re-editions of recognized peer-reviewed books originally published in the region.

The WAC Clearinghouse, Colorado State University Open Press, and University Press of Colorado are collaborating so that these books will be widely available through free digital distribution and low-cost print editions. The publishers and the series editors are committed to the principle that knowledge should freely circulate. We see the opportunities that new technologies have for further democratizing knowledge. And we see that to share the power of writing is to share the means for all to articulate their needs, interest, and learning into the great experiment of literacy.

Recent Books in the Series

Alanna Frost, Julia Kiernan, and Suzanne Blum Malley (Eds.), *Translingual Dispositions: Globalized Approaches to the Teaching of Writing* (2020)

Charles Bazerman, Blanca Yaneth González Pinzón, David Russell, Paul Rogers, Luis Bernardo Peña, Elizabeth Narváez, Paula Carlino, Montserrat Castelló & Mónica Tapia-Ladino (Eds.), *Knowing Writing: Writing Research across Borders* (2019)

Sylvie Plane, Charles Bazerman, Fabienne Rondelli, Christiane Donahue, Arthur N. Applebee, Catherine Boré, Paula Carlino, Martine Marquilló Larruy, Paul Rogers & David Russell (Eds.), *Research on Writing: Multiple Perspectives* (2017)

Lisa R. Arnold, Anne Nebel & Lynne Ronesi (Eds.), *Emerging Writing Research from the Middle East-North Africa Region* (2017)

ENGLISH ACROSS THE CURRICULUM: VOICES FROM AROUND THE WORLD

Edited by Bruce Morrison, Julia Chen, Linda Lin, and Alan Urmston

The WAC Clearinghouse
wac.colostate.edu
Fort Collins, Colorado

University Press of Colorado
upcolorado.com
Louisville, Colorado

The WAC Clearinghouse, Fort Collins, Colorado 80523

University Press of Colorado, Louisville, Colorado 80027

© 2021 by Bruce Morrison, Julia Chen, Linda Lin, and Alan Urmston. This work is licensed under a Creative Commons Attribution-NonCommercial-NoDerivatives 4.0 International License.

ISBN 978-1-64215-122-0 (PDF) | 978-1-64215-123-7 (ePub) | 978-1-64642-222-7 (pbk.)

DOI 10.37514/INT-B.2021.1220

Library of Congress Cataloging-in-Publication Data

Names: Morrison, Bruce, 1956– editor.
Title: English across the curriculum : voices from around the world / edited by Bruce Morrison, Julia Chen, Linda Lin, and Alan Urmston.
Description: Fort Collins, Colorado : The WAC Clearinghouse ; Louisville, Colorado : University Press of Colorado, 2021. | Series: International exchanges on the study of writing | Includes bibliographical references.
Identifiers: LCCN 2021012975 (print) | LCCN 2021012976 (ebook) | ISBN 9781646422227 (paperback) | ISBN 9781642151220 (pdf) | ISBN 9781642151237 (epub)
Subjects: LCSH: English language—Rhetoric—Study and teaching—Foreign speakers. | Academic writing—Study and teaching. | Report writing—Study and teaching. | Language arts—Correlation with content subjects. | Second language acquisition.
Classification: LCC PE1128.A2 E4645 2021 (print) | LCC PE1128.A2 (ebook) | DDC 428.0071—dcundefined
LC record available at https://lccn.loc.gov/2021012975
LC ebook record available at https://lccn.loc.gov/2021012976

Copyeditor: Meg Vezzu
Design and Production: Mike Palmquist
Cover Photo: English Language Centre, The Hong Kong Polytechnic University. Used with permission.
Series Editors: Terry Myers Zawacki, Magnus Gustafsson, Joan Mullin, and Federico Navarro
Series Associate Editors: Ana M. Cortés Lagos, Anna S. Habib, and Matthew Overstreet

The WAC Clearinghouse supports teachers of writing across the disciplines. Hosted by Colorado State University, and supported by the Colorado State University Open Press, it brings together scholarly journals and book series as well as resources for teachers who use writing in their courses. This book is available in digital formats for free download at wac.colostate.edu.

Founded in 1965, the University Press of Colorado is a nonprofit cooperative publishing enterprise supported, in part, by Adams State University, Colorado State University, Fort Lewis College, Metropolitan State University of Denver, University of Colorado, University of Northern Colorado, University of Wyoming, Utah State University, and Western Colorado University. For more information, visit upcolorado.com.

Contents

Introduction 3
    Julia Chen and Bruce Morrison

SECTION ONE. ENGLISH ACROSS THE CURRICULUM

1. Supporting Undergraduate Student Learning through Reflective Journal Writing in a Service-Learning Subject: An Interdisciplinary Collaborative Approach....................................... 17
    Felicia Fang and Yammy Chak

2. Gaps in Content-Based English Enhancement in Science and Engineering... 35
    Barbara WY Siu

3. Students' Perceptions of the Use of English in a Core Business Subject for First-Year Business Students......................... 59
    Hannah Y. Lai and King-Wah Pang

4. Engaging and Empowering Scientific Writers in Different Disciplines... 73
    John Blake and William R. Holden III

5. Helping Students from Different Disciplines with their Final Year/Capstone Project: Supervisors' and Students' Needs and Requests 91
    Julia Chen, Christy Chan, Vicky Man, and Elza Tsang

SECTION TWO. CONTENT AND LANGUAGE INTEGRATED LEARNING

6. Impacts and Challenges of a Mobile App for Improving Final-Year Project Proposal Writing: A Case from a Hong Kong University.... 109
    Grace Yuk Wan Lim and Ivan Wang-Hei Ho

7. Teacher Perspectives on Content and Language-Integrated Learning in Taiwan: Motivations, Implementation Factors, and Future Directions..127
    Jeffrey Hugh Gamble

8. GREATCLIL Camps Integrating School-Based Curricula: An Analysis of Learning Motivation in Remote Areas of Taiwan ... 149
    Ai Chun Yen

Contents

9. Testing the Effect of Asynchronous Discussions in a Language and Content-Integrated Hybrid Course 171
   Sinh Ngoc Dang

10. Theatrical Texts in Content and Language Integrated Learning 187
    Alan Thompson

Section Three. Writing Across the Curriculum

11. WAC and Critical Thinking: Exploring Productive Relationships . . . 207
    Mike Palmquist

12. Critical Thinking, Writing, and Language Learning: A Report from Northwest China 223
    Matthew Overstreet

13. Using the Onion Model to Scaffold the Case Analysis Genre in Information Systems 239
    Maria Pia Gomez-Laich, Thomas D. Mitchell, Silvia Pessoa, and Michael Maune

14. Beyond "Coping" to Natural Language Work: A Case Study at a Transnational Campus 255
    Jay Jordan

15. Correctness Revisited: How Students (Mis)Identify and Comment on Error in Peers' Drafts 271
    Chris M. Anson

16. The Praxis of Innovation in Writing Programs 293
    Andy Frazee and Rebecca E. Burnett

17. The (Transnational) Past, Present, and Future of the Writing Across the Curriculum Movement 311
    Martha A. Townsend, Terry Myers Zawacki, Mike Palmquist, and Julia Chen

Contributors 331

ENGLISH ACROSS THE CURRICULUM: VOICES FROM AROUND THE WORLD

§ Introduction

Julia Chen and Bruce Morrison
THE HONG KONG POLYTECHNIC UNIVERSITY

In December 2018, The Hong Kong Polytechnic University (PolyU) hosted the Second International English Across the Curriculum (EAC) Conference, with over 100 presentations, colloquia, and participants from 20 countries as well as mainland China and Macau. Both the first and second conferences were planned with three major goals in mind: one, to announce that writing across the curriculum (WAC)—in the form of EAC—is once more a feature of the Hong Kong tertiary landscape, framed by a policy of biliteracy and trilingualism and featuring complicated relationships between politics and language education decisions (Chen, 2020); two, to learn from those who have had considerable experience developing EAC, WAC, and content and language integrated learning (CLIL) initiatives in various international contexts; and three, to provide a platform for exchanging scholarship of teaching and learning on disciplinary literacy, especially in contexts where English is learned as an additional language (EAL).

For many participants, the EAC conferences were their first introduction to pedagogical movements that embed writing and speaking in content courses with a view to heightening faculty and students' awareness of the need for disciplinary literacy development. In many parts of Asia, the continent with the highest number of indigenous languages (Eberhard et al., 2020), the mother tongue is most often a language other than English, and the learning of English is often limited to generic English language lessons. Some schools and universities employ English as the medium of instruction (EMI), despite studies showing the benefits of mother tongue instruction and a strong correlation between academic achievements and learning in the mother tongue (Benson, 2004; Kosonen, 2005; Parba, 2018; Perez & Alieto, 2018). The use of EMI is often driven by socio-political, ideological, and economic reasons, including government policies, parent-driven demands, resourcing justifications, globalisation efforts, identity negotiations, and future study and career advances (Baldauf Jr. et al., 2011; Evans, 2017; Hu & McKay, 2012; Kosonen, 2005; Lin & Man, 2009; Parba, 2018; Rahman & Pandian, 2018). However, even in EMI institutions, where content subjects are taught in English, language use itself is not generally considered a part of learning content, and literacy in the disciplines is little developed.

DOI: https://doi.org/10.37514/INT-B.2021.1220.1.3

Exigence for English Across the Curriculum

The teaching of English tends mainly to take the form of compulsory English language subjects, which are often generic in nature even at university level. Owing to limited curriculum space in the undergraduate programme, academic English subjects are usually taken only in the first or second year. While such English courses are valuable in laying the linguistic foundation for academic pursuit, they may not be adequate for students, especially those studying at an EMI university, to then effectively apply these recently acquired generic academic English language skills in their major subjects.

In the hope of increasing students' exposure to English and their opportunities to use the language in authentic learning contexts, a number of schools and universities where English is not the mother tongue have introduced content-based language-learning. This is done in the belief that "content and language create a symbiotic relationship" (Stoller, 2008, p. 59) that helps students more effectively learn both the content and the language appropriate to content dissemination and discussion. Schools and universities in various contexts (Cheyne & Rummel, 2015; Ito, 2018; Suwannoppharat & Chinokul, 2015; Thuy, 2016; Tsou, 2018) employ a Content and Language Integrated Learning (CLIL) approach, which accords a strong focus on both content and the language of instruction in a content course (Coyle, 2007; Marsh, 2012). The implementation of this dual-focused approach has spread quickly in Europe and in some parts of Asia, with an aim to create multilingual citizens who can function in cross-cultural situations (European Commission, 2010). It is, however, often implemented in less than half of the school curriculum, and finding suitable teachers who can teach the content and have language teaching qualifications is a challenge (Dalton-Puffer, 2011).

Another challenge of an approach that places equal emphasis on content and language lies in the curriculum. It is not always possible to rewrite content courses so that there is explicit emphasis on both content and language learning in the same lesson throughout the duration of the course. It is more feasible to introduce some language elements without disrupting the flow of the content course and without changing the course design or its outcomes. Thus, when a funding opportunity arose in 2013 at The Hong Kong Polytechnic University, a community of practice (CoP) was established. Unlike attempting to develop CLIL, which with its dual focus would cause very considerable upheaval to the undergraduate curriculum and meet resistance in the Hong Kong university context, the CoP would build a cross-disciplinary community of teachers for EAC, a localized version of WAC that is more relevant for the Hong Kong tertiary context. Integral to the notion of

WAC, and by extension EAC, is that writing skills (or in the case of EAC, writing and speaking literacy skills) are acquired not only in language courses, but at different points in the curriculum via disciplinary courses offered by disciplinary experts (Keifer et al., 2000–2018). Unlike CLIL, in WAC and EAC, the content often remains the main focus of the content courses that are mediated through English, and students are given the additional language support that they need to successfully learn the content and complete the written and spoken course assessments in the target language.

Two subsequent grants, including one for a four-university project, enabled the organisation of two international EAC conferences, in 2015 and 2018. Although they were held in Hong Kong, speakers and presenters came from different continents, and their presentations resonated with both new EAC endeavours as well as mature WAC and CLIL curricula alike. For instance, many institutions mandate the use of English for academic studies but have a tight curriculum that does not allow the inclusion of more than a minimal number of standalone English proficiency or writing courses to support students in their acquisition of language and literacy skills for academic success. In such a context, EAC can be a feasible and valuable complement to existing English for Academic Purposes and English for Specific Purposes courses as the department-centered approach integrates the learning of writing into discipline courses. EAC brings together English teachers and academic faculty to help their students learn and perform better in course-embedded assessments. Faculty often feel frustrated with their students' poor writing or oral presentations, but do not know how—or feel they are not in a position—to address these problems. As non-native speakers of English themselves, many faculty have reservations about their own English language ability as well as about their competence to help students with their English, viewing the latter as the job of English teachers (Annous & Nicolas, 2015; Chen et al., 2020; Goldsmith & Willey, 2016). To address faculty concerns and enhance the academic literacy that their students need in their discipline (Wingate, 2018), English teachers can "work hand in hand with faculty members to draw students' attention to disciplinary academic English when they complete assignments in their content courses" (Chen, 2020, p. 121).

However, even when English teachers seek collaboration from faculty, it is not easy to implement EAC/WAC/CLIL (hereafter EAC). There are common issues that institutions face, especially in EAL educational contexts and including those that have a large body of international students in countries where English is the main and official language. Institutional restrictions, such as education policies and the lack of curriculum space, determine how much (or little) room there is for creative flexibility in offering language or literacy support. Even when the overall institutional environment favours experimentation with EAC, those leading the EAC effort still face numerous challenges, such as manpower (especially when the support of graduate teaching assistants that is afforded in some institutions [e.g., Lannin & Townsend, 2020] is scarce or non-existent), resources, departmental support, and the extent to which disciplinary academics are willing to collaborate in discussing and designing the EAC intervention and linking EAC materials to disciplinary knowledge. Another issue that EAC practitioners face is that in situations where the EAL learners' proficiency is low but the expected output is fairly genre-specific and demanding (e.g., a review or a capstone report), EAC support cannot solely focus on higher order constructs, such as organisation and genre, but also has to address lower order concerns (Zawacki & Cox, 2011) as learners grapple with basic grammatical problems before they can develop literacy and rhetorical skills. To compound this situation, when student motivation is low, scaffolding the development of language skills can be doubly hard; and it can be challenging to find an opportune time to introduce the EAC intervention for greater impact. The fact that language teachers may not have relevant disciplinary content knowledge means that they will have to devote time to the analysis of disciplinary genre and discourse features as well as to student writing and speaking performances in order to prepare EAC materials that will not be too general but will be useful to students taking different majors. The multiple issues that EAC teams face signal the need for faculty professional development (Zemliansky & Berry, 2017); and in this digital age, some thoughts can also be given to the use of technology and multimodal activities (Hill, 2014) to achieve EAC goals and continue EAC programmes.

After the design and development of EAC support materials, challenges remain upon implementation. Under the quality assurance culture pervasive in education around the world, EAC teams are expected to evaluate the effectiveness of their intervention and conduct scholarship of teaching and learning to collect and analyse data, in order to inform future practices and reiterations. Even bigger challenges relate to securing continuous funding, addressing EAC programme vulnerabilities (Townsend, 2012), identifying where EAC will be housed (Smith, 1988), and ultimately determining how it can be sustained. These considerations resonate in different forms at various educational levels, from schools (Mullin & Childers, 2020), through undergraduate studies (Nielsen, 2019), to doctoral programmes (Rogers et al., 2015). To justify and support the continuation of EAC, there is a pressing need for EAC initiatives to find an operational model that engages faculty in a trusted relationship with language teachers that can lead to a win-all situation for themselves, their students, and EAC more broadly (Routman, 2014). It is also crucial for EAC to show its educational value, including its effects on enriching the student learning experience, and, through conducting writing tests and textual analysis, any improvement in student performance (Chen et al., 2020). Learning analytics, increasingly used in many aspects of education evaluation, can bring to bear a further possible suite of tools to identify needs, gaps, and areas for further development (Palmquist, 2020).

Practitioner efforts and the challenges faced helping students develop language and literacy skills in their discipline studies are shared by EAC, WAC, and CLIL scholars in many parts of the world. The papers presented at the first and second International Conferences on English Across the Curriculum offered insights into both the enthusiasm and the concerns of teachers and other practitioners from different countries as they drew on EAC/WAC/CLIL principles and practices in developing their localized models with passion in response to their unique linguistic and multifaceted cultural contexts to meet their respective situational needs and challenges.

The Volume

We are pleased that the EAC conferences have provided a platform for the exchange of lessons learnt, learning of new strategies and directions, and sharing of experiences. The organising committee of the second EAC conference decided it was important to capture some of the richness of ideas and practice that emerged from the conference presentations by researchers and educators from around the world. The editorial panel, comprising Bruce Morrison and Julia Chen together with PolyU colleagues Linda Lin and Alan Urmston, considered manuscripts submitted on a wide range of topics and, after a carefully monitored process of blind review, finally selected 17 for *English Across the Curriculum: Voices from Around the World*. We believe this volume will speak to not only practitioners who work in the same cities as the writers but also to scholars elsewhere in the global village, whether they are considering starting an EAC-like initiative or are already involved in an established WAC/CLIL programme.

Section One: English Across the Curriculum

Five of the authors of papers in the first section work in Hong Kong, with the sixth a previous resident. This demographic indeed reflects the points outlined earlier in this introduction with regard to the Hong Kong roots of the present iteration of EAC. The papers focus on the experience of an EAC approach based primarily on the perceptions of students, from various disciplines and at various stages of their academic careers, with issues relating to the necessary collaboration between language centre and subject host department teachers of central importance.

The first three papers focus on EAC initiatives that aim to support undergraduate students' use of English appropriate to the different disciplines in which they are studying and for potential contexts in which they may find themselves working in the future. The students in Felicia Fang and Yammy Chak's study are supported by teachers from the English Language Centre in collaboration with the subject content teacher with the aim of enhancing and operationalising the discipline-related academic writing skills needed for the writing of a reflective journal. Bringing a perspective from an academic from the field of civil engineering, in the next paper, Barbara Siu's primary aim is devising content-based strategies to support the enhancement of her students' language skills as they studied within an engineering curriculum where communication is multimodal. While reporting the positive effects perceived by students involved in her project, she also reveals challenges familiar to many language enhancement initiatives, particularly in relation to the limited opportunities for language practice and a lack of student motivation. Effective language is recognised as crucial to success in the business world, and effectively bringing this to students' attention is one way of raising extrinsic student motivation. Hannah Lai and Anthony Pang examine the perceptions of Faculty of Business students regarding the explicit inclusion of language use in the assessment rubric of a core business subject.

The next three papers in this section turn the EAC focus to support of post-graduate and final-year undergraduate students. Working in a research institute in Japan, John Blake and William R. Holden III report on how student scientific writers are supported in writing for publication. An approach incorporating writing courses and face-to-face writing conferences is supplemented with online support and tools that enable automated 24/7 feedback. Blake and Holden's focus on the importance of online support and feedback for students is also reflected in the last two papers in this section, both of which relate to the development of a mobile app for final-year undergraduates. Introducing the development of an app to support students in their writing of a capstone project, Julia Chen and her team identify the need to support students in the writing of probably the longest report they will have had to complete and then explain the research processes employed to collect stakeholder data and analyse the areas of capstone report writing that present the greatest challenge for students. In their paper, Grace Lim and Ivan Ho present the data from an evaluation of the app, which aims to enhance

Introduction

students' project proposal writing through the provision of language tips and their project management skills through a project scheduling tool.

Section Two: Content and Language Integrated Learning

Asia again provides the background for the four papers in this section, focusing on CLIL initiatives hosted in very differing educational contexts. These range from large-scale studies including nearly 4,000 pupil participants from across Taiwan, to a comparative study of CLIL-based and more traditionally taught classes in Vietnam, and the impact of the use of theatrical texts in a class in Japan.

The first two papers in this section have their home in Taiwan. Reporting on a two-year project, Jeffrey Gamble examines CLIL implementation across Taiwan, investigating the beliefs, attitudes, and challenges of English teachers involved. This teacher-focused investigation is then complemented by a large-scale study by Ai Chun Yen, whose focus is on the motivation of students participating in CLIL summer camps and those in camps following a "traditional" curriculum. Ai Chun Yen finds stronger intrinsic and extrinsic motivation amongst the students following a CLIL-focused curriculum, with students more positive about developing language competence and able to retain strong recognition of the importance of the content being taught.

The last two papers in this section report on a CLIL intervention in a course taught in Vietnam and Japan, respectively. Sinh Ngoc Dang explores the effects of introducing asynchronous discussion into a hybrid course that included American economic history and English language in the syllabus, concluding that student academic performance was enhanced when compared to that in a more "traditional" class. Also introducing a new language-focused element into his class with the use of theatrical texts as content learning resources, Alan Thompson examines the effects of learners' hearing, practising, and reflecting on the texts.

Section Three: Writing Across the Curriculum

Unsurprisingly, while two chapters focus on studies carried out in China (Chapter 12) and Qatar (Chapter 13) respectively, all but one of the chapters in this section hail from U.S. universities. The section is bookended by a paper from Mike Palmquist based upon his plenary presentation and one from Martha Townsend, Terry Zawacki, Mike Palmquist, and Julia Chen that draws upon the end-of-conference panel discussion in which they participated.

Critical thinking is quite rightly considered to be a necessary precursor to effective academic writing. In his chapter, Mike Palmquist considers the role of three types of WAC learning and teaching activities that promote critical thinking and contribute to a student's disciplinary and language learning. Matthew Overstreet focuses on enhancing critical thinking instruction in a university in Northwest China by drawing upon WAC principles. While he found that the need for such an innovation was well-recognised, he also encountered a number of significant structural and cultural obstacles. Recognising the need for critical analysis in the development of a case analysis in the field of information systems, Maria Gomez-Laich and her team based at Carnegie Mellon University Qatar present an example of how students' academic writing might be more effectively scaffolded through employing interdisciplinary modeling of the writing process.

Jay Jordan and Chris Anson both examine different aspects of tertiary student language awareness. In his chapter, Jay Jordan analyses the ways that "Alice," an undergraduate Korean student, used "coping strategies" that were aimed at providing professors with what she believed they required, and strove to pursue "natural" language acquisition. He further reflects on the nature of transnational education and the roles that student and instructor interactions play. Chris Anson's study reveals that one in four "errors" identified by students in their peers' drafts were not in fact errors, and only one in ten errors made were identified. He points towards instructional ideology and written genre as influencing the accuracy of error identification.

The final two papers focus on WAC as a movement, the first in terms of the role for innovation in individual writing programs, the second in terms of examining the past and present of WAC, and considering its future. Andy Frazee and Rebecca Burnett discuss innovation as a transformational element in writing programmes, impacting not only the programme, faculty, and students, but also the innovators themselves. Within the context of the mission of a writing centre creating "a space for innovation," they first discuss characteristics of faculty professional development before going on to examine characteristics of the learning and teaching process, and then suggest questions that other writing centre programmes might consider when trying to make innovation a more central aspect of their centre's mission and work. After discussion of one specific element that might be seen as central to WAC, the volume concludes with a paper that expands on the conference's closing plenary session where Martha Townsend, Terry Zawacki, Mike Palmquist, and Julia Chen take a more panoramic view, presenting their takes on the development of the WAC movement and the trails it might potentially follow.

Concluding Remarks

The chapters in this volume testify to challenges faced, opportunities presented, and a passion displayed for embedding academic English literacy in content/discipline subjects in institutions around the world. They also illustrate the persistence of teachers in creating and shaping valuable learning experiences and ongoing support for their students. At the time of writing, the four-university team that put together the first EAC Conference in Hong Kong has now become a five-university team that has received a further government grant to enhance students' academic English for capstone/final-year projects via the development of a mobile app, so as to provide a technologically-supported writing environment (Palmquist, 2003) for the digital generation. The volume editors are hopeful that more localised forms of EAC might blossom and flourish around the world in the endless pursuit of providing better language and literacy education for students.

Acknowledgements

We would like to thank our other two editors, Linda Lin and Alan Urmston, as well as Belle Choi, whose tireless efficiency has been very instrumental in this volume reaching publication. We are also thankful to the WAC Clearinghouse, a beacon in the expansion of the WAC movement, with its open-access journals and books that provide invaluable resources for those keen to bring EAC, WAC, and CLIL to their home institution. Their support and belief in us have been pivotal in the volume's compilation.

References

Annous, S. & Nicolas, M. O. (2015). Academic territorial borders: A look at the writing ethos in business courses in an environment in which English is a foreign language. *Journal of Business and Technical Communication, 29*(1), 93–111.

Baldauf Jr., R. B., Kaplan, R. B., Kamwangamalu, N. & Bryant, P. (2011). Success or failure of primary second/foreign language programmes in Asia: What do the data tell us? *Current Issues in Language Planning, 12*(2), 309–323.

Benson, C. (2004). *The importance of mother tongue-based schooling for educational quality*. Background paper for the EFA Global Monitoring Report 2005. UNESCO.

Chen, J. (2020). EAP in Hong Kong. In H. Terauchi, J. Noguchi & A. Tajino (Eds.), *Towards a new paradigm for English language teaching: English for specific purposes in Asia and beyond* (pp. 115–126). Routledge.

Chen, J., Chan, C. & Ng, A. (2020). English across the curriculum: Four journeys of synergy across disciplines and universities. In B. Spolsky & H. Lee (Eds.),

Localizing global English: Asian perspectives and practices (pp. 84–103). Routledge

Cheyne, P. & Rummel, E. (2015). Materials development for a Japanese university CLIL class. *ELTWorldOnline.com, Special Issue on CLIL*. http://blog.nus.edu.sg/eltwo/?p=4858.

Coyle, D. (2007). Content and language integrated learning: Towards a connected research agenda for CLIL pedagogies. *International Journal of Bilingual Education and Bilingualism, 10*(5), 543–562.

Dalton-Puffer, C. (2011). Content-and-language integrated learning: From practice to principles? *Annual Review of Applied Linguistics, 31*, 182–204.

Eberhard, D. M., Simons, G. F. & Fennig, C. D. (Eds.). (2020). *Ethnologue: Languages of the world* (23rd ed.). SIL International. http://www.ethnologue.com.

European Commission. (2010). *European language policy and CLIL: A selection of EU-funded projects*. www.edu.xunta.gal/centros/cpicruce/system/files/clilbroch_en.pdf.

Evans, S. (2017). Language policy in Hong Kong education: A historical overview. *European Journal of Language Policy, 9*(1), 67–84.

Goldsmith, R. & Willey, K. (2016). "It's not my job to teach writing": Activity theory analysis of [invisible] writing practices in the engineering curriculum. *Journal of Academic Language & Learning, 10*(1), A118–129.

Hill, A. (2014). Using interdisciplinary, project-based, multimodal activities to facilitate literacy across the content areas. *Journal of Adolescent & Adult Literacy, 57*(5), 450–460.

Hu, K. & McKay, S. L. (2012). English language education in East Asia: Some recent developments. *Journal of Multilingual and Multicultural Development, 33*(4), 345–362. https://doi.org/10.1080/01434632.2012.661434.

Kiefer, K., Palmquist, M., Carbone, N., Cox, M. & Melzer, D. (2000–2018). *An introduction to writing across the curriculum*. Fort Collins, CO: The WAC Clearinghouse. Retrieved from http://wac.colostate.edu/resources/wac/intro.

Ito, Y. (2018). CLIL in practice in Japanese elementary classrooms: An analysis of the effectiveness of a CLIL lesson in Japanese traditional crafts. *English Language Teaching, 11*(9), 59–67.

Kosonen, K. (2005). Education in local languages: Policy and practice in South-East Asia. In UNESCO, *First language first: Community-based literacy programmes for minority language contexts in Asia* (pp. 96–134). UNESCO.

Lannin, A. & Townsend, M. (2020). Graduate student perspectives: Career development through serving as writing-intensive GTAs. In M. Brooks-Gillies, E. G. Garcia, S. H. Kim, K. Manthey & T. G. Smith (Eds.), *Graduate writing across the disciplines: Identifying, teaching, and supporting* (pp. 95–119). The WAC Clearinghouse; University Press of Colorado. https://doi.org/10.37614/ATD-B.2020.0407.2.04.

Lin, A. M. Y. & Man, E. Y. F. (2009). *Bilingual education: Southeast Asian perspectives*. Hong Kong University Press.

Marsh, D. (2012). Content and language integrated learning (CLIL): A development trajectory. Retrieved from https://core.ac.uk/download/pdf/60884824.pdf.

Mullin, J. A. & Childers, P. B. (2020). Still natural? A response to "The natural connection: The WAC Program and the high school writing center." *The Clearing House: A Journal of Educational Strategies, Issues and Ideas, 93*(6), 271–276.

Nielsen, K. (2019). Peer and self-assessment practices for writing across the curriculum: Learner-differentiated effects on writing achievement. *Educational Review*. https://doi.org/10.1080/00131911.2019.1695104.

Palmquist, M. (2003). A brief history of computer support for writing centers and writing-across-the-curriculum programs. *Computers and Composition, 20*(4), 395–413.

Palmquist, M. (2020). Learning analytics in writing instruction: Implications for writing across the curriculum. In L. E. Bartlett, S. L. Tarabochia, A. R. Olinger & M. J. Marshall (Eds.), *Diverse approaches to teaching, learning, and writing across the curriculum: IWAC at 25*. The WAC Clearinghouse; University Press of Colorado. https://wac.colostate.edu/books/perspectives/iwac2018.

Parba, J. (2018). Teachers' shifting language ideologies and teaching practices in Philippine mother tongue classrooms. *Linguistics and Education, 47,* 27–35. https://doi.org/10.1016/j.linged.2018.07.005.

Perez, A. L. & Alieto, E. (2018). Change of "tongue" from English to a local language: A correlation of mother tongue proficiency and mathematics achievement. *The Asian ESP Journal, 14*(7.2), 132–150.

Rahman, M. M. & Pandian, A. (2018). The chaotic English language policy and planning in Bangladesh: Areas of apprehension. *Social Sciences & Humanities, 26*(2), 893–908.

Rogers, P., Zawacki, T. & Baker, S. (2016). Uncovering challenges and pedagogical implications in dissertation writing and supervisory practices: A multimethod study of doctoral students and advisors. In S. Simpson, N. Caplan, M. Cox & T. Phillips (Eds.), *Supporting graduate student writers: Research, curriculum, and program design* (pp. 52–77). University of Michigan Press.

Routman, R. (2014). *Read, write, lead: Breakthrough strategies for schoolwide literacy success*. ASCD.

Smith, L. Z. (1988). Why English departments should "house" writing across the curriculum. *College English, 50*(4), 390–395. Retrieved from https://www.jstor.org/stable/pdf/377611.pdf.

Stoller, F. L. (2008). Content-based instruction. In V. Deusen-Scholl & N. H. Hornberger (Eds.), *Encyclopedia of language and education: Vol 4. Second and foreign language education* (2nd ed., pp. 59–70). Springer Science/Business Media.

Suwannoppharat, K. & Chinokul, S. (2015). Applying CLIL to English language teaching in Thailand: Issues and challenges. *Latin American Journal of Content and Language Integrated Learning, 8*(2), 237–254. https://doi.org/10.5294/laclil.2015.8.2.8.

Townsend, M. A. (2012). WAC program vulnerability and what to do about it: An update and brief bibliographic essay. In T. M. Zawacki & P. M. Rogers (Eds.), *Writing across the curriculum: A critical sourcebook* (pp. 543–556). Bedford/St. Martin's.

Thuy, L. N. T. (2016). Reconsidering the first steps of CLIL implementation in Vietnam. *European Journal of Language Policy, 8,* 29–56. https://doi.org/10.3828/ejlp.2016.4.

Tsou, W. (2018). Implementing content language integrated learning (CLIL) in Taiwan: A review study. *PIM 1st International Conference.* https://conference.pim.ac.th/thai/wp-content/uploads/2017/09/K-EDUCATION-IN-THE-DIGITAL-AGE.pdf.

Wingate, U. (2018). Academic literacy across the curriculum: Towards a collaborative instructional approach. *Language Teaching, 51*(3), 349–364.

Zawacki, T. M. & Cox, M. (2011). Introduction to WAC and second language writing. *Across the Disciplines, 8*(4), 1–11. https://doi.org/10.37514/ATD-J.2011.8.4.19.

Zemliansky, P. & Berry, L. (2017). A writing-across-the-curriculum faculty development program: An experience report. *IEEE Transactions on Professional Communication, 60*(3), 306–316.

Section One. English Across the Curriculum

1 Supporting Undergraduate Student Learning through Reflective Journal Writing in a Service-Learning Subject: An Interdisciplinary Collaborative Approach

Felicia Fang and Yammy Chak
THE HONG KONG POLYTECHNIC UNIVERSITY

Abstract: This chapter reports the findings from the preliminary evaluation of an English Across the Curriculum (EAC) initiative in a Hong Kong university to implement discipline-specific academic English language support materials in a service-learning subject adopting an interdisciplinary collaborative approach. Student survey results, focus group interviews with both students and content teachers, and written reflections by students are presented and analysed. Findings indicate that students and teachers generally acknowledge the value of this interdisciplinary collaboration to improve the learning experience and the quality of assignments. Challenges that the EAC team has encountered in the process of collaborating are also discussed. Compared with previous studies, this chapter attempts to contextualise the strategy for integrating the teaching of content for a service-learning subject with discipline-specific academic English writing skills to undergraduate students with English as a Second or Foreign language (ESL/EFL) in Hong Kong.

Keywords: writing across the curriculum, English Across the Curriculum, service-learning, reflective journal writing, language tips

A number of studies in the last couple of decades have reported success in using reflective activities to support student learning in service-learning subjects in higher education (e.g., Hatcher & Bringle, 1997; Rogers, 2001). In Hong Kong, service-learning has gained increasing popularity. Through intentionally connecting community service activities to educational objectives in the university curriculum, service-learning programmes aim to cultivate students' social awareness and responsibility, nurture their sense of care and compassion for the underprivileged, and promote prosocial behaviours and life-long learning (Fang & Chak, 2018). Reflection activities are considered indispensable to effective service-learning as they enhance students' ability to connect their service activities to content learnt in the subject (Bringle & Hatcher, 1999), and the importance of using continuous academic reflection in service-learning programmes is well documented. It is believed that reflection activities help to consolidate the service experience and nurture the intellectual and cognitive development of students involved in the service activities (Eyler, 2002). Previous studies have reported practices and impacts of implementing academic reflection activities in service-learning subjects in a range of disciplines such as business, language, and medicine (Eyler, 2002). The reported benefits of implementing academic reflective journals include enhancing the learning skills for service-learning, developing more complex understanding of a particular topic, and centering students in the learning process (Cheng et al., 2016; Eyler, 2002; O'Connell & Dyment, 2011). Challenges have, however, also been observed in implementing reflective journals in the higher education context, including those related to the ethics of assessing personal reflections, lack of training provided to the student writers, the time required, and superficial reflections (Crème, 2005; O'Connell & Dyment, 2011; Wingate, 2011).

English Across the Curriculum

The writing across the curriculum "movement" originated in the North American and Australian higher education contexts in the mid-1970s (Wingate, 2011). Ursula Wingate (2011) reported three discipline-specific academic writing intervention initiatives involving the concerted effort of English language teachers and subject teachers in the disciplines of business and applied linguistics in a UK university. Wingate's findings illustrate how undergraduate and postgraduate students benefited from tailored support in developing academic writing skills within their disciplines. In the higher education sector in Hong Kong, the importance of critical academic writing skills in successfully completing different discipline courses has been generally recognised among English language educators and subject teachers in recent years. Tertiary students from different disciplines are expected to engage critically with, comprehend, and deploy written source materials in writing tasks. However, such critical writing skills within the disciplines are not necessarily skills that students have developed through the generic English for Academic Purposes (EAP) subjects that they are required to take. While such generic subjects introduce students to basic features and structures of academic writing and the particular referencing style accepted within the major area of their study, they are often inadequate in preparing students for specific academic writing tasks within their discipline or in other disciplines that students are less familiar with (Chen, 2020). Developing survival academic reading and writing skills may be even more challenging when students are ESL/EFL learners who have entered EMI (English medium of instruction) universities following the local mainstream CMI (Chinese medium of instruction) secondary schooling system prevalent in Hong Kong (Cheng et al., 2014; Morrison & Evans, 2014).

To attempt to address the inadequacy of generic foundation EAP courses and alleviate concerns of content teachers over the lack of academic study skills of students within different disciplines, researchers from four universities in Hong Kong initiated a small community of practice (CoP) project on a start-up government fund in 2013, which then continued to be supported by a four-institution professional development fund provided by the government in 2014 (Chen, 2020; Chen et al., 2021; Palmquist et al., 2018). The project team from The Hong Kong Polytechnic University, where the authors work, decided to extend its focus on writing to both the writing and speaking skills needed by students in fulfilling their disciplinary assessment tasks. The EAC CoP Team (as they will henceforth be referred to as) then introduced teachers from the English Language Centre and disciplinary content teachers within the university to the development of students' academic writing and speaking skills within disciplinary subjects through writing development workshops (Chen et al., 2021). Once content teachers had seen the value of language tips relevant to their disciplines, this complementary approach to enhancing learners' productive skills in academic English gained wider acceptance and support among content teachers. This acceptance helped to build a small interdisciplinary community of English language teachers and content teachers with shared interests and beliefs in supporting students in disciplinary academic literacy. The EAC Team received further funding from the government's Language Enhancement Grant for the 2016–2019 triennium. With this funding, collaboration was implemented in more than 20 disciplinary subjects, resulting in the production of abundant disciplinary academic literacy resources in the form of language tips and checklists across a range of genres. In an anonymous survey conducted by the team, over 90 percent of participating content teachers commented positively on the relevance and importance of language materials developed for their subjects and identified improved performance in student writing (Chen et al., 2021). While these materials were useful, examining the reflective activities in service-learning subjects within the disciplines was needed. One contribution to this body of research is the study on academic service-learning reflection that follows.

Reflection Activities in Academic Service-Learning

The use of personal reflections has been reported across a wide range of academic disciplines (e.g., Boud, 1999; Cheng et al., 2016; Mann et al., 2009; O'Connell & Dyment, 2011). Academic service-learning differs from other forms of community service in that it has educational benefits for students involved in the service process (Bringle & Hatcher, 1999). In academic service-learning subjects, reflective activities provide a mechanism for students to interpret their service experience in light of the intended learning outcomes of the service-learning subject and to make a connection between the service activities and educational content learnt in the classroom. Constant reflection on their service experience enhances students' understanding of the course content, the discipline, and a sense of civic responsibility (Bringle & Hatcher, 1999).

While teaching professionals have applauded the promise of personal reflections, such as captured moments for critical reflection and creativity in the learning process and a more positive teacher-student relationship, for both student writers and instructors, researchers have reported potential challenges associated with their use. Timothy O'Connell and Janet Dyment (2011) remarked that students often fail to demonstrate a high level of reflective and critical thinking in the reflective essays, which is one of the intended learning outcomes of reflective writing in academic disciplines. Crème (2005), drawing on his experience in an action research project, raised another issue—the question of honesty, which his students faced when they were asked to "honestly acknowledge mistakes and lack of understanding" in their learning journals (p. 293). Crème concluded that students may choose to record selected experiences that are more favourable to the subject teachers, who are also assessors of their work, instead of taking the risk of producing a comprehensive, original record of their learning experience.

Interdisciplinary Collaboration

Collaboration has been recognised as a significant factor leading to successful educational changes in Hong Kong schools (Li et al., 2017), and interdisciplinary collaboration has been adopted in a range of settings, including social work and education (Bronstein, 2003). Interdisciplinary collaboration refers to a team comprising members from different disciplines who bring to the collaboration their expertise that is complementary to each other, share a common purpose in what they intend to achieve, and work towards achieving the same goal (Bronstein, 2003; Parker-Oliver et al., 2005). Such collaboration involves communication and connection among team members in achieving a task that is sustained by mutual trust, distributed power, shared belief, and pride in achieving their common goal (Bronstein, 2003; Pugach, 1992; Viggiani et al., 2002). In the educational sector, Marleen Pugach (1992) pointed out that effective collaborative activities would create a more effective learning environment for students and serve other stakeholders in the community more efficiently.

Laura Bronstein (2003) proposed a model for interdisciplinary collaborative research and practice. Five components leading to the positive outcome of the task are included in this model: Interdependence, Newly Created Professional Activities, Flexibility, Collective Ownership of Goals and Reflection on Process. Interdependence refers to the dependency of the participants on each other to achieve the target. Participants are expected to fully understand and respect the professional roles that are played by both themselves and their peers in the collaboration. Newly Created Professional Activities refer to collaborative activities that "can achieve more than could be achieved by the same professionals acting independently" (Bronstein, 2003, p. 300). It is an essential element of collaboration in a service-learning subject, which expects changes in student learning and reflection on their community service. Flexibility is defined as the "deliberate occurrence of role-blurring" (Bronstein, 2003, p. 301). The importance of flexibility, involving professionals from multiple disciplines in collaboration, is echoed by various scholars in the field of social work. Instead of a clear hierarchy of roles, members in a collaborative activity often assume more indistinct roles and are more likely to compromise depending on the situation and needs of the team. According to Bronstein, Collective Ownership of Goals means collaborators' active engagement in the process of working together, including in discussion and decision-making, taking responsibility for their part of the collaborative work, and supporting each other throughout the process. In social work, it is crucial to attend to different stakeholders who are involved in aspects of service delivery, not only the voice of the professionals. Finally, Reflection on Process highlights the conscious effort of the professionals from different disciplines during the collaboration to build effective working relationships, in aspects such as thinking and exchanging ideas about their working relationship and incorporating feedback. Challenges addressed by previous researchers include managing conflicts within the team, self-evaluation, and the use of feedback.

Bronstein's (2003) interdisciplinary model was deemed appropriate for this project as it was to be based on an extensive meta-analysis of studies in social work and fit the kind of direct service that stakeholders are committed to in the service-learning subject studied. It could optimise the collaboration between content teachers in applied social sciences and English language teachers. This model could also raise the collaborators' awareness of opportunities provided by such collaboration and address potential challenges underlying the process of multi-disciplines working together more efficiently.

The Process

Context

This chapter examines an initiative developing and providing discipline-specific academic English language support to facilitate assignment preparation in a service-learning subject for undergraduate students in a Hong Kong university. The service-learning subject aims to promote the holistic development of undergraduate students and nurture their intrapersonal and interpersonal competencies and positive social development through serving underprivileged children of migrant workers in first- and second-tier cities in mainland China. The two-semester subject is delivered through lectures, seminars, workshops, and direct service activities and includes systematic academic reflective activities. Students are required to continuously reflect on their learning and service experience and complete two reflective journals. During the first semester, students attend lectures and seminars on service-learning and child development and examine risks and protective factors for children who are socially and economically disadvantaged. In the second semester, students attend five intensive training workshops on curriculum development, lesson planning, and practical teaching skills before providing a total of 40 hours of direct service activities to the underprivileged children and adolescents at a five-day summer camp. Over 500 university students took this subject and provided direct service to over 2,300 migrant children during the period of this preliminary evaluative study.

The Interdisciplinary Collaborative Process in Promoting English Across the Curriculum

The EAC Team was formed in January 2016 and comprised content teachers in social work and English language teachers from the language centre of the same university. The team members from the language centre reached out to the content teachers and invited them to an initial meeting to share their expectations of reflective essays. An interdisciplinary approach, based on Bronstein's (2003) interdisciplinary collaborative framework, was adopted to enhance the support for students in completing the subject assignments.

Newly Created Professional Activities

The EAC Team initiated the collaboration hoping to provide tailor-made support for students completing academic writing assignments and service in the social work discipline. Involving content teachers from the onset proved more productive than relying solely on language teachers to develop language tips—as is the case in the generic EAP courses taught within the university. Language tips refer to a set of supplemental discipline-specific English language materials developed and provided to the students in the EAC project. They cover various topics related to academic reflective journal writing and academic presentations, which students are required to complete in the subject. The language tips provided in this subject are illustrated in Appendix A. Content teachers had the opportunity to share their observations and views with their language teaching colleagues regarding desired features of successful personal reflective stories and skills needed to develop relevant academic literacy competencies. By maximising the expertise of team members from different disciplines, it was assumed that this team would achieve more than could have been achieved by the content teachers or language teachers alone.

Interdependence

Based on the information collected in the initial meeting, language teachers then developed the initial version of the supplemental language materials and circulated them for further discussion. Over the next few months, the content teachers worked collaboratively with the language teachers to discuss and refine the materials. There were also several rounds of discussion on the language materials involving members of the collaborative team and students through a post-course survey until the first official version of the language tips became available to students in 2016–2017. During this work together, members came to understand each other's perspectives and built respect for the professional knowledge each contributed.

Flexibility

When different views arose, this collaboration engaged in a process of "productive compromises" (Bronstein, 2003, p. 301). Content teachers collected student feedback when they had piloted the initial version of the language tips. Comments from students were reflected to the EAC Team, discussed, and incorporated in the revisions. No hierarchy of roles was assumed, and collaborators shared responsibility in making further revisions to the materials. The team eventually developed the second version of language tips for students who enrolled in the course in 2017–2018.

Collective Ownership of Goals

Content teachers within the social work discipline were actively involved in the process. They shared responsibility for the development, refinement, and further development of the materials, in activities such as sharing and discussing students' sample work with the language teachers and collecting formal and informal feedback on the materials from their students. Content teachers also participated in the critical decision-making process at all stages. In other words, content teachers were involved in not only developing and commenting on the language materials but also in the gathering, analysing, and communication of comments from student writers, which is essential to assuring the quality of the tailor-made language tips and their relevance to students within this discipline.

Reflection on Process

The EAC Team developed a close working relationship throughout the collaborative process. Content teachers reflected on and thoroughly discussed their work and included comments from their colleagues in the initial and further development of the language materials. Content teachers were also keen to evaluate their teaching activities during the process, implementing new pedagogies as a result of the feedback collected from students and for collaborating on student interviews and discussions with language teachers.

The Preliminary Evaluation

This section presents results from the preliminary evaluative study that the authors conducted on the EAC initiative to implement supplemental language tips between 2016 and 2018. Both authors of this chapter have been members of the EAC Team from the onset. One author is a language teacher from the English Language Centre and the other is a content teacher within the discipline of applied social sciences.

Formal and informal feedback was collected during the process of working together throughout the two academic years. Data used for this preliminary evaluation were collected between 2016 and 2018, including responses from two student surveys administered during the last teaching sessions during the two academic years and three focus group interviews conducted with students when they had completed the course. Students who had taken this course were also asked to write a short reflection on their experience using the language tips during the service-learning subject course. One-to-one interviews were conducted with the content teachers.

Three hundred sixty-four students responded to the surveys (response rate: 61.8%). Eighteen students participated in three focus group interviews. Regarding the short reflection on their experience and perceptions of the language support provided by the EAC Team, five completed student reflections were collected. Two content teachers were also interviewed and shared their views on the EAC collaboration. Findings from these processes are discussed below to illuminate the significance of the interdisciplinary collaborative approach in a service-learning subject.

Changes in Collaborators' Perceptions of Reflection Activities and Reflective Writing

Findings concerning changes in content teachers' perceptions of the continuous collaboration emerged from the interviews with content teachers. One content teacher commented about her experience in the EAC project, stating that it "enriched my perception of reflective writing, especially in terms of the professionalism and academic standard . . . and as an instructor, I should focus more on the reflective level of students." This is in marked contrast to her perception before the interdisciplinary collaboration started, when she viewed "the level of in-depth reflection [as] the only key thing in the reflective writing." This teacher also pointed out that she "gained more ideas about writing a high-quality reflection with professional and academic use of English, from planning, to use of tense and language," and now she is "reviewing students' work from different angles." The interview comments suggest that content teachers have found this collaboration to be an opportunity for themselves to shape their own perceptions of reflective journal writing in their discipline in addition to supporting their students' ongoing learning.

Perceptions of Collaborating with Colleagues

When interviewed about their experience in the process of working together, both content teachers responded positively to engaging colleagues from the English Language Centre. One subject teacher commented that "it was a pleasant experience to work towards a common goal to improve students' reflective work." Another content expert with substantial experience in social work commented that their language teaching colleagues were "helpful and professional." Overall, there was appreciation of colleagues' effort concerning developing students' discipline-specific academic literacy skills for the reflective assignments, their willingness to share ideas with colleagues from the other discipline, and their carefully managed class visits to talk to students about the reflective journal writing in the discipline.

Perceptions of the Supplemental Language Materials

Content teachers perceived the usefulness of the supplemental materials unanimously, commenting highly positively during the interview focusing on the supplementary language tips, such as the provision of content-related vocabulary. One content expert remarked during the interview that "some students, especially science and engineering students, had no idea about how to effectively express their reflection using appropriate words and phrases in English. The tips can help by giving them some concrete ideas." As students enrolled in this service-learning subject are from a wide range of academic disciplines within the university, it is important that they are able to communicate ideas using appropriate content-related vocabulary in their reflective journals.

Similar to the teacher comments, over three-quarters of students who responded to the surveys reported that they had used the language tips (Table 1.1). Most participants commented in focus group interviews and written reflections that they had used the supplemental language materials despite the tight schedule and limited time working on the reflective journal assignment. Students generally saw the value of the content-related academic writing tips and described these tips as "reader-friendly," "useful," and "solving problems that are commonly encountered in writing a reflective journal."

In terms of student perceptions about the usefulness of the language tips, survey results across years of the evaluation are comparable. Over 90 percent of students in the survey rated the language tips on reflective journal writing useful or very useful. An overwhelming majority of students were satisfied with the reflective tips, and in particular, almost a third of students who completed the survey in the second year were highly content with the reflective journal writing tips.

In addition, 97 percent of all students who responded to the surveys agreed that the reflective tips helped improve the quality of their reflective journal in two different ways. One student noted in the written reflection that "I do not think the quality [of my reflective journal two] will be the same without the reflection tips." Specifically, the supplemental language tips on reflective journal writing seem to give students direction on how to write a reflective journal and information about how to structure paragraphs in an academic reflective journal. A student commented that the reflection tips "provided a suggested structure for me to follow ... [and it] gave me a very clear direction and sequence for completion." Another student noted in his written reflection that "... at first, I felt confused and uncertain on how to write my journal, but the tips for journal gave a lot of idea of direction on how I should write and what I should include. It helps brainstorm ideas and familiarize myself with the journal."

Table 1.1. Selected end-of-semester student survey results

Survey Questions	Responses		Total Responses
Q1. Did you use the language tips for your assignments?	Yes (177)	No (48)	225
Q3. How would you rate the usefulness of the tips?	Useful or Very useful (163)	A little useful (14)	177
Q4. In general, did the language tips help you improve the quality of writing Reflective Journal 2?	Yes (171)	No (6)	177

Perceptions of Changes in Students' Reflective Writing

Student comments from the focus group discussions and written reflections indicate that the provision of content-related writing tips helped them make connections between their involvement in the service process, verbal reflective activities during direct service, and the post-service written reflective journal assignment. A student commented about "the planning part of the tips" in particular. Although she struggled with "many ideas and points which I would like to include in my reflection journal" at the beginning, this student felt that the language tips helped her "choose a particular experience or story during the service camp and elaborate how it affected me and what my feeling was towards this experience." In other words, making effective use of the tips in the initial planning stage seems to help students interpret and consolidate the service-learning experience, which aligns with the intended learning outcomes of this subject that emphasise learning through purposeful and continuous reflections (Jones, 2001).

Changes in students' reflection activities were also observed by the content teachers involved in the collaboration. One content expert reflected during the interview that "students feel more confident about the reflection tasks and their competence in self-exploration and disclosure is enhanced because of the solid language materials on hand." Another content expert talked about noticing changes in students' use of English and appropriateness of the format of their reflective journals. In the content teachers' view, students who previously "asked about the use of language in the reflective assignments" seem to be "clearer about how to write a good reflective journal" and can deal with issues such as choices of tense, ways of citing sources, and expressing their point of view with greater confidence when relaying their service experience.

It is interesting to note that some students reflected during the interviews and recorded in their written reflections that they would like to see supplemental language materials be developed for the first reflective journal writing assignment as well. There are two reflective journals assessed in this subject. The first is a shorter reflective essay that requires students to reflect on their personal psycho-social development using one of the topics discussed in the four lectures and service planning in the first semester. The second is a more extended reflective journal which is submitted when students have finished the service camp in the second semester. Currently, supplemental language tips have only been developed to support the second reflective journal writing assignment as the content teaching team decided to focus the collaboration on the more challenging writing task. One student commented that "at the time I started to type my journal one, I did not have any idea about it in the beginning that I wanted the English Language Centre to offer me some tips or advice." A similar concern was reflected during the interview with a content teacher. Having read and marked hundreds of students' written reflections, this content teacher observed that her students sometimes struggle with appropriate vocabulary (e.g., emotion words and phrases) to describe their experience in the service-learning process effectively in their reflective journals. A lack of vocabulary may explain the seemingly lack of a higher level of reflective critical thinking, especially for ESL/EFL students (O'Connell & Dyment, 2011). As demonstrating a reasonable level of critical reflection in the written assignments is one of the intended learning outcomes of academic reflective journal writing, the EAC Team needs to attend to this issue with vocabulary when refining the language tips in the future.

Challenges

This interdisciplinary collaborative project highlights several challenges that EAC projects in this context and WAC projects in other places have encountered. One major challenge involves language teachers' level of involvement in the preparation and delivery of the language support materials due to limited funding. The service-learning subject in this study runs for two semesters every year. Compared with the relatively large number of students taking the subject each of the two semesters, the team of language teachers responsible for class visits and material development is relatively small. With limited time off to work on the EAC project, language teachers could not prioritise further development of the EAC materials to improve students' academic writing skills within the discipline. More support from the university and departments is necessary to ensure more sustainable collaboration and to maximise benefits for students.

Another major challenge relates to the time management skills of students. This is consistent with the findings from Bruce Morrison and Stephen Evans (2014). Multi-tasking and, therefore, spending limited time on one writing assignment is often the case for university students. In our questionnaire survey, 14.2 percent of students ($n=225$) noted that while they had spent a significant amount of time preparing the service trip and direct service activities, they devoted somewhat limited time to the reflective essay writing. Some students even admitted that they wrote the 1,000-word essay in less than two days when they had returned from the intensive service trip. A lack of devotion of time to writing has been reported as a side effect of journal writing assignments (O'Connell & Dyment, 2011). As writing quality reflective journals is a time-consuming activity, students should be advised on the importance of planning their assignments early enough in the semester and provided with more practical tips regarding meeting deadlines and ensuring the quality of their essays.

From the course administration perspective, assignment submission dates perhaps need reconsideration. Students are given less than a week to reflect on their service experience and submit the assignment. While acknowledging that the assignment submission is in the summer term when students have fewer other academic commitments, the timing of the assignment and the service trip warrants reconsideration in future operations.

Conclusions and Implications for Teaching

The majority of students enrolled in this service-learning subject use English as a second or foreign language. The findings from this preliminary evaluative study demonstrate the benefits of incorporating content-specific academic English language tips for students through interdisciplinary collaboration. It is also evident that a deep level of involvement of disciplinary content teachers is crucial to the successful implementation of content-specific language materials in a disciplinary subject (Chen et al., 2021). Both students and teachers interviewed appraised the opportunities for students to develop intellectually and linguistically due to the implementation of EAC in the continuous academic reflective writing activities. Students reported having benefited from looking at their essays from different perspectives. Comments from content teachers also illustrate the possible impact of the collaboration on content teachers themselves, as one teacher noted that it shaped her perceptions of high-quality academic reflective writing. These findings echo those reported by Chen et al. (2021) in their anonymous survey across four universities concerning how content teachers have benefited from the implementation of EAC in ways such as making use of the EAC materials developed in their marking. At the same time, results from the preliminary evaluation also suggest the need for a further refinement of the language tips.

We are aware of the need for further evaluation beyond the two-year EAC collaboration described in this chapter. We propose conducting a subject outcome evaluation in the next administration of the service-learning subject. This subsequent evaluation will employ both quantitative and qualitative methods, including a larger-scale student survey; follow-up semi-structured interviews with both students and content teachers; observations of students' reflective activities before, during, and after the direct service; and more systematic analysis of student work produced during the implementation of EAC in the subject (Braun & Clarke, 2006; Cresswell, 2014; O'Connell & Dyment, 2011; Punch & Oancea, 2014). We would hope to gain insights and teaching wisdom, through a methodologically more flexible approach, into the impact of an EAC initiative to enhance discipline-specific academic literacy in a service-learning subject on students' holistic development in real-life problem-based situations.

Acknowledgements

The study reported in this chapter is funded by the Hong Kong Polytechnic University, project title: "English Across the Curriculum" (LEG 16–19). We thank Dr. Grace Lim and Ms. Anna Cheung from the Hong Kong Polytechnic University for their assistance with the administration of the student surveys. We are also immensely grateful to Dr. Julia Chen, Dr. Bruce Morrison, and Dr. Alan Urmston from The Hong Kong Polytechnic University for their comments on an earlier version of this chapter.

References

Boud, D. (1999). Avoiding the traps: Seeking good practice in the use of self-assessment and reflection in professional courses. *Social Work Education*, *18*, 121–132.
Braun, V. & Clarke, V. (2006). Using thematic analysis in psychology. *Qualitative Research in Psychology*, *3*(2), 77–101.

Bringle, R. & Hatcher, J. (1999). Reflection in service learning: Making meaning or experience. *Evaluation / Reflection, 23*, 179–185. https://digitalcommons.unomaha.edu/slceeval/23.

Bronstein, L. R. (2003). A model for interdisciplinary collaboration. *Social Work, 48*(3), 297–306.

Chen, J. (2020). EAP in Hong Kong. In H. Terauchi, J. Noguchi & A. Tajino (Eds.), *Towards a new paradigm for English language teaching: English for specific purposes in Asia and beyond* (pp. 115–126). Routledge.

Chen, J., Chan, C. & Ng, A. (2021). English across the curriculum: Four journeys of synergy across disciplines and universities. In H. Lee & B. Spolsky (Eds.), *Localizing global English: Asian perspectives and practices* (pp. 84–103). Routledge.

Cheng, G., Law, E. & Wong, T. (2016, December). *Investigating effects of automated feedback on EFL students' reflective learning skills* [Paper presentation]. IEEE International Conference on Teaching, Assessment, and Learning for Engineering, Bangkok, Thailand. https://ieeexplore.ieee.org/document/7851798.

Cheng, W., Chan, M., Chiu, H., Kwok, A., Lam, K. H., Lam, K. M., Lim, G. & Wright, R. (2014). *Enhancing students' professional competence and generic qualities through writing in English across the curriculum.* The Hong Kong Polytechnic University. https://www.researchgate.net/publication/269397173_Enhancing_students%27_professional_competence_and_generic_qualities_through_writing_in_English_across_the_curriculum.

Crème, P. (2005). Should student learning journals be assessed? *Assessment & Evaluation in Higher Education, 30*(3), 287–296.

Cresswell, J. W. (2014). *A concise introduction to mixed methods research*. Sage.

Eyler, J. (2002). Reflection: Linking service and learning—Linking students and communities. *Journal of Social Issues, 58*(3), 517–534.

Fang, F. & Chak, Y. (2018, December). *Integrating supplementary language materials to support learners in their assignments in a service learning subject: An Evaluation of 2016–2018* [Paper presentation]. 2nd International Conference on English Across the Curriculum, Hong Kong.

Hatcher, J. & Bringle, R. G. (1997). Reflection: Bridging the gap between service and learning. *College Teaching, 45*(4), 153–158.

Jones, S. (2001). Where's the learning in service-learning? *The Journal of Higher Education, 72*(2), 256–258.

Li, L., Hallinger, P., Kennedy, K. J. & Walker, A. (2017). Mediating effects of trust, communication, and collaboration on teacher professional learning in Hong Kong primary schools. *International Journal of Leadership in Education, 20*(6), 697–716.

Mann, K., Gordon, J. & MacLeod, A. (2009). Reflection and reflective practice in health professions education: A systematic review. *Advances in Health Sciences Education, 14*, 595–621. https://link.springer.com/content/pdf/10.1007%2Fs10459-007-9090-2.pdf.

Morrison, B. & Evans, S. (2014). Challenges faced by non-native undergraduate student writers in an English-medium university. *The Asian ESP Journal, 10*(1), 136–174.

O'Connell, T. & Dyment, J. (2011). The case of reflective journals: Is the jury still out? *Reflective Practice: International and Multidisciplinary Perspectives, 12*(1), 47–59.

Palmquist, M., Zawacki, T., Townsend, M. & Chen, J. (2018, December). *The future of writing across the curriculum: Building on a strong foundation* [Plenary panel discussion]. 2nd International Conference on English Across the Curriculum, Hong Kong.

Parker-Oliver, D., Bronstein, L. R. & Kurzejeski, L. (2005). Examining variables related to successful collaboration on the hospice team. *Health & Social Work, 30*(4), 279–286.

Pugach, M. C. (1992). Uncharted territory: Research on the socialization of special education teachers. *Teacher Education and Special Education, 15*(2), 133–147.

Punch, K. F. & Oancea, A. (2014). *Introduction to research methods in education*. Sage.

Rogers, R. R. (2001). Reflection in higher education: A concept analysis. *Innovative Higher Education, 26*(1), 37–57.

Viggiani, P. A., Reid, W. J. & Bailey-Dempsey, C. (2002). Social worker-teacher collaboration in the classroom: Help from elementary students at risk of failure. *Research on Social Work Practice, 12*(5), 604–620.

Wingate, U. (2011). Using Academic Literacies and genre-based models for academic writing instruction: A 'literacy' journey. *Journal of English for Academic Purposes, 11*(1), 26–37.

Appendix A: An Example of the Language Tips

Body paragraphs

The body paragraphs reveal a good variety of your ideas on your chosen topic.
Each of your body paragraphs should follow a clear progression of ideas as illustrated below:

Topic sentence	e.g. *The five-day service teaching enhanced my problem-solving skills.*
⬇	
Supporting details (e.g. examples, theories, elaboration)	e.g. *On the first day, problems occurred due to the imperfection of lesson planning. For example, the time for the activities was underestimated and the children in the class were not well managed because of my soft voice. I was a bit disappointed with my performance on the first day. When I reflected on this day, I realised that I had relied solely on instant response from students rather than preparation for the problems beforehand and strategies to deal with them. Therefore, I changed my strategies in lesson preparation after day one and had more strategic preparation on the lesson after.*
⬇	
Concluding sentence	e.g. *Teaching these days reminded me that to deal with problems, I really should think of the problems that might occur in advance and prepare for the strategies.*

Practice:
Write a body paragraph of your reflective essay using the structure recommended.

What is your topic sentence?
_____

What are the supporting details?
_____
_____
_____

What is your concluding sentence?
_____

Appendix B: An Example of the Reflective Journal Checklist

Reflective Journal Checklist
In my reflective journal, the following are included:

☐	I have given detailed information about this personal experience.
☐	I have presented a careful analysis of my personal experience.
☐	There is connection between theory and real life experience.
☐	There is demonstration of self-awareness and learning through this reflection.
☐	The language used is academic and formal.
☐	I have acknowledged all the works (e.g. journals, books, online materials) I used.
☐	There is a reference list at the end.
☐	All the references used in my text are included in the reference list.
☐	My referencing style is consistent (e.g. APA 6th edition).

Appendix C: End-of-Semester Survey for Students (Part related to the reflective journal writing assignment)

1. Did you refer to the English tips provided by the ELC for your assignments?
2. How much time did you spend on the following English tips provided by the ELC?
3. How would you rate the following English tips provided by the ELC?
4. In general, did the above English tips provided by the ELC help you improve the quality of writing Reflective Journal 2 in this subject?
5. The English tips on writing provided by the ELC were not so helpful because . . .
6. Have you consulted ELC's Writing Assistance Programme (WAP) for writing Reflective Journal 2 in this subject?
7. My writing grade is usually . . .

2 Gaps in Content-Based English Enhancement in Science and Engineering

Barbara WY Siu
THE HONG KONG POLYTECHNIC UNIVERSITY

Abstract: In the fields of science and engineering, teaching and assessment habitually makes use of calculations and drawings rather than extended writing or oral presentations. Although the ability to communicate eloquently in the disciplinary context is required of students, the development of language skills is often contracted out to language teaching units. This chapter reports on a project that aimed to devise content-based strategies to enhance students' English language skills within a technical curriculum. In a baseline survey conducted to understand students' habits and views about English, respondents self-reported a general confidence in their language use for the purpose of learning their discipline, but noted difficulties in speaking and, to a lesser extent, writing, with the fluency of both affected by deficiencies in grammar and vocabulary. Moreover, it was found that the target students' motivation for language improvement was highly instrumental, based on obtaining better jobs or better grades. The study reveals some systemic problems, such as the lack of opportunities for more extensive use of language in teaching and assessment in technical disciplines and an overall lack of motivation among students.

Keywords: English Across the Curriculum, writing across the curriculum, engineering education, science education, university education

Language Needs of Tertiary Students in Hong Kong

Most university students in Hong Kong are ESL (English as a Second Language) learners who began learning English in kindergarten. English may or may not have been the principal medium of instruction in their primary and secondary schools, but passing the English subject in the public examination is a compulsory university admission requirement (Hong Kong Examinations and Assessment Authority, 2019). Second language (L2) proficiency is crucial for students' adaptation to university studies and for their academic success, and one of the reported difficulties in the school-to-university transition is the use of English as the medium for teaching and learning (Evans & Morrison, 2012). Several studies conducted in Hong Kong have highlighted the need for additional language support for L2 learners in the areas of academic writing and speaking, receptive and productive vocabulary, technical vocabulary, comprehension of lectures, and conforming to the specialised culture and conventions of the academic community (Evans & Green, 2007; Evans & Morrison, 2011).

How English is Valued in the Teaching and Assessment of Science and Engineering

Desmond Allison (1992) noted in an earlier study at the University of Hong Kong that the English ability of engineering students was much weaker than that of their counterparts in the arts. This phenomenon is related to the value placed on English by students and teachers in science and engineering. Surveys of tertiary students in Hong Kong (Evans & Green, 2007; Evans & Morrison, 2011, 2012) revealed that the core subjects in the undergraduate programme focus mainly on the disciplinary content and place little or sometimes no weight on English in teaching or assessment, which creates the impression that English is not important to success in these subjects. Rosalie Goldsmith and Keith Willey (2016) observed that although writing remains the main form of assessment at universities (not limited to those in Hong Kong), the practice of writing continues to be marginalised, particularly in technical disciplines such as engineering. Students are neither interested in, nor value, writing, and there is a systemic issue of writing practices not being considered developmental or intrinsic to the engineering curriculum.

The Language of Science Shapes the Use of English in Teaching and Assessment Practices

Science and engineering students are required to navigate between scientific and colloquial English in learning and communication (Lee et al., 2013). The importance of language in science (and engineering) education has been widely discussed (Wellington & Osborne, 2001; Yore et al., 2003), and English language competence is an accreditation requirement of various professional associations (Accreditation Board for Engineering and Technology, 2016; The Hong Kong e.g., Institution of Engineers, 2013).

Language shapes and is shaped by disciplinary practices and epistemologies across a wide range of specialisations, from the sciences to arts and humanities

(Kuteeva & Airey, 2013). As noted by Fang (2005), "scientific genres are typically multimodal and scientific meanings are often conveyed through a combination of words, images, diagrams, and mathematical/graphical signs" (p. 336). This multimodality is in contrast to humanities and arts disciplines in which words constitute the primary mode of communication. This affects how science and engineering contents are taught. In the earlier stages of science and engineering education, the assessment of students' ability to "remember," "understand," and "apply" (ref. Bloom's taxonomy—Bloom, 1956 as cited in Lasley, 2010) academic knowledge and skills can be expediently assessed via accuracy in calculations (symbols), drawings, or keywords because little interpretation or elaboration is required. Conventional science and engineering classrooms create the impression that the ability to understand the concepts and express ideas in calculations or diagrams is imperative, whereas linguistic knowledge can be seen as merely supplementary. The opportunity for language use does not improve significantly when students reach university level, where they are expected to demonstrate the ability to "analyse," "evaluate," and "create" (ref. Bloom's taxonomy—Bloom, 1956 as cited in Lasley, 2010) in the disciplinary context. Rebecca Essig and colleagues (2018) reviewed undergraduate civil engineering textbooks and assessment practices and found that writing was still minimal. This finding is echoed by my previous study (Siu, 2019), which examined the undergraduate engineering curriculum in Hong Kong. In technical disciplines, writing practices are assessed but not taught or practised, but propositional knowledge is taught, practised, and assessed (Goldsmith & Willey, 2016).

As a result, for science and engineering students, common assessment items such as written assignments, tests, and examinations usually require them only to demonstrate their understanding via calculations and drawings, or at most bullet points or keywords. One may argue that these students very often need to perform experiments and write laboratory reports, both of which demand substantial writing to describe the procedures and explain the results. However, in a companion study by Siu (2019), students reported that most teachers simply assign zero weightings to language use in laboratory reports, while others even simplify the task to the completion of laboratory worksheets, upon which students are only required to write numbers and perform fill-in-the-blanks tasks. In a typical engineering curriculum, case studies, design projects, student research projects, and capstone projects usually occur only in the final year. Group discussions or presentations are considered a luxurious use of class time, so engineering students are likely to participate in about two oral presentations within their core subjects throughout their four years of university life. To sum up, students in the science and engineering disciplines have limited opportunities for language use and development, despite its importance.

Outsourcing of Language Instruction

Experiences, both overseas (such as in Goldsmith & Willey, 2016) and locally (such as in Allison, 1992), describe a status quo in the development of writing (or language use, more generally) within the disciplines, with instruction tending to be outsourced to language teaching units. Students take a handful of courses that focus on academic and (often) professional English, and the core subjects that take up most of the students' curriculum time focus almost entirely on technical concepts. Some content teachers might feel that "it's not [their] job to teach writing" (Goldsmith & Willey, 2016, p. 126) or might not feel confident in providing direct instructions about disciplinary writing. These factors have shaped the conventions of language use in science and engineering education: English has been relegated to a less important position in teaching and assessment, despite the expectations of other stakeholders.

English Across the Curriculum

In Hong Kong tertiary institutions, language improvement efforts have seen a move from remedial teaching to language enhancement (Allison, 1992) and later to a content-driven, English Across the Curriculum (EAC) approach (Evans & Green, 2007), which might be presented in the form of English for Academic Purposes (EAP) courses infused with discipline-related materials (Evans & Morrison, 2011). That language enhancement is more effectively achieved within the disciplinary context (Murray & Hicks, 2014), with writing and speaking support integrated into the curriculum is not a new idea. Indeed, the writing across the curriculum (WAC) movement is "based on the premise that writing is highly situated and tied to a field's discourse and ways of knowing, and therefore writing in the disciplines is most effectively guided by those with expertise in that discipline" (INWAC Ad Hoc Working Group, 2018).

Writing serves a variety of purposes, and students improve as learners and thinkers when teachers integrate writing as frequently as possible across the curriculum (Kiefer et al., 2018). For students, EAC promotes engaged student learning, critical thinking, and a greater facility with communication across rhetorical situations. A variety of writing and speaking activities/tasks not only enhances students' language competence, it also helps academically by providing students with a better understanding of the course content and by improving their ability to develop critical ideas about what they have learnt. Language competence and a deeper understanding of course content then enable students to interact with others effectively (i.e., communicate well) in the disciplinary context. Teachers also benefit from EAC: marking becomes less time-consuming and less daunting due to the introduction of alternative types of shorter writing tasks; teachers can better gauge students' learning via more frequent interaction and instant feedback; as students gain competence in subject content and critical thinking, they can better achieve course goals; and teachers are recognised for their scholarship in teaching and learning (Patterson & Slinger-Friedman, 2012).

Despite ample evidence of the effectiveness of EAC/WAC in humanities, social sciences, and business disciplines (see Cheng et al., 2014 for local examples in Hong Kong), EAC/WAC in science and engineering is emerging and rarely studied (Essig et al., 2018). An Australian review (Dunworth et al., 2014) found that successful language enhancement at universities required strong leadership to ensure consistent policy and allocation of resources and significant involvement of both discipline teachers and language experts. Mutual recognition and collaboration in the design of lectures and assessments that target the discourse of the discipline were found to be the most effective and practical ways of helping to ensure tertiary language enhancement. This contrasts with the status quo in most science and engineering disciplines, in which the language elements are almost entirely contracted out to language experts.

In the study of EAP in science and engineering, Okhee Lee et al. (2013) noted the substantial difference between the language of science and everyday discourse, and suggested the need for a shift from the "sheltered model" in content-based language enhancement strategies. In the sheltered model, teachers receive some training in language pedagogies and are then expected to focus on both content objectives and language objectives in their teaching. For science and engineering disciplines, Lee et al. (2013) proposed a further shift to focus on creating a "language-in-use" environment that emphasises what students "do" with language as they engage in scientific enquiry and discursive practices. In that way, both content learning and language learning are promoted.

Project Background

Compartmentalisation of English teaching and discipline teaching has resulted in a lack of opportunities for students to develop skills in thinking about and presenting disciplinary knowledge in an L2. The project of which this study forms a part aims to develop a content-based language enhancement scheme for students of science and engineering subjects at The Hong Kong Polytechnic University. The main objective is to strengthen students' abilities in reading, writing, and speaking in the disciplinary context. This is to be achieved by incorporating English enhancement components into the technical subjects.

The entire project spans one and a half years. This chapter reports on the first phase of implementation, which involved content-based strategies targeting (i) comprehension of technical vocabulary, (ii) understanding and writing discipline-specific assignment types, and (iii) pronunciation. These content-based strategies were piloted in several subjects offered in the Department of Civil and Environmental Engineering.

This chapter highlights the major observations from a student survey and reveals the perceived obstacles to language enhancement in the fields of science and engineering. The survey results help to identify specific content-based resources that can address students' problems and, by helping to understand students' attitudes and self-help habits, suggest ways to better engage students in the language enhancement effort to counteract the view, deeply rooted in science and engineering education, that "language is only supplementary."

Student Survey

This chapter reports on the findings from pre- and post-course student surveys in the first semester of project implementation. These surveys help to develop a background understanding of

- students' attitudes towards learning and enhancing their English, including how students perceived their own English and the importance they place on English; and
- students' difficulties in learning and using English, and their attempts at self-help.

Survey Description

The pre- and post-course student survey questionnaires consisted of 25 and 26 questions, respectively, and were divided into three main themes:

- Section 1: Evaluate the change in students' self-evaluated confidence/competence in the use of English in the disciplinary context. This section consisted of 17 questions about students' self-evaluation of their competence in the disciplinary context with regard to reading comprehension (seven questions), technical writing (six questions), and presentation skills (four questions), reported on a five-point Likert scale.
- Section 2: Evaluate the change in students' awareness of the importance of English. This section consisted of four questions about students' awareness of the importance of English for various purposes, reported on a five-point Likert scale.

- Section 3: Understand students' specific difficulties in learning/using English, English-learning habits, and self-help solutions. This section consisted of two five-point Likert scale questions regarding students' habits using dictionaries and translation sites (e.g., Google Translate) and two open-ended questions focusing on students' major difficulties when communicating in English and what they do when they encounter English language problems.

In the post-course questionnaire, one question (Question 26) was added to collect students' opinions on and suggestions for the project website. The full questionnaire is available in the appendix.

The survey was conducted in two undergraduate-level subjects in the Department of Civil and Environmental Engineering:

- Subject one was in the field of hydraulics. It was a second-year core subject with a class size of 94. It was a highly technical, calculation-intensive subject with lectures, tutorials, and laboratory sessions.
- Subject two was in the field of construction law. It was a common final-year core subject for students from several undergraduate programmes in the department. The subject content was technical but mostly descriptive. The class size was 240. About half of the students entered university after the public examination Hong Kong Diploma of Secondary Education (HKDSE), on which the minimum language requirement is for students to attain level three in the HKDSE English paper; the other half were students who had matriculated from other higher diploma or associate degree programmes, for which the minimum language requirement is only level two in HKDSE English.

The pre- and post-course surveys were printed, and hardcopies were distributed to students in lectures. In subject one, the subject lecturer made the return of the survey voluntary, and there were 54 and 30 returns in the pre- and post-course surveys respectively, with corresponding response rates of 57 percent and 32 percent. In subject two, returning the surveys was compulsory, and there was a higher response rate with 208 (87%) and 221 (92%) returns for the pre- and post-course surveys respectively.

Students' Self-Evaluations of English Competence

Table 2.1 to Table 2.3 show students' pre- and post-course self-evaluations of their English competence or confidence in reading comprehension, technical writing, and speaking in the academic/disciplinary context. Following these, the overall ratings before and after the courses are compared (see Figure 2.1). The question statements were in the form of "I can fully understand . . ." or "I am confident in . . . ," and the responses were given on a five-point Likert scale ranging from 1 (*strongly disagree*) to 5 (*strongly agree*). The key observations are as follows.

Generally Positive Confidence Levels

Students reported above-neutral self-confidence in reading, writing, and speaking in English in the academic/disciplinary context. Their level of confidence generally ranged between 3 (*neutral*) to 4 (*agree*) out of 5 in both the pre- and post-course surveys.

Areas of Confidence

As shown in the aggregate scores in Figure 2.1, in overall terms, students felt most confident in speaking, marginally less confident in writing, and least confident in reading.

- Reading: Students felt most confident in understanding tutorial notes and least confident in understanding vocabulary/sentences in textbooks and legal and official documents.
- Writing: Students felt most confident in writing with a topic sentence and least confident in using different English vocabulary.
- Speaking: Students felt most confident in answering questions in English and least confident in holding group discussions in English.

Improvements in Self-Confidence Post-Course

Students in both subjects displayed statistically significant improvements in self-confidence in the post-course survey for most items. This supported the belief underlying EAC that English language enhancement should be content-driven: when students better understand the disciplinary content, they also display higher self-confidence in the use of English. Nonetheless, in items of which self-help materials had been provided to students (technical vocabulary taken from reading materials and aids in comprehending assignment instructions and writing assignments, as marked by the symbol "+" in the respective items in Table 2.1 to Table 2.3), greater improvements in self-confidence were observed (i.e., a larger increase was seen in the ratings from the pre- to post-course survey). These findings confirmed the contribution of the content-based language enhancement approach used in this project.

Table 2.1. Self-evaluation of reading

Subject 1				
Statement: I can fully understand ...[1]		N	Mean	Difference (Post–Pre)
English vocabulary in textbook[+]	Pre	55	3.1091	0.7576**
	Post	30	3.8667	
English sentences in textbook	Pre	55	3.2909	0.5758*
	Post	30	3.8667	
English lecture notes	Pre	55	3.1455	0.5879**
	Post	30	3.7333	
English tutorial notes	Pre	54	3.3704	0.5296**
	Post	30	3.9000	
English assignment questions	Pre	55	3.3273	0.4394*
	Post	30	3.7667	
Quiz and exam questions	Pre	55	3.2909	0.2758
	Post	30	3.5667	
English laboratory instruction	Pre	54	3.4444	0.4222*
	Post	30	3.8667	
Average of all "Reading" in subject 1	Pre		3.2826	0.5126
	Post		3.7952	
Subject 2				
Statement: I can fully understand ...[1]		N	Mean	Difference (Post–Pre)
English vocabulary in textbook[+]	Pre	210	3.0600	0.2100
	Post	223	3.2700	
English sentences in textbook	Pre	210	3.1400	0.1300
	Post	223	3.2700	
English lecture notes	Pre	210	3.3048	0.1033
	Post	223	3.4081	
English tutorial notes	Pre	208	3.3077	0.1587
	Post	223	3.4664	
English assignment questions	Pre	208	3.2837	0.2724**
	Post	223	3.5561	
Quiz and exam questions	Pre	208	3.1779	0.0789
	Post	222	3.2568	

Table 2.1. Self-evaluation of reading (continued)

Subject 2				
Statement: I am confident in ...[1]		N	Mean	Difference (Post–Pre)
English legal and official document	Pre	210	2.9857	0.2206**
	Post	223	3.2063	
Average of all "Reading" in subject 2	Pre		3.1800	0.1677
	Post		3.3477	

1. All responses were given on a five-point Likert scale (1 = strongly disagree; 5 = strongly agree).
* Results significant at level of significance; ** results significant at level of significance;
+ items where discipline-specific materials were developed and provided to students.

Table 2.2. Self-evaluation of writing

Subject 1				
Statement: I am confident in ...[1]		N	Mean	Difference (Post–Pre)
Writing assignments in English	Pre	55	3.2909	0.6091**
	Post	30	3.9000	
Summarising major ideas in a paragraph	Pre	55	3.2545	0.6788**
	Post	30	3.9333	
Using different English vocabulary	Pre	55	3.2909	0.5758**
	Post	30	3.8667	
Writing with a topic sentence	Pre	55	3.4909	0.4091**
	Post	30	3.9000	
Reporting on figures findings in English	Pre	55	3.3091	0.5909**
	Post	30	3.9000	
Writing laboratory reports in English+	Pre	55	3.3636	0.6364**
	Post	30	4.0000	
Average of all "Writing" in subject 1	Pre		3.3333	0.5833
	Post		3.9167	
Subject 2				
Statement: I am confident in ...[1]		N	Mean	Difference (Post–Pre)
Writing assignments in English	Pre	210	3.0476	0.2887**
	Post	223	3.3363	
Summarising major ideas in a paragraph	Pre	210	3.3571	0.1541
	Post	223	3.5112	

Table 2.2. Self-evaluation of writing (continued)

Subject 2				
Statement: I am confident in ...[1]		N	Mean	Difference (Post–Pre)
Using different English vocabulary	Pre	210	2.8810	0.406**
	Post	223	3.2870	
Writing with a topic sentence	Pre	210	3.4857	0.0638
	Post	222	3.5495	
Reporting on figures findings in English	Pre	210	3.2476	0.2098**
	Post	223	3.4574	
Writing case study critics in English+	Pre	208	3.0240	0.2540**
	Post	223	3.2780	
Average of all "Writing" in subject 2	Pre		3.1738	0.2294
	Post		3.4033	

1. All responses were given on a five-point Likert scale (1 = strongly disagree; 5 = strongly agree).
* Results significant at level of significance; ** results significant at level of significance;
+ items where discipline-specific materials were developed and provided to students.

Table 2.3. Self-evaluation of speaking

Subject 1				
Statement: I am confident in ...[1]		N	Mean	Difference (Post–Pre)
Asking questions in English	Pre	55	3.3636	0.5364**
	Post	30	3.9000	
Group discussion in English	Pre	55	3.3818	0.5848**
	Post	30	3.9667	
Presentation in English	Pre	54	3.3333	0.5667**
	Post	30	3.9000	
Average of all "Speaking" in subject 1	Pre		3.3606	0.5811
	Post		3.9417	
Subject 2				
Statement: I am confident in ...[1]		N	Mean	Difference (Post – Pre)
Answering questions in English	Pre	210	3.2619	0.1885**
	Post	222	3.4505	
Asking questions in English	Pre	210	3.2762	0.2058**
	Post	222	3.4820	

Table 2.3. Self-evaluation of speaking (continued)

Subject 2				
Statement: I am confident in . . . [1]		N	Mean	Difference (Post–Pre)
Group discussion in English	Pre	210	3.1905	0.2465**
	Post	222	3.4369	
Presentation in English	Pre	210	3.2381	0.2214**
	Post	222	3.4595	
Average of all "Speaking" in subject 2	Pre		3.2417	0.2155
	Post		3.4572	

1. *All responses were given on a five-point Likert scale (1 = strongly disagree; 5 = strongly agree).*
* *Results significant at level of significance;* ** *results significant at level of significance.*

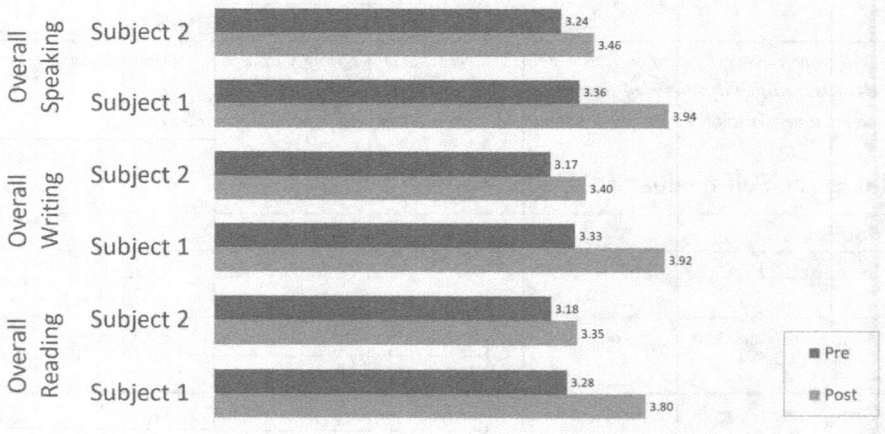

Figure 2.1. Overall ratings for reading, writing and speaking.

Difference Between Student Groups

Junior undergraduate students (subject one) showed higher levels of self-confidence in English and a larger improvement in self-confidence in the post-course survey than their final-year counterparts (subject two). This was possibly because half of the final-year class was made up of students who matriculated from higher diploma or associate degree programmes (alternative pathways to degree programmes) and thus had weaker English backgrounds. That group of students tended to strongly focus on achieving high GPAs in the technical subjects in order to matriculate to the degree programme and thus may have paid less attention to improving their English.

Awareness of the Importance of English

The second section of the survey examined students' awareness of the importance of English language skills. The results are summarised in Table 2.4.

Students were well aware of the importance of English for instrumental purposes, such as learning, handling assessment tasks, and getting jobs, as was evident from the high mean scores of close to or above 4 (*agree*). Final-year students (subject two) were highly aware of the importance of good English from the start of the semester, and this remained unchanged considering normal statistical variations. Junior undergraduate students (subject one), on the other hand, showed a statistically significant increase in their awareness of the importance of English in the post-survey.

The reported motivations for good English skills were all instrumental in nature and related to extrinsic pragmatic benefits; for example, achieving a better GPA to graduate with a good honours degree and thus getting professional recognition. These instrumental motivations were stronger among final-year students, for which "getting a job" appeared to be the most important consideration, based on the highest mean scores.

Table 2.4. English awareness

Subject 1				
Statement: I think good English is important for...[1]		N	Mean	Difference (Post–Pre)
Reading course materials	Pre	54	3.7037	0.4963**
	Post	30	4.2000	
Writing technical reports	Pre	54	3.8148	0.4185*
	Post	30	4.2333	
Presenting my ideas	Pre	54	3.7778	0.4556*
	Post	30	4.2333	
Getting a job	Pre	54	3.8148	0.4519*
	Post	30	4.2667	
Subject 2				
Statement: I think good English is important for...[1]		N	Mean	Difference (Post–Pre)
Reading course materials	Pre	208	4.0192	0.0170
	Post	221	4.0362	
Writing technical reports	Pre	208	4.0865	−0.0367
	Post	221	4.0498	

Table 2.4. English awareness (continued)

Subject 2				
Statement: I am confident in . . . [1]		N	Mean	Difference (Post–Pre)
Presenting my ideas	Pre	207	4.0773	-0.0592
	Post	221	4.0181	
Getting a job	Pre	208	4.1154	-0.0336
	Post	220	4.0818	

1. All responses were given on a five-point Likert scale (1 = strongly disagree; 5 = strongly agree).
* Results significant at level of significance; ** results significant at level of significance.

Difficulties with English and Self-Help Solutions

The final section of the survey consisted of open-ended questions about difficulties in learning or using English, and what students do if they encounter difficulties.

Difficulties in Learning or Using English

Table 2.5 summarises students' self-reported difficulties in learning and using English. Although students displayed higher self-confidence in speaking, followed by writing and reading (as discussed above), when they were asked open-ended questions about the specific difficulties they have, most replies concerned speaking, followed by vocabulary, grammar, and writing. Few replies focused on reading, and none were related to listening. It can be concluded that students acknowledged more difficulties in productive skills (speaking and writing) than in receptive skills (reading and listening).

In addition to reporting difficulties concerning their abilities, some students added comments about the learning environment, such as "(a lack of speaking) opportunities" or the "English atmosphere." Subject lecturers saw passive learning, or students' shyness to express their opinions, as the major reason for the students' perceptions of a poor English atmosphere.

Table 2.5. Students' self-reported English difficulties

Category	Subject 1	Subject 2
Reading	Comprehension	Reading speed Comprehension (e.g., understanding questions) Legal language
Writing	Essay writing	Academic writing (e.g., essay) Professional writing Technical writing

Table 2.5. Students' self-reported English difficulties (continued)

Category	Subject 1	Subject 2
Speaking	Opportunities Accent	Pronunciation Presentation skills Casual conversation Complete utterance Confidence Group discussion Speaking opportunities
Listening	-	-
Grammar	Sentence structures Grammar	Sentence structures Grammar Complete sentence Tenses
Vocabulary	Terminology Meanings Word choice	Word meanings Legal vocabulary Spelling Jargons Situation use
Others	Professional English English is not their first language	English atmosphere English is not their first language Organisation Expression of ideas Logic Reliance on translation sites

Self-Help Strategies

When students first learnt English, they were taught to consult a dictionary when they encountered words that they did not know. Their knowledge of specific words and phrases is largely sufficient for learning and understanding, but students need more than words and phrases to express themselves in extended paragraphs or in oral presentations, and dictionaries are not so helpful in this regard. As internet services become increasingly popular and convenient, it is interesting to see whether students' strategies have changed.

Students' habits in using dictionaries and translation sites (such as Google Translate) to assist in writing are summarised in Table 2.6, and the self-help strategies provided in response to the open-ended question are summarised in Table 2.7.

- Use of dictionaries: When students did not know a word, most either agreed or strongly agreed that they would look it up in a dictionary. The level of agreement with regard to using a dictionary was higher

among more senior students (subject two), whilst around 30 percent of junior undergraduates (subject one) had a neutral view.
- Use of translation sites: When students did not know how to express themselves in written English, most reported that they would use a translation site. Nonetheless, the level of agreement was lower than that for the use of a dictionary, which demonstrates that students were more sceptical about the value of translation sites.
- The most popular self-help solution reported by students was the use of dictionaries, followed by the internet, but the combined results of "Internet" and "Google" surpassed that of "Dictionary." A small number of students reported they would seek help from the subject teachers, ask their friends, or contact the English Language Centre.

Table 2.6. Students' use of dictionaries and translation sites

When I do not know a word, I will look up dictionaries	Subject 1		Subject 2	
	Frequency	Percent	Frequency	Percent
5 - Strongly agree	8	14.5%	54	25.7%
4 - Agree	25	45.5%	97	46.2%
3 - Neutral	17	30.9%	42	20%
2 - Disagree	2	3.6%	13	6.2%
1 - Strongly disagree	2	3.6%	2	1%
Missing	1	1.8%	2	1%
Total	55	100%	210	100%
	Mean = 3.65 Std. deviation = 0.914		Mean = 3.90 Std. deviation = 0.890	
When I do not know how to write, I will use translation sites	Subject 1		Subject 2	
	Frequency	Percent	Frequency	Percent
5 - Strongly agree	10	18.2%	43	20.5%
4 - Agree	19	34.5%	82	39%
3 - Neutral	16	29.1%	48	22.9%
2 - Disagree	7	12.7%	26	12.4%
1 - Strongly disagree	2	3.6%	7	3.3%
Missing	1	1.8%	4	1.9%
Total	55	100%	210	100%
	Mean = 3.52 Std. deviation = 1.059		Mean = 3.62 Std. deviation = 1.056	

Table 2.7. Students' self-reported strategies

Subject 1		Subject 2	
Students' solutions	Votes	Students' solutions	Votes
Dictionary	8	Dictionary	44
Internet	3	Internet	43
Google	8	Google	24
Ask friends	5	Ask friends	23
Translation sites	4	Translation sites	14
Ask teachers	3	Ask teachers	11
		Consultation	5
		Read articles	4
		Ask native speakers	3
		Ask teaching assistants	3
English Language Centre (ELC)	1	ELC tutors	2
Centre for Independent Language Learning (CILL)	1	CILL	1
		Read reference books	1
		Revision	1
		Siri	1
		Wild guess	1
		Write down vocabularies	1
YouTube	1		
Wikipedia	1		

Discussion and Conclusions

Despite the importance of language and communication skills for students in the fields of science and engineering, a compartmentalisation of language learning and content learning has been observed in technical disciplines. The teaching, learning, and assessment of technical content habitually use symbols (calculations) and drawings much more often than words. Writing and speaking practice activities are therefore marginalised. This chapter has reported results from a student survey conducted as part of a project that aims to devise content-based language enhancement strategies for the science and engineering disciplines.

The student survey was conducted to understand students' self-evaluation of their abilities in English and their attitudes, major difficulties, and self-help strategies. Generally, students were fairly confident in their use of English in the academic/disciplinary context. They felt most confident in speaking, followed by writing, and then reading. However, when they were asked in open-ended questions to identify the most difficult issues in learning or using English, most replies were related to speaking, followed by writing, vocabulary, and grammar. This is not a contradiction but rather serves as indirect evidence that the current teaching practice does not demand much productive language use. As a result, students have high confidence in handling the (minimal) kind of speaking required. Apart from the difficulties concerning their English language ability, students also reported that the (classroom) atmosphere did not facilitate the use of English or improvement in its use. The subject lecturers commented that students' passive learning attitudes and/or shyness in expressing their views could be attributed to the "poor English atmosphere."

Students clearly recognised the importance of English for instrumental purposes, such as learning, handling assessment tasks, and getting jobs. Therefore, if "good English" is not aligned with these instrumental purposes, most students would not devote time and effort to them. The low usage of project materials and low engagement rates in voluntary language enhancement activities provided clear evidence for this.

Self-Regulation in Language Enhancement

Content-based language enhancement strategies are not about promoting language to serve as a core learning objective in science and engineering subjects; essentially, they are about technical subject teachers playing a role in fostering self-regulated language learning. Rebecca Oxford and Carol Griffiths (2016) consolidated the definitions of L2 learning strategies and identified self-regulation as one of the key learning "strength factors." Barry Zimmerman (1990) defined students' self-regulated learning as involving three features: (i) their use of self-regulated learning strategies, (ii) their responsiveness to self-oriented feedback about learning effectiveness, and (iii) their interdependent motivational processes. Empirical evidence presented by Zimmerman (1990) also suggested that self-regulation leads to higher academic achievement. Self-regulated learning requires more than cognitive skills; it also requires a motivational component, and the motivation is domain specific. Ulrich Schiefele (1991) echoed the view that "interest" is a content-specific motivational characteristic that has an important bearing on the quality of learning results and the learning experience, and stimulates the use of deep learning strategies. Furthermore, Zimmerman (1990) noted that self-regulated learners have the option not to self-regulate if they are not sufficiently eager to achieve a particular learning outcome. Problems in self-regulation typically arise when discrepancies occur between short-term and long-term outcomes.

The above discussion about self-regulated language learning leads to two conclusions that are relevant to this chapter. First, if interest or motivation is domain specific, it is almost certain that the status quo of diminished importance of language in technical subjects is undermining students' motivations for language improvement, and is thus not conducive to language enhancement. Second, when students' academic success in subjects is predominately dependent on their ability to demonstrate their knowledge via calculation and drawing rather than via writing or oral presentation, conflicts arise between short-term and long-term outcomes, as described in the preceding paragraph. Although effective communication skills may lead to the eventual reward of better career opportunities, most students choose to spend their time focusing on technical content for more immediate rewards, which causes problems with self-regulation in language learning.

The Way Forward for Language Enhancement in Science and Engineering

In an effort to help science and engineering students enhance their English via a content-based approach, the following four actions are considered essential:

- devising useful language enhancement materials that target students' specific areas of weakness,
- integrating these materials into respective technical subjects,
- soliciting cooperation from subject teachers, and
- stimulating students' motivation and engagement.

Of these, stimulating students' motivation and engagement is the most difficult to achieve but the most crucial element of success. The findings reported in this chapter suggest that the current subject and curriculum design cannot provide motivation for students to deploy self-regulated language learning or to sustain their self-regulation.

Lacking opportunities for more extensive use of English in teaching and assessment, and students' low levels of motivation are systemic issues that cannot be solved with piecemeal efforts. In the future development of this project, in addition to devising other types of content-specific language-enhancement materials, efforts are required to create more opportunities for students to practise English at the subject and curriculum levels. A long-term plan should be developed to consistently incorporate sufficient writing and speaking tasks throughout a programme, and students should be required to complete more challenging language tasks as they progress.

Acknowledgement

The study in this chapter is funded by the Language Enhancement Grant of the Hong Kong Polytechnic University (LEG16–19/LS/CEE1).

References

Accreditation Board for Engineering and Technology. (2016). *Criteria for accrediting engineering programs, 2016–17*. http://www.abet.org/accreditation/accreditation-criteria/criteria-for-accrediting-engineering-programs-2016-2017/#objectives .

Allison, D. (1992). From "remedial English" to "English enhancement" (So, what else is new?). *Hongkong Papers in Linguistics and Language Teaching*, *15*, 15–29.

Cheng, W., Chan, M., Chiu, H., Kwok, A., Lam, K. H., Lam, K. M. K., Lim, G. & Wright, R. (2014). *Enhancing students' professional competence and generic qualities through writing in English across the curriculum*. The Hong Kong Polytechnic University.

Dunworth, K., Drury, H., Kralik, C. & Moore, T. (2014). Rhetoric and realities: On the development of university-wide strategies to promote student English language growth. *Journal of Higher Education Policy and Management*, *36*(5), 520–532. https://doi.org/10.1080/1360080x.2014.936088.

Essig, R. R., Troy, C. D., Jesiek, B. K., Buswell, N. T. & Boyd, J. E. (2018). Assessment and characterization of writing exercises in core engineering textbooks. *Journal of Professional Issues in Engineering Education and Practice*, *144*(4), 04018007. https://doi.org/10.1061/(asce)ei.1943-5541.0000378.

Evans, S. & Green, C. (2007). Why EAP is necessary: A survey of Hong Kong tertiary students. *Journal of English for Academic Purposes*, *6*, 3–17. https://doi.org/10.1016/j.jeap.2006.11.005.

Evans, S. & Morrison, B. (2011). Meeting the challenges of English-medium higher education: The first-year experience in Hong Kong. *English for Specific Purposes*, *30*, 198–208. https://doi.org/10.1016/j.esp.2011.01.001.

Evans, S. & Morrison, B. (2012). Learning and using English at university: Lessons from a longitudinal study in Hong Kong. *The Journal of Asia TEFL*, *9*(2), 21–47.

Fang, Z. (2005). Scientific literacy: A systemic functional linguistics perspective. *Science Education*, *89*(2), 335–347. https://doi.org/10.1002/sce.20050.

Goldsmith, R. & Willey, K. (2016). "It's not my job to teach writing": Activity theory analysis of [invisible] writing practices in the engineering curriculum. *Journal of Academic Language & Learning*, *10*(1), A118-A129.

Hong Kong Examinations and Assessment Authority. (2019). *Entrance requirements for undergraduate programmes.* http://www.hkeaa.edu.hk/en/recognition/hkdse_recognition/local/.

INWAC Ad Hoc Working Group. (2018). Statement of WAC Principles and Practices. https://wac.colostate.edu/principles/.

Kiefer, K., Palmquist, M., Carbone, N., Cox, M. & Melzer, D. (2018). *An introduction to writing across the curriculum.* The WAC Clearinghouse. https://wac.colostate.edu/resources/wac/intro/.

Kuteeva, M. & Airey, J. (2013). Disciplinary differences in the use of English in higher education: Reflections on recent language policy developments. *Higher Education, 67*(5), 533–549. https://doi.org/10.1007/s10734-013-9660-6.

Lasley, T. (2010). Bloom's taxonomy. In T. C. Hunt, J. C. Carper & T. J. Lasley (Eds.), Encyclopedia of educational reform and dissent (pp. 107–109). SAGE Publications, Inc. https://www.doi.org/10.4135/9781412957403.n51.

Lee, O., Quinn, H. & Valdés, G. (2013). Science and language for English language learners in relation to next generation science standards and with implications for Common Core State Standards for English language arts and mathematics. *Educational Researcher, 42*(4), 223–233. https://doi.org/10.3102/0013189x13480524.

Murray, N. & Hicks, M. (2014). An institutional approach to English language proficiency. *Journal of Further and Higher Education, 40*(2), 170–187. https://doi.org/10.1080/0309877X.2014.938261.

Oxford, R. L. & Griffiths, C. (2016). Bringing order out of chaos. In R. Oxford & C. Griffith (Eds.), *Teaching and researching language learning strategies: Self-regulation in context* (2nd ed.) (pp. 84–103). Routledge.

Patterson, L. M. & Slinger-Friedman, V. (2012). Writing in undergraduate geography classes: Faculty challenges and rewards. *Journal of Geography, 111*(5), 187–193. https://doi.org/10.1080/00221341.2011.617833.

Schiefele, U. (1991). Interest, learning, and motivation. *Educational Psychologist, 26*(3–4), 299–323. https://doi.org/10.1080/00461520.1991.9653136.

Siu, B. W. Y. (2019). Science and engineering students' English competence and motivation in improving English: Voices from teachers and students [Unpublished manuscript].

Snow, C. E. (2010). Academic language and the challenge of reading for learning about science. *Science, 328*(5977), 450–452. https://doi.org/10.1126/science.1182597.

The Hong Kong Institution of Engineers. (2013). *Professional accreditation handbook (engineering degrees).* https://hkie.org.hk/en/quali/criteria/.

Wellington, J. J. & Osborne, J. (2001). *Language and literacy in science education.* Open University.

Yore, L., Bisanz, G. L. & Hand, B. M. (2003). Examining the literacy component of science literacy: 25 years of language arts and science research. *International Journal of Science Education, 25*(6), 689–725. https://doi.org/10.1080/09500690305018.

Zimmerman, B. J. (1990). Self-regulated learning and academic achievement: An overview. *Educational Psychologist, 25*(1), 3–17. https://doi.org/10.1207/s15326985ep2501_2.

Appendix

Pre-course Questionnaire

Think about your learning experience in the first two lessons. Please circle the suitable number for Question 1 to 23 and answer Question 24 to 25 below.

Reading comprehension

	Strongly agree	Agree	Neutral	Disagree	Strongly disagree
1. I can fully understand the English <u>vocabulary</u> in textbook.	1	2	3	4	5
2. I can fully understand the English <u>sentences</u> in textbook.	1	2	3	4	5
3. I can fully understand the English <u>lecture notes</u> (e.g. lecture notes and Powerpoint slides)	1	2	3	4	5
4. I can fully understand the English <u>tutorial notes</u> (e.g. worksheet)	1	2	3	4	5
5. I can fully understand the English <u>assignment questions</u>.	1	2	3	4	5
6. I can fully understand the <u>quiz and exam questions</u>.	1	2	3	4	5
7. I can fully understand the English <u>laboratory instruction</u>.	1	2	3	4	5

Technical writing

	Strongly agree	Agree	Neutral	Disagree	Strongly disagree
8. I am confident in writing <u>assignments</u> in English.	1	2	3	4	5
9. I can <u>summarise major ideas</u> in a paragraph in English.	1	2	3	4	5
10. I can use different English <u>vocabulary</u> in my writing.	1	2	3	4	5
11. I usually start writing with a <u>topic sentence</u>.	1	2	3	4	5
12. I have no difficulties reporting on <u>figures/findings</u> in English.	1	2	3	4	5
13. I am confident in writing <u>laboratory reports</u> in English.	1	2	3	4	5

Presentation skills

	Strongly agree	Agree	Neutral	Disagree	Strongly disagree
14. I am confident in <u>answering questions</u> in English.	1	2	3	4	5
15. I am confident in <u>asking questions</u> in English.	1	2	3	4	5
16. I am confident in <u>group discussion</u> in English.	1	2	3	4	5
17. I am confident in <u>presentation</u> in English.	1	2	3	4	5

Gaps in Content-Based English Enhancement

English awareness

	Strongly agree	Agree	Neutral	Disagree	Strongly disagree
18. I think good English is important for reading course materials.	1	2	3	4	5
19. I think good English is important for writing technical reports.	1	2	3	4	5
20. I think good English is important for presenting my ideas.	1	2	3	4	5
21. I think good English is important for getting a job.	1	2	3	4	5
22. When I do not know a word, I will look up dictionaries.	1	2	3	4	5
23. When I do not know how to write, I will use translation sites (e.g. Google Translate).	1	2	3	4	5

24. What are your major difficulties in English?

25. When you have English problems, what will you do?

Post-course Questionnaire

Think about your learning experience in the first two lessons. Please circle the suitable number for Question 1 to 25 and answer Question 26 below.

Reading comprehension

	Strongly agree	Agree	Neutral	Disagree	Strongly disagree
1. I fully understand the English vocabulary in textbook.	5	4	3	2	1
2. I fully understand the English sentences in textbook.	5	4	3	2	1
3. I fully understand the English lecture notes (e.g. lecture notes and Powerpoint slides)	5	4	3	2	1
4. I fully understand the English tutorial notes (e.g. worksheet)	5	4	3	2	1
5. I fully understand the English assignment questions.	5	4	3	2	1
6. I fully understand the quiz and exam questions.	5	4	3	2	1
7. I fully understand the English laboratory instruction.	5	4	3	2	1

Technical writing

	Strongly agree	Agree	Neutral	Disagree	Strongly disagree
8. I am confident in writing assignments in English.	5	4	3	2	1
9. I can summarise major ideas in a paragraph in English.	5	4	3	2	1

10. I can use different English <u>vocabulary</u> in my writing.	5	4	3	2	1
11. I usually start writing with a <u>topic sentence</u>.	5	4	3	2	1
12. I have no difficulties reporting on <u>figures/findings</u> in English.	5	4	3	2	1
13. I am confident in writing <u>laboratory reports</u> in English.	5	4	3	2	1

Presentation skills

	Strongly agree	Agree	Neutral	Disagree	Strongly disagree
14. I am confident in <u>answering questions</u> in English.	5	4	3	2	1
15. I am confident in <u>asking questions</u> in English.	5	4	3	2	1
16. I am confident in <u>group discussion</u> in English.	5	4	3	2	1
17. I am confident in <u>presentation</u> in English.	5	4	3	2	1

English awareness

	Strongly agree	Agree	Neutral	Disagree	Strongly disagree
18. I think good English is important for <u>reading course materials</u>.	5	4	3	2	1
19. I think good English is important for <u>writing technical reports</u>.	5	4	3	2	1
20. I think good English is important for <u>presenting my ideas</u>.	5	4	3	2	1
21. I think good English is important for <u>getting a job</u>.	5	4	3	2	1
22. I find the English Hub (i.e. the website shared in class email) useful.	5	4	3	2	1
23. I find the 'wordcloud' of vocabulary useful.	5	4	3	2	1
24. I find the reading tips useful for understanding assignment questions.	5	4	3	2	1
25. I find the writing tips useful for writing a case study report.	5	4	3	2	1

26. What other resources and/or services do you want to get from the English Hub website?

3 Students' Perceptions of the Use of English in a Core Business Subject for First-Year Business Students

Hannah Y. Lai and King-Wah Pang
THE HONG KONG POLYTECHNIC UNIVERSITY

Abstract: English literacy and communication skills are crucial to business graduates for their future career development, and Hong Kong universities emphasize language competency across the curriculum to develop students as effective communicators. In the Faculty of Business at The Hong Kong Polytechnic University, each core subject includes an individual English language writing task, contributing to at least 15 percent of the overall subject assessment. This chapter reports on a study investigating the ongoing English Across the Curriculum collaboration between the Faculty and the English Language Centre. The study examined student perceptions of the use of language as a grading criterion in a core business subject, as well as the usefulness of assessment language support materials. The findings indicate that most students used the language materials and reported improvements in their case study reports. However, some did not recognize the central importance of language competency, believing that language skills and professional knowledge are separate entities.

Keywords: collaboration, use of English, perceptions, business students, higher education

Introduction

Internationalization has been adopted as one of the core objectives of higher education for the 21st century in Hong Kong as well as in other parts of the world. In recent years the world of education has been tremendously affected by economic, cultural, and technological changes, and this has contributed to the current internationalization trends in higher education (Yemini & Sagie,

2016). The university student population has increased and become more heterogeneous than ever before in terms of academic, linguistic, and cultural background (Dafouz & Smit, 2016). In the Asia-Pacific region, an important indicator of the extent to which a university is "internationalized" is the university's capacity to deliver programs in English (Wang et al., 2017).

The use of English as a medium of instruction (EMI) is a growing global trend in universities outside the major English-speaking countries in the world. The reasons for this trend include the increase in student mobility, the need to increase university rankings, and the fact that English is the principal language of research (Evans & Morrison, 2017). In Hong Kong, about 16 percent of the student population in universities are non-local students, including international students and mainland Chinese students (Yu & Wright, 2017).

Interdisciplinary Collaborations

As the English language is considered the lingua franca in the realms of scientific research, academic publication, and international business, more higher education institutions are offering programs in English (Hammond, 2016). However, studies reveal questions about the importance of English in the higher education classroom. University students report that their professors focus only on content and do not correct students' language errors, which negatively affects students' English writing and speaking skills (Ament & Pérez-Vidal, 2015). This issue highlights the need for teachers from different disciplines to work together to optimize the undergraduate learning experience. With a better understanding of students' perceptions of English writing in their courses, English teachers, discipline teachers, and students can bridge the gap between students' understanding of writing and that of teachers, and students can be better prepared for the globalized workplace upon graduation.

Indeed, both interdisciplinarity and collaboration are deemed "mantras for change in the 21st century" (Klein & Falk-Krzesinski, 2017, p. 1055). However, collaboration among disciplines in universities seems uncommon in Hong Kong (Braine, 2001). One reason for this lack of collaboration could be that the focus in higher education courses is mainly on covering content (Clughen & Connell, 2012; Zhu, 2004). Another cause could be that professors feel territorial about their area of expertise (Becher & Trowler, 2001; Pawan & Ortloff, 2011; Zhu, 2004). Some English teachers, likewise, may feel similarly and even be skeptical about embedding language use in content subjects (Fulwiler, 1988). Samer Annous and Maureen Nicolas (2015) maintain that this paradigm of "tribes and territories" (p. 104) is now outdated, and it hinders the students' development of all the skills that are crucial to be competitive in modern life. The lack of collaboration among departments could also be partly a result of the reward system, as Julie Klein and Holly Falk-Krzesinski (2017) posit that universities should take steps "to establish greater clarity in assigning credit . . . in response to the challenge of judging individual contributions in collaborative research" (p. 1057).

Another challenge faced by collaborators in different disciplines is that collaborating researchers in different fields may use different words to describe the same phenomena because "what we see is largely dependent on what we have been trained to see" (Dixon & Dougherty, 2010, p. 3). Thus, individuals from different academic disciplines who work together will find themselves "always slightly at cross purposes" (Dixon & Dougherty, 2010, p. 3). It is, therefore, important for teachers from different disciplines to be aware of their differences and appreciate that they look at students' writing through different lenses. Together, they can provide students with an improved learning experience and successful outcomes.

Writing Practices

Studies conducted in Hong Kong and other regions show that students benefit from content courses that include the use of language as one of the assessment criteria, as well as from collaboration between English language teachers and content-area teachers (Bacha, 2012; Evans & Morrison, 2011; Jackson, 2005; Pawan & Ortloff, 2011). Marcelo Gaspar and colleagues (2017) conducted a "collaborative pedagogical experiment" (p. 209) in a Portuguese school of engineering for one semester, and suggested that collaboration between teachers "can take place in various situations, which may be globally classified as co-teaching" (p. 211). They conclude that the dedicated design strategies used in the team-teaching approach "contributed positively to the students' learning processes" (p. 214). While the teachers reported positive feedback about combining content with language, students stated they had more motivation for language learning, and that the discussion exercises, presentations, and writing activities helped to develop their communicative skills.

While team teaching may be beneficial to students' learning, collaboration between teachers can be difficult. David Lasagabaster (2018) notes the need for "strenuous efforts" to develop content teachers into "new advocates of this language and content integration" (p. 413), with the time required for collaboration a hindering issue. Shari Lughmani et al. (2016) conducted studies in three universities in Hong Kong, and found team teaching to be "the deepest form of collaboration" (p. 31). They maintain that different forms of collaboration can lead to greater integration of English in content subjects and increase mutual understanding between content teachers and language teachers.

In a study conducted at one Hong Kong university, 20 teachers from four faculties were interviewed about their students' writing and their feedback to students (Hyland, 2013). The study revealed that even though some subject tutors who "recognize the importance of writing conventions" do provide students support with their writing assignments, "students cannot always depend on this" (p. 252). The "information about faculty writing practices, about subject teacher beliefs, and about learner performance . . . form a key part of the context of writing at university" (p. 252). With a better understanding of university students' perceptions of the integration of language into discipline-specific subjects, teachers from different departments can collaborate and work together more effectively. To provide students with a better understanding of effective writing in their field of studies and to prepare students for the workplace, the study reported in this chapter aimed to explore business students' perceptions of integrating English and communication skills in a content subject.

Background and Context of the Current Study

Hong Kong, an international finance and logistics center, attracts a significant number of multinational enterprises to engage in business and in many cases to establish their headquarters in the city. To supply competent professional young talent to the market, universities in Hong Kong emphasize students' literacy and communication skills. A common learning outcome for university undergraduate programs is to develop students as effective communicators. Graduates are expected to be able to skillfully connect and establish positive relationships with different people across a range of professional and personal contexts. They are also expected to communicate effectively in English and Chinese, both orally and in writing, in professional/work-related contexts. Lughmani et al. (2016) explored English Across the Curriculum (EAC) initiatives in Hong Kong universities and collaboration between English language teachers and general education teachers and the faculties of social sciences and engineering. Studies, however, have not yet investigated the collaboration between English language teachers and teaching staff from business faculties.

In order to develop students' language skills, the Faculty of Business at The Hong Kong Polytechnic University adopted a policy in 2008 that mandated every subject should contain a significant element of individual writing tasks in English. This chapter reports on a collaborative EAC project between a business faculty subject instructor and the English Language Centre (ELC). The study pertained to an assessment which accounted for 15 percent of the overall course grade in one business course. The students were required to select one case from a list of six and write an essay that addressed the questions included at the end of the case description.

The Study

The study was conducted in the second semester of the 2018–2019 academic year. The co-investigator from the ELC prepared guidelines and a checklist to help students with various aspects of English writing. The guidelines included information on the structure, coherence, and referencing style of a case study report. The checklist aimed to help students include all necessary items in their case study report before submitting the assignment.

Questionnaire survey

One hundred and seventy-four business students who took LGT2106 "Principles of Operations Management" in the second semester of the 2018–2019 academic year participated in this study, and more than 90 percent were first-year students. The students were enrolled in four classes taught by four business content teachers, and all were required to write the case study report as one of their assessments. The ELC co-investigator offered a briefing session to all classes on how to use the checklist and guidelines two weeks before their assignment submission.

After students submitted their assignment, they were invited to complete a questionnaire (see Appendix). The questionnaire was designed to explore how business students felt about integrating English into a core business subject. Both open-ended questions and closed questions were used in the survey. Hard copies of the questionnaires were distributed in class by the four business content teachers one week after the case study report was due. These teachers collected the questionnaires at the end of the class and passed the completed questionnaires to the ELC instructor. The student responses were then analyzed.

Findings and Discussion

Students were first asked if they were aware of the weighting of the assignment with regard to their use of English (40 percent of the total marks). About 56 percent (97 respondents) reported that they did know the weighting.

However, as shown in Table 3.1, among the 97 respondents who reported they knew the weighting, only 68 respondents actually knew the correct percentage. Therefore, only 39 percent of all respondents (174 respondents) knew the correct weighting of English in the assignment. The students' responses to this question ranged from 10 percent to 100 percent. This result indicates that only a small proportion of students were aware of the importance of language competency in this business core subject. This could be because of the nature of this core subject—Principles of Operations Management. The subject's intended learning outcomes focus on students' ability to recognize the key techniques and concepts in operations management, and to apply various quantitative models and approaches to inform decision-making in a real business situation. With the emphasis on quantitative models and application in this subject, the students might not focus on their use of English in the case study report.

Table 3.1. Student awareness of the weighting for language use

Awareness of weighting for language use	Students
Stated knowing the weighting for language use.	97 (55.7%)
Stated the correct weighting	68 (39.1%)
Stated the incorrect weighting	29 (16.6%)
Stated not knowing the weighting for language use.	77 (44.3%)
Total	174 (100%)

Table 3.2. Student perceptions of the appropriateness of the weighting for language use (for those 97 students who were aware of a weighting for language)

Appropriate	Students
Yes	52 (53.61%)
No	40 (41.24%)
Missing answer	5 (5.15%)
Total	77 (100%)

Among those respondents who reported they knew the correct percentage, around 54 percent of them (52 respondents) thought that the weighting was appropriate, while 41 percent thought that it was inappropriate, as shown in Table 3.2. However, after checking the feedback of those respondents who thought the weighting was appropriate (52 respondents), only 27 of them actually knew the correct weighting (i.e., 40 percent), which means that more than 48 percent of the respondents' comments on the appropriateness of the weighting were made based on their wrong judgement of the weighting. This result made it difficult for us to analyze students' perceptions of the importance of language use. Nonetheless, it could clearly be concluded that the students were not aware of the importance of the use of English in this subject.

Students' Perceptions of the Weighting

The common reasons given by those students who thought the weighting was appropriate included "Language is important," "Essay structure, organization and presentation are important for Business students," "Essay should be reader friendly and easy to understand," and "It's important to have clear expression, generation and elaboration of ideas in writing essay." Among those respondents who thought that the weighting was inappropriate, most of them thought that it was too heavy, while only a few respondents thought that the weighting was too low. The reasons for claiming the weighting to be too heavy included "Content and ideas are more important" and "This subject is a major discipline subject instead of a language subject."

We further asked the students if the weighting affected their preparation for writing the essay. Around 80 percent (77 respondents) thought that the weighting had "some" or "a lot" of impact on their writing of the essay, as shown in Table 3.3. Even though some students did not agree with the high weighting of their use of English, they acknowledged that their language competency affected their academic performance in this business subject.

Table 3.3. Effect of the weighting for language use on students' preparation of the case study report (for those 97 students who were aware of weighting for language)

Effect	Students
A lot	22 (22.68%)
Some	55 (56.70%)
Little	13 (13.40%)
No change	7 (7.22%)
Total	97 (100%)

Effectiveness of the Language Tips and Checklists

Close to three-quarters of the respondents reported referring to the guidelines and checklist while they were writing the essay. As displayed in Table

3.4, a large majority of the students who had referred to the language tips found them useful. In particular, over 95 percent of the students found the tips on writing the case study report very useful or useful. This could be because most first-year undergraduate students have not written a business case study report before and they focused specifically on the language appropriate for the assignment. The tips on coherence, use of references, referring to sources, and the quick referencing guide for academic writing (APA 6th Edition) were also described as very useful and useful by over 80 percent of the students. In addition, around 80 percent of the students found the report writing checklist and the referencing checklist very useful or useful.

Table 3.4. Student perceptions of the effectiveness of the English tips

Tips	Very useful/ Useful	Not useful	Did not use
Writing a Case Study Report	95.32%	3.91%	0.78%
Coherence in Academic Writing	85.94%	10.94%	3.13%
Use of References in Academic Writing	83.59%	10.94%	5.47%
Referring to Sources in Academic Writing	82.03%	13.28%	4.69%
A Quick Referencing Guide for Academic Writing (APA 6th Edition)	85.15%	10.16%	4.69%
Report Writing Checklist	82.82%	9.3%	7.81%
Referencing Checklist	78.13%	13.28%	8.59%

Over 96 percent of the students reported finding the language tips provided by the ELC helpful in improving their case study reports. Those students who did not find the language tips useful reported that they found the tips too general ($n=3$), or they did not know how to use them to improve their case study report ($n=1$). This could be because there were six cases for students to choose from, and students might have found the tips more relevant to some cases but not others.

Among the students who did not refer to the language tips, nearly 40 percent of them mentioned time as a reason (see Table 3.5). Over 20 percent of the students stated that they felt that their English was good enough. Another 20 percent of the students commented that they either did not know the language tips were available, or they did not know where to find them. Even though the language instructor conducted briefings in all the classes and told students how to access the language tips on the Blackboard learning management system, some students might have been absent on the day of the briefings, which resulted in them not knowing where they could find the guidelines and checklists. Less than five percent of the students stated that they did not care about their language use, or that their grades would not be affected. The remaining 20 percent of the students who did not refer to the language tips stated that they have seen similar language tips in other courses, or they forgot to use the language tips, or they believed that writing a well-structured report required an excessive amount of time.

Table 3.5. Students' reasons for not referring to English tips

Reasons	Students
My English is good enough.	10 (23.26%)
I didn't have time.	16 (37.21%)
I didn't know they were available.	6 (13.95%)
I didn't know where to find them.	3 (6.98%)
I don't care about my language use.	1 (2.33%)
My grade will not be affected.	1 (2.33%)
Others: I have made use of it with my ELC 1012 notes. I already take ELC class this semester and the two are similar. The English tips provided are very basic, that university students should have known (previously written assignment). I thought I know it already.	9 (20.93%)

Conclusion

The aim of this study was to explore business students' perceptions of the value of integrating English and communication skills into a content subject. The results show that students have mixed feelings about the weighting of the use of language in their case study report assessments. Some students reported that they did not use the English tips because the guidelines/tips were similar to those used in their other ELC classes or that they were too general.

In light of the student feedback, we have designed an assessment rubric with clear grading criteria. In addition, we have gathered samples of students' case study reports, analyzed them, and revised the English tips accordingly. We have also made changes to the tips for the case study report by specifically stating which part of the tips applies to which case study. It is hoped that more students will pay attention to the use of language in this course and that more students will find the revised English tips relevant and helpful for their case study reports.

There are two main limitations of this study. One is that LGT 2106 is only one of the Bachelor of Business Administration (BBA) core subjects and that it is more quantitative in focus compared with other BBA core subjects. The other BBA core subjects are more qualitative in nature, and students are given more written assignments that allow them to practise their English language skills. Another limitation is that this is a small-scale study that involved a small percentage of BBA students in the university. There are around 500 first-year students taking this subject every year. The subject is offered both in the fall and the spring semesters, and this study was conducted with students who took the subject only in the spring semester, which accounts for about 50 percent of the population.

While this survey is a small-scale study of first-year business students, the nature of the findings may be transferrable to other disciplines and students in other years of study. An important perspective for future research would therefore be to investigate students' perceptions of the use of English in other academic disciplines. Future research could also consider investigating final-year students' perceptions on the use of English in their capstone projects and their confidence in applying their language skills in the workplace. With this extension, we would be able to better understand students' journeys of growing awareness of the importance of language competency for their study and future career.

Acknowledgement

The study in this chapter was funded by the Language Enhancement Grant of The Hong Kong Polytechnic University, English across the curriculum (LEG 16–19).

References

Ament, J. R. & Pérez-Vidal, C. (2015). Linguistic outcomes of English medium instruction programs in higher education: A study on economics undergraduates at a Catalan university. *Higher Learning Research Communications, 5*(1), 47–68.

Annous, S. & Nicolas, M. O. (2015). Academic territorial borders: A look at the writing ethos in business courses in an environment in which English is a foreign language. *Journal of Business and Technical Communication, 29*(1), 93–111.

Bacha, N. N. (2012). Disciplinary writing in an EFL context from teachers' and students' perspectives. *International Journal of Business and Social Sciences, 3*, 233–256.

Becher, T. & Trowler, P. R. (2001). *Academic tribes and territories: Intellectual enquiry and the culture of disciplines* (2nd ed.). SRHE; Open University.

Braine, G. (2001). When professors don't cooperate: A critical perspective on EAP research. *English for Specific Purposes, 20*(3), 293–303.

Clughen, L. & Connell, M. (2012). Writing and resistance: Reflections on the practice of embedding writing in the curriculum. *Arts and Humanities in Higher Education, 11*(4), 333–345.

Dafouz, E. & Smit, U. (2016). Towards a dynamic conceptual framework for English-medium education in multilingual university settings. *Applied Linguistics, 37*(3), 397–415.

Dixon, M. A. & Dougherty, D. S. (2010). Managing the multiple meanings of organizational culture in interdisciplinary collaboration and consulting. *Journal of Business Communication, 47*(1), 3–19.

Evans, S. & Morrison, B. (2011). Meeting the challenges of English-medium higher education: The first-year experience in Hong Kong. *English for Specific Purposes, 30*, 198–208.

Evans, S. & Morrison, B. (2017). English-medium instruction in Hong Kong: Illuminating a grey area in school policies and classroom practices. *Current Issues in Language Planning, 18*(3), 303–322. https://doi.org/10.1080/14664208.2016.1270106.

Fulwiler, T. (1988). Evaluating writing across the curriculum programs. *New Directions for Teaching & Learning, 36*, 61–75.

Gaspar, M. R., Regio, M. M. & Morgado, M. M. (2017). Lean-green manufacturing: Collaborative content and language integrated learning in higher education and engineering courses. *Journal of Education Culture and Society, 2*, 208–217.

Hammond, C. D. (2016). Internationalization, nationalism, and global competitiveness: A comparison of approaches to higher education in China and Japan. *Asia Pacific Education Review, 17*, 555–566.

Hyland, K. (2013). Faculty feedback: Perceptions and practices in L2 disciplinary writing. *Journal of Second Language Writing, 22*, 240–253.

Jackson, J. (2005). An inter-university, cross-disciplinary analysis of business education: Perceptions of business faculty in Hong Kong. *English for Specific Purposes, 24*, 293–306.

Klein, J. T. & Falk-Krzesinski, H. J. (2017). Interdisciplinary and collaborative work: Framing promotion and tenure practices and policies. *Research Policy, 46*, 1055–1061.

Lasagabaster, D. (2018). Fostering team teaching: Mapping out a research agenda for English-medium instruction at university level. *Language Teaching, 51*(3), 400–416.

Lughmani, S. D., Gardner, S., Chen, J., Wong, H. & Chan, L. (2016). English across the curriculum: Fostering collaboration. *ELTWO: Special Issue on 5th CELC Symposium Proceedings, 2016*, 19–33.

Pawan, F. & Ortloff, J. H. (2011). Sustaining collaboration: English-as-a-second language and content-area teachers. *Teacher and Teacher Education, 27*, 463–471.

Wang, Y., Yu, S. & Shao, Y. (2017). The experiences of Chinese mainland students with English-medium instruction in a Macau University. *Educational Studies, 44*(3), 357–360.

Yemini, M. & Sagie, N. (2016). Research on internationalization in higher education—exploratory analysis. *Perspectives: Policy and Practice in Higher Education*, 20(2–3), 90–98.

Yu, B. & Wright, E. (2017). Academic adaptation amid internationalization: The challenges for local, mainland Chinese, and international students at Hong Kong's universities. *Tertiary Education and Management*, 23(4), 1–14. https://doi.org/10.1080/13583883.2017.1356365.

Zhu, W. (2004). Faculty views on the importance of writing, the nature of academic writing, and teaching and responding to writing in the disciplines. *Journal of Second Language Writing*, 13, 29–48.

Appendix: Post-Questionnaire for LGT 2106 (Principles of Operations Management) Students

The purpose of this questionnaire is to collect your views about the use of English in content subjects at the Hong Kong Polytechnic University. All information given in this questionnaire will be kept with strict confidence and be accessible only to the research team members. By filling in this questionnaire, you agree that we can use the given information for teaching and research purposes.

Circle the appropriate answer and/or write in the space provided.

8. Do you know the weighting for language use in the case study report?
   Yes, _____ %   No, I don't know. (Go to Q4)

9. Do you think this weighting is appropriate?
   Yes,   No,
   because _____

10. How did this weighting affect your preparation of writing the case study report (i.e., the attention that you paid to language use)?
    A lot   Some   Little   No change

11. Did you refer to the English tips provided by the ELC while writing the case study report?
    Yes   No (Go to Q8)

12. How would you rate the following English tips provided by the ELC? (3=Very useful; 2=Useful; 1=Not useful; DNU=Did not use)
    Tips (1) on Writing a Case Study Report   3 2 1 DNU
    Tips (2) on Coherence in Academic Writing   3 2 1 DNU

Tips (3) on Use of References in Academic Writing	3 2 1 DNU
Tips (4) on Referring to Sources in Academic Writing	3 2 1 DNU
Tips (5) A Quick Referencing Guide in Academic Writing (APA 6th edition)	3 2 1 DNU
Tips (6) Report Writing Checklist	3 2 1 DNU
Tips (7) Referencing Checklist	3 2 1 DNU

13. In general, did the English tips provided by the ELC in Q5 above help you improve the quality of writing the case study report?

    Yes, a lot. **(The end. Thank you!)** Yes, some. **(The end. Thank you!)** Not really. (Go to Q7)

14. The English tips provided by the ELC were not so helpful because . . . (You can choose more than 1 item.)
    i. I know these language-related topics really well.
    ii. I didn't know how to use the tips for my case study report.
    iii. I found other English resources more helpful, e.g., _____ _____
    iv. Other reasons: _____ _____

(The end. Thank you!)

15. I didn't refer to the English tips provided by the ELC because . . . (You can choose more than 1 item.)
    i. My English is good enough.
    ii. I didn't have time.
    iii. I didn't know they were available.
    iv. I didn't know where to find them.
    v. I don't care about my language use.
    vi. My grade will not be affected.
    Other reasons: _____

4 Engaging and Empowering Scientific Writers in Different Disciplines

John Blake
UNIVERSITY OF AIZU

William R. Holden III
JAPAN ADVANCED INSTITUTE OF SCIENCE AND TECHNOLOGY

Abstract: Postgraduate students of various scientific disciplines are often required to write research articles in English. Writing for publication is an onerous task, especially when English is an additional language. This chapter describes how scientific writers from three disciplines (information, materials, and knowledge science) are engaged and empowered at a small national research institute in Japan. Based on a comprehensive needs analysis, a three-pronged approach was adopted, comprising credit-bearing courses, face-to-face writing conferences, and online support. Corpus-informed materials were developed in-house for a suite of credit-bearing courses that form the mainstay of the formal curriculum. All courses are hybrid, blending onsite instruction with online learning activities. The courses are eclectic in approach, drawing on concepts such as flipped classrooms and activity-based learning. Face-to-face writing conferences are arranged for writers who submit drafts of articles or chapters for feedback. During these meetings, tutors provide discipline-specific constructive advice. In addition, writers are introduced to online resources and in-house tailor-made tools to assist their writing. Tools harnessing string searches, such as a corpus-based error detector, are used to enable writers to receive automated feedback on their work anytime.

Keywords: scientific writing, curriculum design, needs analysis, corpus-informed materials, disciplinary variation

This chapter describes how scientific writers are engaged and empowered at a small national research institute in Japan. All the writers are studying for research degrees in materials, information, or knowledge science. Their graduation is contingent on having research articles (RAs) accepted for publication in academic journals or conference proceedings. To get published,

DOI: https://doi.org/10.37514/INT-B.2021.1220.2.04

articles need to convince reviewers of the novelty, substance, and significance of the research as well as adhere to generic expectations in terms of language and rhetoric. While breaking these generic expectations may result in rejection, simply meeting them is no guarantee of acceptance, since an excellently written paper with poor science should still be rejected by reputable venues.

The entry barrier to novice scientists is especially high. Not only do they have to deal with the intrinsic difficulties of their research field, but they also need to navigate their way into their specific discourse community to learn its forms and values (Gee, 2007). Writing for publication is an onerous task *per se*. The difficulty is exacerbated when English is an additional language (Flowerdew, 2008), and particularly so when writers may not possess the requisite vocabulary (Evans & Morrison, 2011). The dominance of English as the language of science compels researchers who want to disseminate their research widely to publish in English (Englander, 2006; Lillis & Curry, 2010). Writers need to understand the dialogic nature of RAs (Fryer, 2013) and strategies for dealing with pit bull reviewers (Walbort, 2009) and rejection (Habibie & Hyland, 2019). The journey along the cline from the periphery to expert writers at the core of the community of practice is long and arduous (Lave & Wenger, 1991; Li, 2007; O'Neill, 2001). This is evidenced by reflective accounts of the transition (Casanave & Vandrick, 2003) and numerous case studies (e.g., Canagarajah, 2015). There are many risks, notably the high rejection rates, but there are also many rewards in writing for publication (Habibie & Hyland, 2019). The primary reward, however, for doctoral candidates is the ability to graduate.

Writing conventions vary greatly among disciplines (Lillis & Turner, 2001; Trowler & Becher, 2002), and this was found to be the case for the three disciplines of materials, information, and knowledge science; in fact, even within these disciplines there is notable variation. The disciplinary variation occurs at all levels from the research paradigm, discoursal conventions, and move structure through to lexical choice. This presents a challenge to teachers of writing who, due to timetabling limitations, need to teach classes offered to students from all three disciplines. An English for Specific Purposes (ESP) approach (Dudley-Evans & St. John, 1998) was adopted to address the diverging needs of different sets of writers.

This chapter first presents a case study by describing its learning and teaching context and constraints. It then details the interdisciplinary variation discovered among the three disciplines. The next section describes the approach, needs analysis, course design, and writing lab, after which examples of the corpus-informed materials and the online resources developed are provided. The final section reflects on the program design and shares some of the evaluations given by students.

Learning and Teaching Context

Researchers have long noted the shortcomings of English language education in Japan (Fujimoto-Adamson, 2006; Koike & Tanaka, 1995). In addition, the failure to provide discipline-specific ESP instruction was initially addressed approximately two decades ago and is also well documented (Orr, 1998). A recent study by Leigh McDowell and Cassi Liardét (2019) investigated the research writing processes of Japanese materials scientists drafting manuscripts for publication in English, and discovered that materials science researchers are five times as likely to publish in English as in Japanese. Yet, few graduate programs in Japanese universities in the fields of science, technology, engineering, and mathematics offer programs to prepare graduate students to write research articles.

This case study is set in the Japan Advanced Institute of Science and Technology (JAIST), a research institute offering postgraduate degrees. The cosmopolitan campus has one of the largest percentages of non-Japanese students among Japanese universities. According to its website (JAIST, 2019), approximately half of the student body are international students. Although most research laboratories operate in Japanese, laboratories with non-Japanese speaking professors or students tend to use English as the *lingua franca*. To fulfil the institution's graduation requirements, all doctoral candidates are required to have between one and three RAs accepted for publication. The specific requirements vary by laboratory. The complexity and sophistication of RAs (Chang & Kuo, 2011; Swales, 1990) provides a challenge to which students need to rise to graduate, and which is arguably the *raison d'être* for the establishment of the new English language program.

Interdisciplinary Variation

To help writers, it is necessary to understand the target genre. A detailed knowledge of the target genre and disciplinary variations enables writing teachers to provide accurate actionable advice, saving novice writers valuable time and increasing their likelihood of getting published in a timely manner. The ideal scenario is one where the teacher is a specialist in both English and the specific scientific discipline. A reasonable alternative is for an English language specialist to work closely with a discipline specialist. However, given various constraints in the introductory phase of the development of the program, securing cooperation was not an option.

Pedagogic advice provided by teachers and textbooks is often rather prescriptive, and may not reflect the descriptive reality. For example, textbooks frequently advise scientists to adopt an introduction-method-results-discussion (IMRD) model for research abstracts, yet short RAs in some engineering and information science sub-disciplines make use of a two-move result-method model (Blake, 2015). The assumption that all research articles follow the same framework is flawed and leads to such over-generalizations. Advice based on descriptive analysis may more closely reflect the type of writing that is actually published rather than an idealized envisaged form of writing. Some scholars (Gee, 1996; Wingate et al., 2011) argue that discipline-specific literacy practices are best taught by discipline teachers. Laurence Anthony (2011) states that non-specialists can teach scientific writing using a process-orientated approach rather than a product-orientated approach. This is achieved by supplementing the generic teaching materials with data-driven learning using corpora that the students compile themselves. However, tutors who are also armed with disciplinary knowledge are better placed to offer actionable advice.

To gain a clear picture of discipline-specific expectations, rhetorical organization, and lexico-grammatical patterns in each discipline, a corpus-based approach to materials development was adopted for this project. Two corpora were created: a published RA corpus comprising approximately 1,000 articles and a draft RA corpus consisting of around 200 articles. The published RA corpus included RAs co-written by JAIST faculty-students from the university repository, conference proceedings of top-tier conferences, and research articles from Institute of Electrical and Electronics Engineers (IEEE) journals.

The corpus, which was divided into knowledge, materials, and information science subcorpora, was drawn upon extensively in the creation of discipline-specific course materials. Knowledge science is an emerging discipline resulting from the demands of a knowledge-based economy to address problems in collecting, synthesizing, coordinating, and creating knowledge (Nakamori, 2011). Materials science focuses on the structure, properties, and application of materials (Nasirpouri, 2017). Information science focuses on problems in the collection, storage, retrieval, and use of information stored as bits, or binary digits (Saracevic, 2009).

Through developing corpus-based materials and investigating the corpus using standard techniques and tools, such as keyword analysis, frequency analysis, and keyword-in-context concordance line analysis, the authors became familiar with the linguistic idiosyncrasies of each of the three domains. This corpus-based knowledge combined with the insights gained from working with authors in the writing lab and the classroom led to a clearer understanding of the commonalities and differences among the three disciplines. The authors identified eight areas in which disciplinary variation impacts research writing, which are described below.

Reasoning

Knowledge science relies on arguments based on samples and uses inductive reasoning to generalize to larger populations, which is reflected in the higher incidence of hedging when making claims. Information science relies on laws and mathematical proofs, while materials science relies on the constant nature of physical elements. Falsifiability, or the principle that a proposition or theory cannot be considered "scientific" unless it is possible to empirically show it to be false, is what fundamentally separates knowledge science from materials or information science. This explains why deductive reasoning tends to dominate in information and materials science.

Document Preparation

Unlike knowledge and materials scientists, information scientists tend to prepare research documents in plain text using LaTeX rather than formatted text in word processors, such as Microsoft Word. LaTeX documents look more like HTML code than writing until they are compiled into a pdf. This means that the use of typical methods to provide feedback on Microsoft Word documents, such as track changes and insert comment features, is not possible.

Text Recycling vs. Plagiarism

Text recycling, or "language re-use" (Flowerdew & Li, 2007), is frequently used in the method and result sections in materials science, with only minor changes being made to the variables and values. The extensive use of boilerplate text as evidenced in the corpus of published articles frees up writers from having to reinvent different ways to describe very similar methods. Much research in materials science uses standard methods and produces results which vary only in the numerical quantities and names of materials. Some sub-disciplines within information science appear to permit text recycling in the introduction section as well, based on the reuse of text in the corpus of published articles. This results in widespread lift-and-switch, or patch writing (Wette, 2010) in which writers copy and paste whole sections and only change the names of variables and values. Some publications (e.g., *IEEE Transactions on Nanotechnology* and *IEEE Transactions on Computer-Aided Design of Integrated Circuits and Systems*) specify that 30 percent of content should be new for an article to be considered for submission, which by implication means that 70 percent of the content need not be.

Citation Practices

Citation practices differ among the disciplines (Leydesdorff et al., 2016). Knowledge science articles tend to use name-date citation styles, such as APA, while the other two disciplines invariably use numerical citation systems. Examination of hundreds of manuscripts produced by the three departments has shown that quotations are used in knowledge science, but almost never used in materials science and information science, even when exact words are copied.

Page Layout

Knowledge science articles may be written in single-column templates, whereas the other two disciplines use double-column templates (e.g., IEEE and ACM templates). Figures inserted in the double-column format tend to be inserted in portrait rather than landscape. Template instructions sometimes forbid landscape figures but, even when permitted, placement of landscape figures involves more intricate coding in LaTeX, and novice writers in information science who have not fully mastered LaTeX tend to choose the easier portrait option.

Generic Conventions

Information science and materials science manuscripts tend to display greater adherence to predictable generic conventions in their structure, organization, and development, whereas manuscripts in knowledge science tend to exhibit greater variation. There are several possible explanations for this. Generic conventions are more firmly established in the first two fields than in the latter due to the fact that the former are well-known disciplines found at universities and research institutions worldwide, and because there exists an identifiable hierarchy of research publications in these fields and their subfields. Likewise, conventions in natural and applied science articles are less flexible than those in the social sciences. In addition, research strategies in the natural sciences are anchored in "concentrated knowledge clusters," whereas those in the social sciences are more frequently adapted to numerous "small isolated knowledge clusters" (Jaffe, 2014, p. 1).

Lexical Coherence

Similarly, the information science and materials science manuscripts examined display a more coherent set of lexis and rhetorical devices than do manuscripts from knowledge science. For example, the descriptions of the materials and methods follow similar patterns and use similar lexical items in materials science articles, while knowledge science articles do not. The simplest explanation for the discrepancy is that the taxonomies of the first two fields are clearly delineated: every scholar involved in a particular field of research shares and employs a broad overarching vocabulary and a vocabulary specific to their specialization. Because knowledge science is an emerging interdisciplinary field that comprises areas as diverse as knowledge management, perceptual information processing, media technology, data mining, and ethnography, there is little in the way of a shared vocabulary, and manuscripts tend as a result to follow the lexical conventions of a particular sub-specialization.

Research Abstracts

Research abstracts vary greatly among the three disciplines. Materials science is particularly notable since graphical abstracts are frequently used in top-tier journals (Hendges & Florek, 2019; Lane et al., 2015). The move structure of research abstracts also varies greatly, with abstracts in knowledge science tending to have lengthy introductions and less emphasis on results. Abstracts in materials science and information science are more results focused. The organization of the typical rhetorical moves of introduction (I), purpose (P), method (M), results (R), and discussion (D) (Bhatia, 1993) vary dramatically. The default order of IMRD is rarely followed in information science. Some moves may be omitted, e.g., IMR. In a corpus study of scientific research abstracts, John Blake (2015) noted that pairs of moves may be repeated, especially MRMR in wireless communication, a sub-discipline of information science. In this move pattern, the first result tends to be the new algorithm and the second result the proof that the algorithm is superior to previous algorithms. Some moves may be inverted, such as RM in both materials science and information science.

Course Design

A writing in the disciplines model (Carter et al., 2007; Wingate, 2012) was considered but was not possible at the outset. In this model, discipline specialists and language specialists work together to help novice writers acquire the requisite skill set in a timely manner and, as noted above, this was not feasible in the introductory phase of the program. An alternative approach was therefore needed to meet the needs of the novice writers. We adopted an ESP-driven eclectic approach by selecting teaching methods and materials most appropriate to achieve the aims for a particular student or cohort of students rather than rigidly adhering to a single theoretical framework. This is in line with Ken

Hyland (2019), who notes that a core strength of ESP is the ability to overcome "the theory-practice divide [and make] visible academic and professional genres to students" (p. 1). Central to the ESP framework is the importance of conducting a detailed needs analysis coupled with genre analysis (Swales, 1990). Genre analysis is a key component, arming teachers with specific knowledge of text types. Teachers and materials developers use this knowledge to make explicit the language and rhetorical features that are usually acquired through extended exposure to such texts over time. Only through investigating the genre can teachers understand the form, format, and functions that learners need to become familiar with and master. A primarily social constructivist approach was adopted in which students and teachers worked together on draft manuscripts, enabling students to move from the periphery to the core of their specific discourse community, or community of practice.

Target-context related and learning-context related needs analysis surveys (Bocanegra-Valle, 2016; Hutchinson & Waters, 1987) were used to gain a fuller picture of the perceived needs, wants, and lacks of the students (Allwright, 1982). Primary data collection methods included questionnaires, focus interviews, and observation. Secondary data sources, such as course syllabi for content subjects, lab rosters, and laboratory publications housed in the university repository, were collected and analyzed. From the surveys, we discovered that the primary difference in responses to the needs analysis surveys was not between different disciplines but between different mother tongues, with approximately half the Japanese respondents indicating that research writing in English was unnecessary, while the non-Japanese respondents universally stated that publishing in English was very important to their academic and career prospects. Analysis of the secondary data revealed that 20 percent of the labs produced 80 percent of the research output in English. Based on the extensive needs analysis, a three-pronged approach was adopted, comprising credit-bearing courses, individual conferencing in a writing lab, and provision of online resources.

A suite of credit-bearing courses forms the mainstay of the formal curriculum. These courses are supplemented with online resources and a writing lab that offers individual consultations. All the credit-bearing courses are hybrid, blending onsite instruction with online learning activities. The courses are eclectic in approach, drawing on concepts such as flipped classrooms and activity-based learning. Students, thus, do the majority of their "learning" outside of the classroom. This allows class time to be devoted to activities that require students to recall and reinforce knowledge, and to develop and practice a repertoire of skills that facilitate their familiarity with and competence in research writing. Students typically watch lectures or short "how-to" videos online, or undertake reading assignments, take notes, or complete a set of questions or tasks, and submit answers on a learning management system prior to class.

Three scientific research writing courses were developed, focusing on pre-writing, developmental writing, and research writing. The pre-writing course introduces students to the writing of scientific research documents. Students who successfully complete this course learn to analyze authentic research documents for structure, organization, language, and common features. Students on the developmental writing course produce a detailed summary or synthesis of an authentic RA that follows appropriate stylistic and linguistic conventions, and a move structure/outline which can be used as the basis for planning a future original RA. Students on the research writing course produce a manuscript for a short RA documenting original research that adheres in structure, style, and content to articles in a specific publication they have targeted. This course adopts a process-approach, engaging and empowering students to draft a manuscript of publishable quality.

The writing lab provides individualized support to writers. Students submit manuscripts for review prior to attending the writing lab. One-to-one writing conferences follow a learner-centered approach, with the learner initially identifying up to five aspects that they suggest the tutor focus on (e.g., coherence, clarity, noun phrases). Most students submit short research articles that have been vetted for content by their supervisor. The writing lab tutors provide advice based on both the learner's request and the tutor's evaluation of the research article. Constructive advice is provided on how to improve the student's ability to write in general or how to improve a particular piece of writing. During these meetings, tutors provide both generic and, where possible, discipline-specific advice. However, when the tutor is unsure about practices in a particular discipline or publication, learners are advised to consult their supervisor.

The online resources that were provided for students consisted of various tools and reference materials that could help students draft and edit their manuscripts. Some tools were proprietary, such as the plagiarism detection software, while others were open access, such as the academic writing suggestion machine (AWSuM) developed by Atushi Mizumoto (2017). Tailor-made tools were also created, including a move visualizer for research abstracts and a corpus-based error detection tool.

Materials and Online Resources

The courses make use of tailor-made materials that are corpus-informed to minimize the disjuncture between prescriptive advice and the descriptive reality of specific disciplines. Sections from authentic research articles were chosen based on their clarity, language, and ability to provide a generic model for the analysis of authentic documents from various fields. As most incoming students are unfamiliar with the structure, organization, and language of research documents, familiarization with the prototypical genre characteristics of research documents and the way that the structure works to provide a retrospective account of the research was deemed appropriate. The concept of moves and steps (Swales, 1990) within sections is introduced, accompanied by a limited set of lexical bundles indicative of each of the functions of these various moves and steps in the development of the article. Students initially analyze a generic RA and then apply the same analytical techniques to the corresponding section of an authentic RA from their discipline.

Figure 4.1 shows one of the tasks that students complete on the generic RA. This generic research abstract follows the IMRD organization, illustrating how a research abstract can encapsulate the key sections of a research article. Figure 4.2 shows a research article in the field of information science, which was annotated by a student taking the pre-writing course. The student was able to identify the different moves within the abstract and label the functions of each of the paragraphs in the introduction. Many tasks in the writing course encourage students to analyze RAs in their specific discipline.

Figure 4.3 shows a task that focuses students on the need for repetition of key ideas. Students use the task to identify the sections of their selected RA that display repetition. The teacher of writing then focuses students on how sentences can be summarized as clauses, clauses as noun phrases, and noun phrases shortened even to nouns. This provides less grammatically aware writers with a systematic way to approach summarization.

Section	Function in text
Move 1. Background	established context of and motivation for the research
Move 2. Purpose	presents the aim or goal of the paper
Move 3. Method	information on the design, procedure, analysis, etc.
Move 4. Results	results, findings or product
Move 5. Conclusion	applications or wider implications of the results

Task: Identify the sentences that belong to each move in this abstract.

Authorship in publications establishes accountability, responsibility, and credit. Misappropriation of authorship undermines the integrity of the authorship system, but accurate data on its prevalence are limited. This paper aims to determine the prevalence of articles with gift authors and ghost authors in peer-reviewed medical journals. A total of 809 corresponding authors (1179 surveyed, 69% response rate) of articles published in 1996 in 6 peer-reviewed, general medical journals responded. A total of 156 articles (19%) had evidence of gift authors; 93 articles (11%) had evidence of ghost authors; and 13 articles (2%) had evidence of both. In conclusion, a substantial proportion of articles in peer-reviewed medical journals demonstrate evidence of gift authors or ghost authors.
Adapted from: Annette Flanagin, RN, et.al. Prevalence of Articles with Honorary Authors and Ghost Authors in Peer-Reviewed Medical Journals. JAMA, July 15, 1998—Vol 280, No. 3

Figure 4.1. Analysis of rhetorical moves in a generic research abstract.

Engaging and Empowering Scientific Writers

Figure 4.2. Discipline-specific function analysis.

Abstract	Abstract
Intro	Background
	Hypothesis or research questions
	Preview
Methods	Description of method
Results	Key data
	Key data summary
Discussion	Explanations, generalisations, comparisons and contrasts
	Summary
Conclusion	Summary
	Extension to other domains, contexts
References	List of cited works
Appendices	Place to insert details that only interest some readers

Task: Compare your specialist paper to the table and determine whether it includes summaries in the same sections. What phrases are used to signal these moves?

Figure 4.3. Discipline-specific summary analysis task.

Move Visualizer

To enable writers to discover move patterns prevalent in research abstracts in their discipline, a visualizer was created to automatically highlight rhetorical moves in a corpus of 500 research abstracts collected from five journals recommended by discipline specialists. The abstracts were annotated by hand, and specialist informants were consulted to verify the accuracy. Figure 4.4 shows a screenshot of an abstract from *Transactions on Wireless Communication*, a sub-discipline of information science. The moves are color-coded to enable students to notice the patterns. Typical patterns are linear (e.g., IMRD) and cyclic (e.g., MRMR), but non-linear patterns (e.g., RM) can also be seen in this corpus.

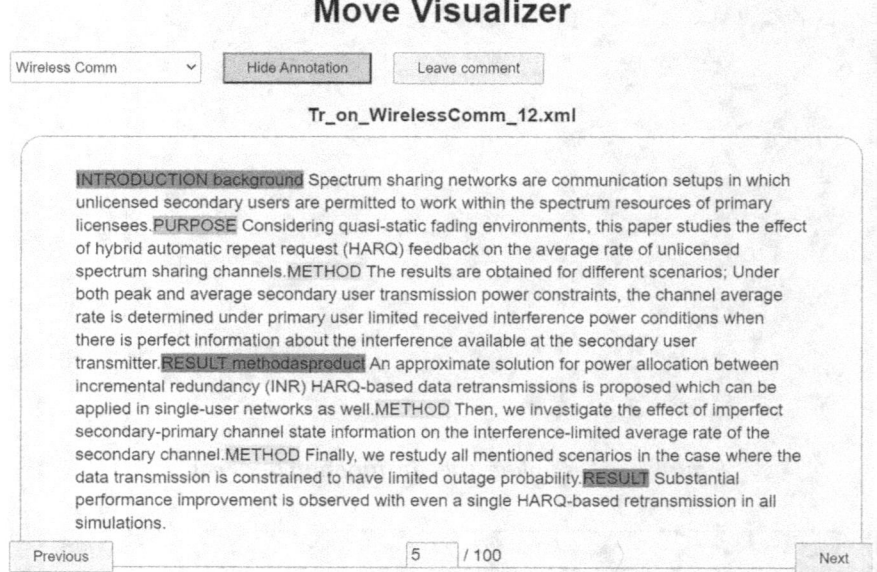

Figure 4.4. *Move visualizer showing an annotated abstract.*

Corpus-Based Error Detector

Error-free research articles have a higher chance of acceptance than those permeated with lexical, grammatical, or genre-related errors. A review of the pedagogic literature on scientific writing in English housed in the research institute was conducted. This survey revealed that most sources mentioned three main criteria: accuracy, brevity, and clarity, while some sources noted two additional criteria: objectivity and formality (see Table 4.1). Although these criteria are inextricably intertwined, each one can be used as a filter through which feedback on research writing can be given. Scripts to parse for these common errors were incorporated into the error detector. The common errors were identified using the corpus of 200 draft RAs submitted for internal review to the writing lab. Errors were classified manually into five categories, namely accuracy, brevity, clarity, objectivity, and formality. Feedback from ten student users of the latest version of the error detector was positive, with all students noting improvement in the accuracy of their final manuscripts. One student submitted nine drafts of a manuscript to the error detector and received a total of 227 actionable suggestions (Blake, 2020).

Tutors in the writing lab therefore do not need to deal with errors that can be automatically detected, and so can spend more time on dealing with higher level issues rather than predictable surface-level errors.

Table 4.1. Criteria for scientific research writing

Criteria	Typical errors
Accuracy	Factual, numerical, and language errors
Brevity	Verbosity
Clarity	Vagueness and ambiguity
Objectivity	Overly personal and emotional
Formality	Unexplained abbreviations, contractions, and informal terms

Source: In-house writing course

Conclusion

Response to the materials and courses collected on student evaluation forms has been very positive. Students frequently commented on the usefulness and practicality of these courses, and stated that they feel they can write more fluently and coherently. The real success, however, is not related to the student feedback questionnaires, but in enabling students to get published. Numerous students have attributed their success in this respect to the research writing program and the tutors in the writing lab. In addition to sending emails thanking tutors for their help, students leave comments on the writing lab record. Some of their comments are reproduced below verbatim:

> Student 1: Thank you for your reviewing of my conference paper in this October. The result comes today, and my paper has been accepted! I know that my paper would not have been accepted without your help.

> Student 2: Thank you for help me to improve the quality of my paper. I really liked the quick response from the professor and of course I really appreciate all his comments.

> Student 3: I have learnt a lot of things that I never knew before. One important thing I have learnt . . . is that using

short and simple terms can make your writing become more powerful than using some difficult terms or vocabularies.

Student 4: Comments and suggestions were so practical and specific that I could use them directly.

Numerous students who have taken writing courses and participated in the writing lab secured their required publications, gained their doctoral degrees, and started their professional or academic careers. This itself is the main driver of satisfaction for the teachers of writing in this program.

Thanks to the positive word-of-mouth feedback from students completing writing courses and participating in one-to-one writing conferences, some discipline specialists now work directly with writing lab tutors. Students enrolled in the research writing courses benefit from language advice from the writing tutor in tandem with advice from their research supervisor. The initial ESP approach has slowly started to transform into a writing-in-the-disciplines approach.

The corpus-informed tailor-made materials provide authenticity and minimize the disjuncture between prescriptive advice and the descriptive reality of specific disciplines. The focus of the pre-writing course is on enabling learners to understand the generic characteristics and language features of scientific research articles. For the more advanced courses, the focus is on engaging and empowering students to develop knowledge and skills that will better enable them to write their own research articles. As shown in the materials section, students were able to apply the knowledge of structure, language, and organization learned in the classroom on generic materials to authentic research documents from their own field.

In this context, engaging and empowering students means focusing on enabling them to develop, both under supervision and on their own, in order to meet the external needs and demands of their academic and professional communities of practice. Students' efforts are guided, encouraged, and supported by writing center faculty and their disciplinary supervisor, but students remain in charge of both the development of their skills repertoire and the documents needed to satisfy the requirements of the course and an external audience. Finally, the focus of the writing courses is on initiating and developing students as members of their specific discourse community, so that they can participate knowledgeably, competently, and confidently.

Novice writers are engaged in reading, analyzing, and understanding the form, format, and function of each of the sections of RAs in their respective disciplines. The credit-bearing courses provide the foundation on which writers build. The individual one-to-one writing consultations help writers improve their draft research articles, while the tailor-made online tools help individualize the learning to each specific discipline. By focusing on the five filters of accuracy, brevity, clarity, objectivity, and formality, writers have a tangible framework through which to assess the language of their draft RAs. Following this approach, writers are empowered to draft RAs that adhere to the generic integrity, expectations, and conventions of their community of practice.

References

Allwright, R. (1982). Perceiving and pursuing learner's needs. In M. Geddes & G. Sturtridge (Eds.), *Individualisation (pp. 24–31)*. Modern English Publications.
Anthony, L. (2011). Products, processes and practitioners: A critical look at the importance of specificity in ESP. *Taiwan International ESP Journal, 3*(2), 19–50.
Bhatia, V. K. (1993). *Analyzing genre: Language use in professional settings.* Longman Publishing.
Blake, J. (2015). Prescriptive-descriptive disjuncture: Rhetorical organisation of research abstracts in information science. In F. Formato & A. Hardie (Eds.), *8th International Corpus Linguistics Conference* (pp. 377–378). Lancaster University.
Blake, J. (2020). Genre-specific error detection with multimodal feedback. *RELC Journal, 51*(1), 179–187. https://doi.org/10.1177/0033688219898282.
Bocanegra-Valle, A. (2016). Needs analysis for curriculum design. In K. Hyland & P. Shaw (Eds.), *The Routledge handbook of English for academic purposes* (pp. 560–576). Routledge.
Canagarajah, A. S. (2015). "Blessed in my own way:" Pedagogical affordances for dialogical voice construction in multilingual student writing. *Journal of Second Language Writing, 27,* 122–139. https://doi.org/10.1016/j.jslw.2014.09.001.
Carter, C., Ferzli, M. & Wiebe, E.N. (2007). Writing to learn by learning to write in the disciplines. *Journal of Business and Technical Communication, 21*(3), 278–302. https://doi.org/10.1177/1050651907300466.
Casanave, C. P. & Vandrick, S. (Eds.). (2003). *Writing for scholarly publication: Behind the scenes in language education.* Erlbaum.
Chang, C.F. & Kuo, C.H. (2011). A corpus-based approach to online materials development for writing research articles. *English for Specific Purposes, 30*(3), 222–234. https://doi.org/10.1016/j.esp.2011.04.001.
Dudley-Evans, T. & St. John, M. J. (1998). *Developments in English for specific purposes: A multi-disciplinary approach.* Cambridge University Press.
Englander, K. (2006). Revision of scientific manuscripts by non-native-English-speaking scientists in response to journal editors' criticism of the language. *Journal of Applied Linguistics, 3*(2), 129–161. https://doi.org/10.1558/japl.v3i2.129.
Evans, S. & Morrison, B. (2011). Meeting the challenges of English-medium higher education: The first-year experience in Hong Kong. *English for Specific Purposes, 30*(3), 198–208. https://doi.org/10.1016/j.esp.2011.01.001.

Flowerdew, J. (2008). Scholarly writers who use English as an additional language: What can Goffman's "stigma" tell us? *Journal of English for Academic Purposes*, *7*(2),77–86. https://doi.org/10.1016/j.jeap.2008.03.002.

Flowerdew, J. & Li, Y.Y. (2007). Language re-use among Chinese apprentice scientists writing for publication. *Applied Linguistics*, *28*(3), 440–465. https://doi.org/10.1093/applin/ammo31.

Fryer, D. L. (2013). Exploring the dialogism of academic discourse: Heteroglossic engagement in medical research articles. In G. Andersen & K. Bech (Eds.), *English corpus linguistics: Variation in time, space and genre* (pp. 183–207). Rodopi.

Fujimoto-Adamson, N. (2006). Globalization and history of English education in Japan. *Asian EFL Journal*, *8*(3), 259–282.

Gee, J. P. (1996). *Social linguistics and literacies: Ideology in discourses, critical perspectives on literacy and education* (2nd ed.). Routledge.

Gee, J. P. (2007). *Social linguistics and literacies: Ideology in discourses* (3rd ed.). Taylor & Francis.

Habibie, P. & Hyland, K. (2019). Introduction: The risks and rewards of scholarly publishing. In K. Hyland & P. Habibie (Eds.), *Novice writers and scholarly publication: Authors, mentors, gatekeepers* (pp. 1–10). Palgrave Macmillian. https://doi.org/10.1007/978-3-319-95333-5.

Hendges, G. R. & Florek, C. S. (2019). The graphical abstract as a new genre in the promotion of science. In M.-J. Luzón & C. Pérez-Llantada (Eds.), *Science communication on the internet: Old genres meet new genres* (pp. 59–79). John Benjamins. https://doi.org/10.1075/pbns.308.04hen.

Hutchinson, T. & Waters. A. (1987). *English for specific purposes.* Cambridge University Press.

Hyland K. (2019) English for specific purposes: Some influences and impacts. In X. Gao (Ed.), *Second handbook of English language teaching.* Springer. https://doi.org/10.1007/978-3-030-02899-2_19.

Jaffe, K. (2014). Social and natural sciences differ in their research strategies, adapted to work for different knowledge landscapes. *PloS One. 9*(11), e113901. https://doi.org/10.1371/journal.pone.0113901.

Japan Advanced Institute of Science and Technology (JAIST). (2019). *About JAIST.* https://www.jaist.ac.jp/english/about/outline/foreigner-student.html.

Koike, I. & Tanaka, H. (1995). English in foreign language education policy in Japan: Toward the twenty-first century. *World Englishes*, *14*(1), 13–25.

Lane, S., Karatsolis, A. & Bui, L. (2015, July). Graphical abstracts: A taxonomy and critique of an emerging genre. In *Proceedings of the 33rd Annual International Conference on the Design of Communication* (pp. 1–9). ACM. https://doi.org/10.1145/2775441.2775465.

Lave, J. & Wenger, E. (1991). *Situated learning: Legitimate peripheral participation.* Cambridge University Press.

Leydesdorff, L., Bornmann, L., Comins, J. A. & Milojević, S. (2016). Citations: Indicators of quality? The impact fallacy. *Frontiers in Research Metrics and Analytics*, *1*(1). https://doi.org/10.3389/frma.2016.00001.

Li, Y. (2007). Apprentice scholarly writing in a community of practice: An intraview of an NNES graduate student writing a research article. *TESOL Quarterly, 41*(1), 55–79. https://doi.org/10.1002/j.1545-7249.2007.tb00040.x.

Lillis, T. & Curry, M. J. (2010). *Academic writing in a global context*. Routledge.

Lillis, T. & Turner, J. (2001). Student writing in higher education: Contemporary confusion, traditional concerns. *Teaching in Higher Education, 6*(1), 57–68. https://doi.org/10.1080/13562510020029608.

McDowell, L. & Liardét, C. L. (2019). Japanese materials scientists' experiences with English for research publication purposes. *Journal of English for Academic Purposes, 37*, 141–153. https://doi.org/10.1016/j.jeap.2018.11.011.

Mizumoto, A. (2017). Initial evaluation of AWSuM: A pilot study. *Vocabulary Learning and Instruction, 6 (2)*, 46–51.

Nakamori Y. (2011) Introduction. In Y. Nakamori (Ed.), *Knowledge science—Modeling the knowledge creation process* (pp. 1–10). CRC Press.

Nasirpouri, F. (2017). *Electrodeposition of nanostructured materials*. Springer.

O'Neill, D. K. (2001). Knowing when you've brought them in: Scientific genre knowledge and communities of practice. *The Journal of the Learning Sciences, 10*(3), 223–264.

Orr, T. (1998). ESP for Japanese universities: A guide for intelligent reform. *The Language Teacher, 22*(11). https://jalt-publications.org/tlt/articles/2428-esp-japanese-universities-guide-intelligent-reform.

Saracevic, T. (2009). Information science. In M. J. Bates (Ed.), *Encyclopedia of library and information sciences* (3rd ed., pp. 2570–2585). Taylor and Francis.

Swales, J. M. (1990). *Genre analysis: English in academic and research settings*. Cambridge University Press.

Trowler, P. & Becher, T. (2002). Academic tribes and territories: Intellectual enquiry and the cultures of discipline (2nd ed.). Open University Press.

Walbort, V. (2009). Are we training pit bulls to review our manuscripts? *Journal of Biology, 8*(3), 24.

Wette, R. (2010). Evaluating student learning in a university-level EAP unit on writing using sources. *Journal of Second Language Writing, 19*(3), 158–177. https://doi.org/10.1016/j.jslw.2010.06.002.

Wingate, U. (2012). 'Argument!' Helping students understand what essay writing is about. *Journal of English for Academic Purposes, 11*(2), 145–154. https://doi.org/10.1016/j.jeap.2011.11.001.

Wingate, U., Andon, N. & Cogo, A. (2011). Embedding academic writing instruction into subject teaching: A case study. *Active Learning in Higher Education, 12*(1), 69–81. https://doi.org/10.1177/1469787410387814.

5

Helping Students from Different Disciplines with their Final Year/Capstone Project: Supervisors' and Students' Needs and Requests

Julia Chen
THE HONG KONG POLYTECHNIC UNIVERSITY

Christy Chan
CITY UNIVERSITY OF HONG KONG

Vicky Man
HONG KONG BAPTIST UNIVERSITY

Elza Tsang
THE HONG KONG UNIVERSITY OF SCIENCE AND TECHNOLOGY

Abstract: A capstone project (CP) demands mastery of a broad range of skills, such as formulating research questions, synthesizing and cross-referencing previous literature with current findings, and writing up the study in the longest report students have probably ever written. The study reported in this chapter is part of a government-funded five-university project on co-developing a mobile app for supporting CP writing in various disciplines. This project is grounded in the belief that the ubiquitous and interactive nature of mobile learning could enrich learning and supervision experience (Källkvist et al., 2009), which in turn would lead to higher student satisfaction (Del Río et al., 2018). To develop a mobile app that helps supervisors and students, a dual-method approach was employed to gather both subjective and objective stakeholder feedback data via focus group interviews and by analysing CP reports from three disciplines to reveal common writing problems (Flowerdew, 2018). Results show that the introduction section, the literature review and the discussion sections, research mapping, and referencing are four major areas of concern.

Keywords: English across the curriculum, capstone project, mobile app, student needs, textual analysis

One key feature of the new four-year undergraduate curriculum in Hong Kong's tertiary education is the explicit requirement for a capstone project (CP) as a means to provide undergraduate students with a culminating experience that equips them with the employment proficiencies, such as problem-solving, presentation, and organizational skills (Cranmer, 2006; Washer, 2007; Zinser, 2003), needed for a knowledge-based society (Education Commission, 2000). Research has shown that at least four factors are important for the successful completion of the CP: quality supervision, good time management, strong communication skills, and affordances of technology. Supervision is largely a one-on-one activity that can be conducted on campus or in online settings (Jaldemark & Lindberg, 2013). Although supervision support for students varies across disciplines and supervisors, good quality supervisor-supervisee communication helps students reach CP milestones, such as setting suitable research objectives (Greenbank & Penketh, 2009). Good time management is the second key factor. Belinda Ho (2003) reports that students respond differently to the same time management advice given by their supervisors, and good planning is a key to completing a project on time. A further requirement for a successful CP is strong communication skills. Both first-language (L1) and second-language (L2) students "may be lacking in specialized reporting and English skills" and would benefit from a language intervention and enhancement program (Blicblau & Dini, 2012). The CP process can provide training in the language skills required in industries where students will find jobs; indeed, some students have reported "communication and presentation skills being improved" as part of their capstone experience (Thomas et al., 2014, p. 588).

The fourth factor relates to the affordances of technology. The last decade has witnessed an increasing number of studies on the use of technology for mediating capstone project supervision, largely due to the wide adoption of learning management systems. For example, Marie Källkvist and colleagues (2009) report student and supervisor satisfaction with virtual learning spaces and communication tools. The availability of digital tools increases the possibility for multimodal supervision, which can benefit from the employment of analytics to "give the 'big picture' of student engagement" (Stoneham & Essop, 2014, p. 5). Increased online interaction with supervisors can also lead to higher student satisfaction (Del Río et al., 2018).

Further advances should bring together these four factors in situations where technology is used to mediate and facilitate supervision, deliver core competencies and communication training, and enhance CP planning management, which is the aim of the current study.

Background

An examination of the background of Hong Kong university students can provide insight into their struggles during the CP writing process. An increasing number of Hong Kong university students come from CMI (Chinese as medium of instruction) schools as the number of EMI (English as medium of instruction) schools has dropped dramatically from 90 percent to 25 percent since 1997 (Evans & Green, 2007; Fan, 2001). The MOI (medium of instruction) fine-tuning policy has had a substantial bearing on university students' academic communication ability (Chen, 2020), which has become a primary concern for both students and academics (Littlewood & Liu, 1996), given the perceived need for fluent English to succeed academically in university (Hyland, 1997). Numerous studies have reported that CMI students, when compared with their EMI counterparts, generally demonstrate lower competence and confidence in English and encounter greater difficulties in understanding subject-specific vocabulary, writing academic texts (Evans & Morrison, 2011), articulating complex ideas in English grammatically (Evans & Green, 2007), and adjusting to the academic demands of their key study area (Evans & Morrison, 2018).

Despite the language needs of CMI students, the Hong Kong undergraduate curriculum leaves limited classroom contact hours for EGAP (English for general academic purposes) and ESAP (English for specific academic purposes) courses. This is especially the case in the sophomore and senior years in nearly all the government-funded institutions, as shown in Table 5.1.

EGAP training is essential for helping students "navigate their school-to-university transition and acculturation process" in English-medium universities (Chen, 2020, p. 119) and acquire academic skills such as argument structure, academic register, and referencing and citation in the freshman year. Recent studies have also noted the effectiveness of EGAP training in enhancing undergraduate students' general academic English skills. Evidence from Peter Crosthwaite's (2016) corpus-based study indicates that after one semester of EGAP training, students demonstrate significant improvement in the use of appropriate academic register, such as fewer first-person pronouns, more nominalizations, and better argument structure. Another study (Chen & Foung, 2017) adopted a learning analytics approach to compare the academic writing of students whose university entry English scores were equivalent to International English Language Testing System (IELTS) 6.30–6.51 with that of students with a higher entry score (equivalent to IELTS 6.81–7.77). Results revealed encouraging improvement in the English proficiency level and referencing skills of the former group in comparison with the latter after 13 weeks of EGAP training.

Table 5.1. English courses offered by language centers in eight government-funded universities in Hong Kong

University	Year 1	Year 2	Year 3	Year 4
City University of Hong Kong (CityU)	3 credits EGAP 3 credits ESAP			
The Chinese University of Hong Kong (CUHK)	4 credits EGAP	3 credits ESAP	2 credits ESP	
The Education University of Hong Kong (EdUHK)	3 credits EGAP Writing 3 credits EGAP Speaking			
Hong Kong Baptist University (HKBU)	6 credits EGAP			
The University of Hong Kong (HKU)	6 credits EGAP	6 credits ESAP		
The Hong Kong University of Science and Technology (HKUST)	6 credits EGAP	3 credits ESAP	3 credits ESP	
Lingnan University (LU)	9 credits EGAP			
The Hong Kong Polytechnic University (PolyU)	6 credits EGAP	1–3 credits ESAP		

ESP—English for Specific Purposes

ESP/ESAP training, although deemed equally essential for success in students' senior years, is valued very differently across Hong Kong universities. As presented in Table 5.1, half of the institutions do not offer English training beyond the freshman year, while the other half extend support for faculty-based discipline-specific English (ESP) and/or English for specific academic purposes (ESAP) in the sophomore and senior years. To address the scarcity of curriculum space for ESP/ESAP training and to provide sustainable campus-wide support for enhancing discipline-specific academic literacy, English Across the Curriculum (EAC) initiatives, supported by two government funds, were introduced in four of the eight Hong Kong universities in

2014 and one additional tertiary institution in 2017. One feature of EAC is the collaboration between English teachers and faculty staff to identify the competencies and skills required for successful completion of assignments in content courses, such as the writing of case study reports, capstone project dissertations, and critiques of professional practices (Chen, 2016). Accompanying language support services and resources, including writing consultations, writing templates, and online learning materials, are subsequently developed to supplement the lack of ESP/ESAP materials in the four-year curriculum.

Although EAC resources have been developed with one-off government and university funds, inadequate ESP/ESAP training and support have made the CP writing and supervisory process challenging for students and academics. Keith Thomas et al.'s (2014) study reports that students failed to apply what they learned in their university studies when preparing their CP dissertations, while academics felt that, due to heavy workload and pressure to publish, "being a project supervisor is not easy" (p. 590). Another concern expressed by supervisors relates to the paucity of materials available to support CP supervision. Other than departmental CP procedural documents, academics have no access to structured and clear guidelines on effective CP supervision (Roberts & Seaman, 2018).

One way to address the lack of ESP/ESAP provision in the curriculum and to enhance student and faculty engagement in the CP preparation process is to develop a mobile app which provides instant communication as well as ubiquitous and one-stop English language support for faculty staff and senior-year students. Studies with higher education students have shown that students prefer accessing the internet on mobile devices (Wong et al., 2015) and learning through bite-sized lectures (Koh et al., 2018). In contrast to language learning websites, mobile apps offer more personalized user experiences and foster students' active participation via the use of multimodal materials (Beach & O'Brien, 2014), progress-tracked exercises, and self-management tools. The CP app presented in this chapter, which aims to help students in various disciplines master a broad range of skills required for the successful completion of CP dissertations, is the first attempt to utilize mobile technology to address the gaps and language needs identified in the current delivery of CP in Hong Kong tertiary institutions.

Methodology

The development of a mobile app, called Capstone Ninja, for supporting CP report writing in various disciplines was the primary aim of a government-funded project for five Hong Kong universities. In order to develop such an app that addresses the needs of both CP supervisors and students, this study sets out to examine 1) students' and supervisors' needs and expectations in the CP preparation process and 2) what app functions and language support are expected and needed.

To obtain "a holistic view of student writing needs in a particular context" (Flowerdew, 2018, p. 5), the project team decided to use a dual-method approach in the collection of both subjective and objective data through the gauging of stakeholders' feedback and the analysis of student writing because "a combination of methods is preferred for a target- and present-situation analysis" (Flowerdew, 2018, p. 5).

Focus group interviews were conducted with 12 students and five supervisors of five disciplines (applied physics, computer science, electronic and information engineering, environmental science[1], and humanities), with open-ended questions on the three major issues: the challenges they faced or observed in CP writing, their comments on the app, and suggestions for its future development. The questions were deliberately phrased in this way to allow the respondents to express their views extensively. Responses from students and staff were then compared to see where agreements and differences lay. After that, consent was obtained to analyse nine CP reports from three disciplines[2] (electronic and information engineering, environmental science, and applied physics). The textual analysis of the nine CP reports focused on the four aspects that were identified as areas of concern by students or supervisors in the focus group interviews: 1) the introduction section, 2) the literature review and discussion sections, 3) lack of research mapping, and 4) referencing. A sentence-based approach was employed to examine "sentence-level features, inter-sentential relations, coherence breaks, and functional sentence perspective" (Connor, 1987, p. 680). This method allowed the project team to "target certain features of discourse" and make "data-driven" discovery (Leki, 1991, p. 132). Such a "textual orientation . . . work[s] to actively foster the construction in students of rhetorical schemata which hopefully correspond to those of English-speaking readers" (Leki, 1991, p. 135). Text analysis in the context of CP writing offered a means "to identify common problems" (Flowerdew, 2018, p. 5) for "purposive, tailor-made" materials (Flowerdew, 2018, p. 1).

---

1   The Department of Environmental Science was renamed the Department of Ocean Science in the 2018/2019 academic year. For consistency purposes, this article uses the former to refer to their staff and students.

2   Due to logistical constraints, the research team was not able to collect CP reports produced by students of computer science and humanities at the time of writing.

User Feedback: Findings from Focus Group Interviews with Students and Supervisors

As noted above, students' and supervisors' views were solicited in three major areas: challenges in CP writing, feedback on the app's functions, and suggestions for its future development. The interviews revealed interesting findings, including some commonalities and differences between students and teachers.

Challenges in CP Writing

Both students and supervisors agreed that the content of the final-year project posed the biggest problem for students. Student interviewees reported one common challenge, which was not knowing how to start their CP. They felt that they lacked ideas about their project requirements. Some students found it difficult to decide on a broad area for their final-year project and then narrow it down to a feasible research topic. Students also encountered various problems with finding appropriate literature. For example, a computer science student commented on the huge number of readings he had to do before he could select a focus for his study, whereas a humanities student struggled with locating enough information or sources to support his project. One engineering student expressed his concern about finding a suitable method that could be applied to his project.

These findings were in line with what supervisors found most challenging in CP supervision, which was guiding students on the content and organization of their reports. Students showed a lack of preparedness in undertaking the CP, which often requires intensive reading (Healey et al., 2013). As an engineering supervisor noted, students "may not [have] enough information and may follow some wrong path to reach their goals." A humanities supervisor observed that students were "not doing anything" at the initial research and consolidating stage of their projects. She pointed out that students should have done preliminary work over the summer, but when they finalized their project in September, they were "not ready to do so at all," and ended up changing their projects because they realized that "what they proposed earlier did not work at all." Most of the supervisors emphasized the importance of regular supervisor-supervisee communication. They believed there was a connection between students' (un)preparedness and the (in)frequency of their communication and interaction with their supervisors. The humanities supervisor believed that "if students meet their supervisors regularly, then any problems can be identified, but the motivation for students to initiate meetings is low."

Differences were found in students' and supervisors' perceptions of the most difficult section of the thesis for students. Students felt that the introduction chapter was the most difficult to write because of its important location in the whole report, being the first section that the audience reads. They also felt that the introduction chapter needed to include considerable content, e.g., it must present background information, explain the purpose of the study, and identify the study's contribution to society. None of the supervisors, however, mentioned the introduction section as posing the biggest difficulty for students. While the environmental science and engineering supervisors did find some problems in students' introduction sections, such as the lack of concrete objectives, they observed that their students often had more serious problems with other sections of the report. The engineering supervisor pointed out that the literature review was often very thin and did not contain sufficient relevant in-text citations. The environmental science supervisor reported that the discussion section was problematic, as her students could not include a critical analysis of the findings or do research mapping (i.e., a comparison of their findings with those presented in publications) to highlight the significance of their results. She also recounted how students could not provide concise summaries of "the key point of views in one or two sentences" in the conclusion section, and how some students failed to adhere to proper style guidelines in the references section. The engineering supervisor also mentioned the references section as a problematic area. The problem went beyond formatting conventions to the selection of sources. Students chose poor-quality references that were not appropriate or reported studies that were conducted in contexts that were considerably different from their own.

Another interesting difference between students and supervisors related to students' writing abilities. Students reported that their main worry was content, as they believed this was the aspect that their supervisors would pay most attention to. Organization and overall structure of the paper were also mentioned as areas of concern. Language did not rank as an area of high concern for students. Engineering students considered language as an area of medium-level concern because without good language, they could not express their ideas clearly; however, this was far less a worry than the technical aspects of their projects. While some humanities students showed awareness of the need for an appropriate style and tone in their CP, environmental science and computer science students did not mention language as an area of concern at all.

In contrast, all the supervisors commented on students' writing and other language issues. The humanities supervisor reported that some students simply connected loose and short excerpts from different sources and used them to write a literary analysis with minimal criticism. Similarly, the engineering supervisor noted that students tended to include all kinds of information without "filtering and processing" the content. He remarked that if students had shown him their work "maybe a week" before the submission deadline, he would have taken "a look" at the clarity and organization; however, students "seldom do it." Common language problems that he often saw in students' CP reports included misuse of tenses and reporting verbs, as well as expressing ideas using vocabulary that they did not completely understand. The applied physics supervisor echoed the engineering supervisor's observations, while also noting that he considered CP supervision "a burden" and a time-consuming and challenging task because he did not consider himself "trained" to give feedback on English language or "fix" students' writing problems.

Feedback on the Basic App Version

The second area covered in the interviews concerned the usefulness of the Capstone Ninja app, which received a positive response from students and supervisors alike. Students reported several aspects that they found especially useful, e.g., that the app helped them systematically learn about the requirements and expectations of the different sections of a CP report. They believed that the app was useful for self and flexible learning, and that it was convenient and easy to navigate. Although some respondents felt that some learning modules contained slightly too much information and could be made more appealing, the majority of the students reported that the bite-size learning modules served as handy and quick references for them during the writing process. This finding is in line with the project's rationale of bite-size learning for better learner engagement and aligns with the call for just-in-time support, especially for year-long capstone projects (Omer, 2015). These student views were also in agreement with the comments from supervisors, who perceived the learning modules on the app to be providing helpful assistance to students in acquiring the skills of formatting and organizing a research report. As noted by the environmental science supervisor, the learning materials on the mobile app were "rich" and "enough for students to learn [the content] by themselves."

The convenience in managing the project tasks was another feature that appealed to both students and supervisors. The majority of the supervisors found the self-management tools, such as the to-do list, valuable and useful for planning and checking CP progress. This was echoed by computer science students, who found it easy to set schedules and deadlines on the app. Engineering students viewed the to-do list function on the app as a helpful reminder of their deadlines.

Suggested Features for the Future App Version

One of the features students and supervisors would like to see in future versions of the Capstone Ninja app is a chat function. Student respondents wanted to receive immediate and instant advice on their CP and use such a chat function to alert supervisors about uncooperative group members. Supervisors concurred that a chat function would be a valuable tool to schedule meetings and communicate about simple matters. The engineering supervisor considered the ability to communicate with students via the app a much-welcomed option as he would not want to give his mobile number to students.

Other suggestions made by students included developing content on oral presentations of theses, providing external links to online resources, giving them access to previous students' CP reports, and including pre- and post-learning module interactive questions to motivate them to "scroll" for learning. Supervisors generally favoured the inclusion of more interactive features such as videos and links to online resources. One supervisor also recommended developing an accompanying web version of the app for use in the office.

Textual Analysis of Students' CP Writing Problems

To further investigate the weaknesses in student writing expressed by the CP supervisors, nine CP reports were examined, with particular attention given to four aspects that were identified as areas of concern by students or supervisors in the interviews: 1) writing the introduction section, 2) writing the literature review and discussion sections, 3) doing research mapping, and 4) referencing.

Writing the Introduction Section

A close examination of the CP reports tended to confirm the concerns indicated by the CP supervisors that students' ways of stating research objectives can be "idiosyncratic." For example, the student writing in Excerpt 1 attempted to link the research gap to the project objectives but was not very successful. "The second objective" is confusing, as readers would probably ask how the recommendations relate to the project objectives.

> Everyday Hong Kong and Shenzhen have a food waste enormous production which faces different aspect of challenges. This project objective has two fold. The first objective is to compare the policies and technology of Hong Kong and Shenzhen in food waste problem, especially in recycling

part. The second objective is to give some recommendations in both cities to achieve a more comprehensive approach to food waste treatment. (Excerpt 1: Environment Science CP Report A)

While an introduction usually contains a general background, literature review, and research objectives, novice student writers often struggle with the order of these features. Excerpt 2 shows unnecessary repetition of the objective statement before and after the background.

The goal of the task is to locate the vehicle in a static state with traffic lights and photodiodes through signal transmission. Currently, the Global Positioning System (GPS) is widely used in vehicle positioning through locating the vehicle via four satellites. However, GPS can be inaccurate and may fail to locate a vehicle precisely. . . . Therefore this task tries to improve vehicle locating accuracy with the visible lighting system and traffic lights, to tackle the inaccuracy problems of GPS. (Excerpt 2: Electronic & Information Engineering CP Report B)

Writing the Literature Review and Discussion Sections

One concern raised by supervisors related to students' literature review and discussion sections being too thin, without relevant scholarly substantiation. Indeed, textual analysis corroborates these observations as shown in Excerpt 3 and Excerpt 4 below, where the student claims were not supported by any findings.

Coatings with single element materials and binary materials were rather well investigated, but a little effort has been devoted to the development and research of materials based on multi-element structures such as composite ternary borides of aluminum and magnesium. (Excerpt 3: Applied Physics CP Report B)

Cloud-based, which application is an upcoming trend in the information world, because of shorter implementation times and without additional hardware or software requires. . . . Due to the potential benefits of cloud-based, more and more industries and companies would like to use cloud-based as a tool to finish a different kind of missions. . . . (Excerpt 4: Electronic and Information Engineering CP Report A)

Research Mapping

The analysis of the student reports indicates that most students failed to show the relationship between the findings of the current report and published studies. Experienced writers tactfully show where and how their present work fits into the research map in their field. They also use research mapping to demonstrate the novelty or significance of their findings by showing that there is a lack of such findings in existing research reports. Excerpt 5 illustrates an unsatisfactory attempt at research mapping. While the Germany example was used to contrast the practice in Hong Kong and Shenzhen, no further details were given to substantiate the comparison with previous research findings.

> To increase plastic recycling in Hong Kong, the key to success is how the policies are introduced and implemented.... With the all-rounded strategy, examples like fining those people who throw disqualified refuse into the bins and . . . would be capable of increasing recycling rate. This is what has been done in Germany but not in Hong Kong and Shenzhen. Therefore, a comprehensive strategy is crucial to ensure its efficiency. (Excerpt 5: Environmental Science CP Report C)

In the same way, Excerpt 6 has failed to elaborate on findings from previous research to present similarities in the results obtained.

> Sediment with estimated calendric age of 595 years before present (BP) located at the top of the sediment profile also contradicts with the expectation. This suggests that mangrove in Xi Wan might be not naturally formed. Other results obtained from other research teams of this project (via personal communication) also evidenced the mangrove ecosystem in Xi Wan is a result of reclamation. (Excerpt 6: Environmental Science CP Report B)

Referencing

By making appropriate references to credible sources (i.e., including effective in-text citations), experienced writers engage critically with the text to show how their current research contributes to both the knowledge (Abasi et al., 2006) and their readers, in addition to how it relates to studies in the field (Yates et al., 2005). Such explaining, however, is very challenging for ESL students, whose writing often exhibits features of patchwriting, i.e., the rearranging of words and phrases without truly paraphrasing the original sentences, and demonstrates difficulties in "using the existing literature to back up [their] points" (Pittam et al., 2009, p. 159). Although Excerpt 7 mentions a certain person, no scholarly reference was made to further illustrate the argument.

> During last year, Mr. W. L. Cheuk of the Hong Kong Polytechnic University attempted to apply A* pathfinding algorithm and obstacle avoidance algorithm solve the problems of SLAM and Cooperative-SLAM. . . . MR. W. L. Cheuk focus on enhancing the performance of Single-Robot SLAM, it inspires me very much. (Excerpt 7: Electronic & Information Engineering CP Report A)

Supervisors also commented that students included non-credible in-text citations, e.g., wiki articles, popular science blogs, and news articles. Excerpt 8 cites a newspaper article (深圳商報) written in Chinese, which the supervisor considered inappropriate:

> In Shenzhen, there are two main policies which are . . . and 家庭生活垃圾分類投放指引 (深圳商報, 2017) to mitigate food waste problem. (Excerpt 8: Environmental Science CP Report A)

Another major problem of referencing was inappropriate format:

> For the reference of an alert message, according to Marina & Kenneth, "Emergency vehicles at scene warning message size is 39 bytes." (Excerpt 9: Electronic & Information Engineering CP Report B)

To summarize, a close examination of focus group interview data and textual analysis reveals that writing the introduction, literature review, and discussion sections of a research paper; doing research mapping; and referencing are challenging for students in their CP preparation process. Textual analysis suggests that novice CP report writers need help with situating themselves in the field by demonstrating the importance of their report findings and justifying their significance.

The Way Forward

The findings from the interviews and textual analysis have provided a clear direction for the app's development, which can progress in three major ways.

First, it is clear that the app needs to include more learning content to help develop students' literacy skills in CP report writing. Supervisor feedback and textual analysis indicate the need to strengthen students' writing skills in the following areas: setting the scene well by making the introduction effective, developing a well-structured argument in the literature review and discussion sections, and doing research mapping and referencing effectively. To help students develop these skills, suitable excerpts from previous CP reports and credible publications should be used to illustrate the important concepts. Links to relevant external resources, such as credible websites that teach these skills, can also be incorporated into the app for students' extended learning.

A second area for future development pertains to the communication and self-management functions of the app. Both students and supervisors expressed their wish to use the app as a communication tool. In addition to mass notifications for one-way communication and announcements, a chat function is currently being developed for mutual communication on the app. Given the importance of motivating students to set CP-related goals, the team will explore the feasibility of developing more time-management tools, such as incorporating departmental CP timelines and setting individual milestones.

The third area in the app's development is testing and evaluating. Efforts will be made to expand student and supervisor use of the app, as well as to collect user feedback on the usefulness of the various app functions. One way of doing so is by including a "Comment" function on the app for users to relay their feedback. Another means of measuring the extent of student engagement with the app would be establishing a learning analytics mechanism on the back end that offers a systematic and quantitative approach to facilitate understanding of user mobile behavior.

In sum, Capstone Ninja is a one-of-a-kind mobile app bridging the gap in the provision of ubiquitous, multimodal CP language support for students across the disciplines. This study, which has offered fresh insight into supervisor concerns and supervisee needs, advances the development of English across the curriculum in the digital age.

Acknowledgement

The study reported in this chapter is funded by the Hong Kong Government's UGC Funding Scheme for Teaching and Learning Related Proposals, project title: "Language Enhancement for Capstone Projects Using Interactive Apps."

References

Abasi, A. R., Akbari, N. & Graves, B. (2006). Discourse appropriation, construction of identities, and the complex issue of plagiarism: ESL students writing in graduate school. *Journal of Second Language Writing, 15*(2), 102–117.

Beach, R. & O'Brien, D. (2014). *Using apps for learning across the curriculum: A literacy-based framework and guide.* Routledge.

Blicblau, A. & Dini, K. (2012). Intervention in engineering students? Final year capstone research projects to enhance their written, oral and presentation skills. *International Journal of Engineering Pedagogy, 2*(3), 11–18.

Chen, J. (2016, August). *EAP curriculum evaluation and English Across the Curriculum* [Invited workshop]. JACET Summer Seminar, Kyoto, Japan.

Chen, J. (2020). EAP in Hong Kong. In H. Terauchi, J. Noguchi & A. Tajino (Eds.), *Towards a new paradigm for English language teaching: English for specific purposes in Asia and beyond* (pp. 115–126). Routledge.

Chen, J. & Foung, D. (2017, June). *Does streaming work? A quantitative study of university EAP subjects* [Paper presentation]. Faces of English 2 Conference, Hong Kong.

Connor, U. (1987). Research frontiers in writing analysis. *TESOL Quarterly, 21*(4), 677–696.

Cranmer, S. (2006). Enhancing graduate employability: Best intentions and mixed outcomes. *Studies in Higher Education, 31*(2), 169–184.

Crosthwaite, P. (2016). A longitudinal multidimensional analysis of EAP writing: Determining EAP course effectiveness. *Journal of English for Academic Purposes, 22*, 166–178.

Del Río, M. L., Díaz-Vázquez, R. & Maside Sanfiz, J. M. (2018). Satisfaction with the supervision of undergraduate dissertations. *Active Learning in Higher Education, 19*(2), 159–172.

Education Commission. (2000). *Reform proposals for the education system in Hong Kong.* https://www.e-c.edu.hk/doc/en/publications_and_related_documents/education_reform/Edu-reform-eng.pdf.

Evans, S. & Green, C. (2007). Why EAP is necessary: A survey of Hong Kong tertiary students. *Journal of English for Academic Purposes, 6*(1), 3–17.

Evans, S. & Morrison, B. (2011). The first term at university: Implications for EAP. *ELT Journal, 65*, 387–397.

Evans, S. & Morrison, B. (2018). Adjusting to higher education in Hong Kong: The influence of school medium of instruction. *International Journal of Bilingual Education and Bilingualism, 21*(8), 1016–1029.

Fan, M. Y. (2001). An investigation into the vocabulary needs of university students in Hong Kong. *Asian Journal of English Language Teaching, 11*, 69–85.

Flowerdew, L. (2018). Needs analysis for the second language writing classroom. In J. I. Liontas & TESOL International Association (Eds.), *The TESOL encyclopedia of English language teaching,* pp. 1–6. https://doi.org/10.1002/9781118784235.eelt0523.

Greenbank, P. & Penketh, C. (2009). Student autonomy and reflections on researching and writing the undergraduate dissertation. *Journal of Further and Higher Education, 33*(4), 463–472.

Healey, M., Lannin, L., Stibbe, A. & Derounian, J. (2013). *Developing and enhancing undergraduate final-year projects and dissertations.* The Higher Education Academy,

University of Gloucestershire. https://www.heacademy.ac.uk/system/files/projects/developing_and_enhancing_undergraduate_final-year_projects_and_dissertations_0.pdf.

Ho, B. (2003). Time management of final year undergraduate English projects: Supervisees' and the supervisors' coping strategies. *System, 31*(2), 231–245.

Hyland, K. (1997). Is EAP necessary? A survey of Hong Kong undergraduates. *Asian Journal of English Language Teaching, 7*(2), 77–99.

Jaldemark, J. & Lindberg, J. O. (2013). Technology-mediated supervision of undergraduate students' dissertations. *Studies in Higher Education, 38*(9), 1382–1392.

Källkvist, M., Gomez, S., Andersson, H. & Lush, D. (2009). Personalised virtual learning spaces to support undergraduates in producing research reports: Two case studies. *The Internet and Higher Education, 12*(1), 35–44.

Koh, N. S., Gottipati, S. & Shankararaman, V. (2018). Effectiveness of bite-sized lecture on student learning outcomes. In *4th International Conference on Higher Education Advances (HEAD'18)* (pp. 515–523). Universitat Politècnica de València.

Leki, I. (1991). Twenty-five years of contrastive rhetoric: Text analysis and writing pedagogies. *TESOL Quarterly, 25*(1), 123–143.

Littlewood, W. & Liu, N. F. (1996). *Hong Kong students and their English.* Macmillan Publishers (China) Limited.

Omer. A. (2015, September 21). *Is bite sized learning the future of e-learning?* eLearning Industry. https://elearningindustry.com/bite-sized-learning-future-of-elearning.

Pittam, G., Elander, J., Lusher, J., Fox, P. & Payne, N. (2009). Student beliefs and attitudes about authorial identity in academic writing. *Studies in Higher Education, 34*(2), 153–170.

Roberts, L. D. & Seaman, K. (2018). Good undergraduate dissertation supervision: Perspectives of supervisors and dissertation coordinators. *International Journal for Academic Development, 23*(1), 28–40.

Stoneham, R. & Essop, A. (2014). Supervision tracking: Improving the student and staff experience for projects and dissertations. *Compass: Journal of Learning and Teaching, 5*(9), 1–5. https://journals.gre.ac.uk/index.php/compass/article/viewFile/109/164.

Thomas, K., Wong, K. C. & Li, Y. C. (2014). The capstone experience: Student and academic perspectives. *Higher Education Research & Development, 33*(3), 580–594.

Washer, P. (2007). Revisiting key skills: A practical framework for higher education. *Quality in Higher Education, 13*(1), 57–67.

Wong, K., Wang, F. L., Ng, K. K. & Kwan, R. (2015). Investigating acceptance towards mobile learning in higher education students. In K. C. Li, T. L. Wong, S. K. S. Cheung, J. Lam & K. K. Ng (Eds.), *Technology in education. Transforming education practices with technology.* Springer.

Yates, S. J., Williams, N. & Dujardin, A. F. (2005). Writing geology: Key communication competencies for geoscience. *Planet, 15*(1), 36–41.

Zinser, R. (2003). Developing career and employability skills: A US case study. *Education+ Training, 45*(7), 402–410.

Section Two. Content and Language Integrated Learning

6 Impacts and Challenges of a Mobile App for Improving Final-Year Project Proposal Writing: A Case from a Hong Kong University

Grace Yuk Wan Lim and Ivan Wang-Hei Ho
THE HONG KONG POLYTECHNIC UNIVERSITY

Abstract: Despite recognition of their characteristics of flexibility, mobility, and easy accessibility, the use of mobile devices in higher education is still in its early stages, with few focusing on essay writing. This chapter presents the initial data collected from students piloting an inter-institutionally developed mobile app, Capstone Ninja, for improving their final-year project proposal writing and managing their project schedule. Highlights of the project findings have been detailed in Chapter 5. This chapter focuses on results from pre- and post-app launch interviews which revealed that students were very positive towards the management tool, as it helped them to monitor various schedules easily, whereas their feedback on the learning content was varied. Factors with respect to students' readiness of adoption of the app for learning, their attitude towards this mode of learning, their language proficiency level, and the limitations of the app are explored.

Keywords: mobile learning, mobile app, textual analysis, browse behaviour, final-year project proposal

The increasing ubiquity and accessibility of mobile devices and the wide access to networks globally have encouraged and enabled the development of mobile learning (hereafter referred to as *m-learning*) in education. M-learning refers to "learning across multiple contexts, through social and content interactions, using electronic devices" (Crompton, 2013, p. 4). While m-learning has been studied and applied in education for over two decades, "there is still relatively little knowledge available, especially regarding the use of mobile technology in higher education setting(s)" (Pimmer et al., 2016, p. 492). Given that the largest demographic of mobile device users is 18–29-year-olds, which is also the typical age of college students (Pew Research Center, 2019), it is worth examining the use of this technology among tertiary students. In addition, most m-learning in English focuses on individual language items such as vocabulary, grammatical items, and sentence structure. As shown in Chapter 5, recent research has started to explore the use of a mobile app for enhancing students' capstone project writing.

This chapter presents the initial findings on the use of the mobile app Capstone Ninja by electronic and information engineering students in a Hong Kong university to enhance their project proposal writing, a genre different from that focused upon in the previous chapter. It predominantly aims to explore the effectiveness of the app by studying the correlation between its use and the resulting quality of student writing, using both qualitative and quantitative data. Overall, the project is expected to contribute to our understanding of mobile education in improving students' writing, and students' perceptions of such learning and of mobile app devices.

English Education in Hong Kong Universities

Most tertiary institutions in Hong Kong have adopted English as the medium of instruction, despite the fact that Chinese is used predominantly in students' daily lives (e.g., Evans, 2017; Li, 2009). This is the situation in the authors' university. Nearly half of the freshmen in our university come from Chinese-medium secondary schools and may take a year to adapt to the change in language of instruction (Evans & Morrison, 2018). During their four years of study, students usually take two courses in English for academic purposes (EAP) in Year One and/or Year Two. These courses help equip them with general academic writing and speaking skills needed for their university studies. Between years two and four, students take one more English course of one to three credits which focuses on the language skills needed for their disciplinary study or future profession.

Students are required to complete a capstone/final-year project in the last stage of university education, which accounts for three to nine credits of the total 120-credit degree requirement in their undergraduate studies. They may not receive language support to prepare for their final-year project writing; this is particularly the case for those from the engineering programmes due to their packed curricula. Research in the U.S. university system suggests that students may not transfer the academic English skills learnt in their junior year to the disciplinary subjects in their senior years (Horner, 2014). Therefore, additional language support is important for these engineering students.

Mobile Learning in Higher Education

The pedagogical value of mobile and ubiquitous learning has been studied from several perspectives: in formal education settings (e.g., Frohberg et al., 2009), in work-based environments (e.g., Pachler et al., 2013), and in lifelong learning contexts (e.g., Alina-Mihaela, 2015). The themes examined vary widely, focusing on factors such as educational levels, contexts, subject matter domains, types of mobile devices, learning theories, and geographic distribution.

Mobile devices are characterised by distinguishing attributes such as portability, mobility, connectivity, and individuality (Sung et al., 2016). They provide very considerable potential for improving university students' learning experience and for solving some of the problems students and teachers face in higher education contexts (Wang & Cui, 2016). Their use can increase student autonomy and improve teacher-student interaction if they are integrated well with instructional strategies and pedagogy (Wang & Cui, 2016). This is especially helpful to Chinese students, as they tend to be quieter and more passive in learning, simply following teachers' instructions and teaching in the classroom (Ho, 2001). Some researchers therefore foresee that mobile technologies may radically transform higher education by offering new strategies and resources to enable "pervasive, personal, and connected learning" (Wagner, 2005, p. 43).

Research into m-learning in university education focuses on several areas. Most attention is placed on its impact on students (Crompton & Burke, 2018). Qun Wu (2015) developed a mobile app for students to learn English vocabulary. His results show that students who used this programme significantly outperformed those in the control group in acquiring new vocabulary. Learning vocabulary in this way is regarded by students to be innovative and creative (Agca & Ozdemir, 2013). Zhi Li and Volker Hegelheimer (2013) employed a web-based mobile application, Grammar Clinic, in an ESL writing class for one semester. Their analysis indicates a reduction in errors in final drafts as a result of the gains evidenced in a grammar post-test.

Another important area examined is students' and teachers' perceptions of m-learning (Crompton & Burke, 2018). Some studies have explored the more general views on its use for collaborative learning and communication (see for instance, Kim et al., 2013 and Zou & Yan, 2014, among others). Mohamed Sarrab (2015) analysed in detail science and engineering students' knowledge, acceptance, and use of m-learning. He found that they welcomed the idea of reading an article, submitting their assignment, and setting an assignment reminder using a mobile device. Others are interested in finding out learners' expectations on usage intent, ease of use, and perceptions of the types of mobile devices and applications, as well as the language skills they aim to improve (Fucekova & Metruk, 2018; Hyman et al., 2014). Understanding students' attitudes towards the use of hand-held devices as educational tools is important for informing researchers of their behaviour when engaging in this type of learning. If users view m-learning as having little value, they will be less motivated to engage in the relevant activities (Crompton & Burke, 2018). Thus, one effective measurement of the value of mobile technology in an educational setting is to examine its usability by students in this situation (Swanson, 2018). In addition to finding out perceptions of students, research also shows teachers' positive evaluations regarding the use of m-learning in higher education (Al-Emran et al., 2016) and its value in stimulating interactions between teachers and students (Dascalu et al., 2014).

It is also essential to understand the factors and variables that impact the use of m-learning and its effectiveness for successful implementation. The use of mobile devices has been the central focus of research in m-learning. Chun Lai (2013) examined the factor of self-management, and Ibrahim Arpaci (2015) investigated the influence of culture on mobile learning adoption. It has been argued that the most important factor for the success of m-learning in higher education is the adoption of a model that can integrate the understanding of teaching and learning simultaneously (Alrasheedi et al., 2015). This is shown in Thomas Cochrane and David Rhodes' (2013) reiterative study in which impact of student learning is noted in the pedagogical integration of the mobile technology into a course and assessment.

This chapter addresses the major concerns expressed by the students and supervisors about the appeal and effectiveness of Capstone Ninja in helping students' writing. It considers the mobile app design, the language content, and impact on writing performance as a result of student login activities. Finally, it explores factors that may influence their adoption of the mobile app as well.

Research Objective

The research project, entitled "Language Enhancement for Capstone Projects Using Interactive Apps," is government-funded, involves five participating universities, and is expected to be completed by August 2021 (Chen et al., 2018). It aims to enhance the English communication competence students need for completing their project proposals, interim reports, and final-year project (FYP) reports, as well as the skills they require to verbally present the report results. To achieve these aims, the project has been developing a mobile app called Capstone Ninja, which has multimodal English learning resources, a learning tool, a management tool, and a communication tool for students to communicate with their supervisors. The design is based on the underlying belief that an app should be flexible and able to tailor learning content to individual students. It provides supplementary language support to students who lack formal language input, with a focus on the speaking and writing necessary for completing an FYP report. It also aims to facilitate communication between the supervisor and the supervisee, which may not be effectively achieved using traditional emails. The first version of the app has already been developed and is available for download in the Apple App Store and the Google Play Store.

This chapter discusses the initial findings collected from the early adopters after they tried out the first version of the mobile app. In particular, the data analysis aims to examine whether the app can (1) enhance engineering students' English communication competence needed for completing their FYP proposal and (2) help them to manage their schedule using the management tool.

Research Questions

This study aims to answer the following questions:

1. What are students' opinions on the design and content of the learning tool and the management tool of the app?
2. What are the supervisor's views on the design and functions of the mobile app?
3. Is there a significant difference in the quality of students' final-year project proposal writing which can be attributable to the use of the mobile app?

Methods

A mixed methodology was used in this research study, involving the collection of both quantitative and qualitative data. The first type of quantitative data indicated the improvement in students' proposal writing after the use of the mobile app compared with before. This was measured in terms of the number of rhetorical moves in the writing, including the abstract, study background, literature review, objectives, research methods, project timetable, and bibliographic references. The second type examined student login and active time spent on the app during the writing period. The qualitative data included the pre- and post-app launch interviews with students. Post-app launch interviews were also conducted with the supervisor and the language assessor, who was previously a university language teacher.

Participants

A total of six students and a supervisor from an engineering programme voluntarily participated in this trial. The students were in their final year of study, and the supervisor, who is the co-author of this chapter, is experienced in FYP supervision. This stage of the study lasted around two months, and students were encouraged to use the mobile app for self-learning and time management. The number of users is expected to increase substantially when the app is fully developed (Chen et al., 2018).

Other studies have evaluated mobile applications with a small number of subjects. For example, five adult users were invited to assess the usability of a mobile handwriting application (Yilmaz & Durdu, 2015); three participants were observed in their use of an iPad app (Tavernier, 2016); and two students' first drafts, self- and peer- feedback, and final drafts were analysed when examining the effectiveness of Google Docs (Woodard & Babcock, 2016). To increase the reliability of the results obtained with a small sample, the current study adopted triangulation methods for data collection.

Functions of the Mobile Learning App

The trial mobile app comprised two available functions:

1. The *learning tool* provides general and discipline-related English language resources for different types of FYP-related writing and the oral presentation. The language resources contain information that guides students regarding the rhetorical moves needed in their writing, referencing skills and language features typical in writing.
2. The *management tool* enables students to keep track of deadlines from different parties (department, supervisor, and themselves) and helps them to monitor their schedules.

The third function, a communication tool, is being developed and will be available to users in the next stage of the project. It provides a platform for the supervisor to communicate with the supervisee in real time and for students to communicate with their peers (in the case of a group project). The app is available for download from the Apple App Store and the Google Play Store. Figure 6.1 shows a screenshot of the two main functions available for the trial use and the third function, which is being developed.

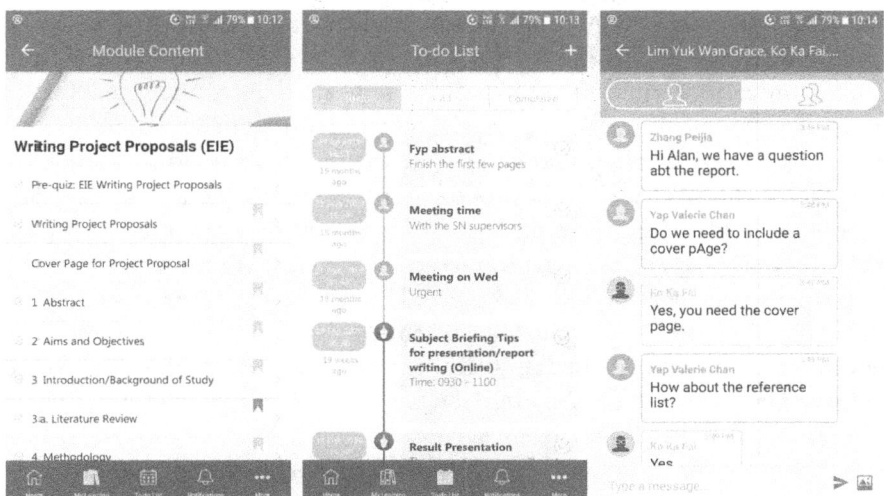

Figure 6.1. Screenshot of three functions of Capstone Ninja

To develop the content for the learning tool, the language team from the authors' university conducted textual analysis on previous students' project proposal writing. Reference was also made to the host department's guidelines on proposal writing; these list the main sections to be included, such as the objectives, introduction/background, method, project schedule, and references. Additional advice was solicited from the participating supervisor, who shared his perceptions of the students' weaknesses and strengths in writing and his views regarding what he felt should be the focus of the project. Finally, the language team incorporated the different ideas and developed the content for the learning tool of the mobile app. The initial design of the management tool was suggested by the students and supervisors in the pre-app survey, while the information for the schedule was provided by the department.

Procedure

Student interviews were conducted before and after they had used the app. The pre-interview was conducted in September 2018 in the first meeting in which the supervisor briefed his six supervisees. These students were asked in a short interview to share their usage intent and attitude toward apps for learning and for social networking. Immediately after this, they were invited to log onto the mobile app, complete the pre-quiz, browse the site, and comment on six areas—app features, app design, to-do-lists, learning modules, chat, and readiness to use the app for FYP writing.

A pre-quiz was administered before students were allowed to read the content; the post-quiz contained the same questions as the pre-quiz but in a shuffled order. Both quizzes asked users to indicate their confidence level for the option chosen. The post-quiz evaluated students' understanding of content and language use in proposal writing. The results revealed that students' language use and knowledge of proposal writing were generally satisfactory, as two-thirds of them answered two questions out of five correctly. All six students attempted the pre-quiz in the briefing, as it was administered in the class, whereas the post-quiz was completed by four students in their free time when they finished reading all the content in this module. Post-interviews were conducted in November 2018 after the proposals were submitted. Three students were available for the interview.

Textual analysis of the six pre-proposals (from the previous year) and post-proposals was conducted by a former English teacher to identify language and writing problems. The results were verified with another experienced language teacher; their inter-reliability ratio was found to be 90 percent. Any disagreement was resolved through negotiation. The qualitative results of the rhetorical moves of the proposals were further processed to identify whether there were similarities or differences in the rhetorical moves in writings after the use of the mobile app. Finally, each student's browse data over the two-month period were retrieved.

The findings from the interview results, quality of student writing, and students' mobile app usage rates are discussed below.

Results and Discussion

This section discusses and examines four types of collected data: (1) perceptions and attitude of students and their supervisor toward the design and application features of the mobile app, (2) number of rhetorical moves in the pre- and post-project proposals analysed by a language teacher, (3) supervisor's and language teacher's evaluation of writings, and (4) students' app browse data.

Comments on Mobile App Design and Functions

Pre-Launch Interview

All six students commented on the app design and applications in the interview. Their responses revealed a mixed attitude toward the use of an app for language learning. In their daily life, they used mobile apps for socialization and for entertainment. For improving English, they rarely used any app; nonetheless, they welcomed free apps such as Grammarly and Dictionary for helping them to proofread essays or verify the meaning of words. A few liked using Sololearn as it enabled them to interact with other learners in virtual contexts, offered different levels of challenges, and even awarded them a certificate. The students were more willing to acquire subject knowledge using apps (e.g., Mimo) and pay for them as well.

Students found functions such as to-do-lists, chat, notification, and bookmark to be very useful. They expected the app to remind them of deadlines and wanted to use it to communicate with their supervisor. They also hoped that the app could synchronise with their phone calendar.

Students' views toward the proposal content were divided. One thought that the content was general and might not be relevant to his topic, whereas another appreciated the language support. They both rated the information on the proposal structure as helpful. However, they found the presentation of the learning unit for proposals unappealing owing to its lack of flexibility in letting them skip sections according to their interests and knowledge level. Similarly, their supervisor suggested that more interactive designs and features be implemented to increase its attractiveness.

Post-Launch Interview

Three of the participants attended the post-interview. All three evaluated the app's management tool favourably, as it allowed them to check the deadlines of their project schedule. One said, "I want(ed) to know what time to submit and when is the next deadline." All of them valued the tool that allowed them to set their own notifications before the deadlines for assignment submissions in the coming months. The students' evaluations of the content of the learning tool varied. All of them rated the information rather positively as "quite useful" and "helpful." They also thought that the app explained the organisation of the report well and provided "an overview and an idea on what to do." This is probably because it fills gaps in their understanding of writing, as the subject guidelines from their department provide little information on either the content or its structure.

However, the students seemed reluctant to spend more time on the app to improve their writing further, as indicated by their browse time within this period. There are a few possible reasons for this. One could be related to their perception of the educational potential of technological resources, a point discussed in Chun Lai and colleagues' (2012) study. The materials may not meet their needs fully.

One student indicated, "The materials are quite useful but I think maybe they are not for everyone. At least I don't feel like I need to read everything." This student's rating on the writing materials is positive but he did not seem to be interested in all of them. His proposal content was rated highly by the supervisor, but the writing style and language were given a mid-range grade by the language teacher. He considered it unnecessary to write a detailed proposal at the early stage of the project as, according to the subject guidelines, the main emphasis should be on its technical information. The low weighting for writing (4% of the overall grade of the entire subject) may also demotivate students from making more of an effort in this regard. This echoes researchers' views that the use of technology is related to the demands of the study situations (Goodyear & Ellis, 2008).

Another student with a fairly good command of English looked for excellent samples of theses on his topic to guide him on writing objectives and developing a good theory. He targeted specific journal articles or A+ graded theses from online sources and was not interested in the app's information on project proposals. The last student used the app for "grammar improvement" but was frustrated at reading "so many English words in the small screen" as this made him feel "uncomfortable," and therefore, he was "not willing to use it." This remark confirmed earlier observations that users could develop a negative experience because of the limitations of the device or the ease of using the tools (Kim et al., 2013; Ting, 2012).

Overall, students' responses to the app were divided. While all were interested in the management tool, they expected more flexible and personalised content that would meet their individual needs. As noted by Mike Sharples (2000), the more the learning becomes student-centred and individualised, the better and more personalised the new technologies will become.

Rhetorical Moves of Proposal Writing

Six copies of pre- and post-intervention proposal writing were graded and textually analysed by the former language teacher. The analysis focused on two main areas: quality of rhetorical moves and referencing skills (e.g., in-text citations and bibliographical list). The rhetorical moves examined were the seven components recommended by the supervisor: abstract, study background, literature review, objectives, research methods, project timetable, and bibliographic references. Some of the sub-moves, for instance, statement of problem and research gap in the move of study background, were further interpreted. The quality of the pre- and post-proposal writing is reported and discussed below.

One way to objectively examine the impact of the mobile app is to analyse the changes in the number of moves in the students' writing after the intervention. In the pre-proposals completed in 2017, five students included six moves, with an embedded literature review in the introduction section following the department guidelines, whereas only one proposal contained all the moves recommended in the mobile app. In the post-proposals written in 2018 after the app intervention, three students included all seven moves; this was in marked contrast to what was observed in the pre-intervention proposals in the previous year. Figure 6.2 summarises these findings.

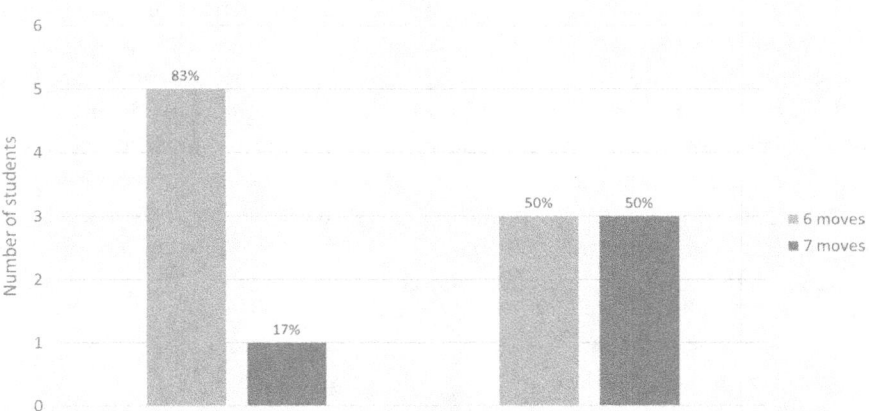

Figure 6.2. Difference in number of moves in the pre- and post-proposals in 2017 and 2018.

As seen in Figure 6.2, three students included all the rhetorical moves in their proposals in 2018 compared with only one in 2017. This may suggest an improvement in the content of post-proposals, as two more students added the abstract section in their writing. These students are unlikely to have learnt about this from their supervisor or from the course guidelines, as both provided no input on proposal writing. They were very likely influenced by the app. The remaining three proposals that did not follow the rhetorical moves suggested were either graded low (C) or very outstanding in performance (A). The supervisor commented that the two weak proposals were very poorly written with little content, and poor organisation and referencing skills. An analysis of the browse time and student activities on the app showed that four students read the content a week before the submission of the proposal, and only three of them decided to incorporate the abstract section. This points to an individual student making a personal learning choice, and/or accepting ideas from the app and ignoring the supervisor's advice in order to make the entire proposal writing clearer and more comprehensive.

Other than the level of motivation to improve writing quality, there are two reasons for students' reluctance to adopt the app content as discussed in the section on the pre-launch interview. Evidence from the browse activity indicates that the two students whose English is very good did not browse the site on proposal writing again after the first login in September during the briefing. They may regard the content as unimportant because it is not the official subject material, or as less authoritative compared with the subject guidelines from the department. In fact, both the project team members and their supervisor encouraged them to use the app, but they did not have to commit to it, as use of the app is optional and is intended for self-learning. Another reason could be related to students' level of English, which may affect their understanding of the materials and their subsequent use in improving their writing. It seems that if students' level of English and knowledge of writing are average, they are more motivated to browse the app. However, the extremely weak students may find the English texts on the app too challenging to read and apply in their writing. Because of the reasons discussed above, students may simply give reasons such as "heavy workload," "tight schedule," and "busy" for not browsing the app.

Feedback on Writing by Supervisor and Language Teacher

The language teacher and the supervisor marked the proposals using their own individual criteria. Therefore, their grades may not be fully comparable. However, it is interesting to note that both shared similar views in their grading and evaluation. Tables 6.1 and 6.2 show the final overall grades given to proposals written without and with mobile app support, respectively.

Table 6.1. Grades given to proposals written without mobile app support

Markers	Performance of proposals written without app support					
	Proposal 1	Proposal 2	Proposal 3	Proposal 4	Proposal 5	Proposal 6
Supervisor	A	A	B+	B+	C	B+
Language teacher	B+	B+	C+	B	C	B

Table 6.2. Grades given to proposals written with mobile app support

Markers	Performance of proposals written with app support					
	Proposal 1	Proposal 2	Proposal 3	Proposal 4	Proposal 5	Proposal 6
Supervisor	B	B+	C	A	B	C
Language teacher	B	B	C+	B+	C+	B

The language teacher and supervisor gave similar grades to most pre- and post-proposals. As shown in Tables 6.1 and 6.2, the grades for the five pre- and post-proposals were very comparable, with half a grade difference at most. Both markers graded pre-proposals one and two high, and pre-proposal five low; however, they varied greatly in their grading on pre-proposal three. Five post-proposals (one to five) were given similar grades. The supervisor gave a wider spread of grades, ranging from C to A, whereas the language teacher gave a narrower range (C to B+). In the authors' university, A+/A/B+ are generally regarded as high, B, as average, and C/C+ as low grades by both the faculty members and the language teachers. It seems that the quality of writing of pre-proposals is better, as higher grades were given overall compared with the post-proposals. According to the supervisor, the students that he supervised the previous year were more motivated and demonstrated a better attitude toward learning. The grades illustrate that the two colleagues' marking seems to align generally even though different criteria were adopted.

The language teacher and supervisor emphasised different aspects of writing when rating the proposals. In general, the supervisor viewed content (e.g., originality of research idea, objectives, research design) to be of primary importance, whereas the language teacher focused on the writing style, rhetorical moves, and quality of in-text citations and referencing skills. This may explain the wide difference in the grades of pre-proposal three and post-proposal six. Pre-proposal three presented a good project idea, although the language and referencing skills were rather weak. By contrast, post-proposal six had a weak project idea and method, but contents were well-organised with appropriate referencing.

It is noteworthy that the supervisor also shared the concerns of the language teacher on the writing style (e.g., logical flow of ideas), organisation of information (e.g., lack of section title, poor use of paragraphs), and the quality of references when evaluating student writing. He further commented that these language problems would affect the final grade of the writing owing to the poor impression they create. The language teacher further noticed that students ignored the logical sequence in presenting the information suggested in the app, with almost all students stating the objectives in the first few lines of the proposals without discussing the background information/problem first. This may lead to readers' difficulty in understanding the development of the project motivation and thereby eventually affect its persuasiveness.

Feedback on Students' Referencing Skills from Language Teacher

Students were advised by the department to cite references properly to avoid plagiarism. However, the language teacher's textual analysis revealed that a substantial number of cited ideas were not acknowledged and that there were inaccuracies in the in-text citations and reference lists. While citations may be satisfactorily presented in well-written proposals, average and poorly-written ones contained a substantial number of unacknowledged texts: e.g., "VLC is an optical wireless communications technology, it carries information by modulating light in the visible spectrum (400nm to 700nm)."

In-text citations were often inaccurate in most proposals and contained grammatical mistakes and problems in the format as indicated by the underlined expressions in this example: "She et al. <u>designed</u> to implement of two Bayesian estimators, namely Kalman filter (KF) and particle filter (PF) to continuously track the trajectory of a moving person [2]." There were other citation problems, including the absence of an in-text citation for a reference listed in the bibliographic references, the inclusion of an in-text citation in the overview of writing, and the absence of a page number in a direct quotation in the APA referencing style. The reliability of the references used can also be an issue. Students cited information from Wikipedia, a non-academic source, thus ignoring the advice given on the app and by their supervisor.

Conclusion and Implications for App Design for Language Learning

This chapter presents the initial feedback from engineering students and their supervisor on the use of the trial version of the Capstone Ninja mobile app. Two functions are available at this stage: the learning tool and the management tool. While students' feedback on the management tool was very positive, feedback on the learning tool content and the app features was divided. Generally, some valued the useful guidance on proposal content, whereas others looked for richer language resources and personalised experiences of use. The app could be more attractive in its features and content.

To meet the genuine need for communication between the supervisor and supervisee, the project team has developed a chat function that enables them to communicate with each other in real time. Additional writing tips for weaker/sophisticated learners have been added to cater to different levels of writing skills among them and expectations in writing quality. The usability of the app has also been improved by enabling learners to pick and choose content to read with a tap icon. Instead of accessing two different electronic devices like before, students only need to login on the app, following which they can read the subject guidelines, contact their supervisor(s), and learn the proposal writing tips all on one device. In addition, some features such as data analytics based on usage conditions are now available fully for helping the project team members to generate a better understanding of the correlation between app usage and students' FYP performance. Finally, gamification based on the learning progress and user scores will be included in the app to increase the interest level in the app. Although the app is tailor-made for FYP writing, the entire design can be adapted for subjects that aim to provide a learning tool, a management tool, and a communication tool between the teacher(s) and the students owing to its easy operability and universality.

Acknowledgement

The study in this chapter is funded by the Hong Kong SAR Government's UGC Funding Scheme for Teaching and Learning Related Proposals, as part of a project entitled "Language Enhancement for Capstone Projects Using Interactive Apps."

References

Agca, R. K. & Ozdemir, S. (2013). Foreign language vocabulary learning with mobile technologies. *Procedia-Social and Behavioural Sciences, 83*, 781–785.

Al-Emran, M., Elsherif, H. M. & Shaalan, K. (2016). Investigating attitudes towards the use of mobile learning in higher education. *Computers in Human Behaviour, 56*, 93–102.

Alina-Mihaela, I. (2015). Mobile technologies for lifelong learning. *Informatica Economica, 19*(2), 112–119.

Alrasheedi, M., Capretz, I. F. & Raza, A. (2015). A systematic review of the critical factors for success of mobile learning in higher education (University students' perspective). *Journal of Educational Computing Research, 52*(2), 257–276.

Arpaci, I. (2015). A comparative study of the effects of cultural differences on the adoption of mobile learning. *British Journal of Educational Technology, 46*(4), 699–712. https://doi.org/10.1111/bjet.12160.

Chen, J., Lim, G., Robbin, J. & Yap, V. (2018, December). *Can a mobile app help students write better final year project proposals?* [Paper presentation]. The 2nd International Conference on English Across the Curriculum, Hong Kong.

Cochrane, T. & Rhodes, D. (2013). iArchi[tech]ture: Developing a mobile social media framework for pedagogical transformation. *Australasian Journal of Educational Technology, 29*(3), 372–386.

Crompton, H. (2013). A historical overview of mobile learning: Towards learner-centred education. In Z. L. Berge & L. Y. Muilenburg (Eds.), *Handbook of mobile learning* (pp. 3–14). Routledge.

Crompton, H. & Burke, D. (2018). The use of mobile learning in higher education: A systematic review. *Computers & Education, 123*, 53–64.

Dascalu, M. I., Bodea, C. N., Lytras, M., De Pablos, P. O. & Burlacu, A. (2014). Improving e-learning communities through optimal composition of multidisciplinary learning groups. *Computers in Human Behaviour*, *30*, 362–371.

Evans, S. (2017). English in Hong Kong higher education. *World Englishes*, *36*(4), 591–610.

Evans, S. & Morrison, B. (2018). Adjusting to higher education in Hong Kong: The influence of school medium of instruction. *International Journal of Bilingual Education and Bilingualism*, *21*(8), 1016–1029.

Frohberg, D., Göth, C. & Schwabe, G. (2009). Mobile learning projects. A critical analysis of the state of the art. *Journal of Computer Learning*, *25*, 307–331.

Fucekova, M. & Metruk, R. (2018). Developing English skills by means of mobile applications. *Information Technologies and Learning Tools*, *66*(4), 173–185.

Goodyear, P. & Ellis, R. A. (2008). University students' approaches to learning: Rethinking the place of technology. *Distance Education*, *29*(2), 141–152.

Ho, I. T. (2001). Are Chinese teachers authoritarian? In D. A. Watkins & J. B. Biggs (Eds.), *Teaching the Chinese learner: Psychological and pedagogical perspectives* (pp. 99–114). CERC & ACER.

Horner, B. (2014). Writing in the disciplines/Writing across the curriculum. In C. Leung & B. Street (Eds.), *English for academic purposes* (pp. 405–418). Routledge.

Hyman, J. A., Moser, M. T. & Segala, L. N. (2014). Electronic reading and digital library technologies: Understanding learner expectation and usage intent for mobile learning. *Educational Technology Research Development*, *62*, 35–52.

Kim, D., Rueckert, D., Kim, E. J. & Seo, D. Y. (2013). Students' perceptions and experiences of mobile learning. *Language Learning & Technology*, *17*(3), 52–73.

Lai, C. (2013). A framework for developing self-directed technology use for language learning. *Language Learning & Technology*, *17*(2), 100–122.

Lai, C., Wang, Q. & Lei, J. (2012). What factors predict undergraduate students' use of technology for learning? A case from Hong Kong. *Computers & Education*, *59*, 569–579.

Li, D. C. S. (2009). Towards 'biliteracy and trilingualism' in Hong Kong (SAR): Problems, dilemmas and stakeholders' views. *AILA Review*, *22*(1), 72–84.

Li, Z. & Hegelheimer, V. (2013). Mobile-assisted grammar exercises: Effects on self-editing in L2 writing. *Language Learning & Technology*, *17*(3), 135–156.

Pachler, N., Pimmer, C. & Seipold, J. (2013). Work-based mobile learning: An overview. In N. Pachler, C. Pimmer & J. Seipold (Eds.), *Work-based mobile learning: Concepts and cases* (pp. 1–48). Peter Lang.

Pew Research Center. (2019, June 12). *Mobile fact sheet*. http://www.pewinternet.org/fact-sheet/mobile/.

Pimmer, C., Mateescu, M. & Gröhbiel, U. (2016). Mobile and ubiquitous learning in higher education settings: A systematic review of empirical studies. *Computers in Human Behaviour*, *63*, 490–501.

Sarrab M. (2015). IETC 2014. M-learning in education: Omani undergraduate students' perspective. *Social and Behavioural Sciences*, *176*, 834–839.

Sharples, M. (2000). The design of personal mobile technologies for lifelong learning. *Computers and Education, 34*, 177–193.

Sung, T., Chang, K. & Liu, T. (2016). The effects of integrating mobile devices with teaching and learning on student learning performance: A meta-analysis and research synthesis. *Computer Education, 94*, 252–275.

Swanson, J. N. (2018, July). Assessing the effectiveness of the use of mobile technology in a collegiate course: A case study in M-learning. *Technology, Knowledge and Learning*, 25, 389–408 (2020). https://doi.org/10.1007/s10758-018-9372-1.

Tavernier, M. (2016). Exploring the suitability of the book creator for iPad app for early childhood education. In D. Churchill, J. Lu & T. K. F. Chiu (Eds.), *Mobile learning design: Theories and application* (pp. 249–270). Springer.

Ting, Y. L. (2012). The pitfalls of mobile devices in learning: A different view and implications for pedagogical design. *Journal of Educational Computing research, 46*(2), 119–134.

Wagner, E. D. (2005). Enabling mobile learning. *EDUCAUSE Review, 40*, 41–52.

Wang, Z. & Cui, Y. (2016). Mobile-assisted language learning in China's College English Education: The reality and research. In D. Churchill, J. Lu & T. K. F. Chiu (Eds.), *Mobile learning design: Theories and application* (pp. 335–381). Springer.

Woodard, R. & Babcock, A. (2016). Designing writing tasks in Google Docs that encourage conversation: An inquiry into feedback and revision. In V. X. Wang (Ed.), *Handbook of research on learning outcomes and opportunities in the digital age* (pp. 1–29). IGI Global. https://doi.org/10.4018/978-1-4666-9577-1.

Wu, Q. (2015). Designing a smartphone app to teach English (L2) vocabulary. *Computers & Education, 85*, 170–179.

Yilmaz, B. & Durdu, P. O. (2015). Heuristic evaluation of a mobile hand-writing learning application. In *2015 9th International Conference on Application of Information and Communication Technologies (AICT)*, (pp. 549–552). IEEE. https://doi.org/10.1109/ICAICT.2015.7338621.

Zou, B. & Yan, X. (2014). Chinese students' perceptions of using mobile devices for English learning. *International Journal of Computer-Assisted Language Learning and Teaching, 4*(3), 20–33. https://doi.org/10.4018/ijcallt.2014070102.

7

Teacher Perspectives on Content and Language-Integrated Learning in Taiwan: Motivations, Implementation Factors, and Future Directions

Jeffrey Hugh Gamble
NATIONAL CHIAYI UNIVERSITY, TAIWAN

Abstract: This chapter reports the findings of a two-year qualitative project exploring how the Content and Language-Integrated Learning (CLIL) approach is interpreted and implemented by English teachers in Taiwan. There is a lack of evidence that such an approach, which places equal emphasis on the language of instruction (English) and the content being taught, is appropriate or feasible for the majority of Taiwanese primary or secondary school classrooms. The project addressed teacher beliefs, attitudes, and conceptions regarding the feasibility and appropriate implementation of CLIL in the Taiwanese context. To evaluate teachers' perspectives, a constructivist grounded-theory approach was adopted, using data co-constructed through group discussions and interviews, and triangulated with survey results from pre-service and in-service teachers, including current CLIL and non-CLIL English teachers, both local and foreign. The primary findings were organized into four main categories: motivations, implementation factors, obstacles, and future potentials for CLIL in Taiwan. Implications include increased investment in teacher training, increased use of students' first language to increase comprehension, and clearer guidelines and greater provision of resources to assist CLIL teachers.

Keywords: content and language-integrated learning, teacher education, foreign language learning policy, teacher beliefs, constructivist grounded theory

This research was prompted by a workshop with in-service teachers who were being asked to engage in Content and Language-Integrated Learning (CLIL) instruction and were, therefore, being trained in teaching using an "English only" approach. After discussion, it became clear that several key factors remained undefined regarding the meaning and implementation of CLIL. First, from the initial meeting with teachers, the rationale or motivation behind the push for CLIL remained unclear. Teachers were originally only aware that they were being required to teach English without using Chinese during class. Later, teachers learned that when teaching other subjects, such as health, using English was a further goal of their local government. Thus, the first consideration was the motivation behind CLIL, as compared to more traditional English as a Foreign Language (EFL) methods, such as content-based instruction (CBI). Furthermore, our discussions led to the issue of how CLIL was to be implemented (the second area investigated by the study) and potential obstacles to implementation (the third area of investigation). Finally, great speculation was aroused through discussions of the potential future of CLIL for Taiwanese teachers and students (the fourth main research area).

CLIL Implementation

CLIL's dual focus is on both language and content, which has been perceived as beneficial to students' linguistic and conceptual development. However, modes and frameworks of implementation vary from teacher to teacher. From most of the successful examples of implementation in the literature, CLIL teachers were required to meet both linguistic and content-related standards and be, as such, proficient in both the language and the subject being integrated (De Graaff et al., 2007; Lasagabaster & Sierra, 2010). In fact, CLIL had been used in Asia, and in Taiwan, in the past, with some success (Yang, 2015, 2018). However, this was at the tertiary level. After further reading, it appeared that these "CLIL" classes were more similar to English as a medium of instruction (EMI), in which academic subjects are taught in English and, as such, did not focus on language as much as content. Moreover, the "English Only" policy being implemented in some areas of the country was based on the value attached to increased exposure to English, particularly from native speaking teachers (Huang & Yang, 2018; Lin et al., 2018). However, the overemphasis on English "immersive" approaches contradicts important findings regarding the importance of the students' first language (L1) in CLIL (see, e.g., Lin, 2015). Similar common, but incorrect, assumptions have been widely held by teachers who viewed CLIL as involving monolingual immersion, which teachers believed did not fit the needs of local students. Overall, CLIL, while taught at workshops in Taiwan since at least 2009, is still generally a vague concept, loosely (and often inaccurately) defined and improperly conflated with monolingual immersion.

Despite a great deal of literature on CLIL, national and local initiatives remain largely "policy-oriented" rather than "practice-oriented" (Chern & Curran, 2019; Luo, 2017; Reynolds & Yu, 2018). Since the infrastructure, linguistic resources, and teaching materials are not yet in place, policy for English-only CLIL instruction is implemented before teachers and students are ready. As such, foreign talent is being hired at an unsustainable pace. Furthermore, there are few concrete implementation guidelines or performance indicators, leaving CLIL teachers unaware of how to conduct a CLIL class. In an attempt to address several "political" issues simultaneously, early learners (first or second grade classes) and remote and rural schools are often selected for CLIL instruction, which means that the learners with the fewest linguistic and school-based resources are being taught CLIL in an English-only manner. As mentioned above, the concepts of "immersion education" and "bilingual education" are also being conflated with CLIL.

Through discussion with teachers during the initial workshop, several important issues fundamental to language learning were raised. Amongst the perceived obstacles to the successful implementation of CLIL in Taiwan was the issue of how students might learn a language without linguistic support from L1. "English Only" CLIL programs would potentially deny students this important resource. Furthermore, intelligibility must take precedence over content acquisition, meaning that the language element of CLIL should be based on students' background knowledge. Additionally, the sustainability of EFL instruction in Taiwan must be considered in terms of local teacher training and placement. Since CLIL is largely a European model requiring a minimum level of target language fluency (for both teachers and students) and a more target language-rich environment, the question to be raised is whether this model can fit the Taiwanese pedagogical context.

A number of core questions emerged, focused on the motivations behind CLIL implementation in Taiwan, the lack of clear implementation factors, and the potential obstacles to successful CLIL programs. Certain issues, in addition to the four categories evaluated by the study (motivations, implementation factors, obstacles, and future directions), were utilized to guide discussions, interviews, and the co-construction of meaning regarding CLIL implementation. As such, the study sought answers to the balance of L1 and L2 in instruction, the roles and collaboration of foreign English teachers (FETs) and local English teachers (LETs), and any resulting impacts on future teacher training.

English Education in Taiwan

English, although having been taught for several decades at the primary level, particularly in private schools, has only been officially mandated in Taiwan since 2001 (Chou, 2013), originally beginning in fifth grade and then, from 2005, beginning in third grade. Some school districts or individual schools offer English learning from the first grade, despite no official mandate from the Ministry of Education. English education policy is characterized by four emphases: 1) individual school autonomy, 2) a focus on oral communication, 3) privatization of textbook publishing, and 4) emphasis on motivation and internationalization (Chen & Tsai, 2012). However, scholars have noted the lack of speaking opportunities, motivation, and intercultural contact as barriers to effective English learning (Yang et al., 2012), a reality that presents a motivation for an increased emphasis on EAC in Taiwan.

Parents are well aware of the need for English proficiency in order for their children to have a competitive advantage in an increasingly global environment where English is already considered the primary international language. However, as noted above, the current reality is that most children are seldom exposed to authentic opportunities for communication in English. Furthermore, it is questionable whether the language generated in either classroom-based English instruction or cram school English classes qualifies as "authentic" according to the definition of Rémi van Compernolle and Janice McGregor (2016). The description of "authenticity" offered by van Compernolle and McGregor (2016) involves familiar language patterns and meanings among users of that language, offering speakers freedom in language use for communicative purposes, rather than an emphasis on specific structural language patterns (an approach too commonly adopted by language teachers through the use of textbooks). In simple terms, children are not exposed to authentic language or language experiences in the classroom, and most Taiwanese children have very few chances for immersion in English environments due to the relatively homogeneous nature of Taiwanese society. This results in both the lack of authentic English learning environments, as well as the lack of intercultural contact (Yang et al., 2012).

Political and Social Pressures Regarding English Language Learning

A study by Yuh Fang Chang in 2008 found that Taiwanese parents were eager to have their children start learning English at an earlier age, such as in preschool, despite the Ministry of Education mandating that English learning start at third grade. Furthermore, parents looked to cram schools for support in terms of their child's English learning, with a strong preference for FETs, regardless of their qualifications. Also, nearly 80 percent agreed that English in the classroom should be taught only in English (Chang, 2008).

Although parents' expectations and demands in terms of English language learning are not grounded in language pedagogy, parents are the voters. As such, several programs promoting either bilingual education or English-only, monolingual language learning have been used by certain politicians, at both the local and national level, as policy platforms. These programs, while criticized by some language experts and many language teachers, have been positively received by parents and non-parents alike, who believe that whole-English teaching and, if possible, native-speaking English teachers, are optimal for language learning. Parents are increasingly expressing their dissatisfaction with traditional English teaching models and, according to a recent poll, over 64 percent believe that more English should be taught in primary and junior high school (Hsu & Hsu, 2019). Likewise, nearly 70 percent of parents enroll their children in cram schools to learn English and 42 percent believe that English should be taught starting in preschool.

The fact that these policies, to a certain degree, are driven by parents' pressure on policy-makers, is reflected in the findings of AI-hua Chen (2011), who notes that pressure from parents and discrepancies at the local, city, or national level create additional tension and a strong pressure towards sweeping reforms in English language educational policy. Among the issues investigated by Chen (2011) are the following five where parents may have the strongest concerns regarding EFL educational policy: differences in ages for starting English language learning, the wide range of English abilities within classes, the lack of teachers with English teaching qualifications, differences in textbook content among publishers, and the balance between learning English and learning other languages (such as Taiwanese, Hakka, and mother tongue aboriginal languages).

Trends towards English across the Curriculum

Under the umbrella of English across the Curriculum (EAC), several interventions have been implemented in Taiwan over the past decades, with varying degrees of success, generally at the tertiary level (e.g., Yang, 2015, 2018). In the past, teachers attempting to adopt a cross-curricular approach towards learning tended to integrate English into other curricular subjects using content-based instruction (CBI) for primary and secondary learners. Until recently, few studies of EAC for elementary or secondary education have been conducted in Taiwan, with limited results, such as improvements in listening (Chou, 2013), or mixed results, such as no difference in attention and engagement but increased language complexity for students taking CBI versus non-CBI courses (Huang, 2011). While several options for EAC have been adopted by primary and secondary teachers, there is a lack of evidence that the CLIL approach (placing equal emphasis on the language of instruction, the native language, and the content being taught) is appropriate or feasible for primary or secondary school classrooms in Taiwan.

Regardless of the mixed results, Jhih-kai Yang and Genevieve Leung (2018) cite several policies which have been implemented in recent years, including plans to make English a second official language. Another recent national policy includes the requirement that every school in Taiwan implement CLIL in school subjects including art, music, and physical education, at least on a trial basis, while local policies, such as that of New Taipei City, have promoted the establishment of bilingual experimental schools which will be staffed by at least one FET (Yang & Leung, 2018).

In December 2018, the Ministry of Education released a *Blueprint for Developing Taiwan into a Bilingual Nation by 2030* (National Development Council, 2018). Among the strategies related to education were the following: "conducting bilingual schooling and relaxed related enrollment regulations," "implementing a teaching mode that allows for flexibility based on student aptitude and English proficiency," and "integrating English into preschool" (p.12). While responding to parental and societal pressure, these strategies contradict years of policy, many of which were based on traditional beliefs, such as the concept that learning English at an early age may interfere with students' L1 development. Further complications include the expectation that bilingual programs are inevitably offered by private schools with more resources, resulting in an imbalance along socio-economic lines, or that by grouping students according to English proficiency, lower-level students would be offered fewer resources and opportunities than those grouped in "advanced" classes. Thus, although the 2030 policy towards bilingualism is seen by many as a step forward, classroom teachers often have a more reserved view towards the feasibility of the policy.

Research Methods

This chapter reports on the evaluation of both in-service and pre-service teachers' perceptions towards the meaning and implementation of CLIL in their classrooms. In order to evaluate teacher perceptions, the study adopted a constructivist grounded theory (CGT) approach (Charmaz, 2006, 2017) by collecting qualitative data, including group discussion and interview transcripts, from various stakeholders. This data was then triangulated with quantitative data (using paper-based and online surveys). CGT, by definition, requires introspection and a recognition of the inherently subjective nature of qualitative research. The approach is used widely in education and other social sciences and is deemed valuable in that the direction of inquiry is guided by collaboration among researcher and participants. When issues such as "teacher perceptions" are being evaluated or, in particular, when new concepts are being uncovered, evaluated, and re-evaluated over a longer period, CGT can provide valuable insights. In addition, cross-checking with participants of ongoing construction of themes and use of codes was included to satisfy the condition of "co-construction." As such, participants served as both co-constructors of knowledge as well as co-evaluators of the findings as they were constructed. That is, the coding and themes being constructed were negotiated and discussed with participants, both overall and through the selection of more experienced or expert participants. The research process is illustrated in Figure 7.1.

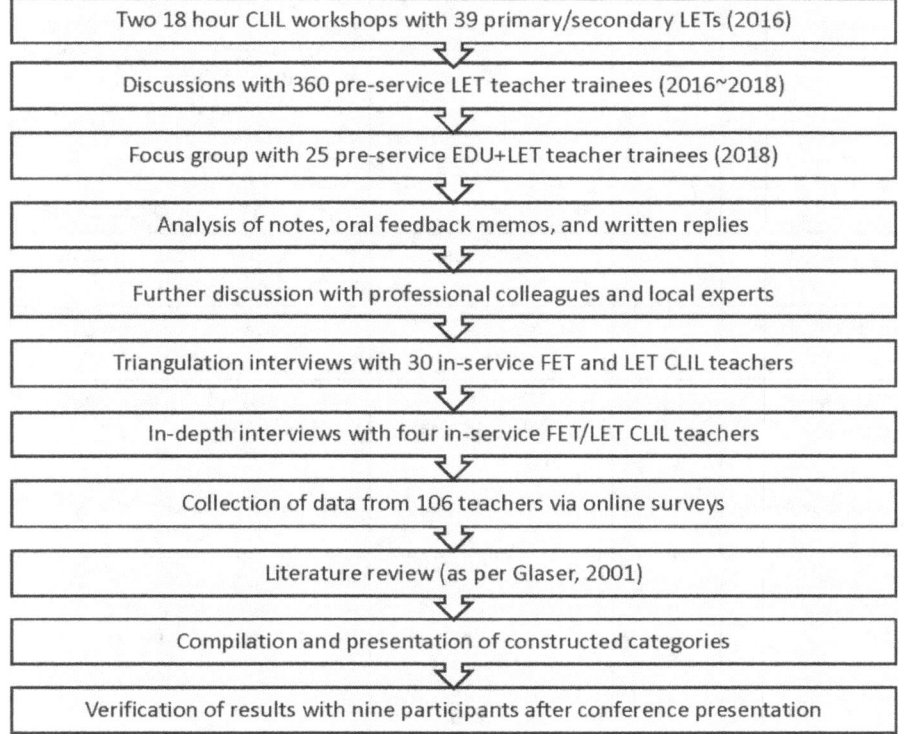

Figure 7.1. Process of data collection and analysis.

Participants

Participants included in-service teachers (including CLIL, content, and English teachers) and pre-service teachers (teacher trainees taught by the researcher/author), as well as the researcher/author himself as a researcher-participant. Participant information is provided in Table 7.1. All participants provided informed consent regarding their participation in the study and the future use of the data collected. Participants were provided with details on the goals and objectives of the study and were invited to discuss the results of the study both during ongoing analysis and once the findings had been written up.

Table 7.1. Participant background information

Stage	Number	Experience	Background
1. CLIL workshops	39	2 to 30 years	In-service LETs attending a required workshop on whole English teaching and CLIL
2. Pre-service teacher trainees	360	2nd through 4th year English teaching majors	Possessing some theoretical background in the Teaching of English to Speakers of Other Languages (TESOL), including CLIL. Some teaching experience
3. Focus groups	25	3rd and 4th year education majors	Some background in CLIL, required to select a subject major
4. Collegial discussions	6	Professors in linguistics or TESOL	Most research CLIL, and all have attended CLIL conferences.
5. Triangulation interviews	30	FET and LET CLIL in-service teachers	At least two years of active CLIL teaching or support
6. In-depth interviews	4	Two FET and two LET CLIL in-service teachers	At least two years of successful CLIL teaching
7. Online survey	106	11 pre-service and 95 in-service teachers	50% have experience teaching CLIL; 20% are FETs
8. Post-conference meetings	9	Two in-service CLIL teachers (one FET, one LET), two pre-service CLIL interns, five CLIL researchers (two master's students, two professors)	Firsthand experience with CLIL teaching or teacher training. Research in CLIL practice in Taiwan

Data Collection

The motivation for the study stems from in-depth discussions from two intensive, 18-hour in-service CLIL training programs for primary and secondary school English teachers ($N = 39$) taking place in 2016, and is further enriched by discussions with pre-service teachers, ranging from first to fourth year TESOL and education majors ($N = 360$). A focus group of 25 pre-service teachers was used to clarify and triangulate the findings of the prior interviews and discussions. After an analysis of the research notes and consultation with local CLIL researchers through collegial discussions ($N = 6$), further triangulation and co-construction of meaning was accomplished through discussions with 30 LET and FET CLIL teachers, in-depth interviews with four in-service CLIL teachers with over two years of experience, and questionnaire feedback from 106 in-service teachers based on the Questionnaire on Teachers' Attitudes, Perceptions and Experiences in CLIL adapted from Jermaine McDougald (2015). Finally, after the preliminary results were presented at an international conference, a core group of nine CLIL experts was recruited to evaluate the process and the results and to share their perspectives, adding nuance to the findings. A timeline of the data collection procedure is provided in Figure 7.1.

Data Analysis

Research was conducted and analyzed employing a constructivist grounded theory approach using constant comparison, reflexive and iterative questioning, flexible approaches matched to the context (e.g., interviews, focus groups, and surveys), theoretical sampling, and a focus on co-construction of meaning. While variants of grounded theory abound in the literature, the perspective adopted by the study is based on the writings of Kathy Charmaz (2006, 2017). A fundamental concept of the adopted approach is based on the famous quotation by Barney Glaser, a pioneer in grounded theory, who wrote, "all is data" (2001, p. 145). As such, all of the data collected through the variety of techniques used, such as interviews, question and answer sessions, assigned reflection reports, researcher notes, messages and emails, survey responses, and many others, are considered valid sources of knowledge that can be used to construct meaning. In terms of the constant comparative method, at first an area of interest was selected, namely the perceptions of pre-service and in-service teachers towards the meaning and interpretation of CLIL in the Taiwanese setting. Then, features, principles, and topics of this area of interest were identified (see the sections below), before making decisions based on initial data collection and areas which still required investigation. Then, the concept of theoretical sampling was applied, wherein individuals or stakeholders who could provide the necessary information to fill gaps or resolve conflicts were selected purposively. Eventually, themes were constructed through continual reflection and data collection, and the relevance of the constructed theoretical structure was re-evaluated.

Findings

The qualitative results of the two-year study are based on a constructivist grounded theory approach to co-construction of themes related to teachers' perspectives on the meaning and implementation of CLIL. In order to organize the findings, four categories were developed, based on the qualitative data obtained from teachers. As noted above, teachers included both in-service and pre-service teachers, as well as both LETs and FETs, and both CLIL and non-CLIL teachers. The four main categories include: motivations, implementation factors, obstacles, and future potentials for CLIL in Taiwan. These categories are specific to the Taiwanese context but do bear some relevance to implementation of CLIL in other non-European settings.

The findings suggest that there are several perceived "meanings" of CLIL and even more modes of implementation. Although there is a lack of consistency in what pre-service and in-service teachers perceive as appropriate CLIL teaching, there is an overall trend towards a recognition of a lack of resources and support, a sense of CLIL as a burden on both LETs and FETs that requires a great deal of collaboration, and a skepticism regarding the sustainability of a "hard" form of CLIL which emphasizes an English-only environment. In fact, based on both qualitative analysis and a comparison of pre-service and in-service teachers, perceptions tended to align for both groups, with no significant differences found between pre-service and in-service teachers. Summaries of findings by category are provided below. Tables are provided which identify themes constructed for each category and a sample of "codes" that were used to tag key participant data (such as interview transcripts, written comments, questionnaire open-ended questions, or email exchanges). These codes were generated in collaboration with participants and used to reflect their frequency in both written and oral records. For each theme, excerpts are provided from pre-service teachers and CLIL teachers (both FET and LET).

Motivations for CLIL Implementation

In terms of motivations for CLIL implementation, two themes were co-constructed: "bilingualism as a present or future requirement" and "perceived benefits of CLIL related to student-centered learning." These two themes, with sample codes and excerpts from the researcher's notes, are included in Table 7.2. Without fail, the perceived goal of CLIL among participants was to develop functional bilingualism as a "requirement." Since teachers in Taiwan are currently required to be functionally bilingual in order to conduct CLIL teaching, the lack of English proficiency (as perceived or as tested) among subject teachers has escalated the hiring of FETs, who, although proficient in English, are often not familiar with the content they are asked to teach or associated national curricular standards. The long-term goal of bilingualism is focused on both students, in the short-term, and all teachers, in the long-term, which is in line with national policy (National Development Council, 2018) and parents' expectations (Chang, 2008; Chen, 2011; Hsu & Hsu, 2019).

Table 7.2. Category 1 findings: Categories, themes, sample researcher codes, and excerpts

Category 1: Motivation for CLIL instruction		
Themes	Sample Codes	Excerpts
A. Bilingualism as a present or future requirement	bilingualism: current, near future, distant future, student, teacher	**1. Pre-service teacher**: "teachers are bound to be required to have bilingual ability" [future; teacher] **2. In-service CLIL FET**: "the lack of English background affects the effectiveness of CLIL" [present; teacher] **3. In-service CLIL LET**: "In the long term, students' English ability should be improved." [future; student]
B. Perceived benefits of CLIL related to student-centered learning	hands-on, critical thinking, motivation, independent thinking, L2 exposure, interaction, breadth of learning, flexibility, language as a tool, scaffolding	**1. Pre-service teacher**: "Curriculum mapping for CLIL should design interesting subject content for students to learn and then motivate students to learn more about the knowledge of that subject extensively by using target language." [scaffolding; L2 exposure; motivation] **2. In-service CLIL FET**: "I can observe the benefits of gradually adding CLIL by starting with the lower grades and adding a grade each year. I find this more successful than adding CLIL to all grades across the board." [scaffolding] **3. In-service CLIL LET**: "CLIL is good as FETs interact with students for more than 45 min per week." [L2 exposure; interaction]

Another perceived benefit of CLIL is the nature of the classes which are taught by CLIL teachers. They are, by definition, cross-disciplinary, using more hands-on learning, requiring independent and higher-order thinking, increasing language use, broadening learning, and providing flexibility within a scaffolded routine, focusing on language as a "tool" rather than subject. The preceding items were included as "codes" and were commonly cited by participants as either current or potential benefits of CLIL. The issue here is that these perceived benefits could be obtained from almost any project/problem-based learning curriculum, as mentioned by teachers participating in the initial 2016 workshops. Thus, the instructional design philosophy of CLIL, rather than its actual implementation, may lead some stakeholders to believe it is an appropriate paradigm for EFL. In fact, reported comprehension difficulties in many CLIL classrooms suggest that language use in CLIL classrooms is not "authentic," according to the principles of a) familiarity with language patterns and meanings and b) freedom in language use for communicative purposes, as characterized by van Compernolle and McGregor (2016).

Current CLIL Implementation Factors

From the current CLIL teachers, some implementation factors became immediately apparent, namely the role of FETs as "resources" and LETs as "guides." FETs were regarded, by themselves and LETs, as "resources." These two themes, with sample codes and excerpts from the researcher's notes, are included in Table 7.3. Their duty was perceived as allaying LETs' fears regarding English language proficiency and lack of preparation time. FETs also self-perceived this role and, while some considered this as a negative role, others embraced it. They were also seen as conveying culture and globalization. In fact, Taiwanese parents have pushed strongly for FETs in schools, with an emphasis on their role as language resources (Chang, 2008). They were often assigned content-creation tasks with relative freedom about what they wanted to teach, although many lacked the background in the subject being integrated with English. Although assessed and evaluated, the FETs often lamented the fact that they were provided with almost no feedback from the professors or administrators assessing them.

In terms of LETs, they were regarded as "guides." They were considered to be the curriculum experts (although that is primarily because they could read the curricular guidelines or content-specific textbooks, which were only available in Chinese). Ultimately, they took the role of "designers" or "co-designers" of content, ensuring that the CLIL courses were in line with national objectives. LETs often considered that their main duty was translating textbooks into English. Overall, some LETs considered their role was to act as guardians of local culture, as an English-only language class may tend to focus on internationalization over localization. While generally supporting classroom instruction in English, the role of LETs as L1 "guides" has been suggested (Lin, 2015).

Table 7.3. Category 2 findings: Categories, themes, sample researcher codes, and excerpts

Category 2: Implementation factors for CLIL instruction		
Themes	Sample Codes	Samples
A. Foreign teachers as CLIL "resources"	foreign teacher, teacher-as-resource, self-confidence, primary teacher, globalization, western culture, content-creators	**1. Pre-service teacher**: "However, because countries have their own curriculum structure learning, it is easy for foreign teachers to misjudge the past learning experience of Taiwan students, which makes the design of curriculum teaching activities too difficult or simple." [content-creators; western culture]
		2. In-service CLIL FET: "Course design should be conducted by CLIL professionals rather than asking new teachers to design." [course design]
		3. In-service CLIL LET: "It appears many schools are simply dumping workload on the foreign teachers, telling them to teach CLIL, and leaving them to do everything without support." [primary teacher; content-creators]
B. Local teachers as CLIL "guides"	local teacher, teacher-as-guide, course design, curriculum, local(ization), translator, assistant, cultural guardians	**1. Pre-service teacher**: "I feel very unfair because my salary is different and my working hours are longer than those of foreign teachers." [local teacher; assistant]
		2. In-service CLIL FET: "Another very problematic aspect is the translation of textbooks into English. It is very time-consuming and often not accurate." [translator; curriculum]
		3. In-service CLIL LET: "CLIL really depends on curriculum and how to help me develop it. Or if the curriculum can be appreciated and supported by all staff." [curriculum; course design]

Perceived Obstacles to CLIL Success

Themes co-constructed for this category include student and teacher rejection, as well as social and systemic factors. Obstacles to the success of CLIL in Taiwan were strongly emphasized throughout the data collection process, but mostly by LETs (pre-service and in-service). Teachers feared rejection of CLIL based on several factors, three of which were most prominent: linguistic factors (language interference with L1 and the complexity/difficulty of L2 content), affective factors (confusion and frustration and incomprehensible input, lack of interest, or "learned helplessness"), and conceptual/developmental factors (such as the lack of appropriate schemata for processing the content provided through CLIL courses which were not matched to their developmental level). These three themes, with sample codes and excerpts from the researcher's notes, are included in Table 7.4. These results mirror those of Kuei-Min Huang's (2011), finding no improvement in motivational factors accompanied by increased language complexity in CLIL classrooms.

Other obstacles included societal or systemic factors, again most often cited by LETs. These include the fact that proficiency gaps are often caused by social and economic factors. The paper-and-pencil test culture of Taiwan was another factor which teachers feared would limit CLIL's future implementation. Likewise, as mentioned in the literature review, Taiwan does not have English as an official language, and English is not commonly used outside of the classroom (Yang et al., 2012). Teachers noted that the policies are often superficial, and that the learning effectiveness and learning motivation of students is often not improved through CLIL programs.

Table 7.4. Category 3 findings: Categories, themes, sample researcher codes, and excerpts

Category 3: Obstacles to CLIL success		
Themes	Sample Codes	Excerpts
A. Student rejection of CLIL	linguistic (interference, complexity, L1) affective (confusion, interest, learned helplessness) conceptual (development, schemata)	1. **Pre-service teacher:** "Students might only learn English for a few months or even never learned English before. How can they learn the content if they don't understand any meaning of English words? I can't imagine how tough will it be for students." [future; teacher] 2. **In-service CLIL FET:** "'English' only is one of the problems . . . and not starting at the same grade level and subject" [linguistic: L1; affective; conceptual] 3. **In-service CLIL LET:** "It is forbidden to speak Chinese. This will actually give students a potential message: Chinese is inferior, English is the first." [linguistic; affective]

Table 7.4. Category 3 findings (continued)

B. Teacher rejection of CLIL	loading, burden, teacher fear, time constraints, lack (resources, support, collaboration)	**1. Pre-service teacher:** "Teachers must prepare lessons with foreign teachers, which will increase the burden on teachers.... Taiwan's education system does not have a perfect plan for students to accept this innovative teaching method." [burden; lack: resources, support]
		2. In-service CLIL FET: "From the beginning we were promised resources and help. We never received any. No books, proper and consistent training" [lack: resources, support]
		3. In-service CLIL LET: "CLIL is more suitable in the ESL context, and the EFL situation is difficult to push. Where are the supporting measures? [burden; lack: support]
C. Social and systemic factors impeding implementation	SES, proficiency gap, test culture, assessment issues, official language, policy first, politics, environment	**1. Pre-service teacher:** "Teachers must think twice about who your students are, their level of English, content knowledge, and requirements. In the elementary school, the students' grades also have a large gap between the high and low level." [proficiency gap; assessment issues]
		2. In-service CLIL FET: "CLIL focuses on background knowledge, but without any how can we teach CLIL [to students without this background knowledge]?" [proficiency gap; environment]
		3. In-service CLIL LET: "It is impossible for Taiwanese students to be completely exposed to the English environment" [environment]

Future Directions for CLIL in Taiwan

Themes co-constructed for this category include "supporting the training of local teachers" and "alternatives to proposed public school intervention." These two themes, with sample codes and excerpts from the researcher's notes, are included in Table 7.5. Through the process of data collection and analysis, it became clear that teacher training of local English and content teachers is required for the future of CLIL in Taiwan. Related to this finding is the need for self-sufficiency and resource-sharing among teachers, schools, and districts. Professionalism and empowerment of local teachers is an investment which is fundamental for the success of CLIL and is a wiser use of resources than the importation of foreign talent (Chen, 2011), which is becoming increasingly difficult to source, as the demand for qualified and certified teachers who are native speakers of English has increased globally. System-level development of theory-based, empirically sound pedagogy for CLIL in the Taiwanese context is needed at the policy level. Such a future for CLIL would need to embrace students' mother tongue and local culture, rather than relegate this to non-CLIL courses.

Other suggestions were provided which seem to suggest that CLIL, as an approach for EFL, can operate in parallel to regular English instruction until the infrastructure and resources are in place for courses to be taught by teachers, with increasing use of LETs and less reliance on FETs, who are confident in both the language and the content. Examples of alternative suggestions for integrating CLIL more effectively and consistently in the future include:

1. providing self-access materials for students, such as non-fiction readers,
2. using "English time" as a small portion of other content courses to allow English language learning to be integrated across the curriculum,
3. opening up the CLIL paradigm to greater use of translanguaging (see Wei & Lin, 2019) by allowing greater use of L_1 for comprehension,
4. letting the private sector expand (e.g., through offering the design and promotion of reasonably priced and localized CLIL teaching resources),
5. by first starting CLIL teaching at the secondary level, before gradually offering courses to younger learners.

Teachers are eager for the benefits of CLIL but are wary of the English-only nature of the pedagogy. While FETs lacked this fear of English, their background and competency in CLIL subjects was often questioned. Teacher training must be emphasized before our teachers can embrace and succeed in any new pedagogy.

The necessity for comprehensibility of input cannot be overstated. Keith Graham et al. (2018), in addressing the mixed results of empirical studies on the effects of CLIL on both language and content outcomes, highlighted two prerequisite conditions for language learning proposed by Krashen's Input Hypothesis (1985): sufficient quantity of target language input and the comprehensibility of this input. Although, according to Graham et al. (2018), most implementations of CLIL will ensure an abundance and variety of target language input; if this input is not comprehensible to students, neither language development nor content knowledge acquisition will be possible. As such, any implementation of CLIL as an "English-only" model will inevitably lead to increasingly overwhelming cognitive demands and negative affect for learners who lack the sufficient linguistic or content background to comprehend the input provided by teachers without L1 support.

Table 7.5. Category 4 findings: Categories, themes, sample researcher codes, and excerpts

Category 4: The future of CLIL in Taiwan		
Themes	Sample Codes	Excerpts
A. Supporting the training of local teachers	self-sufficiency, resource sharing, professional development, training, empowerment, investment, systemic development, accommodate L1	1. **Pre-service teacher**: "Teachers' professionalism and professional communication and expression in professional subjects are still insufficient." [self-sufficiency; professional development] 2. **In-service CLIL FET**: "Subject teachers needs to have more training about how to teach though the target language" [training; self-sufficiency] 3. **In-service CLIL LET**: "More information and training is needed on strategies, not only for CLIL teachers but also for co-teachers." [training; investment]
B. Alternatives to proposed public school integration	alternatives, self-access, parental choice, private sector, new approaches, additional methods	1. **Pre-service teacher**: "I think our MOE shouldn't spend too much money on promoting CLIL because it's not appropriate for Taiwan now. Maybe some bilingual schools can use this method but not in every school." [alternatives; private sector] 2. **In-service CLIL FET**: "Foreign teachers only stay in short intervals and have their own teaching styles, so how do they benefit students?" [new approaches] 3. **In-service CLIL LET**: "I think CLIL could be arranged into "specialty schools," such as private schools." [private sector]

Triangulation with Quantitative Data

Quantitative results from the online survey support the qualitative findings and show a general sense of optimism towards CLIL, but a strong need for methodological, subject-specific, preparatory, material, administrative, and collaborative support. These findings demonstrate that the FET CLIL teachers possess more knowledge of CLIL than LETs when teachers are asked "How much do you know about CLIL?" (p = .02), based on a Likert-type response ranging from 1, "a lot," to 3, "not much," (FET M = 1.77; LET M =

2.17). As such, during interviews, it was found that FETs do most of the CLIL teaching and report greater satisfaction and confidence, despite a greater sense of burden. Burden, in the study, was evaluated by the online survey, adopting a Likert-type scale from 1, "strongly disagree," to 4, "strongly agree." LETs reported significantly lower responses to "CLIL requires a lot of time (lesson planning and teaching)" (FET M = 3.77; LET M = 3.52; p = .02) and significantly higher responses to "CLIL requires more subject knowledge that English language teachers possess" (FET M = 2.86; LET M = 3.47; p = .00). This finding can be explained by reference to the reported role of LETs as "guides," who perceive themselves as having fewer linguistic resources and confidence in CLIL pedagogy, thus teaching less CLIL content and underestimating the amount of time required for CLIL preparation and instruction.

Conclusions and Implications

The issue of CLIL implementation in Taiwan is complex. Through the evaluation of over three years of data collected through interviews, questionnaires, discussion sessions, and reflection reports, several themes related to the key categories of motivation, implementation, obstacles, and future directions were constructed. Principally, the motivations for CLIL implementation are based on the perceived need for Taiwan to become a bilingual (or English-proficient) society in the near future. In combination with the perceived "student-centered" benefits of a CLIL approach, which may or may not be adhered to in classroom settings, this push towards multilingualism is undoubtedly a contributing factor in the trend towards CLIL models of instruction. In terms of implementation issues, the use of FETs as "resources" (namely, providers of English language and culture) for schools to implement CLIL, with local teachers serving as "guides" (such as through translating documents or referring to local curricula) has become the norm. This model of implementation has led to several obstacles for students and teachers alike. Students, when facing the dual pressures of language and content, must overcome linguistic, affective, and conceptual challenges. The CLIL programs currently being offered are also perceived by teachers as lacking in the resources, support, and authentic collaboration necessary for successful implementation. These factors are compounded by societal barriers, which include inequalities in students' English proficiency, as well as factors related to socioeconomic status (and resulting inequality in access to learning resources)—factors which policy makers should consider in future CLIL projects. Turning to potential future directions, teacher training should be the primary concern and receive additional investment. Sustainable development is only possible if local teachers are trained and supported in terms of both linguistic and discipline-specific knowledge and skills. Therefore, unless a critical evaluation of current policy and practice is conducted, with a clarification of the definition, implementation practices, and roles of teachers, CLIL may be relegated to private educational institutions, such as bilingual schools, where ample resources and teacher qualifications are ensured.

Based on the findings, one major "tweak" to the current status-quo interpretation of CLIL by Taiwanese scholars (most of whom recommend English-only environments) is that greater use of translanguaging and L1 are deemed to be beneficial or even necessary for the majority of local teachers. This echoes the work of Amy Lin (2015) who critiques the idealization of "English-only" approaches and over-application of the "maximum input hypothesis." Given the burdens faced by CLIL teachers and the lack of resources, it is essential that materials be either designed (long-term) or imported (short-term) to meet the needs of CLIL teachers, since many local teachers are faced with the challenge of translating local textbooks into English, while following Ministry of Education guidelines.

Furthermore, a slower rollout of CLIL is recommended, with guidelines and training being fundamental to the sustainability of CLIL in Taiwan. Additionally, the current reliance on foreign talent at the expense of local talent is not deemed sustainable, and local teacher training and preparation for CLIL is strongly recommended, along with a careful consideration of the role and future of foreign English teachers in Taiwanese primary and secondary schools. Overall, the research findings reported in this chapter demonstrate that multiple interpretations of the meaning and implementation of CLIL exist simultaneously, even within the same school or classroom, and that a clarification of how EAC can be best applied to achieving the stated policy goals of the Taiwanese government must be undertaken in order to clarify the expected roles of teachers and improve their perceptions towards EAC in their classrooms.

References

Chang, Y. F. (2008). Parents' attitudes toward the English education policy in Taiwan. *Asia Pacific Education Review*, 9(4), 423–435.
Charmaz, K. (2006). *Constructing grounded theory: A practical guide through qualitative analysis*. Sage.
Charmaz, K. (2017). Special invited paper: Continuities, contradictions, and critical inquiry in grounded theory. *International Journal of Qualitative Methods*, 16(1), 1–8.

Chen, A. H. (2011). Parents' perspectives on the effects of the primary EFL education policy in Taiwan. *Current Issues in Language Planning, 12*(2), 205–224.

Chen, S. & Tsai, Y. (2012). Research on English teaching and learning: Taiwan (2004–2009). *Language Teaching, 45*(2), 180–201.

Chern, C. L. & Curran, J. E. (2019). Moving toward content-integrated English literacy instruction in Taiwan: Perspectives from stakeholders. In B. Reynolds & M. Teng (Eds.), *English literacy instruction for Chinese speakers* (pp. 333–348). Palgrave Macmillan, Singapore.

Chou, M. H. (2013). A content-based approach to teaching and testing listening skills to grade 5 EFL learners. *International Journal of Listening, 27*(3), 172–185.

De Graaff, R., Jan Koopman, G., Anikina, Y. & Westhoff, G. (2007). An observation tool for effective L2 pedagogy in content and language integrated learning (CLIL). *International Journal of Bilingual Education and Bilingualism, 10*(5), 603–624.

Glaser, B. G. (2001). *The grounded theory perspective: Conceptualization contrasted with description.* Sociology Press.

Graham, K. M., Choi, Y., Davoodi, A., Razmeh, S. & Dixon, L. Q. (2018). Language and content outcomes of CLIL and EMI: A systematic review. *Latin American Journal of Content and Language Integrated Learning, 11*(1), 19–37.

Hsu, C. W. & Hsu, E. (2019, May 27). *Most parents think English education in Taiwan schools inadequate: Poll.* Focus Taiwan. http://focustaiwan.tw/news/asoc/201805270009.aspx.

Huang, K. M. (2011). Motivating lessons: A classroom-oriented investigation of the effects of content-based instruction on EFL young learners' motivated behaviours and classroom verbal interaction. *System, 39*(2), 186–201.

Huang, S. H. & Yang, L. C. (2018). Teachers' needs in the advancement of communicative language teaching (CLT) in Taiwan. *TESOL International, 13*(1), 100–117.

Krashen, S. D. (1985). *The input hypothesis: Issues and implications.* Longman.

Lasagabaster, D. & Sierra, J. M. (2010). Immersion and CLIL in English: More differences than similarities. *ELT Journal, 64*(4), 367–375.

Lin, A. M. (2015). Conceptualising the potential role of L1 in CLIL. *Language, Culture and Curriculum, 28*(1), 74–89.

Lin, T. B., Wang, L. Y. & Wang, M. W. (2018). Diverse interpretations on nativeness but unanimous subscription to native-speakerism: Identity of future non-native English teachers in Taiwan. *Journal of Asia TEFL, 15*(3), 603–617.

Luo, W. H. (2017). Teacher perceptions of teaching and learning English as a lingua franca in the expanding circle: A study of Taiwan: What are the challenges that teachers might face when integrating ELF instruction into English classes? *English Today, 33*(1), 2–11.

McDougald, J. (2015). Teachers'' attitudes, perceptions and experiences in CLIL A look at content and language. *Colombian Applied Linguistics Journal, 17*(1), 25–41.

National Development Council. (2018). *Blueprint for developing Taiwan into a bilingual nation by 2030.* Executive Yuan.

Reynolds, B. L. & Yu, M. H. (2018). Addressing the language needs of administrative staff in Taiwan's internationalised higher education: Call for an English as a lingua franca curriculum to increase communicative competence and willingness to communicate. *Language and Education, 32*(2), 147–166.

van Compernolle, R. A. & McGregor, J. (2016). Introducing authenticity, language and interaction in second language contexts. In R. A. van Compernolle & J. McGregor (Eds.), *Authenticity, language and interaction in second language contexts*. Multilingual Matters.

Wei, L. & Lin, A. M. Y. (2019) Translanguaging classroom discourse: Pushing limits, breaking boundaries. *Classroom Discourse, 10*(3–4), 209–215.

Yang, J. K. & Leung, G. (2018). The center-periphery constellation of English language co-teaching in Taiwan: Examples from the spectrum of four different classrooms. *Interplay, 4*(1), 31–58.

Yang, W. (2015). Content and language integrated learning next in Asia: Evidence of learners' achievement in CLIL education from a Taiwan tertiary degree programme. *International Journal of Bilingual Education and Bilingualism, 18*(4), 361–382.

Yang, W. (2018). The deployment of English learning strategies in the CLIL approach: A comparison study of Taiwan and Hong Kong tertiary level contexts. *ESP Today: Journal of English for Specific Purposes at the Tertiary Level, 6*(1), 44–64.

Yang, Y. T. C., Gamble, J. & Tang, S. Y. S. (2012). Voice over instant messaging as a tool for enhancing the oral proficiency and motivation of English-as-a-foreign-language learners. *British Journal of Educational Technology, 43*(3), 448–464.

8 GREATCLIL Camps Integrating School-Based Curricula: An Analysis of Learning Motivation in Remote Areas of Taiwan

Ai Chun Yen
NATIONAL DONG HWA UNIVERSITY, TAIWAN

Abstract: Although several studies have suggested the potential of Content and Language Integrated Learning (CLIL) programmes to increase students' learning motivation, there is a shortage of empirical evidence to support this. This chapter presents the results of a study comparing data from traditional primary and secondary formal English (non-CLIL) classes with data from a CLIL-based summer camp intervention based on an innovative curricular model called GREATCLIL. The research was carried out in remote and rural schools in Taiwan and included 107 school camps. The schools were purposely selected due to their reported low levels of English language study pressure and low English learning motivation. The findings support the efficacy of the GREATCLIL camps, as participants' affective filter was lower than during their formal classes, with associated lower amotivation and stronger extrinsic motivation and intrinsic motivation, as learning took place in a relatively anxiety-free environment. Although the GREATCLIL students in the study favoured language competence over content knowledge, the findings clearly indicated that content was considered almost as important in terms of learning motivation and associated learning outcomes.

Keywords: content and language integrated learning, English across the curriculum, English learning motivation, student engagement

Debuting in the mid–1990s, Content and Language Integrated Learning (CLIL) has evolved from merely a method for increasing exposure to a foreign language into an educational approach for language classroom practice adopted widely across Europe, based on the need for multilingual citizens (European Commission, 2010). With a large and growing body of literature, CLIL has gained attention in the Taiwanese primary and secondary education community due to its perceived benefits for developing the English proficiency of English as a foreign language (EFL) students and for equipping global citizens with foreign language skills. According to Wenhsien Yang (2016), this phenomenon can be traced back to the years between 1979 and 2010, when the Taiwanese Ministry of Education (MOE) conducted a nation-wide appraisal of 92 CLIL-based degree programmes. Based on the MOE's report on September 19, 2018, administrators began to develop the "Taiwan into a Bilingual Nation by 2030" policy. The National Development Council was designated to serve as the coordinating agency to propose a blueprint for the implementation of the policy. Thus, CLIL was officially adopted as policy based on the government's blueprint for developing Taiwan into a bilingual nation (National Development Council, 2018).

From a European perspective, CLIL programmes not only introduce students to new concepts through offering courses in a foreign language, but are also aimed at increasing students' confidence and motivation in both the foreign language and their mother language (Bentley, 2010; Järvinen, 2006; Pladevall-Ballester, 2018). David Marsh (2000) notes that CLIL includes subtle aims to help students understand the value of learning a language and developing a "can-do" attitude to language learning. Yet, there is a shortage of studies in Taiwan exploring the design of integrative CLIL programmes, particularly in terms of how specific strategies can be embedded in the learning process for both content and language acquisition. Both EFL educators and students often find themselves frustrated in CLIL classrooms due to inadequate background and training on pedagogical approaches and lack of access to materials, which, in turn, limits the success of CLIL teaching and learning. This issue is significant in countries like Taiwan where there is a strong divergence between content-related and foreign language competencies and a lack of teachers possessing both competencies. Due to the potential impact of the aforementioned frustrations among teachers and learners, this chapter introduces a framework developed as part of a recent study into CLIL-based summer camps, which is intended to help teachers to develop school-based CLIL camp curricula. This chapter also seeks to evaluate whether these teacher-developed CLIL materials can positively influence CLIL campers' learning motivation.

A school-based curriculum is central to the study highlighted in this chapter. In the 1970s a decentralised educational system featuring school-based curricula (SBC) was first introduced in Australia and New Zealand, a model which later influenced other countries (Li, 2006). In Taiwan, teachers have been encouraged to participate in implementing SBC projects subsidized by the MOE since the early 2000s. This chapter advocates for CLIL knowledge integration in SBC contexts, and discusses the evaluation of campers' knowledge, perceptions, and learning motivations. A five-stage GREAT-Cycle framework (Get to know the school; Research and background assessment; Evaluate language and content; Activity design and refinement; Teach and touch students' hearts) was developed, focusing on school-based factors. Teams of volunteer teachers, project supervisors, and school teachers (hereafter, GREATCLIL team) carried out school-based mini projects that involved the design and construction of SBC-based CLIL summer programmes. To shed light on the potential role of school-based CLIL as a motivating factor for English language learning, a longitudinal study was conducted of five-day CLIL camps for primary and secondary school students (Y1-Y12) involving a total of 3,932 student campers and 107 camps, held in Taiwan between 2015 and 2018.

Participants were campers from remote and rural schools, who tend to experience relatively less pressure regarding English study and also demonstrate comparatively lower English proficiency and learning motivation as compared to urban students. In addition to demonstrating lower learning motivation and English proficiency, Taiwanese remote learners are frequently linguistically heterogeneous, speaking Taiwanese, aboriginal languages, Hakka, and new immigrant languages like Vietnamese or Indonesian. Given the noted gaps in English proficiency and motivation among these student campers and the potential influence of school-based CLIL summer programs on students' motivation, the corresponding mechanisms of culture, environment, content, and language were built into the development and implementation of a GREAT-Cycle instructional design.

Literature Review

Content and Language Factors

Phil Ball (2009) regards CLIL as an approach for integrating linguistic and content factors particularly appropriate for language pedagogies focused on thematic or content-based instruction. CLIL can also be viewed as a platform for encouraging and providing opportunities for language and content teachers to exchange teaching practices. CLIL teachers approach language from a different angle as compared to traditional teacher-centred language teachers, who typically focus on teaching the four skills of English as a subject rather than as a tool, and emphasise grammar and drills in order to prepare students for tests (Lasagabaster, 2014). CLIL language is based on the specific discourse of a subject and is not simply lexical. Steve Darn (2006) suggests that

CLIL provides students with the necessary subject-specific tools (including vocabulary) and access to diverse content from different perspectives. According to Darn (2006), David Lasagabaster and Aintzane Doiz (2016), and Jon Merino and David Lasagabaster (2018), CLIL improves overall target language competence and raises awareness of both the mother language and the target language in the subjects taught.

Do Coyle et al. (2010), in an attempt to codify language learning principles, state that CLIL pulls together the threads of existing approaches, such as content-based instruction and language-supported subject learning, as well as immersion and bilingual/ plurilingual education. Its typical context is classrooms where subjects are taught in English by non-native English-speaking content teachers. The aforementioned terms suggest a strong relationship between language learning and subject matter content. This default type of dual purpose for the teaching of content and language at the same time, involving non-native English-speaking content teachers utilizing a more immersive approach, is classified as "strong" or "hard" CLIL (Ball, 2009; Bentley, 2010), with some promising research outcomes reported in those settings (Dalton-Puffer, 2011; Pérez-Cañado, 2012). Ball (2009) identifies five types of CLIL programmes on the "strong/hard" versus "weak/soft" continuum: a) total immersion, b) partial immersion, c) subject/content area classes (reading, language arts, math, science, and social studies), d) language classes based on thematic units, and e) language classes with greater use of content than evidenced in typical language acquisition-based courses. Thus, relatively "harder" forms of CLIL are entirely in the target language, while "softer" forms of CLIL simply have a stronger emphasis on academic or subject-related content than typical EFL courses.

For Darn (2006), CLIL is dependent on the fact that linguistic knowledge becomes the means by which other content is learned, with language being fundamental across curricula, and language acquisition principles being central to both learning motivation and the contextualized nature of language and content. According to Heini-Marja Järvinen (2006), CLIL-type provision has been defined as consisting of a minimum of 20 percent of a class taught in the target language, with instances of classes taught in the target language for less than 20 percent of the time virtually non-existent in terms of CLIL interventions.

Maria Luisa Pérez-Cañado (2012) postulates that a simple ratio of each language used in teaching is a useful quantitative measure for evaluating language use in CLIL-type interventions. However, the danger in using such a ratio is that the role of language in immersion programmes tends to be defined by quantity rather than quality. In fact, CLIL operates, to one degree or another, qualitatively in the language learner's experience. Regardless of the perspective, quantitative or qualitative, adopted for assessing the balance between an emphasis on language and content during instruction, these two constructional mechanisms are fundamental to the implementation of CLIL when considering student motivation.

Environmental Factors

Stephen Krashen's (1985) language acquisition hypotheses, in particular the Input Hypothesis, state that a rich and understandable language environment (comprehensible input) is the only prerequisite for language acquisition. In regard to CLIL pedagogy, Kay Bentley (2010) and Liz Dale and Rosie Tanner (2012) propose different approaches to language learning depending on the relative emphasis placed on content knowledge and linguistic knowledge. Bentley (2010) differentiates language-led, subject-led (modular), and subject-led (partial immersion) CLIL approaches in terms of target language use time during class, with modular approaches similar to the notion of "soft CLIL." Subject-led (partial immersion) approaches are closer in definition to those of early immersion programmes described by Wallace Lambert and Richard Tucker (1972) and Merrill Swain and Sharon Lapkin (1982) in which immersion starts with 100 percent use of the target language, which is gradually replaced by the mother language until the ratio is approximately 50/50. Bentley (2010) considers strong/hard CLIL as the outcome of a series of trials in which the weekly hours of target language teaching are increased until half of the course is taught in that language. In this manner, the more the subject is emphasised, the stronger the CLIL programme.

Dale and Tanner (2012) further ponder the differences between strong/hard and weak/soft CLIL in terms of both instruction and the means for practising CLIL, where subject lessons are taught by either subject teachers or language teachers. They suggest that CLIL teachers and learners require knowledge of the language related to curricular subjects. This can enable learners to understand the subject and communicate ideas, while requiring less formal language use in subjects for which the purpose is everyday communication. Makoto Ikeda (2013) provides a continuum of CLIL approaches (see Figure 8.1) comparing Ball (2009), Bentley (2010), and Dale and Tanner (2012) in terms of content and language use. Considerations of content and language balance also relate to the type of environment in which CLIL is taught, ranging from immersive to thematic, or from language teacher-led to content teacher-led. It is certain that "engaging with and learning cognitively challenging content through another language requires a depth of processing which cannot be attained when the teacher is simply in transmission mode" (Coyle et al., 2010, p. 88).

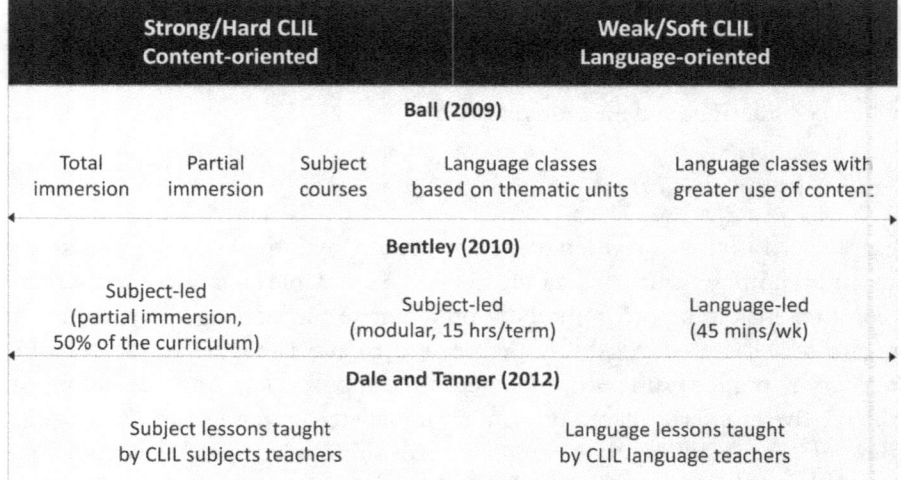

Figure 8.1. CLIL Continuum comparison (Ikeda, 2013, p. 32).

Most scholars agree that language experts are likely to excel in "weak/soft" CLIL, where the goal is the acquisition of language for general discourse and communicative competence, while a strong content background is likely necessary for "strong/hard" CLIL, where learners are expected to gain content knowledge necessary for domain-specific communication. In terms of the balance of content and language learning objectives, Teresa Ting (2011) considers that if a 50:50 content: language ratio is applied to CLIL classes, teachers must consider "whose language does the '50/language' refer to?" (pp. 314–315). In other words, for the 50 percent of learning objectives that are linguistic in nature, one must consider "whose" language is being taught: that of the teacher or learner, of the target language or the mother language. The answer Ting (2011) offers is that the language portion of the CLIL lesson must refer to the target language (such as English) which is, most importantly, familiar or known to the learners; otherwise, input will not be comprehensible (Krashen, 1985). Students will not be motivated if the content and language are incomprehensible. If educators lack the awareness of these differences in the learning environment, it may lead to unsatisfactory learning results in both content and language and a backlash against CLIL.

Cultural Factors

Underpinned by the critical analysis by Cenoz et al. (2014) and by Dallinger et al. (2016), CLIL implementation can be found extensively in Europe, but to a lesser extent in North and South America, Australia, Asia, or Africa, primarily due to a lack of suitable materials. Dario Banegas (2014) found that advertised CLIL-oriented EFL coursebooks have "(1) little correlation between featured subject specific content and school curricula in L1 (non-English), (2) oversimplification of contents and (3) dominance of reading skills development and lower-order thinking tasks" (p. 345). Ball et al. (2015) consider that many materials have no consideration of language or culture support because they are not produced for EFL learners. McDonough et al. (2013) suggest materials should be developed within a framework which considers context (learners and setting), goals, and the syllabus. Following a cognitivist paradigm, materials should be developed in a way that presents learners with a sequence that evolves in complexity and scope to promote both language and, above all, cognitive development (Banegas, 2014). This concern echoes Esther Bosompem (2014), who declares that teacher-developed CLIL materials, rather than published coursebooks, may be more suitable for learners and their contextual needs.

A review of the literature was conducted in order to develop theoretical and practical foundations for the development of the instructional model (GREATCLIL) and the instructional intervention discussed in this chapter. The findings, based on the efficacy of the instructional model, are reported in order to offer recommendations to assist school administrators and teachers in implementing SBC-based CLIL principles and processes. A framework that helps volunteer teachers to design integrative CLIL camp curricula will also be presented and evaluated.

Research Methods

Participants and Setting

Over four years, 605 volunteer student teachers, including those with ambitions to become full-time teachers in the future or with a motivation to use their expertise to provide education in remote areas, were recruited from Taiwanese colleges to serve a total number of 107 remote schools and 3,932 campers (see Table 8.1). The volunteers were required to form teams of six to twelve individuals (with at least half of them being English majors) and submit their service plans for evaluation and selection. All teams prepared a five to ten-minute film in English to demonstrate their service motivation, their expertise, and their verbal English proficiency. Selected teams were assigned project supervisors ($N = 115$) who were highly respected teachers from Taiwanese primary and secondary schools and who were responsible for supervising the volunteers' camp curriculum designs.

Table 8.1. GREATCLIL participation data

Years	Schools	Volunteers	Student Campsers	Project Supervisors
2015	19	134	739	24
2016	29	160	1,113	32
2017	30	167	1,083	30
2018	29	144	997	29
Total	107	605	3,932	115

Development of the GREAT-Cycle Framework

Once the CLIL team (volunteer and supervisor groups) was established, the next step was to agree on a framework for the camp project: **G**et to know the school; **R**esearch and background assessment; **E**valuate language and content; **A**ctivity design and refinement; **T**each and touch students' hearts (see Figure 8.2).

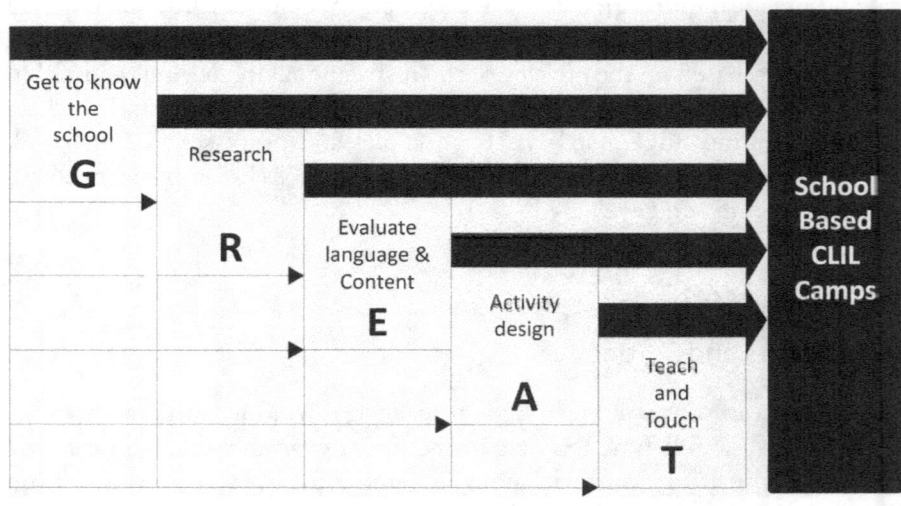

Figure 8.2. Five-stage GREAT-Cycle framework.

The volunteers and their supervisors first visited the school to evaluate students' language levels and understand their SBC before designing their GREATCLIL camps (**G**; Get to know the school). The Taiwanese MOE suggests 19 educational issues for grade schools to develop their SBC: gender equality, human rights, environmental education, ocean education, character education, life education, legal education, technology education, information science education, energy education, safety education, disaster prevention education, career and life planning education, literacy education, outdoor education, multi-cultural education, international education, and aboriginal education. A school-based curriculum approach was adopted, based on Jerome Rotgans and Henk Schmidt's (2011) suggestion that situational interest developed over time is related to academic achievement in an active-learning classroom. The proposed SBC in Chinese was situationally analysed by the volunteers and supervisors who were required to understand that SBC differs depending on local conditions. It is during this stage of doing research (**R**) that elements of SBC (environmental and cultural factors) were integrated with the GREATCLIL camp design (content and language factors).

It is noteworthy that the GREATCLIL framework was based on English language and content learning in conjunction with SBC (**E**; Evaluate language and content). As mentioned earlier, campers' overall English proficiency was relatively low and, in order to ensure comprehensible input for active learning, the English: Chinese ratio for GREATCLIL camps was set at approximately 30:70 to 40:60, which met the minimal requirements Pérez-Cañado (2012) suggests for interventions. In order to gain insight regarding the school-based curriculum, each participating school's English teachers and their school staff (N = 240) were invited to practise the five-stage GREAT-Cycle framework in collaboration with the volunteers since they knew more about the schools' SBC. The GREATCLIL camp activities were designed to scaffold language and content knowledge acquisition (**E**; Evaluate language and content & **A**; Activity design). Overall, the four-year GREATCLIL camp curricula could be viewed as a continuum of practices, depending on who was involved and whether they were "selecting," "adapting," or "creating" SBC objectives to meet local contexts. The language, instructional content, and activities included in the GREATCLIL camps were designed to increase campers' motivation and confidence to learn the school-based curriculum content through English with ease and to foster motivation towards English in the future (**T**; Teach and touch).

Content, Language, Environment, and Culture Considerations

The GREATCLIL camp curricula focused on the SBC (mainly from the MOE's 19 educational issues), language, environment, local and international culture, English language learning, indoor and outdoor instructional activities, and scaffolding for promoting successful learning. Major school-based factors, including the sociolinguistic environment, language gaps, the amount of exposure to GREATCLIL camps, the neighbourhood environment, and the local culture around the school or community, were taken into account by the GREATCLIL framework (see Figure 8.3).

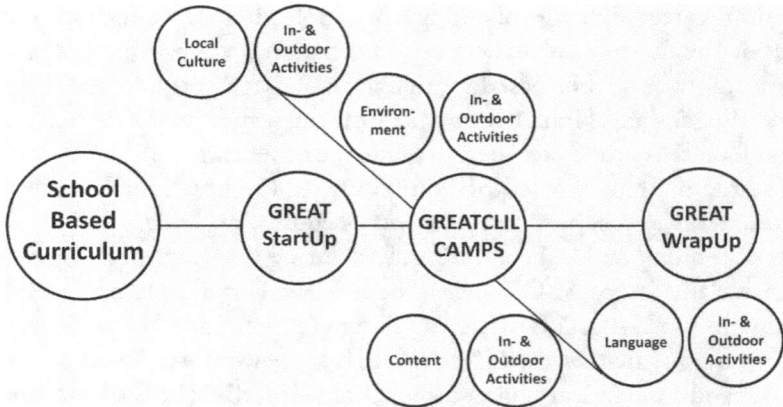

Figure 8.3. GREATCLIL camp curriculum model.

This model helped the GREATCLIL team select and design materials to enhance campers' learning autonomy, competence, and relatedness (positive motivational factors). This was critical, since participants needed to visualize how, in terms of content and language, CLIL was presented appropriately for all campers in terms of environment and culture. For the GREATCLIL team, successful camps required a great amount of outdoor and indoor group/team work and cooperative learning using activities such as creative or scientific brainstorms, jigsaw tasks, scavenger hunts, board games, or competitive events. As such, GREATCLIL activities contributed to aspects of team building related to bonding, teamwork, and positive group dynamics. Participants moved progressively through a unit, leading to a group research or presentation task. Group work was organised to ensure that all campers had a role to play, and they were expected to participate in order to increase their learning motivation.

Evaluation of Motivational Factors (Self-Determination Theory)

Motivational psychologists contend that focal issues (i.e., in this case, the content being taught in CLIL courses) should be personally meaningful to students and related to their cultural experiences, goals, and interests. This perspective is consistent with the stance of Jeffrey Albrecht and Stuart Karabenick's (2018) that, in order to make courses relevant, educators must first consider focal issues through which curricula and instructional procedures can be personalised to be relevant and meaningful to students. For the study highlighted in this chapter, it was necessary to examine the difference in campers' learning motivation between GREATCLIL camps (informal

CLIL classes [IF]) and regular English classes (formal non-CLIL classes [F]) in Taiwanese remote areas. These data were collected and analysed by means of a learning motivation questionnaire based on Richard Ryan and Edward Deci's (2000) self-determination theory (SDT). SDT addresses three universal, innate, and psychological needs: competence, autonomy, and psychological relatedness (see Table 8.2).

Table 8.2. Elements of the self-determination theory model

	Extrinsic Types of Motivation		
Amotivation (AM)	Introjected Regulation (IR) Identified Regulation (IDR)		**Intrinsic Motivation (IM)**
Quality of Behaviour	Non-self-determined ──────────────▶		Non-self-determined

The focus of SDT is on the introjected regulation (IR) and identified regulation (IDR) aspects of extrinsic motivation, as well as on amotivation (lack of motivation [AM]) and intrinsic motivation (IM). The placement of intrinsic motivation on the far right is not intended to suggest that extrinsic motivation can shift to intrinsic motivation, as this depends on the intrinsic interest of the activity to the individual. SDT not only distinguishes between motivation and amotivation, but also describes the quality of motivation on a continuum which ranges from a high level of self-determination with a high degree of intrinsic motivation to act, to a low level of self-determination with a high degree of external determination and extrinsic behavioural motivation. Reliability and validity tests on 1) amotivation, 2) intrinsic motivation, 3) extrinsic motivation: introjected regulation (internalized reward-seeking and punishment-avoidance), and 4) extrinsic motivation: identified regulation (self-recognition of the value of a behaviour towards one's development) were run separately for both formal and GREATCLIL classes. The questionnaire was found to be reliable, with Cronbach's α ranging from .722 to .897 (see Table 8.3).

Table 8.3. Cronbach's alpha for the research questionnaire items

Formal Classes (F)				
Domains	Types	Items	Cronbach's Alpha	Cronbach's Alpha Based on Standardized Items N of Items
Amotivation		01, 02, 18	.871	.872
Extrinsic Motivation	IR	05, 09, 16, 04, 07, 13, 08, 10	.778	.773
	IDR	15, 17, 20, 12	.898	.897
Intrinsic Motivation		03, 06, 19, 11, 14	.880	.886

Table 8.2. Elements of the self-determination theory model (continued)

GREATCLIL Camp Classes (informal classes, IF)				
Domains	Types	Items	Cronbach's Alpha	Cronbach's Alpha Based on Standardized Items N of Items
Amotivation		22, 27, 35	.861	.871
Extrinsic Motivation	IR	23, 28, 31, 34, 36, 25, 21, 32	.747	.722
	IDR	37, 38, 40, 33	.831	.835
Intrinsic Motivation		24, 26, 29, 30, 39	.845	.844

All 40 questions (20/20 for formal/informal classes) included a five-point response format that ranged from "very strongly disagree" (scored 1) to "very strongly agree" (scored 5). The concurrent summer camps lasted five days with an average of 30 students (one class) to 60 students (separated into two classes) per school. The pre- and post-test questionnaires were delivered before and after the camps (please see the appendix). It was hypothesised that campers would improve their learning motivation towards English in their formal classes (F) following informal GREATCLIL camp (IF) learning experiences. For both F and IF groups, it was expected that all motivational factors would be significantly influenced by the GREATCIL intervention. It was also assumed that with an increase in extrinsic and intrinsic motivation, amotivation would decrease.

Therefore, it was hypothesised that a significant motivational difference would result following a five-day GREATCLIL camp (see Figure 8.4). Motivation correlations were calculated using Pearson's product-moment correlation coefficient, and significance levels were set at the .05 level. Motivational differences between formal and informal classes were examined using paired t tests, and significance levels were set at the .05 (*, 2-tailed) and .01 (**, 2-tailed) level.

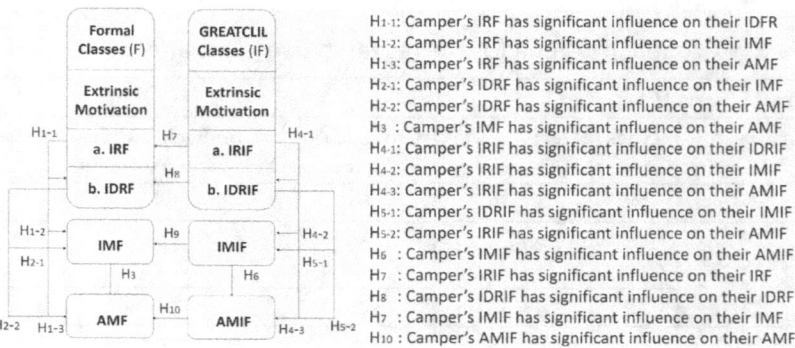

Figure 8.4. Research hypotheses.

Findings

From the pre- and post-tests data of H1-H6 in Figure 8.5, neither campers' identified regulation (IDRF) nor intrinsic motivation (IMF) measured in the IF condition had a significant correlation with their amotivation for formal English classes. Also, the correlation between campers' identified regulation (IDRF) and intrinsic motivation (IMF) was insignificant for the post-test for formal classes. This might be due to the fact that students who are amotivated in certain subjects often demonstrate an unwillingness to act or demonstrate counter-productive behaviour.

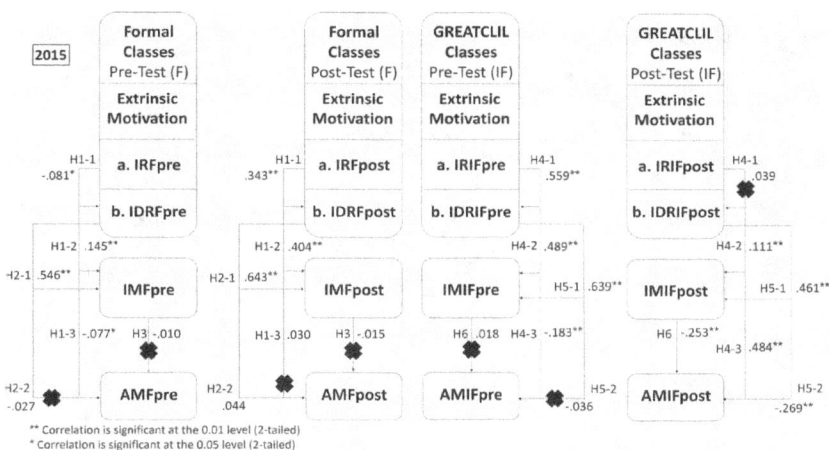

Figure 8.5a. Correlations for learning motivation, 2015

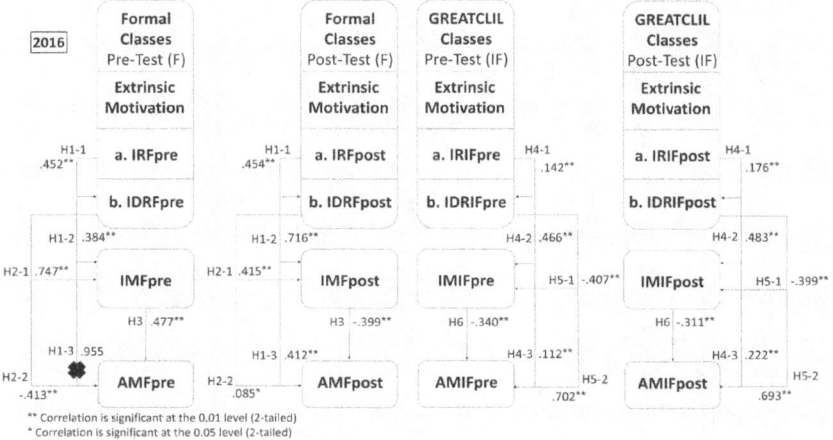

Figure 8.5b. Correlations for learning motivation, 2016

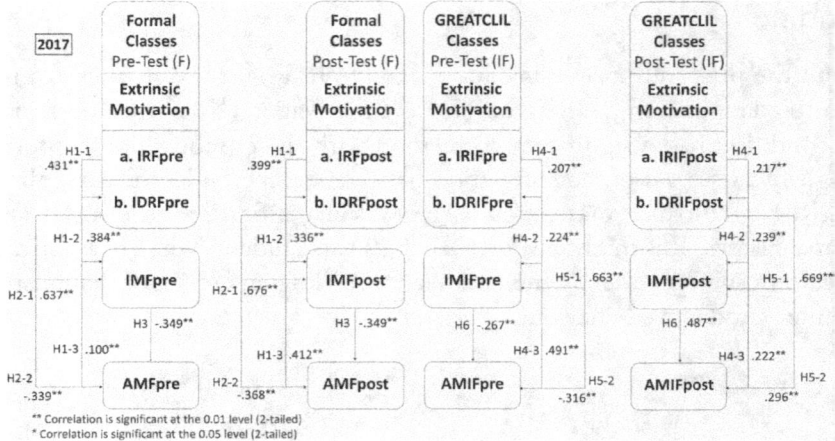

Figure 8.5c. Correlations for learning motivation, 2015

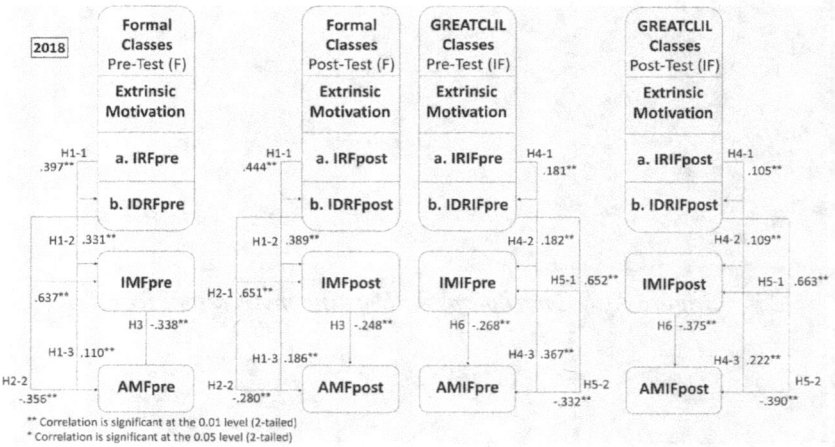

Figure 8.5d. Correlations for learning motivation, 2018

The relative lack of significance of the results could stem from primary and secondary students having a lack of motivation and poor attitude towards English learning in formal classes, which influenced their reported motivation during English summer camps. Similar pre-test results were observed for GREATCLIL classes. Yet, the opposite result was revealed for the post-tests. For the first year of the study, all hypothesised correlations in the model demonstrated statistical significance, supporting the presence of the expected relationships among English learning motivation factors for the 739 participants. It seems that GREATCLIL did impact participants' learning motivation, with negative correlations on the post-test between identified regulation and amotivation (H5–1) and intrinsic and amotivation (H6), confirming that their amotivation decreased as their extrinsic or intrinsic motivation increased.

The year 2015 was the first time campers attended a GREATCLIL summer camp. Behavioural routines like morning dance, camp yields, and team cheers were regularly repeated, creating an established pattern that brought a sense of continuity. Participants identified and recognised that a behaviour was beneficial toward their camp activities and learning development, and would adopt those learning behaviours as their own. These behaviours were not required but, rather, were performed willingly as part of their camp experience. Establishing campers' identified regulation is important for changing learning behaviours and increased interest or the need to succeed. While increased IR was a positive result, the ultimate outcome was a decrease of amotivation and an increase in intrinsic motivation. As a learner-centred approach, CLIL is an active learning method wherein teachers act as facilitators and the responsibility for engagement and reflection is placed upon learners. Therefore, from 2016 on, when the GREATCLIL teams visited schools, students' opinions on issues affecting the local context were elicited, which allowed for better future preparation for the stages of G,R,E, and A to meet students' learning needs, including environmental and cultural factors. Participants' motivational factors demonstrated significant inter-correlations from the 2016 data except for introjected regulation and amotivation on the pre-tests for both formal and informal classes (H1–3 & H4–3).

When students worked together to learn and expand their GREATCLIL knowledge in 2017, they were more likely to become invested and motivated to complete camp tasks and activities. While intrinsic motivation focuses on building upon students' inner feelings, sometimes students require external reinforcement to increase their enthusiasm towards GREATCLIL. According to Deci and Ryan (2002), introjected regulation inspires learners to engage in behaviours not because they want to, but because they fear not to, out of a sense of external obligation. Since GREATCLIL camps provided team members with an agreed mission that provided a framework for all team efforts, they experienced a deep commitment to group decisions and actions. This sense of belonging was enhanced and reinforced when the team spent time developing team norms or relationships which had previously been activated in formal classes; thus, a difference was found not only for GREATCLIL camp experiences but also in formal English classes. For every year other than 2016, the results of correlation analysis for intrinsic and amotivation factors were very similar, although subjects' introjected regulation or identified regulation did not always significantly correlate with their amotivation on the pre- and post-tests.

Apart from 2015, after GREATCLIL camps, participants' extrinsic motivation was not significantly correlated with amotivation, but was significantly correlated with intrinsic motivation. That is, external incentives did not decrease their amotivation. Also, from the first year on, participants' intrinsic motivation and amotivation were significantly correlated on post-tests. Noticeable motivational differences between pre-tests and post-tests were also observed for all years. These motivational differences contribute to the literature by providing empirical support for the motivational potential of CLIL-integrated English summer camps. The correlational results among motivations for all years echo Deci and Ryan's (2002) self-determination theory, which stresses that externally focused or motivated behaviours could naturally develop into a self-controlled behaviour based on learners' interest in, perceived usefulness of, and competence in that specific behaviour or activity, resulting in autonomous learning. The positive findings in Figure 8.6 most likely result from the fact that learning took place in a relatively anxiety-free environment. From camp observations, students were keen to learn content area knowledge that they were already familiar and confident with, so they favoured content knowledge over language competence. It seems clear that content was almost as important for both learning motivation and language outcomes, confirming the critical role of content-based English language camps, in particular for remote school students.

Conclusions and Implications

In terms of the correlations among motivational factors, the results were consistent over all four years. Participants' overall introjected regulation was significantly correlated with both intrinsic motivation ($p < .01$) and amotivation ($p < .01$), while extrinsic motivation: identified regulation was positively correlated with intrinsic motivation ($p < .01$) and negatively correlated with amotivation ($p < .01$). Compared to motivation in formal classes, participants' affective filter was lowered to a greater extent during GREATCLIL camps, such that their amotivation decreased between the pre-test and post-test ($p < .01$, all years except 2017), while their extrinsic motivation: introjected regulation ($p < .05$, all years except 2016), extrinsic motivation: identified regulation ($p < .05$, all years except 2017), and intrinsic motivation ($p < .01$, all years except 2017) increased over the five-day GREATCLIL camps.

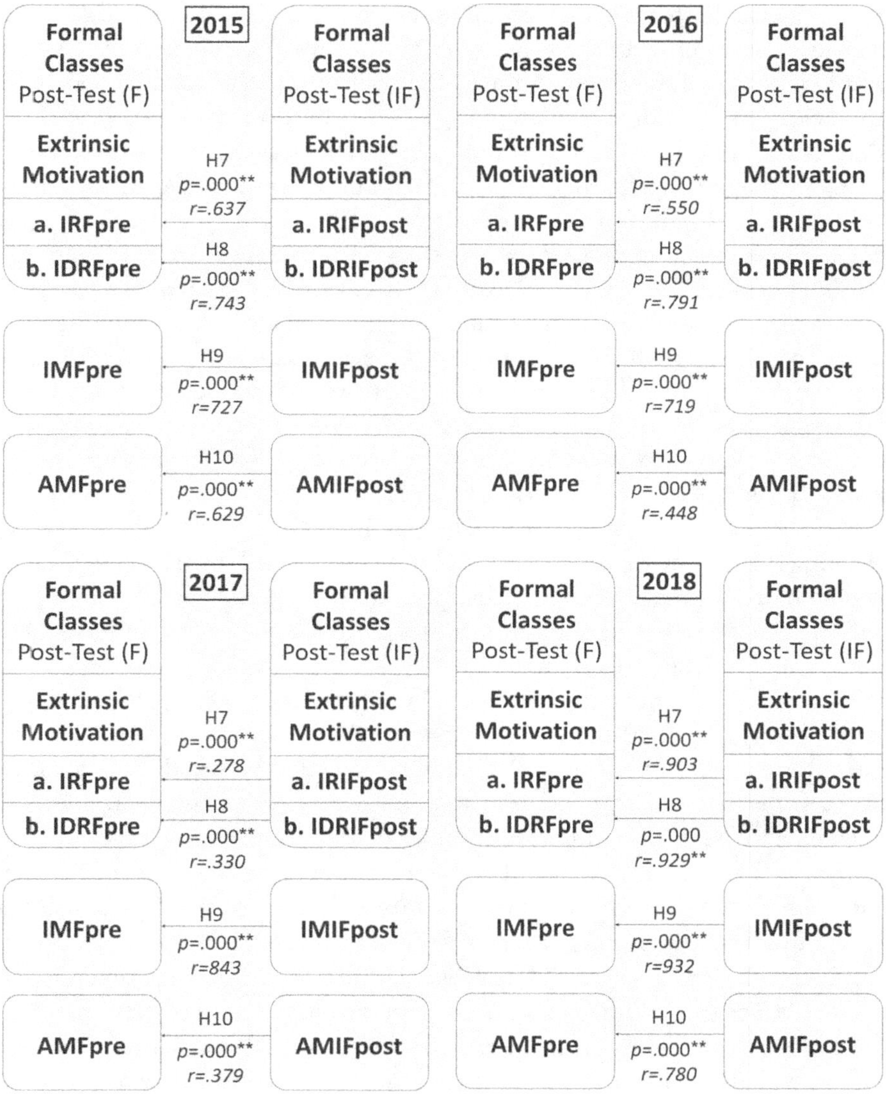

	2015			2016	
Formal Classes Post-Test (F)		Formal Classes Post-Test (IF)	Formal Classes Post-Test (F)		Formal Classes Post-Test (IF)
Extrinsic Motivation a. IRFpre b. IDRFpre	H7 $p=.000**$ $r=.637$ H8 $p=.000**$ $r=.743$	Extrinsic Motivation a. IRIFpost b. IDRIFpost	Extrinsic Motivation a. IRFpre b. IDRFpre	H7 $p=.000**$ $r=.550$ H8 $p=.000**$ $r=.791$	Extrinsic Motivation a. IRIFpost b. IDRIFpost
IMFpre	H9 $p=.000**$ $r=727$	IMIFpost	IMFpre	H9 $p=.000**$ $r=719$	IMIFpost
AMFpre	H10 $p=.000**$ $r=.629$	AMIFpost	AMFpre	H10 $p=.000**$ $r=.448$	AMIFpost

	2017			2018	
Formal Classes Post-Test (F)		Formal Classes Post-Test (IF)	Formal Classes Post-Test (F)		Formal Classes Post-Test (IF)
Extrinsic Motivation a. IRFpre b. IDRFpre	H7 $p=.000**$ $r=.278$ H8 $p=.000**$ $r=.330$	Extrinsic Motivation a. IRIFpost b. IDRIFpost	Extrinsic Motivation a. IRFpre b. IDRFpre	H7 $p=.000**$ $r=.903$ H8 $p=.000$ $r=.929**$	Extrinsic Motivation a. IRIFpost b. IDRIFpost
IMFpre	H9 $p=.000**$ $r=843$	IMIFpost	IMFpre	H9 $p=.000**$ $r=932$	IMIFpost
AMFpre	H10 $p=.000**$ $r=.379$	AMIFpost	AMFpre	H10 $p=.000**$ $r=.780$	AMIFpost

Figure 8.6. Correlations for learning motivation, 2015–2018 (H7–H10)

Intrinsic motivation can be a key to student achievement. However, extrinsic motivation dominates classrooms for the remote area students evaluated in this project. Since the GREATCLIL team were not their regular teachers, these volunteers and the GREATCLIL model also served as external factors. When amotivated, students were unable to generate the energy and concentration needed to participate in and benefit from the activities provided by their teachers. Rather than setting up reward systems, the GREATCLIL team established a camp culture of discovery and a stress-free environment where everyone was free to try new things. The team needed to validate and build upon campers' identified regulation toward their intrinsic motivation to complete GREATCLIL tasks, not by promising them an external incentive, but by giving them choices to participate freely, without pressure, in all camp activities.

Due to the significant correlations among all variables, it is deemed essential to utilise these variables in order to track and evaluate changes in language attitudes and mastery among GREATCLIL campers over time in a more systematic way and to better evaluate the relationships among motivation types over time. Further explanation of these correlations among motivation factors for both formal and informal classes will allow researchers and educational authorities in different language learning contexts to develop future language policies based on a coherent and consolidated theoretical framework. The initial success in GREATCLIL coordination not only calls for external support and incentives, but also for internal resources, agreement on teaching loads, time to experiment, and relationship and team building. Likewise, the methodological and pedagogical innovations associated with CLIL and the change in teaching patterns raises team issues of control, personality clashes, and resistance to advice.

Many of the camp activities the volunteers designed for GREATCLIL camps were, in fact, of intrinsic interest to at least some campers, based on the culture, environment, and SBC factors evaluated before the camps. One effect of presenting these activities within a system of extrinsic incentives is to challenge the intrinsic interest in these activities or tasks for those campers who were familiar with them and had some initial interest. A central problem with our educational system is its inability to preserve an intrinsic interest in learning and the eagerness for exploration that students innately possess. Applying SBC with specific GREATCLIL mechanisms is recommended as a suitable design for integrative CLIL for future school projects. Elevated need satisfaction and reversal of need frustration were the antidotes to amotivation, which provided rather compelling support for the self-determination theory underlying the GREAT-Cycle process.

The sensitivity of the GREATCLIL intervention to students' home cultures was an important element of the instructional design adopted in this research. Recognising this, GREAT-Cycle could help educators (1) increase their students' comfort, competence, confidence, and relatedness need-satisfaction and (2) mitigate the frustration faced by developing opportunities to foster students' competence, confidence, and relatedness towards the school-based curriculum. The findings of this study have revealed that extrinsic and intrinsic motivations, effort, valence, expectancy, and self-estimation of ability were internally related determinants of drive for learning English across the curriculum. The noted decrease in amotivation likely resulted from a decrease in students' affective filter and an increased willingness to engage in both English language and content-area learning. The increases in both intrinsic and extrinsic motivation demonstrate that the use of CLIL as a strategy for learning is both inherently interesting to learners, while also contributing to their appreciation of the role of learning content and English as a means of gaining comfort as well as engaging in self-improvement and development.

This study was designed to evaluate the efficacy of the GREATCLIL camp model, a novel approach that integrates a variety of cultural, environmental, and school-based contexts, and significantly increased participants' learning motivation, demonstrating both the need and value of English language learning. From this perspective, a school-based GREATCLIL curriculum focusing on 19 educational issues can be viewed as autonomy-supportive content teaching which enriches the motivational aspects of students' functioning via need satisfaction. Anti-autonomy-supportive CLIL teaching may exacerbate the amotivational side of students' functioning via need frustration, while teacher neglect or indifference towards these processes may mute other motivational processes and create a new additional amotivational process, depriving the learner of need satisfaction. This chapter concludes that the twin antidotes of the school-based curricula and GREATCLIL camps described here worked towards decreasing amotivation, boosted learning need satisfaction, and reduced need frustration. As such, it is recommended that similar interventions could be profitable for future research in order to test the utility of expanding the GREAT-Cycle model design principles described in this chapter for regular or informal English classes.

Acknowledgement

The study in this chapter was funded by Taiwan's Ministry of Education under the project titles "2014 Youth English Service Camp," "2015 Youth English Service Camp," "2016 Youth English Service Camp," "2017 Youth English Service Camp," and "2018 Youth English Service Camp."

References

Albrecht, J. R. & Karabenick, S. A. (2018). Relevance for learning and motivation in education. *The Journal of Experimental Education, 86*(1), 1–10. https://doi.org/10.10 80/00220973.2017.1380593.

Ball, P. (2009). Does CLIL work? In D. Hill & P. Alan (Eds.), *The best of both worlds?: International perspectives on CLIL* (pp. 32–43). Norwich Institute for Language Education.

Ball, P., Kelly, K. & Clegg, J. (2015). *Putting CLIL into practice*. Oxford University Press.

Banegas, D. L. (2014). An investigation into CLIL-related sections of EFL coursebooks: Issues of CLIL inclusion in the publishing market. *International Journal of Bilingual Education and Bilingualism, 17*(3), 345–359. https://doi.org/10.1080/136 70050.2013.793651.

Bentley, K. (2010). *The TKT course: CLIL module*. Cambridge University Press.

Bosompem, E. G. (2014). Materials adaptation in Ghana: Teachers' attitudes and practices. In S. Garton & K. Graves (Eds.), *International perspectives on materials in ELT* (pp. 104–120). Palgrave Macmillan.

Cenoz, J., Genesee, F. & Gorter, D. (2014). Critical analysis of CLIL: Taking stock and looking forward. *Applied Linguistics, 35*(3), 243–262.

Coyle, D., Hood, P. & Marsh, D. (2010). *CLIL: Content and language integrated learning*. Cambridge University Press.

Dale, L. & Tanner, R. (2012). *CLIL activities: A resource for subject and language teachers*. Cambridge University Press.

Dallinger, S., Jonkmann, K., Hollm, J. & Fiege, C. (2016). The effect of content and language integrated learning on students' English and history competences—Killing two birds with one stone? *Learning and Instruction, 41*(1), 23–31.

Dalton-Puffer, C. (2011). Content-and-language integrated learning: From practice to principle? *Annual Review of Applied Linguistics, 31*, 182–204.

Darn, S. (2006). *Content and language integrated learning (CLIL): A European overview*. ERIC Clearinghouse. https://eric.ed.gov/?id=ED490775.

Deci, E. L. & Ryan, R. M. (2002). *Handbook of self-determination research*. University of Rochester Press.

European Commission. (2010). *European language policy and CLIL: A selection of EU-funded projects*. http://www.edu.xunta.gal/centros/cpicruce/system/files/clil broch_en.pdf.

Ikeda, M. (2013). Does CLIL work for Japanese secondary school students? Potential for the 'weak' version of CLIL. *Internal CLIL Research Journal, 2*(1), 31–43. http://www.icrj.eu/21/article3.html.

Järvinen, H. M. (2006). *Language in content instruction. Issues in promoting language and learning in CLIL type provision*. https://www.academia.edu/1222532 /Language_in_content_instruction._Issues_in_promoting_language_and _learning_in_CLIL_type_provision.

Krashen, S. (1985). *The input hypothesis: Issues and implications*. Longman.

Lambert, W. E. & Tucker, G. R. (1972). *Bilingual education of children: The St. Lambert experiment*. Newbury House.

Lasagabaster, D. (2014). Content versus language teacher: How are CLIL students affected? In R. Breeze, C. L. Saíz, C. M. Pasamar & C. T. Sala (Eds.), *Integration of theory and practice in CLIL* (pp. 123–141). Brill Rodopi.

Lasagabaster, D. & Doiz, A. (2016). CLIL students' perceptions of their language learning process: Delving into self-perceived improvement and instructional preferences. *Language Awareness, 25*(1–2), 110–126.

Li, H. (2006). School-based curriculum development: an interview study of Chinese Kindergartens. *Early Childhood Education Journal. 33*(4):223–229.

Marsh, D. (2000). *Using languages to learn and learning to use languages.* University of Jyväskylä.

McDonough, J., Shaw, C. & Masuhara, H. (2013). *Materials and methods in ELT: A teacher's guide* (3rd ed.). Wiley-Blackwell.

Merino, J. A. & Lasagabaster, D. (2018). CLIL as a way to multilingualism. *International Journal of Bilingual Education and Bilingualism, 21*(1), 79–92.

National Development Council. (2018). *Bilingual nation.* https://www.ndc.gov.tw/en/Content_List.aspx?n=D933E5569A87A91C&upn=9633B537E92778BB.

Pérez-Cañado, M. (2012). CLIL research in Europe: Past, present, and future. *The International Journal of Bilingual Education and Bilingualism, 15*(3), 315–341. https://doi.org/10.1080/13670050.2011.630064.

Pladevall-Ballester, E. (2018). A longitudinal study of primary school EFL learning motivation in CLIL and non-CLIL settings. *Language Teaching Research, 23*(6), 765–786. https://doi.org/10.1177/1362168818765877.

Rotgans, J. I. & Schmidt, H. G. (2011). Situational interest and academic achievement in the active-learning classroom. *Learning and Instruction, 21*(1), 58–67.

Ryan, R. M. & Deci, E. L. (2000). Self-determination theory and the facilitation of intrinsic motivation, social development, and well-being. *American Psychologist, 55*, 68–78.

Swain, M. & Lapkin, S. (1982). *Evaluating bilingual education.* Multilingual Matters.

Ting, Y. L. T. (2011). CLIL … not only not immersion but also more than the sum of its parts. *ELT Journal, 65*(3), 314–317. https://doi.org/10.1093/elt/ccr026.

Yang, W. (2016). An investigation of learning efficacy, management difficulties and improvements in tertiary CLIL (content and language integrated learning) programmes in Taiwan: A survey of stakeholder perspectives, *LACLIL, 9*(1), 64–109. https://doi.org/10.5294/laclil.2016.9.1.4.

Appendix: Pre- and Post Tests: Motivation in Learning English in Formal English Classes and GREATCLIL Camps.

The pre- and post-test surveys are available in English and Mandarin on the book's website at https://wac.colostate.edu/books/international/eac2018.

9 Testing the Effect of Asynchronous Discussions in a Language and Content-Integrated Hybrid Course

Sinh Ngoc Dang
VNU-University of Languages and International Studies, Hanoi, Vietnam

Abstract: The method of teaching delivery has been found to have significant impact on students' learning. "Hybrid" or "blended" courses that mix face-to-face and online instructional methods have gained popularity in education, including in the field of language learning and teaching. There is an increasing number of studies that have explored the methodology of constructing a hybrid class for English language teaching and its potential benefits for student learning. However, little has been studied with regard to using a hybrid course where English and content subjects are integrated. The purpose of the research described in this chapter was to test the effect of asynchronous discussions on learning outcomes of students within a hybrid course and to compare the effectiveness of the course with a more traditional one. In both types of courses, American economic history and English language were learnt simultaneously. A regression model was used to analyze the quantitative data obtained from investigating both types of course formats. The study finds that the incorporation of online discussion forums into an English and content-integrated course can help improve student academic performance.

Keywords: language across the curriculum, English and content integration, economics education, asynchronous discussion, hybrid course

The use of English as the medium of instruction at universities in non-English speaking countries has been growing, due in large part to the impact of globalization and the dominance of the English language generally (Altbach, 2004; Johnson, 2009). As a result, English language and content-integrated learning and teaching has been widely used at international universities to meet the needs of the modern market and economy (Arnó-Macià & Mancho-Bares, 2015; Coleman, 2006; Ljosland, 2005). English Across the Curriculum (EAC) focuses on a twin purpose: learning the target language and the content of a specific subject at the same time. "This dual character is a cognitive challenge for teachers as well as for students as it is substantiated by the combination of language teaching with the context" (Leshchenko et al., 2018, p.17). Elisabet Arnó-Macià & Guzman Mancho-Bares (2015) found that "the language proficiency of both lecturers and students was perceived as the main challenge to CLIL (Content and Language Integrated Learning) implementation" (p. 68). However, in this study, English language proficiency was not such a challenge for the lecturer since he had been a lecturer of English before he became a lecturer of economics. What made it difficult for the lecturer in this study was teaching the relevant English language and content of a specific subject within one semester. The 2015 study by Arnó-Macià and Mancho-Bares indicated that "it's not so much that they [students] learn the language (although they learn technical vocabulary), but that they lose the fear of using the language, that they feel the need to use the language" (p. 68). Thus, it was seen as important to encourage the students to use English to study the subject content. In this study specifically, students were expected to use the technical English of history and economics to acquire knowledge of the specific subject—American economic history—as well as read and write specialized texts, and communicate in academic and professional situations.

The policy of the university where this study was conducted requires students to take several English language courses at university level, with the aim of students reaching level B1[1] after two years. Therefore, when the students took content subjects, they had already reached B1 level, which the university considers the minimum English level for students to pursue content subjects successfully. Hence, students were able to use English for general communication, but found that they did not have enough time to learn both English and the content of the specific subject in the classroom. The challenge therefore that both lecturers and students faced was how to achieve the dual focus on learning English and the content of a specific subject in the classroom.

Vocabulary learning is an essential part of the foreign language learning process, and it is a crucial concern of a language and content-integrated

---

1   B1 level: "Intermediate," the third level in the Common European Framework of Reference

course, as Kara Warburton (2015) recognized when she noted that "one cannot easily distinguish between general language and special language" (p. 362). Specialized vocabulary in economics is, however, different from vocabulary used in everyday language, and it acquires specific meanings when used in a particular academic or professional context. Many words with general meanings for everyday use, when combined together to form a concept concerned with economics and business, have a very abstract meaning: for instance, *consumer price index* (CPI) or *gross domestic product* (GDP). A single word that students are already familiar with may also have a very different meaning in economics and business: for instance, *derivative*, generally meaning "using or taken from other sources; not original,"[2] in economics means "a contract between two parties which derives its value/price from an underlying asset."[3] Normally, students need to memorize the technical words and their meaning in English supported by the meaning in their mother tongue. In a typical lecture in this course, the focus was on the specific subject content together with the introduction of new technical English necessary for the students to understand and acquire the content from the specialized texts. This left inadequate time for students to use the new technical English that they had just learnt to improve their productive English skills and foster their autonomy in building their vocabulary knowledge during the class. Students, therefore, needed to spend more time to fulfil the dual purpose of this course—English and content integration—beyond the classroom and beyond the course. A platform for students to discuss what they had learnt during the class so that they could use the technical English to understand the content of the specific subject and improve their English skills appeared to have been needed.

Technology has changed our approaches to teaching and learning in general and foreign language teaching and learning in particular, and much has been written about the practice of using technology in the classroom (Lin, 2007; Martyn, 2003; Massoud et al., 2011). Although online instruction in a hybrid course, which incorporates face-to-face and online instructional methods, has potential drawbacks, such as less direct interaction with instructors and other students and a difficulty in maintaining academic standards, studies have demonstrated that students can learn effectively in the hybrid course format (Gratton-Lavoie & Stanley, 2009; McGee & Reis, 2012; Vignare, 2007). Regarding the academic performance of students in the hybrid course, there have been studies that found test scores to be higher or slightly higher for hybrid students than students enrolled in the same course in a face-to-face

---

2   Yourdictionary.com
3   http://Investopedia.com

format in the fields of, for example, microeconomics (Gratton-Lavoie & Stanley, 2009), biology (Riffell & Sibley, 2005), and language (Chenoweth & Murday, 2003). For language across the curriculum courses, little or no research has been conducted to compare the effectiveness of hybrid and face-to-face courses.

This study is an attempt to investigate the effect of using a hybrid format in an EAC course. In this study, a "hybrid course" is one that combines face-to-face with asynchronous online discussion. Asynchronous discussion is online discussion progressing at students' own pace when they post to a forum or a discussion board. This is also referred to as "asynchronous learning." With asynchronous online discussion, students can engage in discussions with each other online, while also reviewing and participating in discussions with others at times convenient to them. Asynchronous online discussion can be used as a tool for fostering critical thinking skills and for including different learning styles and personalities, as well as helping to improve the potential for student learning and knowledge sharing (Brewer & Brewer, 2010; Brookfield, 2005; Kienle, 2009). For the course in this study, the purpose of the integration of asynchronous online discussion forums with traditional face-to-face instruction is to assist students in the integration of complex course materials with English language resources to broaden students' knowledge of a specific subject content while, at the same time, improving their English skills beyond the classroom and beyond the course.

Aims of the Research

There has been substantial research on hybrid/online course formats in education in general and in English language teaching in particular (Allen & Seaman, 2011; Bonk, 2011; DePraeter, 2014; Hammer, 2012; Harris et al., 2009; Jochum, 2011; Klimova & Kacetl, 2015; McNeil, 2016; Rubio & Thoms, 2012; Willekens & Gibson, 2010). However, what these studies lack is a method to statistically test the effect of employing a hybrid course model on student learning outcomes. Moreover, little or no research has been conducted on using a hybrid course where English and content subjects are integrated. To address these gaps, this study constructs a regression model to measure the effect of asynchronous discussions on learning outcomes within a hybrid course in which American economic history and English language were learnt simultaneously. This chapter, therefore, contributes to the literature by testing whether or not online asynchronous discussions in a course which integrates disciplinary content and English can truly further students' learning of the specific subject content while also improving their English language skills.

Research Design and Empirical Analysis

Data and Methodology

Following a quantitative approach, the study was conducted using data collected from 110 students taking an American economic history course integrated with English learning. The students specialize in international studies and foreign trade, and they are required to take most content subjects in English after they have reached B1 level of English. The course in this study is designed in such a way that students receive face-to-face instruction for three hours a week, but also use online resources beyond the classroom that they can access via a webpage prepared by the author. The study investigated four classes, with 25 to 35 students in each class. Student populations were self-selected, and the instructor randomly determined which classes would be taught in hybrid mode. Two hybrid classes comprised 56 students, while 54 students were enrolled in the two traditional classes. The two student populations comprised full-time students, and they did not differ much in the ratio of males to females[4]. All students were in their third year at the university, and all of them owned a computer and had Wi-Fi internet access at home and at the university. They could also complete work in a campus computer lab or in other facilities that have computers, such as the university library. All four classes, which were assumed to be of the same English level since students had reached B1 level, were taught in English by the same instructor with the same content, texts, and assignments but using two different modes of delivery: traditional and hybrid.

To test the effect of asynchronous discussion on learning outcomes, both traditional and hybrid classes were taught simultaneously and received the same active-learning activities in class, which included lectures, discussions in pairs or groups, and student presentations on chosen topics related to the subject materials. The only difference was that with the hybrid classes asynchronous discussions were conducted online, while with the traditional classes the students met outside the classroom in groups and conducted discussion face to face—or in any other manner since it was impossible for the instructor to supervise their discussions outside the classroom. The instructor divided the traditional class students into separate discussion groups and asked them to inform him of the time and place they met for discussions. Students in the classes which were chosen for asynchronous discussions were added to the webpage prepared by the instructor in such a way that students of the traditional classes could not access it.

---

4   In each class, males accounted for around 10 percent of the students.

The course was designed around a specific set of materials in a standard format and was conducted over a 15-week semester. There was a required textbook for the course and PowerPoint lecture presentations with accompanying lecture notes, all of which were in English and available to students. These materials constituted the course content, and English was taught and learnt simultaneously with those course materials. For the hybrid classes, the blog of online resources and the Facebook page were used to complement course readings with links to various news articles, podcasts, and videos relevant to the materials being discussed. Questions for discussions prepared by the instructor were posted to the blog. Students were also free to post questions regarding course materials, and both the instructor and other students would respond to these questions. The language used for the asynchronous online discussions had to be English. For the traditional classes, the students were provided with the same complementary materials and questions for discussion. The advantage of asynchronous discussions in a hybrid class over face-to-face discussions in a traditional class is that students of the hybrid class can study and review the complementary materials and participate in discussions with others at times convenient to them. It is also possible for the instructor to track the discussions of all students in the hybrid class.

One student post often encouraged other students to give comments as in the following example:

> **Task:** The picture on page 429 of the textbook we are using is a scene from the movie "It's a Wonderful Life." The authors say that Mary Bailey (Donna Reed) turns over the money she has saved for a second honeymoon to George Bailey (Jimmy Stewart), so he can end the run on his savings bank. The Federal Reserve should have handled the crisis (the Great Depression) the way Mary did. Explain the reasons why the authors of the textbook say so.
>
> **Student A:** The author mentioned the Federal Reserve should have handle the crisis by spending more instead of holding more reserves. The reason is that by spending more on public works such as building schools, road construction, etc. will create more jobs while also facilitate the flow of money in the economy.
>
> **Student B:** The reason is that by spending more on public works such as building schools, road construction, etc. will create more jobs while also facilitate the flow of money in the

economy. This is fiscal policy—the work of the government.
The Fed enacts the monetary policy.

In this way, students were given the time and an online learning environment where they could use the concepts of the specific subject and technical English they had learnt during the class to read, listen, or watch, and write. This appears to have helped both the instructor and students to fulfil the dual purpose of the course: learning the subject content and English at the same time.

In both the hybrid and traditional classes, students were given various homework assignments for which they were given a limited timeframe for completion. There were also four quizzes and two tests,[5] which were graded and used as data for this study. The same quizzes and tests given to both types of students were based on tests from textbooks and/or the College Board.[6] For economics, the test questions were taken from textbooks purchased by the instructor. The economics textbooks included a CD with test questions and a webpage for online access to the test question banks. For history, test questions were taken from American economic history textbooks and the standardized history tests designed by the College Board. In order to motivate students to follow the discussions on the blog for the hybrid classes and discussions outside the classroom for the traditional classes, students of both types of class were given a quiz on the materials provided by the instructor every two weeks. All the quizzes and tests were closed-book, and no outside help of any sort was allowed. Tests and quizzes were monitored strictly by the instructor face-to-face in the classroom with supervision from a non-academic colleague. For the quizzes and tests, the instructor wanted to assess not only basic knowledge gains from the content subject, but also students' ability to comprehend the concepts in English. The content of all quizzes and tests was based directly on the objectives and assessment requirements stated in the course syllabus (sample test questions can be found in the appendix). The students' oral presentations and essays were graded based on a rubric for assessment which has two

---

5 The four quizzes consisted of multiple-choice questions and short reading comprehension texts. Each quiz checked the students' understanding of one or two chapters in the textbook. The two tests included a mid-term test which was the oral presentation and a final test which consisted of different types of questions: multiple-choice, short-answer, and essay-writing questions.

6 The College Board is an American not-for-profit organization that was formed in December 1899 as the College Entrance Examination Board to expand access to higher education. The College Board develops standardized tests and curricula used by K–12 and post-secondary education institutions.

parts: part one measures the integrated language-content knowledge and part two measures the English speaking and writing proficiency. The content-language integrated results of these two tests were then combined with the results of the quizzes to create a set of data. The separate speaking and writing results were combined to create another set of data. Following the Vietnamese grading system, the grade scale of the quizzes and tests is from 1 to 10[7]. For example, if the test consisted of ten multiple-choice questions, each correct answer would be given one point. Therefore, if a student answered all ten questions correctly, he or she would get a full grade of ten points, which is equivalent to 100 percent (4 point-scale) in the U.S. grading system. If a student made no attempt to complete the test or answered all questions incorrectly, he or she would receive a zero. As a measurement of attainment, students' scores from all the quizzes and tests were averaged to produce an overall score out of 10, and this score was used as data for the regression. The speaking and writing scores, from the students' oral presentations and essay writing, were also averaged to produce another overall score for the purpose of measuring the students' English speaking and writing proficiency in this study.

Regression Model and Empirical Analysis

It is assumed that the greater the number of online interactions and discussions of the course materials, the higher the average score each student should receive. To test this hypothesis, the following linear regression model was adopted:

$$\text{Grade}_t = \beta_0 + \beta_1 \text{hybrid}_t + \beta_3 \text{asynch}_t + \beta_3 \text{attend}_t + \beta_4 \text{male}_t + \varepsilon_t,$$

where *Grade* is the student's average test score, *asynch* is the variable that measures the number of discussions and comments to articles or questions that the student made, and *attend* is a variable measuring the students' attendance percentage. β is the coefficient and ε denotes the error term. Two dummy variables are added to the model: *hybrid* is a dummy variable measuring if the class is the hybrid one, and *male* is a dummy variable measuring if the student is male. A dummy variable (or an indicator variable) is a numeric variable that represents categorical data, such as gender, race, age, or another particular grouping. Regression results are easiest to interpret when dummy variables take the values of 0 and 1. A person is given a value of 0 if they are in the control group (the reference group) or a 1 if they are in the treated group. Once a categorical

---

7 https://photos.state.gov/libraries/vietnam/8621/pdf-forms/VN-Grading-System.pdf.

variable has been recoded as a dummy variable, the dummy variable can be used in regression analysis just like any other quantitative variable. For example, in this study, the variable *hybrid* represented the treated group where students were in the hybrid classes, while the reference group consisted of students in traditional face-to-face classes. In the analysis, each dummy variable of the treated group is compared with the reference group. In this study, a positive regression coefficient means that the grade is higher for the treated group than for the reference group; a negative regression coefficient means that the grade is lower. The following table (Table 9.1) presents the summary statistics for all variables.

Table 9.1. Summary statistics

Variable	Observation	Mean	Std. Dev.	Min	Max
grade	110	6.62	1.64	0	9
hybrid	110	0.49	0.50	0	1
asynch	110	4.25	3.76	0	10
absent	110	8.08	2.94	0	10
male	110	0.15	0.36	0	1

A regression analysis is a form of predictive modelling technique estimating the relationships between a dependent and one or more independent variables. The regression model in this study includes *grade* as the dependent variable to measure the effect of asynchronous online discussions in an English language and content-integrated hybrid course. *Hybrid* was used to measure whether in a hybrid course the students could earn higher grades on the tests. Whether or not the asynchronous online discussion is beneficial to the student was not confirmed through previous studies when considering courses that serve the dual purpose of learning subject content and enhancing English language skills. Therefore, the *asynch* variable was included in the model to denote the extent of students' participation in asynchronous online discussions. It is assumed that such discussions can help students further their knowledge of the course content and improve their English language skills at the same time, and as such, this variable was expected to be positive. The variable for attendance (*attend*) was also included to proxy for student motivation: the higher the attendance, the higher the grade. The variable for gender (*male*) was added in the final analysis. In another study, it had been found that male students perform on average 7.5 points better than their female classmates in a microeconomics hybrid class (Gratton-Lavoie & Stanley, 2009).

To estimate the linear model proposed above, the method of ordinary least squares (OLS) was used. OLS is widely used in many scientific fields, and it can be utilized for estimating the unknown parameters in a linear regression model. The results from the OLS model are presented in three tables: Table 9.2 shows the effect of a hybrid class in a content and English-integrated course, Table 9.3 presents the effect of asynchronous online discussions within the hybrid class, and Table 9.4 shows the effect of asynchronous online discussion on English proficiency.

The analysis of the results is based on the regression coefficient (Tables 9.2, 9.3, and 9.4, column 2) since it provides the expected change in the dependent variable (here: *grade*) for a one-unit increase in the independent variables (all other variables in the regression model). P-value is also used in the analysis for the statistical significance. The p-value is the probability of finding the observed results when the null hypothesis of a study question is true: $p < 0.05$ (5%) means less than one in 20 chance of being wrong, and $p < 0.001$ (0.1%) means less than one in 1,000 chance of being wrong (see Tables 9.2, 9.3, and 9.4, column 5). Conventionally 5%, 1%, and 0.1% levels for the statistical significance are used, and if the p-value is greater than 5%, it is considered statistically non-significant due to weak evidence.

According to the estimates, the *hybrid* variable is positive and significant at p-value of less than one percent on the content and English-integrated learning. It is obvious that students in the hybrid class performed better and received grades approximately 1.2 points higher than students of the traditional class (see Table 9.2, column 2, row 2). As all quizzes and tests were graded following the scale from 1 to 10, this means that the test results of students in the hybrid classes were on average 1.2 out of 10 points (or 12 out of 100 percent) higher than those of students in the purely face-to-face ones. When the results on the English proficiency test are separated from the grades on the integrated tests, the *hybrid* variable becomes insignificant (see Table 9.4, row 2), perhaps due to weak evidence.

Table 9.2. The effect of a hybrid class in a content and English-integrated course

Variables	Coefficient	Std. Error	T-Ratio	P-Value	Sig.
hybrid	1.18	0.24	4.91	0.000	***
attend	0.26	0.04	6.46	0.000	***
male	-0.07	0.33	-0.22	0.825	
_cons	3.92	0.37	10.63	0.000	***
R-Squared	0.3677	Adjusted R-squared	0.3615	Number of Observations	110
F (3, 116)	23.46				

Note: *** $p<0.01$, ** $p<0.05$, * $p<0.1$

Table 9.3. The effect of asynchronous online discussion within the hybrid class

Variables	Coefficient	Std. Error	T-Ratio	P-Value	Sig.
asynch	0.11	0.03	3.37	0.00	***
attend	0.26	0.04	5.93	0.00	***
male	-0.17	0.35	-0.48	0.64	
_cons	4.09	0.38	10.65	0.00	***
R-Squared	0.31	Adjusted R-squared	0.30	Number of Observations	110
$F_{(3, 116)}$	17.82				

Note: *** $p<0.01$, ** $p<0.05$, * $p<0.1$

Table 9.4. The effect of asynchronous online discussion on English proficiency

Variables	Coefficient	Std. Error	T-Ratio	P-Value	Sig.
hybrid	0.00	0.13	0.00	0.99	
asynch	0.20	0.18	2.77	0.00	***
attend	0.21	0.15	1.44	0.05	**
male	-0.01	0.33	-0.22	0.39	
_cons	8.03	0.13	61.46	0.00	***
R-Squared	0.37	Adjusted R-squared	0.3615	Number of Observations	110
$F_{(3, 116)}$	23.46				

Note: *** $p<0.01$, ** $p<0.05$, * $p<0.1$

Another variable, which is the main variable of interest, together with the *hybrid* variable, is *asynch*. This variable is both positive and significant at *p*-value of less than one percent. The estimates show that for each additional discussion on the blog, a student raised their grade by more than 0.1 point on the English and content-integrated tests (see Table 9.3, column 2, row 2) and by around 0.2 point on the English proficiency test (see Table 9.4, column 2, row 3). This means that between two students, the one that was more involved in the asynchronous online discussions would perform slightly better in the course. They would achieve approximately 0.1 out of 10 points on the English and content-integrated tests and 0.2 out of 10 points on the English proficiency test higher than the grade earned by the student who was less involved in the asynchronous online discussions. This estimate seems to be insubstantive if a student only contributed to one or two discussions. This is probably due to the fact that those students who were not actively involved in the asynchronous online discussions could still observe and read the discussions from other students who were more involved and hence could improve their understanding of the subject content and improve their English. However, the greater the contribution a student made to discussions, the higher the grade they could earn compared with the grades of students who were inactive.

Also, as expected, the attendance rate was very significant in determining a student's grade, with p-value of less than one-percent level. All else constant, the estimates show that the more frequently a student attended class, the higher the grade they could earn from the course. If a student increased their attendance by ten percent, their test grade would increase by about 2.6 out of 10 points for both types of classes (see Tables 9.2 and 9.3, column 2, row 3). For the English proficiency test, attendance was also significant at the five-percent level, and students could raise their grade by around 0.2 point (see Table 9.4, column 2, row 4).

For the gender variable (*male*), in contrast to Chiara Gratton-Lavoie and Denise Stanley's (2009) findings, male students in this study performed on average about 0.1 point lower than their female classmates in both class types (see Tables 9.2 and 9.3, column 2, row 4). However, this variable was non-significant (p-value > 5%; see Tables 9.2, 9.3, and 9.4, column 5, row 4). The non-significance of the *male* variable was probably because the ratio of male and female students in this study was low, males accounting for only around ten percent of the students.

The R-squared statistic for the OLS model in this study is approximately 0.38, which is on the low side of acceptable, but this study showed other statistically significant predictors (e.g., the p-value). The significance coefficients are, therefore, still valuable.

Conclusions

Teaching and learning in a course where English and content subjects are being taught simultaneously is challenging. One of the challenges is that the technical English of the course may impede students' comprehending of the course materials. This chapter has shown that a hybrid class in an EAC course, where face-to-face instruction is combined with asynchronous online discussions of course-related materials, has in fact helped to improve student academic performance in the subject. This is likely due to increasing involvement and motivation of students in the hybrid course, where self-regulatory cognition, learner autonomy, learning community, and critical thinking skills play important roles in the development of hybrid classes.

Overall, conclusions from the above estimates indicate that asynchronous online discussions helped students in an EAC course receive higher grades than those in the traditional class with regard to both the content subject and English proficiency. Within the hybrid class, students also improved their test performance when they were actively involved in the asynchronous online discussions when compared to those who were inactive.

What this research disregarded but which can be considered for further research is the relationship between students' technological skills and success in hybrid courses. Other important factors to be considered when conducting asynchronous online discussion in hybrid classes are the ways to choose the complementary course materials for students to review online and the types of questions to post to the blog for students' asynchronous discussions. It is also crucial to ensure that students read, listen, or watch the complementary course materials posted by the instructor and participate in the online discussions. This chapter hopefully contributes to the efforts of the language across the curriculum movement in fulfilling the dual focus of content and language learning.

Acknowledgments

I would like to thank my students for their participation in the study, and the anonymous reviewers for their generous and thoughtful feedback.

References

Allen, I. E. & Seaman, J. (2011). *Going the distance: Online education in the United States*. Sloan Consortium.

Altbach, P. (2004). Globalization and the university: Myths and realities in an unequal world. *Tertiary Education and Management, 10(1)*, 3–25.

Arnó-Macià, E. & Mancho-Barés, G. (2015). The role of content and language in content and language integrated learning (CLIL) at university: Challenges and implications for ESP. *English for Specific Purposes, 37*, 3–73.

Bonk, C. J. (2011). *The world is open: How web technology is revolutionizing education*. Jossey-Bass.

Brewer, P. D. & Brewer, K. L. (2010). Knowledge management, human resource management, and higher Education: A theoretical model. *Journal of Education for Business, 85*, 330–335.

Brookfield, S. (2005). *Discussion as a way of teaching: Tools and techniques for democratic classrooms*. Jossey-Bass.

Chenoweth, N. A. & Murday, K. (2003). Measuring student learning in an online French course. *CALICO Journal, 20(2)*, 285–314.

Coleman, J. (2006). English-medium teaching in European higher education. *Language Teaching, 39*, 1–14.
DePraetere, T. (2014). Online Learning Is About Activities. *Elearning industry*. https://elearningindustry.com/members/thomas-de-praetere.
Gratton-Lavoie, C. & Stanley, D. (2009). Teaching and learning principles of microeconomics online: An empirical assessment. *Journal of Economic Education, 40*(1), 3–25.
Harmer, J. (2012). *Essential teacher knowledge. Core concepts in English language teaching*. Pearson Education Limited.
Harris, J., Mishra, P. & Koehler, M. (2009). Teachers' technological pedagogical content knowledge and learning activity types: Curriculum-based technology integration reframed. *Journal of Research on Technology in Education, 41*(4), 393–416.
Jochum, C. J. (2011). Blended Spanish instruction: Perceptions and design—A case study. *Journal of Instructional Psychology, 38*(1), 40–47.
Johnson, A. (2009). The rise of English: The language of globalization in China and the European Union. *Macalester International, 22*(12), 131–168.
Kienle, A. (2009). Intertwining synchronous and asynchronous communication to support collaborative learning—System design and evaluation. *Education and Information Technologies, 14*(1), 55–79.
Klimova, B. F. & Kacetl, J. (2015). Hybrid learning and its current role in the teaching of foreign languages. *Procedia—Social and Behavioral Sciences, 182*, 477–481.
Leshchenko, M., Lavrysh, Y. & Halatsyn, K. (2018). The role of content and language integrated learning at Ukrainian and Polish educational systems: Challenges and implication. A*dvanced Education, 9*, 17–25. https://doi.org/10.20535/2410-8286.133409.
Lin, H. (2007). Blending online components into traditional instruction: A case of using technologies to support good practices in pre-service teacher education. *Journal of Instructional Delivery Systems, 21*(1), 7–16.
Ljosland, R. (September, 2005). *Norway's misunderstanding of the Bologna process: When internationalization becomes anglicisation* [Paper presentation]. Bi- and Multilingual Universities: Challenges and Future Prospects, Helsinki University. https://pureadmin.uhi.ac.uk/ws/portalfiles/portal/422495/Ljosland_Helsinki.pdf.
Martyn, M. (2003). The hybrid online model: Good practice. *Educause Quarterly, 1*, 18–23.
Massoud, A., Iqbal, U. & Stockley, D. (2011). Using blended learning to foster education in a contemporary classroom. *Transformative Dialogues: Teaching & Learning Journal, 5*(2), 1–11.
McGee, P. & Reis, A. (2012). Blended course design: A synthesis of best practices. *Journal of Asynchronous Learning Networks, 16*(4), 7–22.
McNeil, M. (2016). Preparing teachers for hybrid and online language instruction. *Issues and Trends in Educational Technology, 4*(1), 3–15.
Riffell, S. & Sibley, D. (2005). Using web-based instruction to improve large undergraduate biology courses: An evaluation of a hybrid course format. *Computers & Education, 44*, 217–235.

Rubio, F. & Thoms, J. J. (2012). Hybrid language teaching and learning: Looking forward. In F. Rubio & J. Thoms (Eds.), *Hybrid language teaching and learning: Exploring theoretical, pedagogical and curricular issues* (pp. 1–9). Heinle Cengage Learning.

Vignare, K. (2007). Review of literature blended learning: Using ALN to change the classroom — Will it work? In A. G. Picciano & C. D. Dziuban (Eds.), *Blended learning: Research perspectives* (pp.37–63). Sloan Consortium.

Warburton, K. (2015). Managing terminology in commercial environments. In H. J. Kockaert & F. Steurs (Eds.), *Handbook of terminology* (pp.361–392). John Benjamins.

Willekens, R. & Gibson, P. (2010). Hybrid courses and student engagement: Opportunities and challenges for community college leaders. *International Journal of Educational Leadership Preparation*, 5(1), 1–14.

Appendix: Sample Test Questions

Choose the best answer:

Question 1: Classical economics is a school of thought in economics that flourished, primarily in Britain, in the late 18th and early-to-mid 19th century. Its main thinkers are held to be Adam Smith, Jean-Baptiste Say, David Ricardo, and Thomas Robert Malthus...

If you are a classical economist, which statement would you support?

    a. Let the economy work out its own problems
    b. The more the government spends to improve the economy, the better
    c. The government should be involved to help during recessions
    d. The government is the key to economic success

Questions 2, 3, 4:

> "Wherefore, security being the true design and end of government, it unanswerably follows that whatever form thereof appears most likely to ensure it to us, with the least expense and greatest benefit, is preferable to all others. . . . Here too is the design and end of government, Freedom and Security."
>
>   – Thomas Paine, *Common Sense*, 1776

> "Governments are instituted among Men, deriving their just powers from the consent of the governed. That whenever any Form of Government becomes destructive of these ends, it is the Right of the People to alter or to abolish it, and to institute new Government, laying its foundation on such principles and

organizing its powers in such form, as to them shall seem most likely to affect their Safety and Happiness."

– Thomas Jefferson, *Declaration of Independence*, 1776

Question 2. The excerpts were written in response to the

   a. British government's attempt to assert greater control over the North American colonies.
   b. British government's failure to protect colonists from attacks by American Indians.
   c. failure of colonial governments to implement mercantilist policies.
   d. failure of colonial governments to extend political rights to new groups.

Question 3. The ideas about government expressed by Paine and Jefferson are most consistent with which of the following?

   a. The concept of hereditary rights and privileges
   b. The belief in Manifest Destiny
   c. The principle of religious freedom
   d. The ideas of the Enlightenment

Question 4. The principles expressed by Paine and Jefferson best account for which of the following features of the United States during and immediately after the American Revolution?

   a. The development of factions and nascent political parties
   b. The rapid expansion of frontier settlements
   c. The relatively limited powers of the Articles of Confederation
   d. The growth of conflict between wealthy elites and poor farmers and laborers

Essay question: Explain the various theories of what caused the Great Depression. Why did it last so long?

10 Theatrical Texts in Content and Language Integrated Learning

Alan Thompson
GIFU SHOTOKU GAKUEN UNIVERSITY, JAPAN

Abstract: This chapter describes an ongoing case study that investigates the use of excerpts from theatrical texts (ranging from ancient to modern and originating in multiple cultures) as resources in Content and Language Integrated Learning (CLIL) at a Japanese university. After reviewing research on the suitability of literary texts for content and language learning, on the benefits of repeated aural/oral practice, and on learning effects related to dramatic process or performance, a rationale is presented. To wit, theatrical texts, as language learning materials, are engaging models of sustained spoken interactions which provide practice in hearing and producing the stress, rhythm, and intonation patterns of natural English, and raise awareness about grammar/meaning and pragmatics/use relationships. As resources for content learning, the texts serve as springboards for learning world cultural history and the role of theatre itself. The second half of the chapter includes a description of the teaching practice with a specification of the instruments used to observe the effect of learners hearing, practising, and considering the texts in aural/oral mode. This is followed by some preliminary findings—focusing on real-time learner responses, attitudes towards content and language learning through theatrical texts, and measurable gains in prosodic awareness and its effect on retention of content learning.

Keywords: theatre, content and language integrated learning, aural-oral learning, language learning, cultural history

The well-liked texts of literature have value in learning contexts. That is, they engage the imagination, sustain interest, and provide a valid context for encountering language in use—poetry for rhythm and intonation, plays for conversation, and even deliberately artful features of language for illustrating how grammar works (Brumfit & Carter, 1986; Falvey & Kennedy, 1997; Teranishi et al., 2015). Theatrical texts, especially, are meant to entertain, and, unlike some prose and poetry, they usually do so without placing too great a cognitive burden on the receiver, who is, after all, conceived first and foremost as a viewer of a story unfolding on stage. Actors and fans alike are generally supposed to enjoy repeatedly hearing, reading, or reciting the lines of popular plays.

In language learning, willing or even gleeful repetition is a much sought-after state of affairs, so theatrical texts are apt for exploitation in language practice activities. And across the curriculum, greater familiarity with meaning- and culture-rich texts—and with their contexts and implications—can be conducive to the discovery of insights by the content learner. To take advantage of these inherent advantages, a set of learning materials has been developed using as its main resources adapted/translated excerpts from theatrical texts—ranging from ancient Roman comedy, through early modern English and French theatre, to modern Japanese and American plays (see Appendix A for a list of source materials). These are used in listening, reading-aloud, and improvisation activities, while supplementary material provides cultural context and prompts discussion.

The case study described in this chapter comprises a teaching practice (based on these materials) together with observations of the pedagogical effects. The teaching practice proposed here differs from many uses of literature in education in that it investigates the effectiveness of theatrical texts not primarily as reading materials but rather in the spoken mode for which they were intended, with an important aim being the enhancement of students' (noticing and production) abilities in listening, in reading aloud, and in rehearsed and semi-rehearsed speaking with natural prosodic features. Also, the focus is on the effect of the texts themselves, and not on the process nor the performance of drama (unlike Kao & O'Neill, 1998; Maley & Duff, 2005). Drama activities are welcome and natural complements to the use of theatrical texts and, as summarised below, evidence exists of their benefits. Yet, as the inclusion of drama activities as a set of manipulable variables was not felt to be feasible, there is no attempt to observe the effects of this or that method of dramatisation. The intent here, rather, is to observe the effect of learners hearing, practising, and considering the texts in aural/oral mode.

Language and Content Learning through Theatrical Texts

The aptness of literature for language and content learning has mostly been asserted, intuited, or presumed (and often disputed). There has been, however, some empirical support from a variety of educational contexts, at least for relations that, even if not causal, show some promising concurrences between the experience of literary texts and language and content learning.

Suitability of Literary Texts for Language Learning

Literary texts are not unrepresentative of everyday language practice. All texts, approached without context, can be initially baffling, and since literature is often picked up and read in this way, it has a reputation for being "difficult" and "different," a distinction from other genres (such as social media chats, technical manuals, and advertising wordplay) that is perhaps not deserved. While literary and everyday texts alike contain many differences in register and style, corpus studies have found no empirical distinctions between them (e.g., Biber & Conrad, 2009) that would justify conceptualising "literary" and "everyday" as separate macro-genres. Rather, "what is distinctive about language use in literature, if anything is distinctive, is that far from being a highly specialised use of language, any register can be found in a literary text, and . . . typically a mixture of registers are indeed found"; "all of life is there" (Hall, 2015, pp. 31, 44). Likewise, metaphor and the supposed formal aspects of literature (e.g., parallelism, neologism) are all revealed to be common in everyday speech (Carter & McCarthy, 1995). Even the formal features of poetry—word truncation ("For *oft*, when on my couch I lie"[1]) or marked word order ("a train-band captain *eke was he*"[2])—are present in everyday speech, often for similar reasons—for example, rhythm ("see you this *aft*") or emphasis ("*this* I must see").

Literature may be said to differ in that, as Geoffrey Leech (1969) observes, it often carefully foregrounds certain linguistic features (by repetition, rhythm, or rhyme) to highlight meanings or set up, e.g., equivalences and contrasts, while everyday speech only does so occasionally and in a more clichéd manner ("No news is good news"). There is some evidence that these marked grammatical usages, repetitions, and literary features are more noticeable to the language learner than unmarked, more frequent wordings. Tomohide Ishihara and Akira Ono (2015), for example, report that with literary texts students' attention was drawn more to the surface structure of sentences (not only to the gist of the passage), and David Hanauer (2001) asserts that "the central argument for using poetry reading as a task is that poetry is a natural discourse context that directs the reader's attention to textual features . . . while staying within a meaning construction framework" (p. 298). It is

---

1 William Wordsworth, *Daffodils*.

2 William Cowper, *The Diverting History of John Gilpin*. (In unmarked order, the line might be "He was eke [also] a train-band [militia] captain.")

not unreasonable to assume that this foregrounding function contributes to form-focused learning, and does so not in isolation, but as an integral part of a meaning construction activity—following the story or thoughts of the author. The momentary struggle with a marked form, which is faced by the hearer/reader in order to keep up with the story, "helps learners notice linguistic properties of the input they otherwise might not notice" (Ellis, 1995, p. 89). Or, as Hanauer explains Henry Widdowson's (1975) idea, "the de-familiarization of language used in poetry destabilizes the learners' familiar relation of words to world and sets them on a search for gaps in their own linguistic knowledge of the target language" (Hanauer, 2001, p. 298).

The point that should be taken from the benefits asserted above is not that literary texts are superior to everyday speech for language learning, but that, like everyday language, they provide a necessary complement to the contrived texts that are often presented to language learners (used to foreground a given learning point), adding interest by virtue of their authenticity and inventive foregrounding of forms. In addition, literary texts are actually easier to manage in a learning situation than naturally occurring interactions, which can and are used to provide exposure to everyday speech. There are issues of difficulty and the need for contextualisation (see below)—and these are issues with everyday speech as well—but as Kazuko Takahashi (2015) asserts, literary texts are, even if simplified and adapted, authentic materials, made by authors with non-instructive intentions for real audiences.

A prime advantage of theatrical texts, specifically, is that they are, self-evidently, extended examples of conversations, and (based on their popularity with real-world audiences) they are presumed capable of sustaining interest, and therefore immersive. This is still probably the most common argument made in their favour, as texts "that evoke familiar experiences but 're-present' them in a new light and with greater clarity" (Falvey & Kennedy, 1997, p. 2). While other arguments, such as authenticity and form-focus, can bolster the case for theatrical texts, this argument for their use—that learners will enjoy the conversations—remains key.

Empirical investigation of impressionistic claims of learner enjoyment is theoretically possible, but valid constructs are elusive and teacher-researcher bias is a conspicuous concern. Some research, moreover, suggests obstacles and challenges to the use of literary texts: with their vocabulary range, complexity, non-standard usages, and cultural references, they are difficult and potentially bewildering, and therefore not enjoyable (Edmonston, 1995; Hall, 2015; Martin & Laurie, 1993).

Against these cautions, there is some evidence for the positive effects of Readers' Theatre (RT; reading aloud of a story in parts, dramatised or not) in first language education, including improved attitudes to recreational reading (Smith, 2011) and greater expressiveness (Martinez et al., 1999). In additional language education, Muhammad Kabilan and Fadzliyati Kamaruddin (2010) noted enhanced learner understanding and increased interest and motivation to learn literature, while Carolyn La Von Bridges (2008) noted improved retelling skills. It is unclear if these effects are due to the use or appeal of literary texts, or to specific aspects of the activity of RT, i.e., repetitive reading aloud.

Repeated Aural/Oral Practice in Language Learning

Despite an association with non-meaningful drills, the beneficial effects of frequent repetition on the development of language processing are increasingly acknowledged. As Nick Ellis (2002) states, "much of language learning is the gradual strengthening of associations between co-occurring elements of the language and that fluent language performance is the exploitation of this probabilistic knowledge" (p. 173). The same researcher is quick to note, however, that conscious registration or noticing (Schmidt, 1990) as well as explicit instruction play important roles in initiating these associations. In the field of communicative language teaching (CLT) methodology also, it is recognised that repeated practice is desirable but often lacking.

Although one component of fluency is automatic, smooth, and rapid language use, there are no provisions in current CLT methodologies to promote language use to a high level of mastery through repetitive practice. In fact, focused practice continues to be seen as inimical to the inherently open and unpredictable nature of communicative activities (Gatbonton & Segalowitz, 2005).

Elizabeth Gatbonton and Norman Segalowitz (2005) urge that repetitive practice be incorporated, to improve automaticity, in a way that preserves the communicative nature of language use. Aural/oral practice with theatrical texts might aid in attaining this goal. There is some empirical backing for the idea that the lack of conscious concentration that often accompanies frequent repetition may have benefits. Studies at the Massachusetts Institute of Technology have suggested that overly conscious analysis of input and practice material can hinder acquisition of morphological patterns, while relying on procedural memory (developed through repetition) leads to better results (Massachusetts Institute of Technology, 2014).

Repetitive practice (rehearsing) with theatrical texts may be helpful in conscious learning as well, in assisting learners' noticing of linguistic features embedded in striking language usages, and providing opportunities for form-focused instruction and practice that are inherent in any first encounter with a conversation in a play. Over and above the benefits of literary foregrounding as outlined above, this kind of form-focused instruction (centred on a text) is integrated with later learning and practice activities (viz. conversations) that, in turn, resemble the conditions where the language is expected to be used, where the words and patterns need to be retrieved—a condition for what is known as *transfer appropriate processing* (Spada & Lightbown, 2008).

Further, the activity of repetitive practice, in and of itself, resembles the situations in which learners probably hope to use the skills they are gaining. Although the words "repetition" and "recitation" may bring to mind rather dull activities, there is much behaviour based on repetition that is central to participating in everyday conversation, which Deborah Tannen (1989) calls "involvement." As Geoff Hall (2015) paraphrases the idea, "repetition, 'echoing', representing the speech of others, . . . and other parallelisms [are present] in everyday conversation" (p. 34).

Positive effects of repetitive practice have been observed and reported. Miharu Fuyuno et al. (2014) observed a transfer of beneficial features of speaking (e.g., phrase stress, rhythm, and pauses) from practice on set recitation texts to spontaneous speaking skills. Motoko Ueyama (2017), similarly, noted that drama activities involving repeated practice improved Japanese learners' paralinguistic and prosodic proficiency. Some evidence from Readers' Theatre studies, in addition to the attitudinal effects noted above, suggest that repeated aural/oral practice leads to faster rates of reading aloud, fluidity, and phrasing (Bridges, 2008; Kabilan & Kamaruddin, 2010; Martinez et al., 1999). Similarly, Sandra Bidwell (1990), Jennifer McMaster (1998), and Timothy Rasinski (1988) cite research that demonstrates "that in order to develop fluency, students need opportunities for repeated reading of the same material" (McMaster, 1998, p. 578). The question for this study is whether using theatrical texts avoids the obvious pitfall of repetition identified by Jan Hulstijn (2001): "rereading or relistening to an old text will seldom be motivating to students because it does not contain any new information and therefore does not arouse their curiosity" (p. 283).

Effects Related to Dramatic Process or Performance

Dramatic investment (learners' attempts to think through, feel, and/or act out the mental and emotional states of the characters) is likely to attend any aural/oral practice with theatrical texts, and, although there is no attempt in this study to observe the effects of such investment, some of the intuited and attested benefits are summarised here.

Drama activities are said to facilitate individual contributions to the learning environment, develop social competences, and enhance affective responses to learning (Dubois & Tremblay, 2015; Maley & Duff, 2005). Dramatisation, or simply pairing language with physical activity, aids in the internalisation of prosodic features (Dubrac, 2013), and "physical activity and emotional involvement . . . can lead to improved retention of language structures and vocabulary" (Giebert, 2014, pp. 141–142). Thus, practice with drama can lead to richer, more varied vocabulary (MacFadden, 2010).

There are also attested improvements in terms of psychological attitude—namely, students' perceived gains in self-confidence, spontaneity, and self-expression (Stern, 1983). Many have observed enhanced prosodic proficiency (e.g., Dubrac, 2013; Fuyuno et al., 2014; Ueyama, 2017) and heightened linguistic awareness (McMaster, 1998; O'Gara, 2008). Overall, drama appears to foster holistic and durable learning through physical and emotional involvement and reduces psychological obstacles to learning. Again, however, one must keep in mind that studies of the effects of drama have been conducted by teacher-researchers with an affinity for theatre and therefore susceptible to bias.

Learning Across the Curriculum through Theatrical Texts

Detailed consideration of the noted benefits of theatrical texts for content learning is beyond the scope of this chapter. Having said that, three general advantages can be stated and a brief illustration given of how theatrical material has been used by the author in a course on business communication.

The first advantage is that when theatre draws attention to relevant concepts in world cultural history (features of culture and their strengths, issues, and problems), it is through the experiences of the characters. Learning from these texts, then, is visceral as well as intellectual; the text is a way of gaining experience, not learning about experience. The second is that literature enables authentic participation in culture. In a CLIL framework, "an artistic activity paired with a language activity will allow the student to develop a multitude of competences, for example, to exercise his/her critical judgement, to display his/her creative thinking, and to communicate appropriately" (Dubois & Tremblay, 2015, p. 132; my translation). When using a theatrical text that is an authentic element of the culture, readers or reciters are, in Mikhail Bakhtin's (1981) formulation, taking part in discourse, in the ongoing conversations of others, through their encounter with the text, then by "expropriating it, forcing it to submit to one's own intentions and accounts" (p. 294). A third point is that intercultural diffusion through literature (such as reading theatrical pieces from a variety of cultures in English) is not in any way bizarre, but is rather a very commonplace condition. Itamar Even-Zohar (1978/2012) notes the disproportionately significant contributions of peripheral texts to most cultural milieux, while Claire Kramsch (1997) attests to the "thrill in trespassing [on] someone else's territory" (p. 256) which accompanies reading as a nonnative.

Specifically, the author has previously had success using theatrical texts to spur reflection on business communication strategies in a course for undergraduate university students. A scene from Molière's *The Imaginary Invalid*, where a doctor is seeking to take charge of a new patient, serves as an example of framing a meeting—including managing perceptions of self, business partner, and meeting objectives—through situational arrangements and speech patterns. The famous scene in Shakespeare's *The Merchant of Venice* of a borrower and lender deciding the terms of a loan was used to show differing ways of managing a position in a negotiation—pressing for response, redirecting attention, and keeping a fall-back position. In contrast to prescriptive teaching of strategies for the various stages of business communication, students were encouraged to work out their own guiding principles as they considered the effects of differing personalities and strategies on the outcomes of the scene, and to apply those principles to situations that are nearer at hand.

The Teaching Practice

Rationale

In view of the promising concurrences between theatrical texts and CLIL learning noted above—that they provide authentic, meaningful, and integrated form-focused learning of content and language, that occasional marked or inventive wordings assist the learner in noticing form-function relationships (grammar-meaning and pragmatics-use relationships), and that interest sustained by the text enables repeated aural/oral practice—a teaching practice utilising play excerpts was imagined. The essence of this method is encouraging fascination and therefore repeated practice with the texts, and so the preparation of the texts, as learning materials, is a crucial step. By careful excerpting and by translation/adaptation, the materials sought to demystify texts that contained unfamiliar registers or cultural references, and explicit instruction of some cultural concepts and linguistic features was included to show how meanings in a story are developed in a theatrical text. The instructor also made clear to learners the underlying assumption that interest sustained by the text enables and encourages repeated practice, even to the point, if learners were to "buy in" to the method, of developing familiarity and automaticity with the text sufficient for a polished performance.

While there was no intention to play down the importance of dramatic activities in drawing out learners' intrinsic resources and motivation (Maley & Duff, 2005), the present focus is directed elsewhere, namely, onto how the use of lively theatrical texts themselves enables or enhances the content to be learned/discussed, grammatical awareness, and prosodic features/patterns to be practised. Nonetheless, the teaching practice takes seriously the idea (suggested by Giebert, 2014 and others) that physical activity can help words and patterns be retained, not merely as isolated mental abstractions but as ingrained parts of the learner's physical routines and emotional temperament. Such physical activity may include moving, gesturing, as well as articulating stress, rhythm, and intonation, together with even moderate emotional involvement with repeated rehearsal of a part.

To summarise, when viewed within a CLIL framework, a teaching practice based on theatrical texts is proposed to have the following specific advantages.

As language learning materials, theatrical texts are engaging models of sustained spoken interactions,

- providing practice in hearing and noticing the phonetic and prosodic patterns of conversational English speech;
- motivating learners to practice producing natural English prosody—stress, rhythm, and intonation patterns; and
- (through the above practice) raising awareness about grammar/meaning and pragmatics/use relationships, and their relationships to prosodic patterns (e.g., stress, breath/intonation groups).

As resources for content learning, theatrical texts serve as spurs to learning through the examination of the play's cultural background, supporting a content syllabus covering world cultural history topics (including those such as slavery, roles of women/men, and attitudes towards medicine and science) and the development and role of theatre itself.

Deployment in Learning Environments

Following the adaptation or translation of texts for readers of multicultural backgrounds and the conception of learning points germane to the texts, a series of seven workshop-format lessons were developed. At the time of writing, four have been implemented.

The learning environments are (i) an undergraduate CLIL course for English-language majors at a Japanese university, entitled *World Cultural*

History through Theatre, Poems, and Speeches (~10 students), (ii) an English Listening skills course at the same university (~35 students), and (iii) an elective workshop series at an Australian university (~15 participants). In these venues, the theatrical texts are deployed (with background material and discussion activities, and with audio recordings—commercially available, public domain, or recorded as part of this project) in a series of learning activities. These activities are selected, sequenced, and recycled to suit the needs in each learning environment, and include:

- listening tasks (holistic and focused; with and without bi-modal reading accompaniment);
- shadowing and reading aloud;
- comprehension checks and meaning-focused explanations to repair comprehension gaps;
- practice in producing English prosodic patterns of stress, rhythm, and intonation;
- analysis and translation of repeated and/or pivotal lines in the text, and highlighting of relationships between prosody and grammar/pragmatics;
- rehearsed recitation and (quasi-)improvised performance; and
- group performances of excerpts with introductory and debriefing presentations dealing with the cultural contexts of the excerpts.

The activities put more focus on form (verbal, phrasal, and prosodic form) than there is commonly in Readers' Theatre. This was evidenced in more repetition and varied modes of practice, and activities aimed at noticing grammatical patterns and their relation to prosody. With such balanced emphases on form, meaning, and context, on listening ability and spoken production, than from one macro-activity (i.e., practice centred on the theatrical text), all the desiderata of regular and frequent repetition of input, meaning focus, and integrated form focus can feasibly be achieved.

Evaluation of the Practice

Summary of Data Collected

As the teaching practice is implemented, its effectiveness is being evaluated by a variety of qualitative probes and quasi-quantitative measures.

Qualitative

- real-time learner response (observations noted by researcher directly after each session)

- attitudes towards content and language learning through theatrical texts (probed by questionnaires modelled on Norton & Vanderheyden [2004]; see Appendix B)
- gains in content and language learning through theatrical texts (probed by questionnaires)

Quasi-Quantitative

- time spent practising language (measured by anonymous wide-angle classroom video)
- changes in listening comprehension level (measured by discrete item and integrative tests) and spoken production ability (measured by a recitation rubric)

At the time of writing, some of the qualitative data have been collected and analysed. The most significant findings are briefly reported below.

Real-Time Learner Response

Some of the observations of real-time learner response showed the benefits of participants perceiving and grappling with language features in the context of repetitive practice with theatrical texts. In an episode during the meaning-focused (story-focused) instruction phase with the author's adaptation of a scene from *Romeo and Juliet*, the underlined clause below caused some confusion.

Mother:	*(entering)* Juliet, are you up?
Juliet:	*(surprised)* Oh, mother. Yes, madam. I am not well.
Mother:	Are you sad about your cousin's death, Or that <u>the villain lives that killed him</u>?
Juliet:	What villain, madam?

A wording of the line that conforms to basic sentence patterns might be "the villain that killed him lives" (with the relative clause "that killed him" adjacent to the head noun "the villain"), and this wording might be less challenging for learners. However, as the relative clause is easily distinguished as a unit prosodically (as an intonation-breath group), the line was translated in a way that preserved the displaced relative clause of the original, with the objective that the challenge of comprehension would help to enhance learners' grammatical sensitivity (namely, here, to seek antecedents for relative clauses).³ Therefore, learners were told that "In poetry and song the phrases sometimes move around. Listen and look for the words that are related in meaning." In this way, as was asserted by Widdowson (1975) and by Hanauer (2001), de-familiarisation through poetry destabilised learners "and set them on a search for gaps" in their understanding, possibly leading to more retentive learning.

In the questionnaire responses, learners explicitly stated that searching for ways of understanding a text is aided by the practice of hearing and producing the prosodic features of the text, indicating that they were aware of the importance of prosody in revealing grammar/meaning and pragmatics/use relationships.

Attitudes towards Content and Language Learning through Theatrical Texts

In the questionnaires, students in the CLIL course and the listening skills course self-reported that they spent more time directly engaged in aural and oral practice than they had in previous comparable learning situations. This impression awaits corroboration from the wide-angle classroom video, but is plausible, due to the nature of the activities, most of which require repeated work (analysis or practice) with texts that are longer than those usually found in language learning materials, and appear to be capable of sustaining interest.

Gains in Content and Language Learning through Theatrical Texts

In the questionnaire responses after a session practising a scene from Lorraine Hansberry's *A Raisin in the Sun*, learners reported on the impact the sessions had regarding content and language. In the early familiarisation tasks (listening, shadowing, and comprehension checks), the lines that attracted attention during practice and the lines that were remembered verbatim after practice were those that contained exceptions to basic grammatical language patterns (of the type that might be used in learning materials), as underlined below:

> Beneatha: Oh I like George all right, Mama. <u>I mean</u> I like
> him enough to go out with him <u>and stuff</u>, but—

---

3   The line in Shakespeare's original has a similarly displaced relative clause:
    LADY CAPULET: Well, girl, thou weep'st not so much for his death,
    As that the villain lives that slaughtered him.

Ruth: What does *and stuff* mean?

Beneatha: Mind your own business.

Mama: Stop picking at her, Ruth.

Beneatha: Oh, I just mean I couldn't ever really be serious about George. He's so shallow.

Ruth: Shallow–<u>what do you mean</u> he's shallow? He's rich!

A feature that these remembered lines share is that they were prosodically distinguished from the rest of the conversation, which suggests that repeated listenings and training in prosodic awareness may be assisting in the identification and comprehension of these phrases.

If we turn our attention to content learning, which for this text was focused on the culture and perceptions of African Americans in the US, it was clear that learners also showed sensitivity to the cultural questions raised by characters' words and actions without direction from the instructor. Several lines in the text prompted learners to make independent observations or pose questions. Some comments revealing learners' responses to cultural aspects from the play are listed below:

"Daughter argues hardly [strongly] with Mama."

"Beneatha wants to be free, to go out, to experience."

"Mama said 'God willing!' a lot."

"Mama was afraid of god."

"Beneatha thinks follow God or not follow God is decide[d] yourself."

In response to this play excerpt, learners also perceived in the text (of characters or implied by the author) attitudes relating to slavery, to religious freedom, and to arranged marriages.

Conclusion

These preliminary findings illustrate that there is promise for the idea of using theatrical texts as a basis for Content and Language Integrated Learning. Several concrete effects can plausibly be attributed to the special conditions entailed by engagement with theatrical texts.

- More time was spent engaged in aural/oral learning in the target language—due perhaps to interest being sufficiently sustained for extended and repeated analysis and practice.
- Linguistic patterns were noticed in their prosodic form, assisting with their retention—due perhaps to the primary mode of reception of these texts being aural/oral.
- Unfamiliar linguistic patterns were comprehended inductively, with and without assistance by the instructor—due perhaps to the de-stabilising effect of marked poetic patterns, and to greater attention to aural/oral prosodic form.
- Content learning points (aspects of cultural history) were observed independently, without indication by instructors—due perhaps to sheer fascination with the theatrical texts.

Quantitative evaluative measures and further qualitative findings are anticipated and will be reported in a subsequent study.

References

Bakhtin, M. M. (1981). Discourse in the novel (C. Emerson & M. Holquist, Trans.). In M. Holquist (Ed.), *The dialogic imagination: Four essays by M. M. Bakhtin* (pp. 259–422). University of Texas Press.

Biber, D. & Conrad, S. (2009). *Register, genre, and style*. Cambridge University Press.

Bidwell, S. M. (1990). Using drama to increase motivation, comprehension, and fluency. *Journal of Reading, 34*(1), 38–41.

Bridges, C. L. (2008). Effects of readers' theatre on English language learners: A strategy for oral language and reading improvement. *TNTESOL Journal, 1,* 20–29.

Brumfit, C. & Carter, R. (1986). *Literature and language teaching*. Oxford University Press.

Carter, R. & McCarthy, M. (1995). Discourse and creativity: Bridging the gap between language and literature. In G. Cook & B. Seidlhofer (Eds.), *Principle and practice in applied linguistics: Studies in honour of H. G. Widdowson* (pp. 303–322). Oxford University Press.

Dubois, J. & Tremblay, O. (2015). L'enseignement par le théâtre en classe de français au Québec: État des lieux et pistes didactiques. *Lidil. Revue de linguistique et de didactique des langues, (52),* 129–152.

Dubrac, A. L. (2013, July 8). *Using theatre techniques in the language classroom* [Conference presentation]. 8th Drama and Education IDEA World Conference, Paris.

Edmonston, W. (1995). The role of literature in foreign language learning and teaching: Some valid assumptions and invalid arguments. *AILA Review, 12,* 42–55.

Ellis, N. C. (2002). Frequency effects in language processing: A review with implications for theories of implicit and explicit language acquisition. *Studies in Second Language Acquisition, 24*(2), 143–188.

Ellis, R. (1995). Interpretation tasks for grammar teaching. *TESOL Quarterly, 29*(1), 87–105.

Even-Zohar, I. (2012). The position of translated literature within the literary polysystem. In L. Venuti (Ed.), *The translation studies reader* (pp. 199–204). Routledge. (Original work published 1978)

Falvey, P. & Kennedy, P. (1997). *Learning language through literature: A sourcebook for teachers of English in Hong Kong*. Hong Kong University Press.

Fuyuno, M., Hama, N., Myall, J. & Yukimaru, N. (2014). Effects of the experience of English recitation on Japanese EFL learners: Towards multi-modal English speaking skills education. *Annual Review of Language Learning and Teaching, 4*, 15–28.

Gatbonton, E. & Segalowitz, N. (2005). Rethinking communicative language teaching: A focus on access to fluency. *Canadian Modern Language Review, 61*(3), 325–353.

Giebert, S. (2014). Drama and theatre in teaching foreign languages for professional purposes. *Recherche et Pratiques Pédagogiques En Langues de Spécialité. Cahiers de l'Apliut, XXXIII*(1), 138–150.

Hall, G. (2015). *Literature in language education*. Palgrave Macmillan.

Hanauer, D. I. (2001). The task of poetry reading and second language learning. *Applied Linguistics, 22*(3), 295–323.

Hulstijn, J. H. (2001). Intentional and incidental second language vocabulary learning: A reappraisal of elaboration, rehearsal and automaticity. In P. Robinson (Ed.), *Cognition and second language instruction* (pp. 258–286). Cambridge University Press.

Ishihara, T. & Ono, A. (2015). The effects of literary texts on students' sentence recognition: Translation tasks and comprehension tasks. In M. Teranishi, Y. Saito & K. Wales (Eds.), *Literature and language learning in the EFL classroom* (pp. 140–150). Palgrave Macmillan.

Kabilan, M. K. & Kamaruddin, F. (2010). Engaging learners' comprehension, interest and motivation to learn literature using the reader's theatre. *English Teaching: Practice and Critique, 9*(3), 132–159.

Kao, S.-M. & O'Neill, C. (1998). *Words into worlds: Learning a second language through process drama*. Ablex.

Kramsch, C. (1997). Guest column: The privilege of the nonnative speaker. *PMLA, 112*(3), 359–369.

Leech, G. N. (1969). *A linguistic guide to English poetry*. Longman.

MacFadden, P. (2010). *Using theatre arts to enhance literacy skills at the second grade level* [Doctoral dissertation, University of California, Irvine and University of California, Los Angeles]. ProQuest. https://search.proquest.com/docview/822194466.

Maley, A. & Duff, A. (2005). *Drama techniques: A resource book of communication activities for language teachers* (3rd ed.). Cambridge University Press.

Martin, A. L. & Laurie, I. (1993). Student views about the contribution of literary and cultural content to language learning at intermediate level. *Foreign Language Annals, 26*(2), 188–207.

Martinez, M., Roser, N. L. & Strecker, S. (1999). "I never thought I could be a star": A reader's theatre ticket to fluency. *The Reading Teacher, 52*(4), 326–334.

Massachusetts Institute of Technology. (2014, July 21). *Try, try again? Study says no: Trying harder makes it more difficult to learn some aspects of language, neuroscientists find*. ScienceDaily. https://www.sciencedaily.com/releases/2014/07/140721142211.htm.

McMaster, J. C. (1998). "Doing" literature: Using drama to build literacy. *The Reading Teacher, 51*(7), 574–584.

Norton, B. & Vanderheyden, K. (2004). Comic book culture and second language learners. In B. Norton & K. Toohey (Eds.), *Critical pedagogies and language learning* (pp. 201–221). Cambridge University Press.

O'Gara, P. (2008). To be or have not been: Learning language tenses through drama. *Issues in Educational Research, 18*(2), 156–166.

Rasinski, T. (1988). Making repeated readings a functional part of classroom reading instruction. *Reading Horizons, 28*(4), 250–254.

Schmidt, R. W. (1990). The role of consciousness in second language learning. *Applied Linguistics, 11*(2), 129–158. https://doi.org/10.1093/applin/11.2.129.

Smith, D. M. (2011). *Readers theatre: Its effectiveness in improving reading fluency, student motivation, and attitudes toward reading among second-grade students* [Doctoral dissertation, The Pennsylvania State University]. Penn State Electronic Theses and Dissertations for Graduate School. https://etda.libraries.psu.edu/catalog/12019.

Spada, N. & Lightbown, P. (2008). Form-focused instruction: Isolated or integrated? *TESOL Quarterly, 42*(2), 181–207.

Stern, S. L. (1983). Why drama works: A psycholinguistic perspective. In J. Oller & P. Richard-Amato (Eds.), *Methods that work* (pp. 207–225). Newberry House.

Takahashi, K. (2015). Literary texts as authentic materials for language learning: The current situation in Japan. In M. Teranishi, Y. Saito & K. Wales (Eds.), *Literature and language learning in the EFL classroom* (pp. 26–40). Palgrave Macmillan.

Tannen, D. (1989). *Talking voices: Repetition, dialogue, and imagery in conversational discourse*. Cambridge University Press.

Teranishi, M., Saito, Y. & Wales, K. (Eds.). (2015). *Literature and language learning in the EFL classroom*. Palgrave Macmillan.

Ueyama, M. (2017). Sougouteki komyunikeeyson nouryoku wo mezasita nihongo onsei kyouiku: Italia ni okeru nihongo engeki katudou no jissen kara [Japanese phonetic instruction aimed at comprehensive communication ability: Implementing Japanese language drama activities in Italy]. *Nihongo onsei komyunikeesyon [Japanese Phonetic Communication], 5*, 35–70.

Widdowson, H. G. (1975). *Stylistics and the teaching of literature*. Longman.

Appendix A: List of Source Materials Used

Plautus, *Mostellaria (The Ghost)*, c. 200 BCE
William Shakespeare, *Romeo and Juliet*, c. 1594–96

William Shakespeare, *The Merchant of Venice*, c. 1596–97
Molière, *Le Malade Imaginaire* (*The Imaginary Invalid*), 1673
Miyazawa Kenji, *Tsuchigami to Kitsune* (*Earthgod and Fox*), 1934
Lorraine Hansberry, *A Raisin in the Sun*, 1959

Appendix B: List of Questions Probing Content and Language Learning through the Theatrical Text *A Raisin in the Sun*

The language of the text:

[*While answering this question, don't look at the script. Don't worry: it's not a test.*]

Do you remember any lines? If so, write them here, as well as you can remember.

- _____
- _____
- _____
- _____
- _____

[*You can look at the script again now. But don't change the lines you wrote above.*]

Were some lines difficult for you? If so, write the difficult lines or phrases here. (You can also add a comment about why they were difficult if you like.)

- _____
- _____
- _____
- _____
- _____

Your character:
- What character (role) did you play?
- What did your character want?
- What did your character fear?

What did you learn about the world?
- What is interesting about the world of *A Raisin in the Sun**?
(*African-American Chicago, 1950s, 60s)
- What was strange or different* about this scene?
(*if you compare it to your world & your life?)
- What about this scene was the same, or similar, to your life?

Your experience:
- Did you enjoy reading this scene? (no! 1 2 3 4 5 yes!)
- Did you enjoy listening & shadowing to this scene? (no! 1 2 3 4 5 yes!)
- Did you enjoy speaking this scene? (no! 1 2 3 4 5 yes!)
- Would you like to use theatrical texts again?
- Do you think using this theatrical text was helpful in learning English? Why or why not?
- Do you think using this theatrical text was helpful in learning about the culture of another time and place? Why or why not?

Section Three. Writing Across the Curriculum

11 WAC and Critical Thinking: Exploring Productive Relationships

Mike Palmquist
COLORADO STATE UNIVERSITY

> Abstract: Writing across the curriculum (WAC) activities are often characterized as useful strategies for enhancing student learning. In this chapter, WAC activities are considered as critical thinking activities. Drawing on Bloom's taxonomy of cognitive skills as modified by Anderson and Krathwohl (2001), three types of WAC activities are described—writing to learn, writing to engage, and writing to communicate—in terms of how they can contribute to both language learning and disciplinary learning.
>
> Keywords: writing across the curriculum, critical thinking, writing to engage, writing to learn, writing in the disciplines, writing to communicate

I began thinking about writing across the curriculum (WAC) in 1987, when I took a graduate seminar on WAC with Richard Young at Carnegie Mellon University.[1] A few years later, almost immediately after I began to work as an assistant professor at Colorado State University, I was drawn into a WAC initiative that focused on how best to implement WAC at a research-intensive university. Our inquiry had been prompted by the realization that our colleagues in other disciplines—and in particular in engineering, where we were then focusing our efforts—understood why they should use writing to support learning and teaching in their courses, but nonetheless chose not to do so. Essentially, our colleagues were telling us, "Yes, morally and ethically, I know I should use writing in my courses. It would be good for them." Still, they would go on to say, "But I don't have the time to do it."

We took this kind of resistance to WAC as a good sign, as a potential opportunity to address the root causes that led to it. We were not alone in

---

[1] This chapter is adapted from the opening keynote at the EAC Conference. By looking at the ways in which writing-across-the-curriculum (WAC) activities intersect with critical thinking activities, I invited listeners to consider the ideas outlined as a framework for examining how WAC activities are structured.

DOI: https://doi.org/10.37514/INT-B.2021.1220.2.11

viewing it in this way. A rich literature on faculty resistance to innovation exists, and there was already, even at that point, only twenty years after WAC had emerged as a higher-education movement, a substantial amount of scholarship about faculty resistance to WAC (see, for example, Couch, 1989; Kaufer & Young, 1993; McLeod & Soven, 1992/2000; and Swanson-Owens, 1986). As a result, since that time, my colleagues and I at Colorado State University have consistently viewed the local context in which we work as the starting point for our discussions of how to reduce the resistance to WAC we encountered among our colleagues in other disciplines.[2] Those discussions, in turn, have led us to explore the connections between writing and critical thinking.

Viewing Writing and Speaking as Transformative Acts

There are many reasons why writing and critical thinking are related. Among them is the role writing plays in assessing learning. In most cases, when we ask someone to demonstrate that they have engaged in critical thinking, we do not use multiple-choice exams. We do it through some sort of performance, often one that involves writing or speaking. We ask people to talk to us about what they are thinking, or we ask them to write it down.

A more important reason is that writing and speaking are transformative acts. Long ago, when my life revolved around competitive running, I gave a series of talks to the American Lung Association Running Club in Minneapolis, Minnesota. The members of the club had suffered heart attacks or some other sort of cardiovascular setback, and they had decided that running was a way to regain their health. The first time I talked with them, I stumbled through my talk. I felt foolish. Running was something I knew well. I was a college track and cross country coach. I was a successful competitive runner. I was part owner of a chain of running stores. But I could not talk clearly about it right away—at least, not for that audience. Later, my talks improved, and I was able to talk about running almost as well as I could do it.

During my graduate studies, I learned why I had struggled to talk about running, something I knew so well. Drawing on the work of Marlene Scardamalia and Carl Bereiter (1987), I began to see writing and speaking as rhetorical acts that involve the transformation of knowledge for a particular audience.

---

2   My thinking about WAC was shaped initially by the work I did with Richard Young, then by my colleagues Kate Kiefer, Dawn Rodrigues, and Don Zimmerman, and later by my colleagues Donna LeCourt, Nick Carbone, Sarah Sloane, and Sue Doe. They stand out among many others for their generosity and thoughtfulness. And since then, of course, I have benefited from extensive conversations with members of the WAC Clearinghouse editorial board and the larger WAC community.

Essentially, as you adapt your message for a particular audience, as you transform your knowledge in ways that allow them to understand your thinking, you engage in an act of cognitive change—a kind of critical thinking. My sense then and now is that, because it involves the thoughtful transformation of knowledge for a particular audience, writing is itself an act of critical thinking.[3]

Faculty in the disciplines at that time seemed to think, and even now some might say, "That's nonsense. Writing and speaking are just the presentation of knowledge." Yet that act of transformation—that act of critical thinking—is central to what we do as teachers of writing, and this has long been recognized by scholars in the WAC community, such as Sue McLeod (1988/2000; McLeod & Maimon, 2000; McLeod et al., 2001), John Bean (1996, 2011), Bill Condon 2001; Condon & Kelly-Riley, 2004; Condon & Rutz, 2012), Marty Townsend (2001; Townsend & Zawacki, 2013), Christine Farris (Farris et al., 1990), and Chris Anson (Anderson et al., 2015, 2016; Anson, 2017; Rutz, 2004), among many others. When we talk about writing in the disciplines, or speaking in the disciplines (the kind of speaking that typically involves prepared presentation or debates or more deliberate kinds of communication), we are talking about transforming knowledge in ways that other people can understand. And through that act of transformation, writers and speakers will come to understand their knowledge and personal experience more deeply themselves.

I would extend this discussion of transforming knowledge into how my thinking about writing across the curriculum has changed over the years. In the United States, when we talk about WAC, we focus on two major approaches: writing to learn and writing in the disciplines, which is sometimes referred to as writing to communicate. As I began to explore WAC and critical thinking many years ago, I felt that those two approaches were not sufficient to explain the different things we can do with writing in our classrooms. Eventually, I came to think of a third—a middle way—I have been learning a little bit of Mandarin Chinese, so it seems appropriate to talk about a middle way: *writing to engage*. Engagement is connection—in this case, connection to knowledge and to the sharing of that knowledge with others; it is transactional.

Understanding and Rising to the Challenge: WAC and Critical Thinking

Since 1991, I have been involved in a range of efforts at Colorado State University to encourage faculty to think about how they can improve their

---

3   I am focusing on writing when I think of critical thinking because it is typically a deliberate and thoughtful act. Speaking can spur us to think critically, but it does not always do so.

teaching and their students' learning.[4] Like most universities in the US, we have worked through the shift from a focus on delivering information during class sessions to trying to do more to engage students during class. This kind of change can take time and, as is the case with many colleges and universities, we have more progress to make. The reasons for this are fairly straightforward and are particularly pressing at research-intensive institutions. In a nutshell, we expect our faculty members to publish, to teach well, to generate funding, to perform service for the university and the profession, and to engage with the local and regional communities we serve.

That is, we expect a great deal. And perhaps we expect too much. If we are to continue to improve teaching and learning, we need to help faculty members adopt strategies that lead to improved pedagogical outcomes without imposing additional burdens. My experience leading teaching and learning efforts at my institution has helped me understand that we can accomplish this by focusing on critical thinking. Simply put, our faculty members—and I think this is typically the case at many institutions in the US and internationally—often view the development of strong critical thinking skills as one of their most important teaching goals.

This understanding is where I began to view the connections between critical thinking and writing as not only the key to reducing resistance to WAC but also as a central part of our efforts to improve teaching and learning. As I noted earlier, the idea that writing is intimately related to critical thinking is perhaps as old as WAC itself. Indeed, it would take several pages to list all of the people who have talked about writing and critical thinking since Barbara Walvoord offered the first WAC seminar in the 1969–70 academic year. That connection, however, tends to be understood in idiosyncratic, often deeply personal terms. Each of us seems to have a slightly different understanding of what critical thinking is and how we can best encourage it. And that is perfectly fine, viewed in a general sense. As I continued to reflect on the connections between writing and critical thinking, however, it seemed as though we could improve both our understanding of those connections and how we shared that understanding with our colleagues across the disciplines so that they, in turn, could engage their students more fully in the learning process.

I began my exploration of the connections between writing and critical thinking by considering what have become traditional reasons to use WAC

---

4   In addition to my work with WAC and writing program administration, I've served as the founding director of our Institute for Learning and Teaching, director of our online and distance learning division, and as Associate Provost for Instructional Innovation.

WAC and Critical Thinking

pedagogies: to help students learn, to improve communication skills, and to prepare students for careers and civic life. But I realized that there were other reasons to adopt WAC. This emerged from my work with faculty on curriculum development and course design (see Figure 11.1). One of the primary goals we shared with faculty members was to *challenge* students. Creating a written document or preparing a presentation, we told them, takes much more effort –and typically results in far deeper learning—than cramming for a multiple-choice exam. A second goal we encouraged them to pursue was to *engage* students with their courses. We asked, for example, "How can we get students to do things that are related to the course, that get them involved in the content of the course, that get them thinking about the approaches and methods used in their disciplines or professions?"

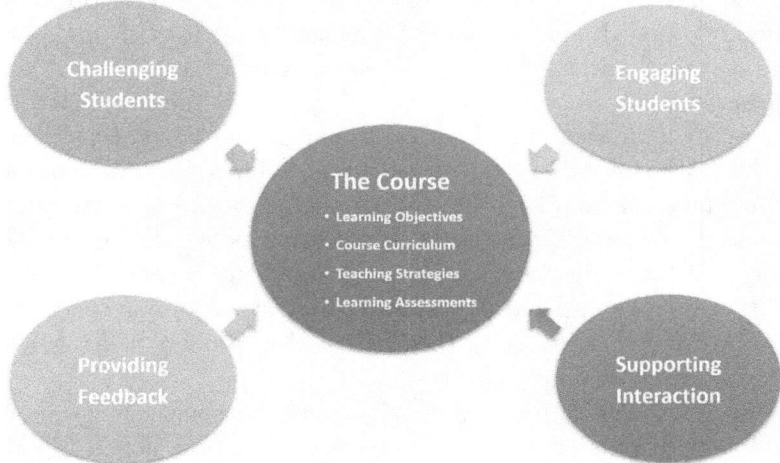

Figure 11.1. Additional reasons to use WAC.

Our third and fourth goals, *supporting interaction* with classmates and instructors and *providing instructor feedback* on student work, were equally important in our curriculum development and course design efforts. To support student efforts to meet the challenges we set for them and to help them engage more deeply with the course, we need to help them work and share their ideas with other students them. And to help them understand how they are performing in the course, we need to provide them with regular and timely feedback.

With this in mind, my colleagues and I at Colorado State University, a group that included Kate Kiefer and Sue Doe, began to think about WAC as a lever for helping our faculty reconsider how we taught and how our students learned. In turn, our focus on WAC became deeply implicated in our efforts to support the development of curricula that engaged students in critical thinking.

Drawing on Critical Thinking Traditions

As I thought about the connections between critical thinking and writing, I began to consider the question of which critical thinking framework to employ. In part because so many of my colleagues across the disciplines were aware of it and in part because of its frequent use by the course designers with whom I was working, I was drawn most strongly to Benjamin Bloom's Taxonomy of Cognitive Objectives as modified by Lorin Anderson and David Krathwohl (2001). This is a robust framework within which to approach critical thinking. It is also one of the main sources of the idea of "higher order" and "lower order" critical thinking skills (see Figure 11.2).

Certainly, other important approaches exist, and they have had strong effects on my understanding of critical thinking. Jean Piaget (1936) and Lev Vygotsky (1978, 1987) have offered influential developmental frameworks. William Perry (1970, 1981) has offered an interesting but often-criticized scheme that aligns individuals with various epistemological positions. Patricia King and Karen Kitchener (1994) have developed a reflective judgment model that is intriguing and powerful. And we can also look to the various conceptions of critical thinking that are based in problem-solving, as John Bean (1996, 2011) has done in his books.

In my work with curriculum development and course design, however, I have found Bloom's taxonomy to be particularly useful. When Bloom was working with his colleagues, he developed terms that reflected a highly conceptual approach to cognitive activities, terms such as *knowledge, comprehension*, and *synthesis*, among others. When Lorin Anderson, who was one of Bloom's students, began to work with the taxonomy, he used verbs to shift the focus from naming to action. The modified taxonomy asks questions such as: Can you *remember* what you just read? Can you *understand* what you have read or experienced? Can you take a theoretical framework that you understood and *apply* it to a real-world situation or a text? Could you take that situation apart, break it down into its bits, and *analyze* it? Could you *evaluate* something? Can you *create* something new? The result of Anderson's work is a more accessible set of terms that describe general classes of cognitive activities (see Figure 11.2) that not only engage students but also can be observed and measured.

After some thought, I modified it again to include an important aspect of the composing process: reflecting (see Figure 11.3).

WAC and Critical Thinking

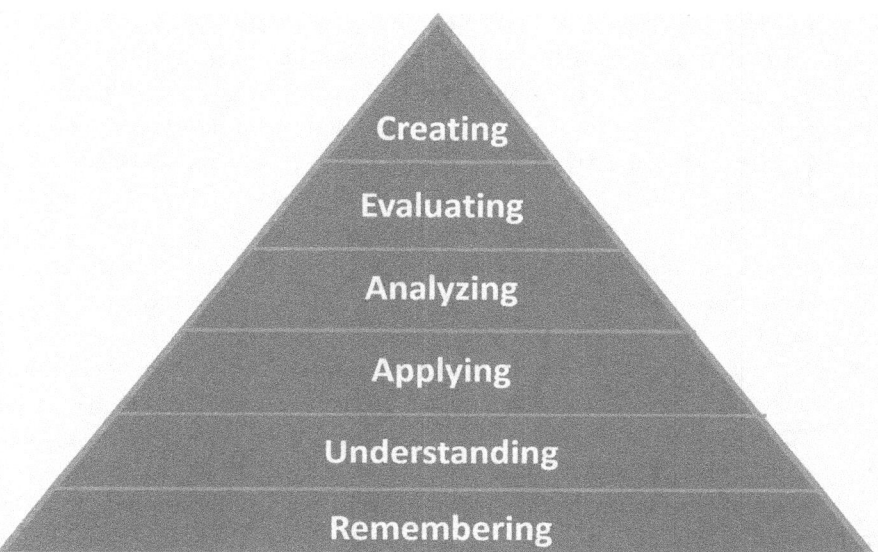

Figure 11.2. Bloom's taxonomy as modified by Anderson and Krathwohl (2001).

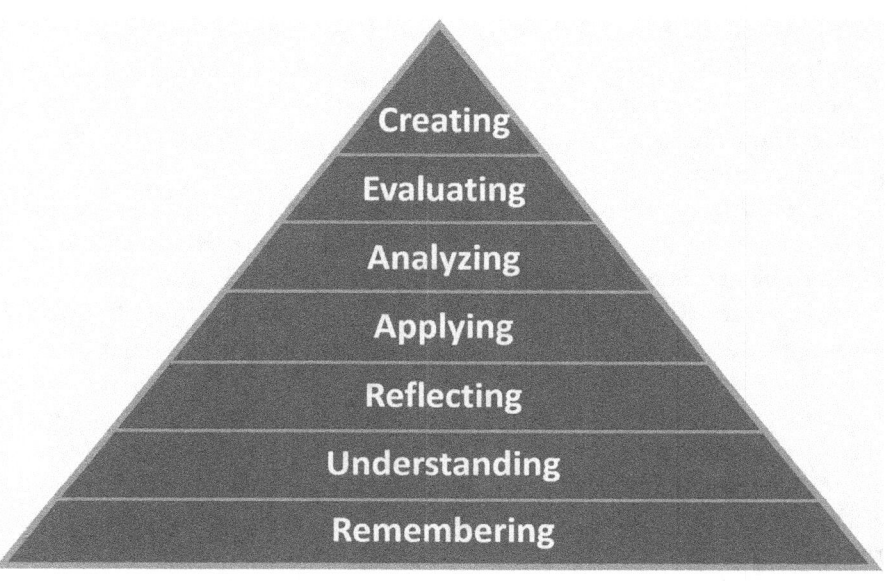

Figure 11.3. Bloom's taxonomy, modified to include the critical-thinking skill reflecting.

I find this list of terms useful. Sometimes, for instance, we assign work to students that is far more complex and demanding than we had intended. Perhaps, like me, you have found yourself thinking, "They just didn't get it." And perhaps this thought is followed by the realization that you've designed an assignment or examination that would challenge even an expert. We can address situations like these by thinking carefully about the kinds of critical thinking we want our students to engage in at a given point in a course. Doing so allows us to design learning experiences that are in line with the knowledge they have gained in the course so far and the kinds of thinking processes we want them to understand and control. We can ask, for example, whether our goal is to help students commit information to memory, to understand a concept, or to get to the point where they can explain their knowledge to somebody else, as we might do if we were drawing on Scardamalia and Bereiter's (1987) idea of knowledge transformation.

Certainly, as with any framework, we can identify problems with Bloom's taxonomy. Despite presenting it as a taxonomy—a set of categories—it signals a hierarchy, one that has led to the popular idea of lower- and higher-order thinking skills. And that hierarchy, at least in Western cultures, carries with it an implied value judgment. I find this problematic, and it is certainly worthy of careful thought. We might ask, for example, whether it is always the case that engaging in a "higher-order" thinking skill (for example, creating something) is more important than engaging in a "lower-order" thinking skill (for example, acquiring knowledge or working to understand something). For teachers and students, I suspect, the answers to questions such as these are heavily dependent on the teaching and learning goals in a particular course.

As teachers, we should view these activities not as if one leads inevitably to the next—although they often build on one another—but rather as a set of thinking activities that we engage in at different points as we learn and then use what we have learned. We should also consider the roles these activities might play in a particular learning situation. For example, our teaching goals in an introductory chemistry course would most likely focus on helping students remember and begin to understand core concepts and perhaps start to apply them. In a more advanced upper-division chemistry course, in contrast, we would probably want our students to engage in analyzing, evaluating, and perhaps creating. Both courses would be challenging, but because the second builds on the first, the nature of the challenge would differ. Notably, the "higher-order" thinking skills required in the advanced course would be impossible, in any meaningful sense, if students could not remember and understand the underlying concepts and processes they learned in the introductory course. It is also worth noting that even advanced students who are already engaging in higher-order thinking skills are likely to return to basic concepts and refresh their understanding of them. In this sense, it seems most useful to view these thinking skills as interrelated and recursive—as types of thinking we move among as we work on particular tasks or engage with particular ideas.

Reconsidering Approaches to WAC

Over the years, as I worked to develop a more expansive understanding of how writing activities and assignments might be used to enhance teaching and learning, I began reconsidering the two dominant approaches to WAC that I referred to earlier: writing to learn and writing in the disciplines. These two approaches are sometimes viewed as not only different but also in conflict with each other, with writing to learn viewed as WAC and writing in the disciplines viewed as something other than WAC—that is, as another approach to using writing altogether. I take the view that writing to learn and writing in the disciplines are best viewed as approaches that fall within the larger framework that WAC provides. I believe they are best viewed as two ends of a spectrum of WAC activities. Figures 11.4 and 11.5 offer brief overviews of the two approaches.

Writing to Learn: Using writing to help students learn course concepts, conceptual frameworks, skills, processes, and so on. It is useful for helping students remember and understand course content, issues, and ideas (as opposed to cramming for exams).

Best characterized as "low-stakes" writing:

- Focus on content; little or no attention to form since students often struggle with new information and ideas
- Limited feedback and comparatively little instructor effort; assignments are typically not graded

Typical activities include:

- In-Class Responses to Prompts
- Reflections
- Summary/Response
- Posts to Discussion Forums and Email Lists
- Definitions and Descriptions

Figure 11.4. Characteristics of writing to learn.

> **Writing in the Disciplines/Writing to Communicate:** Using writing to help students learn how to contribute to discourse within a discipline or profession.
>
> Best characterized as "high-stakes" (typically graded) writing:
>
> - Instructor time is required for designing and responding to student writing.
> - Potential for student academic misconduct
>
> Typical activities include:
>
> - Reports
> - Articles and Essays
> - Presentations
> - Poster Sessions

Figure 11.5. Characteristics of writing in the disciplines/writing to communicate.

Writing to learn focuses largely on the content of the course. It is an aid to learning. It supports reflection. It supports remembering and understanding. Because it is typically seen as low-stakes writing (Elbow, 1997), it does not require a great deal of response from instructors. Some instructors will offer feedback in the form of quick marks on a document, such as check marks or brief notes. Some instructors simply collect the work and offer a general response to the class as a whole at the next class session.

In contrast, most instructors who use a writing-in-the-disciplines approach do so to help their students learn how to engage in discourse within a particular discipline or a profession. In this sense, it can be seen as preparation for professional life. It focuses on learning the disciplinary orientations and conventions that can help the writer become a contributing member of a discipline or profession. In this sense, it is typically what Peter Elbow (1997) calls high-stakes writing.

As WAC scholars, we should help instructors who use a writing-in-the-disciplines approach become aware of two key issues. First, it takes time to design and respond to writing that conforms to disciplinary conventions. If you are working with instructors who are pressed for time, you might turn to discipline-based writing activities, such as poster sessions, which require less response time than assignments such as term papers or longer reports. Students typically work on posters in small groups, and they can be asked to provide feedback on the drafts produced by other groups. During a poster exhibition (such as the final session of a class or during finals week), they can

WAC and Critical Thinking

further respond to questions from the instructor and other classmates. This can reduce the time needed for the instructor to respond without reducing the challenge and complexity of the assignment.

Second, some students might be tempted to plagiarize or engage in other forms of academic misconduct on a major writing assignment—although this is more often the case with common assignment genres, such as term papers, than it is with specialized disciplinary genres. To reduce the possibility of plagiarism in more common assignment genres, instructors can stage an assignment by asking for topic proposals, working bibliographies, source evaluations, and outlines or rough drafts, or some combination of materials like this. This will allow instructors to see what students are working on, and it will likely reduce the potential for academic misconduct.

Remapping WAC to Critical Thinking

To map out the connections between WAC and the thinking skills defined by Bloom and his colleagues, I set up a spectrum from remembering to creating. Then I laid that over the approaches we use in WAC, which are writing to learn and writing in the disciplines (see Figure 11.6). As I did so, I found myself asking, "Where do we draw the line? Where does one shift over? Does this alignment work?" It might be that I was foolish to view WAC activities and assignments as falling along a spectrum. Certainly, I found myself thinking that it did not quite fit.

Writing to Learn	Writing in the Disciplines

Figure 11.6. Mapping WAC to critical thinking.

I mentioned earlier that I have been thinking about a middle way in WAC, a bridge between writing to learn and writing in the disciplines. Certainly, I recognize that engagement occurs all along the spectrum I have set up in Figure 11.6. Writing-to-learn activities can be highly engaging. And there is little doubt that writers can be highly engaged when they write for an audience. Over the years, however, I have come to the conclusion that there is value in naming a set of activities that do not fit neatly into either writing to learn or writing in the disciplines. I am calling this set of activities writing to engage.

Writing-to-engage activities ask students to use language to carry out tasks that are relatively distinct from writing-to-learn and writing-in-the-disciplines activities and assignments. These tasks could work well in a second-year or third-year course. They might even be used in a second-semester first-year course. I like the term because it allows us to fine-tune our understanding of the range of activities we can ask our students to carry out. I recognize, however, that people who have worked in WAC for years—and, in particular, those who have focused on writing to learn for many years—will say, "Well, we do this. This is part of writing to learn." My colleagues Terry Myers Zawacki and Marty Townsend, for example, told me after I had given this talk at the conference that they have long viewed writing to learn in ways that overlap with the notion of writing to engage (personal communication). My response to this perspective is that there is value in parsing our activities more finely. Doing so will allow us to better understand what we are asking our students to accomplish. And this, in turn, will help us assess and ultimately enhance our students' learning experiences. I show how this parsing might be represented in Figure 11.7, which not only shows the alignment between the three approaches to WAC and various cognitive activities but also indicates that these approaches overlap.

Figure 11.7. Remapping WAC to critical thinking.

Writing to engage involves students in cognitive activities—reflecting, applying, analyzing—that they draw on as they begin to engage with the information, ideas, and arguments within a discipline. While students who work on these kinds of writing activities and assignments might not be participating in typical forms of disciplinary discourse, they would certainly be starting to grapple with what their disciplines care about. In contrast to writing-to-learn activities, which tend to focus on work that is typically carried out as learners are exposed for the first time to new information and ideas in a given field, writing-to-engage activities focus more strongly on the work of transforming knowledge they have already gained (Scardamalia & Bereiter, 1987). This process of transformation also has important implications for our understanding of prior learning and transfer (see, for example, the essays in Anson & Moore, 2016). Writing to engage can be seen as a key driver in helping students begin to gain an understanding of writing within a given discipline or profession.

In making a distinction between writing to engage and writing to learn, I want to avoid suggesting that students will not gain new knowledge as they work on writing-to-engage activities or assignments. They certainly will, particularly when a writing task asks them to explore content more deeply. What

I do want to suggest, however, is that writing to engage tends to focus more on the transformation of knowledge—on deepening the connections among what is already known by the writer—than on acquiring new knowledge. There is certainly overlap between these two types of WAC activities, as Figure 11.7 indicates. And it is likely that some activities and assignments that fall near the borders of writing to learn and writing to engage might best be characterized as falling in both categories. Similarly, I see this kind of classification issue coming up at the borders of writing to engage and writing in the disciplines.

I have seen writing-to-engage activities and assignments offered by some of the faculty members I have worked with. In these cases, they have wanted to accomplish more than they could with a typical writing-to-learn activity. For example, a colleague from sociology assigned a short paper that asked students to report on their application of a sociological theory they had been discussing in class to a YouTube video about the interactions among a particular group of people. It seemed fairly straightforward: "You've studied two approaches to this area. Here's a video. Watch it. Pick one of the approaches. Apply it. And then tell me why you didn't pick the other approach." This is not something the students could publish, and it is unlike professional discourse in sociology. But it is useful because it helps students engage with the ideas in the course at a fairly deep level. I describe writing to engage in Figure 11.8.

Writing to Engage: Using writing to help students work with and develop greater control of course concepts, conceptual frameworks, skills, processes, and so on.

Assignments can:

- Build on writing-to-learn activities
- Support a higher level of engagement than writing-to learn assignments
- Range from low-stakes (typically ungraded) to high-stakes (typically graded) assignments
- Focus on reflecting, applying, and analyzing and might include some attention to evaluating

Typical activities include:

- Application of Frameworks to Texts, Media, Cases
- Evaluations of Alternative Approaches and Methods
- Reflections, Critiques, Comparisons
- Proposals, Brief Reports, Progress Reports

Figure 11.8. Characteristics of writing to engage.

Looking Ahead

The writing-to-engage approach stands between the long-standing writing-to-learn and writing-in-the-disciplines approaches to WAC. It not only offers a middle way, so to speak, but also allows instructors who use communication activities and assignments to create meaningful, engaging assignments that are not limited to the genres typical of a given discipline or profession. In this sense, writing to engage aligns with both the *meaning-making writing tasks* construct developed by Paul Anderson, Chris Anson, Robert Gonyea, and Robert Paine (2016) and the findings of Michele Eodice, Anne Ellen Geller, and Neal Lerner's (2017a, 2017b, 2019) Meaningful Writing Project (http://meaningfulwritingproject.net/). It also aligns with work in writing transfer (Anson & Moore, 2016; Winslow & Shaw, 2017). I explore these connections more deeply elsewhere (Palmquist, 2020).

Writing to engage also serves as a potential response to some of the questions explored at the second English Across the Curriculum Conference about how best to enhance student communication skills. Conference presenters—some of whose work is included in this collection—raised important questions about the role of writing and speaking activities and assignments in a wide range of courses, and in particular, in courses that prepared students for careers that involve speaking and writing in English. My hope is that, as a concept, "writing to engage" might prove useful to instructors who are leading these courses and for those working with instructors on language learning pedagogy.

Acknowledgements

I am grateful to the editors of this collection and to Terry Myers Zawacki, Marty Townsend, and Joan Mullin for their thoughtful feedback on drafts of this chapter.

References

Anderson, L. W. & Krathwohl, D. R. (Eds.). (2001). *A taxonomy for learning, teaching, and assessing: A revision of Bloom's taxonomy of educational objectives*. Longman.

Anderson, P., Anson, C. M., Gonyea, R. M. & Paine, C. (2015). The contributions of writing to learning and development: Results from a large-scale multi-institutional study. *Research in the Teaching of English, 50*, 199–235.

Anderson, P., Anson, C. M., Gonyea, R. M. & Paine, C. (2016). How to create high-impact writing assignments that enhance learning and development and reinvigorate WAC/WID programs: What almost 72,000 undergraduates taught us [Special issue on WAC and high-impact practices]. *Across the Disciplines, 13*(4). https://doi.org/10.37514/ATD-J.2016.13.4.13.

Anson, C. M. (2017). Writing to read, revisited. In A. S. Horning, D. Gollnitz & C. R. Haller (Eds.), *What is college reading?* The WAC Clearinghouse; University Press of Colorado. http://doi.org/10.37514/ATD-B.2017.0001.2.01.

Anson, C. M. & Moore, J. L. (Eds.). (2016). *Critical transitions: Writing and the question of transfer.* The WAC Clearinghouse; University Press of Colorado. https://doi.org/10.37514/PER-B.2016.0797.

Bean, J. (1996). *Engaging ideas: The professor's guide to integrating writing, critical thinking, and active learning in the classroom.* Jossey-Bass.

Bean, J. (2011). *Engaging ideas: The professor's guide to integrating writing, critical thinking, and active learning in the classroom* (2nd ed.). Jossey-Bass.

Condon, W. (2001). Accommodating complexity: WAC program evaluation in the age of accountability. In S. H. McLeod, E. Miraglia, M. Soven & C. Thaiss (Eds.), *WAC for the new millennium: Strategies for continuing writing-across-the-curriculum programs* (pp. 28–51). National Council of Teachers of English. https://wac.colostate.edu/books/landmarks/millennium/.

Condon, W. & Kelly-Riley, D. (2004). Assessing and teaching what we value: The relationship between college-level writing and critical thinking abilities. *Assessing Writing, 9*(1), 56–75.

Condon, W. & Rutz, C. (2012). A taxonomy of writing across the curriculum programs: Evolving to serve broader agendas. *College Composition and Communication, 64*(2), 357–382.

Couch, R. (1989). Dealing with objections to writing across the curriculum. *Teaching English in the Two-Year College, 16*, 193–196.

Elbow, P. (1997). High stakes and low stakes in responding to student writing. *New Directions for Teaching and Learning, 69*, 5–13.

Eodice, M., Geller, A. E. & Lerner, N. (2017a). *The meaningful writing project: Learning, teaching, and writing in higher education.* Utah State University Press.

Eodice, M., Geller, A. E. & Lerner, N. (2017b). What meaningful writing means for students. *Peer Review, 19*(1). https://www.aacu.org/peerreview/2017/Winter/Eodice.

Eodice M., Geller, A. E. & Lerner, N. (2019). The power of personal connection for undergraduate student writers. *Research in the Teaching of English, 53*(4). https://scholar.stjohns.edu/english_facpubs/2/.

Farris, C., Wood, P. Smith, R. & Hunt, D. (1990). *Final report on critical thinking in writing intensive courses.* University of Missouri-Columbia, Office of the Provost.

Kaufer, D. & Young, R. (1993). Writing in the content areas: Some theoretical complexities. In L. Odell (Ed.), *Theory and practice in the teaching of writing: Rethinking the discipline* (pp. 71–104). Southern Illinois University Press.

King, P. M. & Kitchener, K. S. (1994). *Developing reflective judgment: Understanding and promoting intellectual growth and critical thinking in adolescents and adults.* Jossey-Bass.

McLeod, S. H. (2000). Translating enthusiasm into curricular change. In S. H. McLeod (Ed.), *Strengthening programs for writing across the curriculum* (pp. 5–12). The WAC Clearinghouse. https://wac.colostate.edu/books/landmarks/mcleod-programs/ (Original work published in 1988 by Jossey-Bass).

McLeod, S. H. & Maimon, E. (2000). Clearing the air: WAC myths and realities. *College English, 62*(5), 573–583. https://www.jstor.com/stable/378962.

McLeod, S. H. & Miraglia, E., Soven, M. & Thaiss, C. (2001). Writing across the curriculum in a time of change. In S. H. McLeod, E. Miraglia, M. Soven & C. Thaiss (Eds.), *WAC for the new millennium: Strategies for continuing writing-across the-curriculum programs* (pp. 1–27). National Council of Teachers of English. https://wac.colostate.edu/books/landmarks/millennium/.

McLeod, S. H. & Soven, M. (Eds.). (2000). *Writing across the curriculum: A guide to developing programs.* The WAC Clearinghouse. https://wac.colostate.edu/books/landmarks/mcleod-soven/ (Original work published in 1992 by Sage)

Palmquist, M. (2020). A middle way for WAC: Writing to engage. *The WAC Journal, 31*, 7–22. https://doi.org/10.37514/WAC-J.2020.31.1.01.

Perry, W. G. (1970). *Forms of intellectual and ethical development in the college years: A scheme.* Holt, Rinehart & Winston.

Perry, W. G. (1981). *Cognitive and ethical growth: The making of meaning.* Jossey-Bass.

Piaget, J. (1936). *Origins of intelligence in the child.* Routledge; Kegan Paul.

Rutz, C. (2004). WAC and beyond: An interview with Chris Anson. *The WAC Journal, 15*(1), 7–17. https://doi.org/10.37514/WAC-J.2004.15.1.01.

Scardamalia, M. & Bereiter, C. (1987). Knowledge telling and knowledge transforming in written composition. In S. Rosenberg (Ed.), *Cambridge monographs and texts in applied psycholinguistics. Advances in applied psycholinguistics, Vol. 1. Disorders of first-language development; Vol. 2. Reading, writing, and language learning* (pp. 142–175). Cambridge University Press.

Swanson-Owens, D. (1986). Identifying natural sources of resistance: A case study of implementing writing across the curriculum. *Research in the Teaching of English, 20*, 69–97.

Townsend, M. A. (2001). Writing intensive courses and WAC. In S. H. McLeod, E. Miraglia, M. Soven & C. Thaiss (Eds.), *WAC for the new millennium: Strategies for continuing writing-across the-curriculum programs* (pp. 233–258). National Council of Teachers of English. https://wac.colostate.edu/books/landmarks/millennium/.

Townsend, M. A. & Zawacki, T. M. (2013). Conversations in process: An observational report on WAC in China. *The WAC Journal, 24*(1), 95–109. https://doi.org/10.37514/WAC-J.2013.24.1.06.

Vygotsky, L. S. (1978). *Mind and society: The development of higher mental processes.* Harvard University Press.

Vygotsky, L. S. (1987). Thinking and speech. In R. W. Rieber & A. S. Carton (Eds.), *The collected works of L. S. Vygotsky, Volume 1: Problems of general psychology* (pp. 39–285). Plenum Press. (Original work published 1934)

Winslow, D. & Shaw, P. (2017). Teaching metacognition to reinforce agency and transfer in course-linked first-year course. In P. Portanova, J. M. Rifenburg & D. Roen (Eds.), *Contemporary perspectives on cognition and writing.* The WAC Clearinghouse; University Press of Colorado. https://doi.org/10.37514/PER-B.2017.0032.2.10.

12 Critical Thinking, Writing, and Language Learning: A Report from Northwest China

Matthew Overstreet
KHALIFA UNIVERSITY, ABU DHABI

Abstract: This chapter details an effort to enhance critical thinking instruction in the language department of a Chinese university. Drawing on core writing across the curriculum (WAC) principles, I argue that critical thinking, in the language-learning classroom, should denote an intersubjective process of reflecting upon and reworking ideas. Language teachers can promote this practice by asking learners to make claims and elaborate upon those claims. After sketching the theoretical justification for such a pedagogy, I discuss potential challenges to this and other pedagogical reform efforts in the Chinese university. Drawing on personal experience, informal interviews, and survey data, I argue that, while enthusiasm for pedagogical innovation is high, significant structural and cultural barriers hinder widespread implementation of progressive, inquiry-based teaching practices.

Keywords: critical thinking, China, active learning, faculty development, writing across the curriculum

For the past two summers, I have been fortunate enough to be a guest of the School of Foreign Languages and Literatures at Lanzhou University, in Gansu province in Northwest China. I was originally asked to use my knowledge of Western (particularly American) college writing practices to help improve the quality of instruction in the department. Once on the ground, this general goal evolved into a more specific one: to provide advice as to how language teachers can help their students "think critically." Among members of the department, I found, critical thinking was almost universally valued. At the same time, teachers had only a vague idea of what it might look like or how to teach it. There was also concern that students might lack critical thinking ability. Indeed, similar concerns about Chinese students are raised in

DOI: https://doi.org/10.37514/INT-B.2021.1220.2.12

the educational literature. A Chinese student, now studying in the UK, sums up prevailing sentiment when they claim that Chinese students "have no idea how to be critical." They further state,

> Apart from reading the materials, [in the UK] you need to argue for or against the existing literature and establish your own argument. Here you need to present evidence and references to support your views and we did not have to do that in China (as cited in Zhang, 2016, p. 10).

For this student, critical thinking is associated with interpretation and assertion, with being able to analyze what others have said and to present evidence-supported claims in response. They clearly feel that their undergraduate education in China left them unprepared for such work. In this chapter, I will discuss my efforts to help remedy this situation. Though I do not claim to dispense any panaceas, I believe my experience can act as a useful point of reference for others interested in using writing to promote critical thought, especially in language-learning courses. I also hope to shed light on the unique challenges educational reform efforts face in the Chinese university.

What is Critical Thinking?

"Critical thinking" is a common term in educational discourse. It is also a notoriously ambiguous one. Across disciplines, "critical thinking" is defined and understood to manifest in a variety of ways. This conceptual indeterminacy might help account for the term's popularity as an educational buzzword. Unfortunately, in my experience, it also hinders efforts to promote critical thought. Without being sure what exactly critical thinking is, how can we promote it? As such, in Lanzhou, my first goal was to better understand the term.

Critical Thinking & WAC

Critical thinking (CT), however it is defined, is near the core of the writing across the curriculum (WAC) project. An influential WAC anthology, for example, notes that WAC aims to help students become better "critical thinkers and problem solvers, as well as better communicators" (McLeod et al., 2001, p. 5). Another articulation holds that WAC ultimately seeks to "promote active learning" and thus "engage students as critical thinkers" (Ochsner & Fowler, 2004, p. 117). In these texts, and throughout the WAC literature, we see a connection between CT and "active learning." CT entails not passive memorization, but doing something with knowledge, putting it to work. Writing, especially in the writing-to-learn context, is seen as a way to make students engage in doing. It provides a space in which to put content knowledge to work.

So writing, active learning, and CT are intimately connected. What might CT look like in practice? Justin Rademaekers (2018) tries to answer this question in his recent article, "Getting Specific About Critical Thinking: Implications for Writing Across the Curriculum." Rademaekers starts from the premise that a general tendency towards critical thought manifests differently in each academic discipline. He then proceeds, via a survey of faculty members, to examine disciplinary differences in thought patterns across several "dimensions" (e.g., whether critical thought is understood to be primarily text-focused or world-focused, objective or subjective). The overall goal is to discover exactly the type of thought each discipline values. Rademaekers believes that this sort of project can help WAC scholars better understand (and thus explain to colleagues and students) differences in disciplinary writing conventions.

Though I see the value in Rademaekers' project, I found his study to be of little use in the situation I faced in Lanzhou. I was working with teachers of English and German. Unlike biologists or economists, they did not see themselves as operating within a well-defined discipline. Also, unlike the scholars Rademaekers surveyed, I found that these teachers often did not have a clear sense of how CT might manifest in their classrooms. Certainly, they could recognize CT "when they saw it," but apart from vague notions such as "logical organization," they had neither the language nor theoretical grounding to describe what they were seeing. As such, I felt I had to step beyond merely describing what they were already doing (which I see as Rademaekers' primary move), and instead provide a pedagogically workable definition of CT, one specifically formulated for their role as language teachers.

Mike Palmquist, in his chapter in this collection and his keynote speech at the 2018 English Across the Curriculum conference in Hong Kong, helps explain why a better understanding of CT could be of great use to language teachers. Drawing on the work of John Bean (2011), Palmquist notes that writing and CT are both transformative acts; they both involve creation and alteration. To better understand their relationship, he discusses CT in regard to Bloom's taxonomy: a model of learning objectives often depicted as a pyramid, with basic cognitive tasks (remembering, understanding) at the bottom and more demanding tasks (analysis, evaluation, creation) at the top. CT entails the activities at the top of the pyramid, i.e., analysis, evaluation and creation. Integrally, though, higher cognitive tasks always implicate lower ones: a student cannot create without remembering, for example. This means that the different levels of the pyramid are mutually sustaining. Thus, it is not that one teaches critical thinking OR helps students memorize content knowledge. Instead, when students engage in CT, they put content knowledge to work. This "putting to work" helps them internalize and remember. When language learners analyze, evaluate, or create texts, for example, it helps them memorize vocabulary and sentence forms. An understanding of CT—and how to promote it—is thus essential to efficient language learning.

Critical Thinking Beyond WAC

To better understand CT, it is useful to examine how the term is defined outside of the WAC literature. The most extensive examination of the topic has been by scholars working in the tradition of informal logic. Speaking broadly, within this tradition, "critical thinking" represents the application of logical rules to everyday claims. Robert Ennis was an early and influential voice. Writing in 1964, Ennis defines critical thinking as "the correct assessing of statements" (p. 599). To help thinkers assess statements correctly, he presents a series of steps they can follow—twelve in total. These include things like identifying and evaluating assumptions and checking to make sure that a statement follows from its premises. According to Ennis, teaching students these competencies will help them avoid common "pitfalls in assessment" (p. 599).

We can call the conception of CT inaugurated by Ennis the procedural approach. As noted, Ennis lays out a series of steps—a procedure—that thinkers can or should follow. For many, the procedural approach defines critical thinking. Tellingly, when the teachers in Lanzhou were asked to identify what CT might entail, their definitions were largely informed by this tradition. Critical thinking involves "using a series of procedures to solve a problem," one teacher wrote in response to a survey I conducted. Another wrote that it demands "judging things logically."

I can see the value of the procedural approach. That said, I doubt its usefulness in a language-learning context. First off, a system like that proposed by Ennis entails memorizing content (logical rules, potential fallacies, etc.). In a standalone logic course this would not be a problem. In a college course built around another set of learning outcomes (such as a language course), this added content becomes an unwanted imposition. More importantly, misapplication of the procedural approach can result in decidedly *non-critical* teaching and learning. Sure enough, Chinese scholar Yu Dong (2015) notes that this is a problem in China. He describes Chinese teachers, driven by top-down demands that they teach critical thought, demanding rote memorization of "thinking rules" and giving multiple-choice tests to ensure adherence. Clearly, this sort of approach does little to trigger higher-order cognitive function and the benefits therein.

Rethinking Critical Thinking

After considering the critical thinking scholarship, I decided that any definition of CT for use in the language-learning classroom should draw not on informal logic, but on the ideas about writing and thinking which underlie the WAC project. As discussed above, when we promote writing across the curriculum, and thus active learning, we are certain we are promoting critical thinking. Why? To answer this question, I turned to one of the first scholars of critical thought—John Dewey, the esteemed American philosopher and progressive educator. For Dewey, thinking always occurs in response to a problem. We are going along, everything is going smoothly, and suddenly a roadblock or incongruity appears. So, we need to identify the problem, identify possible solutions, and select the best solution. This process of identification and selection is thinking. When we do it willfully and self-consciously, we engage in what Dewey (1910) calls "reflective thinking" (his version of critical thinking).

The work of Richard Paul, a contemporary CT scholar, complements the above definition. Writing with Linda Elder (Paul & Elder, 2002), he defines critical thinking, in part, as "the art of thinking about your thinking while you are thinking in order to make your thinking better: more clear, more accurate, more defensible" (p. 316). Here we see an emphasis on thinking about your own thought: what is often called metacognition. To identify and challenge your own conceptions, to rework them into more accurate and defensible forms, Paul calls this critical thinking in the "strong" sense.

For Paul, the reworking of thought is intimately tied to the recognition that a) we always think in systems, and b) that we continually need to strive to transcend any given system, so as to get a better (i.e., more accurate and defensible) view of the world. To this end, he greatly values interaction between different systems. Instead of critiquing "atomic arguments," he believes that critical thinking instruction should work to highlight "argument networks" and provide a space where these networks can be brought into "rational conflict," so as to reveal their blind spots and biases (Paul, 1994, p. 182). We can see here a connection with Dewey. Dewey argues, remember, that we are moved to think when we are presented with a problem, a moment of decision or "forked-road situation" (1910, p. 17). The encounter with other argument networks—and their unique set of proposals—often leads to such moments. Engaging in dialogue with those who think differently, in other words, forces us to think.

Combining the work of Dewey and Paul, a definition of CT in the language-learning classroom starts to emerge. It is centered around problem-posing, dialogue, and reflection. These ideas, of course, have been central to WAC from the very beginning (see Emig, 1977), as has critical thinking. The above analysis helps us see the relationship between these core tenets of our project. Unlike the procedural approach to critical thinking, which posits an individual thinker approaching a static claim, the WAC approach demands reflection and the reworking of thought, spurred by human interaction—the friction between different ways of seeing and asserting. Writing, as a technology, allows for this sort of interaction. Thus writing—and writing across the curriculum—emerge as central to the promotion of critical thought.

Cultivating Critical Thought

In the above section, I referred to the work of John Dewey and Richard Paul to make explicit the definition of critical thinking which, I believe, animates WAC scholarship. I argued that critical thinking, in the WAC context, is an active process that demands reflection on, and the reworking of, ideas. The need to reflect and rework is sparked by human interaction. The question remains, though: how can language teachers create the conditions for productive exchange?

It may seem obvious, but the first step in cultivating critical thought is a simple one: students need to write (or speak). They need to make claims and get feedback. Of course, there are innumerable ways to facilitate communication in the classroom. In Lanzhou, after I presented the above definition of CT to the language teachers, we discussed some possible ways to get students writing and speaking. We considered both writing-to-learn activities and more formal, yet still conversational, "writing-to-engage" activities (see Palmquist, 2018). The teachers seemed to particularly appreciate Gerald Graff and Cathy Birkenstein's (2017) "They Say / I Say" template. This template, I found, provided them an easy-to-remember, general-purpose way to kick-start the thinking process. The basic premise is simple. Students are asked to summarize a claim—the "They Say"—and respond—the "I Say."[1] Of course, the result might be underwhelming, but, as I was quick to ensure my colleagues, that is

---

1 Note how this template moves the student to engage in all three higher-order tasks (analysis, evaluation, creation).

fine. Once a student has stated a claim, a teacher or classmate can engage that student in dialogue and help them achieve a more sophisticated perspective.

What principle should guide this engagement process? As I will discuss in detail in the final section, the proper way to respond to student work was a constant source of worry for our colleagues in Lanzhou. During training activities, they poured over sample essays, trying to formulate the perfect "directed question." Likewise, they worried that peer feedback would be of little value because students may not be knowledgeable about their partner's topic. Considered in light of the definition of CT sketched above, these concerns are misplaced. The goal of dialogue in the thinking process is to spur reflection and reworking. To achieve this end, questions do not need to be particularly complex. Instead, they simply need to encourage more thought. The principle which should guide the engagement process, we can say, is *elaboration*. In short, no matter a student's original position, their dialogue partner needs to encourage them to sustain longer and more detailed—more elaborate—strains of thought. Simple open-ended questions are often a very effective way to achieve this end.

Elaboration spurs reflection because it makes thinking visible. It reveals habits and patterns and assumptions, and very often forces us to rework our ideas. When students engage in revelation, examination, and reworking—when feedback from teachers or peers forces them to do these things—they have, by definition, engaged in critical thought.

There are of course innumerable techniques for making students elaborate. My favorite technique is playing the fool. *Explain. I don't understand. What does this mean? Give examples. Give more details.* Questions are especially useful. *Why is President Xi the best leader? Why should students study hard?* My goal in such questioning is to get the student to reveal the rules of their argument network, show explicitly how different ideas hang together. Of course, in reality, much of the time, I can guess what a student means. I can fill in the blanks. When I play the fool, though, I take pains not to do this work for the student. In turn, they have to push themselves beyond what comes naturally. They have to think.

An example from my own writing classroom demonstrates how effective simple, open-ended questions can be at encouraging critical thought. In this paragraph (part of a longer piece), one of my students, we can call her Anna, makes an argument that, contrary to conventional wisdom, digital media helps promote empathetic relations. She writes,

> Again, I think that Facebook gives people opportunities to share their emotions with others. Moreover, there are a lot of

> examples when people saw posts about others people problems in Facebook and offer help, or when they saw a sad message and cheering someone up. Overall, Facebook creates prosocial behavior and due to everyday usage, it becomes more habitual in the real life.

My response to this paragraph was only one word: how? Anna was given time to revise, and when I next saw her paper, the same paragraph read as follows:

> In addition, I would like to prove my claim using personal experience. I suppose it is logical that media has a positive effect on children's empathy. They do not have enough emotional experience and digital media proposes them a possibility to share their feelings and understand emotions of others. Also, there are a lot of examples when people saw posts about others people problems in social networks and offer help, or when they saw a sad message and cheering someone up. Overall, social media creates prosocial behavior and due to everyday usage, it becomes more habitual in the real life.

In this revision, we see clear evidence of critical thinking as I have defined it. My simple "how?" functioned as a problem in the Deweyian sense. To solve this problem, Anna had to return to her text. She had to reflect on her claim and the reasoning that sustained it. She then had to elaborate. The result is a substantially more complex piece of writing. She has qualified her claim and, integrally, identified a causal mechanism for the social dynamic she proposes. Digital media "has a positive effect on children's empathy," she now argues, because it allows them "a possibility to share their feelings and understand emotions of others." In essence, digital media allows children to practice being social. This is an interesting, fairly original claim. Even if it were not though, this assignment sequence could still be considered a success. CT, as I have defined it, is not about product. Instead, it is about process. When a student reflects upon and reworks their own ideas, that is critical thinking. That is what we should seek.

Elaboration in the Language-Learning Classroom

As noted, my goal in Lanzhou was to develop a simple, flexible method by which language teachers could promote CT. Drawing on WAC principles, I hit upon the formula expressed above: assert and elaborate. Though elaboration via questioning can be a means to encourage critical thought in all writers, it is especially useful—necessary even—when teaching language learners. Richard Paul's (1994) notion of "argument networks" (p. 182) helps explain why.

Consider a Chinese student studying abroad who is asked to analyze the literature in their field and make an argument (a real-life "They Say / I Say" situation). They perform poorly at the task. Perhaps they misread or make irrelevant claims. Why did they perform poorly? In addressing this question, it is useful to remember that every claim, as Paul points out, is in fact part of a network of arguments, an intricate, interconnected web of rules and principles. Some of these principles are stated, but many remain implicit. They exist as tacit knowledge, a sort of operating system for making and judging. Often, in a foreign-language situation, what appears to be a lack of CT is in fact a mismatch between operating systems. Novices are uncertain what principles need to be applied or what applied principles need to be expressly stated. Elaboration helps bring reasoning principles into the open. Once in the open, they can be aligned.

The results of a writing activity I conducted with a group of Chinese graduate students in Lanzhou illustrate this dynamic.[2] The purpose of this activity was to model the sort of pedagogy proposed above. After learning about the "They Say / I Say" format, these students were presented with a controversial text and asked to analyze it and formulate a response. The text was carefully chosen. As one might expect, research shows that CT is more likely when thinkers are personally familiar with a topic (Stapleton, 2001). I also wanted a text that would pose a true problem—something that would challenge the students and force them to make a judgment. "Fooling the Emperor: How is Creativity Misapplied in China," by American academic Yong Zhao (2014), satisfies both these criteria. In this piece, Zhao claims that because of the country's authoritarian system, creativity in China is often misapplied. Instead of engaging in useful innovation, citizens waste their energy trying to "fool the emperor."

The students wrote, in part,

> The essence of Zhao's argument is that Chinese's innovations and creatives are all used in the wrong way, with the wrong purpose of cheating the authorities, rather than making real progress towards productivity. As for us, Zhao's argument seems to be overgeneralized. Though we concede that

---

2   This particular text, as well as the subsequent revision, is a composite of several different student texts from the workshop. The language, argument and overall structure come from the students. I have combined, condensed, and slightly edited their text in order to better illustrate the patterns at play.

several people completely obey authority even at great cost of resources, it doesn't mean that all the efforts, innovations and substantial progress made by the authorities which actually promote the development of China are all cheating.

For instance, five years ago, Lanzhou was one of the most polluted cities in China. . . . Ultimately, a new kind of street sprinkler comes into being which can not only water the street for dust covering, but also spray water vapor for humidity strengthening. Owing to the innovations of the authorities, can pollution in Lanzhou be relieved.

As we see, these students have no problem adopting the formal features of argumentative writing. They also have no problem stating a forceful opinion. On close inspection, though, their argument does not seem to hang together properly. Something is wrong. If we break the text down into parts, we see the problem:

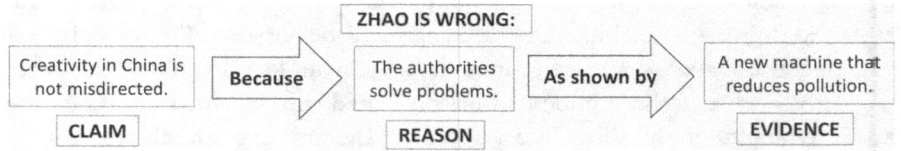

Figure 12.1. Analysis of student text.

Though these students present a claim, a reason for that claim, and supporting evidence, the reason does not necessitate the claim. One could agree that the Chinese authorities are great problem solvers, but also believe that creativity is misdirected. In other words, the text does not accomplish its stated purpose of refuting Zhao's argument. Instead, it refutes an imaginary argument that "efforts, innovations and substantial progress made by the authorities . . . are all cheating." Very likely, this analysis and response, in an American or UK university, would be given a low mark. It would act as further evidence that Chinese students have "no idea how to be critical."

Adopting an elaboration approach to CT instruction, a teacher would move these students to elaborate on their claim. This would be done through questioning. *Where does Zhao say that all progress is cheating? What do you mean by "overgeneralized?"* Given a chance to revise, the students might write something like this:

The essence of Zhao's argument is that Chinese's innovations and creatives are ~~all~~ often used in the wrong way, with

Critical Thinking, Writing & Language Learning

the wrong purpose of cheating the authorities, rather than making real progress towards productivity. As for us, Zhao's argument seems to ~~be overgeneralized~~ *overstate the problem*. Though we concede that ~~several~~ *sometimes* people completely obey authority even at great cost of resources, *many problems are being solved. Creatives are a necessary driving force in solutions*. ~~it doesn't mean that all the efforts, innovations and substantial progress made by the authorities which actually promote the development of China are all cheating~~.

For instance, five years ago, Lanzhou was one of the most polluted cities in China . . . Ultimately, a new kind of street sprinkler comes into being which can not only water the street for dust covering, but also spray water vapor for humidity strengthening. Owing to the ~~innovations of the authorities~~ *creatives of Chinese*, can pollution in Lanzhou be relieved.

When writing in a new language, novice writers often are not sure what reasoning principles need to be expressly stated; they leave out key information, believing that it is implied. In the above writing sample, and its subsequent revision, we see a classic case of this phenomenon. For these students, the existence of the new street sprayer—and the other changes their rapidly developing city has recently undergone—implies great progress, inevitably fueled by great creativity. It did not occur to them to expressly state this link; perhaps the link itself has never even risen to consciousness. Instead, the connection between the authorities, progress, and creativity is purely tacit: a reasoning principle to think with, not about. The elaboration approach moved the students to make this connection explicit. More broadly, in addressing their teacher's questions, they had to think about their own thinking, and in turn their world, and how it emerges in language. And, after doing so, they were able to reformulate their text into what, by conventional argumentative standards, is a perfectly logical chain of ideas. The text now breaks down as follows:

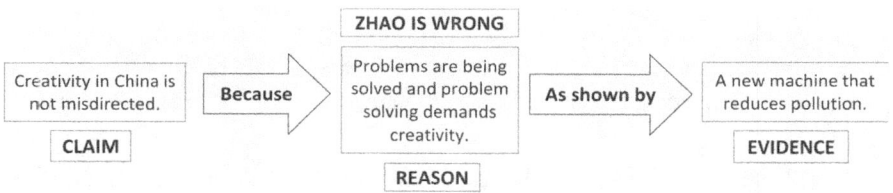

Figure 12.2. Analysis of revised student text.

233

So, these students are not incapable of argumentation, nor operating from a completely alien script. Instead, they simply needed to slow down and examine their thinking patterns for (cultural) blind spots. Questioning forced them to perform this examination. They then reworked their text.[3] The result is a coherent argument with which they can participate in intellectual exchange. That is a fine outcome. More importantly, though, as they rethought and reworked their text, these students engaged in critical thinking. And as we all know, when performed often enough, a practice becomes a habit.

Pedagogical Reform in China: Prospects

In this final section, I would like to present evidence that my work in Lanzhou was successful. Language teachers at Lanzhou University are now utilizing "assert and elaborate" and are seeing marked gains in both their students' CT abilities and general learning outcomes. Unfortunately, such evidence does not yet exist. After a productive two-week session in the summer of 2019, I left Lanzhou. As such, instead of discussing outcomes, I will close this chapter by discussing the potential challenges pedagogical reform efforts—and WAC efforts in particular—face in the Chinese university. My analysis is informed by my own observations, informal interviews with teachers and students, and an online survey completed by participants (n = 20) in the various seminars and workshops I have conducted at Lanzhou over the past two summers.

In her study of the implementation of WAC in China, Dan Wu (2012) notes that within Chinese universities there is "a near-unanimous sense of a need for WAC insights" (xxii). Martha Townsend and Therese Zawacki (2013) echo this claim. My experience indicates that Wu is indeed correct. Throughout my time in Lanzhou, I found both teachers and administrators deeply interested in, and appreciative of, any new insights into pedagogical practices. Core WAC ideas such as writing to learn and the importance of feedback and revision were taken up with great interest. Once introduced to these ideas, Chinese teachers easily adapted them to their particular teaching contexts. I was working with language teachers, remember. They teach large classes (of up to 40 students), typically utilizing a department-issued textbook. In brainstorming sessions, though, they formulated numerous creative ways to introduce writing into their courses. What if students wrote poetry using the vocabulary words from a certain unit, for example? Overall,

---

3   Note that at no point did I discuss the rules of informal logic with the students. Instead, the more "logical" argument structure seen in the revision is simply a result of questioning and elaboration.

there was general agreement that such WAC-inspired activities could further desired learning outcomes.

Unfortunately, despite enthusiasm for pedagogical reform, there are serious impediments to any sort of alteration to conventional Chinese teaching and learning practices. These impediments were made clear during my efforts to promote my WAC-inspired vision of critical thinking. As noted, there is a widespread (though not unanimous) belief that Chinese students lack CT ability relative to their Western peers. This situation has been attributed to China's political system (Zhang, 2016), the country's Confucian legacy (Lloyd, 1996), and linguistic factors (Yoshino, 2004). Yu Dong (2015), for one, rejects all these explanations. He echoes my personal experience when he argues that Chinese students are perfectly capable of engaging in Western-style CT. The problem, as he sees it, is that they are simply not given the chance. Throughout the Chinese system, he notes the persistent use of a "one-way transmission style of pedagogy" (p. 356). This occurs even when teachers claim to value CT. Obviously, this sort of teaching style contravenes the idea of active learning which is so essential to WAC.

What accounts for the prevalence of the "one-way transmission" method in the Chinese system? When asked, Chinese teachers consistently refer to the large size of classes or the demands imposed by high-stakes testing. As one graduate student told me, active learning is simply "not efficient" when trying to help 40 or 50 students pass a required English test. There is, however, a wealth of WAC scholarship devoted to refuting this very point (e.g., Hobson & Schafermeyer, 1994). If anything, active learning practices aim to make instruction more efficient, in that, by putting more responsibility on students, teachers are able to achieve more with less. Also, as we have seen, there is no necessary tradeoff between higher-order and lower-order outcomes. Actively engaging with learning material can, by all accounts, help students remember material more effectively, and thus perform better on exams. A major component of any pedagogical reform effort in China will involve familiarizing teachers with these basic concepts and working with them to adapt active-learning methods to a world of large classes and high-stakes exams.

Apart from the above structural challenges, there are also deep-seated cultural issues which must be overcome if Chinese teachers are to embrace active-learning methods. Again, I find Yu Dong's (2015) perspective particularly insightful. As noted, he rejects the idea that Confucian notions of decorum or the nature of the Chinese language somehow handicap Chinese CT ability. Students cannot engage in critical thought simply because teachers will not let them. Teachers will not let them, he believes, because of the particular conception of knowledge held by educated Chinese. Due to the country's Confucian legacy, "the Truth" exists in an ethereal realm, divorced from practice or evidence-based inquiry. Knowledge is gained by "reading the classical books without looking out the window" (Dong, 2015, p. 362). It is then passed down from teacher to student, expert to novice. In other words, knowledge is something that *is*, rather than something that *is made*. According to Dong, this normative paradigm, derived from a belief system to which few people still openly adhere, shapes Chinese education on an almost genetic level.

With his claim to have identified a single, shared philosophical tradition, Dong could be accused of essentializing Chinese thought. That said, his theory has great explanatory power. He notes that, shaped by "traditional ideas and habits," teachers too often take on the role of "a preacher transmitting infallible knowledge" (Dong, 2015, p. 365). Indeed. Time and time again, I met teachers who felt they had to take on such a role, that it was essential to maintaining authority in the classroom. Any inclination that a teacher might not know the answer to a question—or that a student might be more knowledgeable about a subject than her teacher—was seen as a terrible sin. This strong desire to always know (or be perceived as knowing) deeply informs pedagogical practice.

Earlier I spoke of my difficulties in getting Chinese teachers to respond to student work in a non-directive manner: open-ended questions, or lines of inquiry that might lead to unexpected places, were firmly resisted. I believe that this resistance stems in part from an unwillingness to relinquish the role of knower. From the Chinese perspective, remember, the teacher's role is to transmit knowledge to the student. It is not to help the student create knowledge (because knowledge is not something that is created). Consider some responses to a survey question I posed asking teachers about problems they face when trying to teach critical thinking. Numerous teachers said that they could not teach CT because of their own lack of knowledge about logical rules or processes: "my own logical thinking is poor," one teacher wrote. Another noted that there are "[many] factors which limit my ability to teach critical thinking. For example, if I do not have insight into a problem I cannot guide the students in a proper way." This latter response is telling, in that it posits a single correct answer to whatever problem the student happens to be grappling with. The student can find this answer if guided "in a proper way," by a suitably knowledgeable expert. The idea that there might be multiple correct answers, or that the process of grappling—of making your own "proper way"—might be more important than the end product is not considered. Nor is the idea that a teacher need not be an expert to be a good learning partner. Overall, I found such basic tenets of progressive pedagogy to be utterly unfamiliar to Chinese educators. Whether or not, as Professor Dong claims, a certain conception of knowledge is to blame, proponents of active, inquiry-based learning will have to confront this reality.

Conclusion

My efforts in Lanzhou represent only a tiny sliver of the WAC and WAC-inspired efforts currently ongoing within China. That said, I believe my testimony is valuable in that it presents a snapshot of the situation "on the ground" in the world's biggest university system. All told, I agree with scholars like Dan Wu (2012), who find that Chinese educators are hungry for information about how to improve the learning experience of their students. The rise of high-quality educational scholarship by China mainland authors indicates that the Chinese have much to contribute to the conversation. That said, there are structural and cultural impediments to implementing what we might understand as "best practices" in progressive education. I do not believe that these impediments are impossible to overcome. But it will take continued collaboration. If my own experience is any indication, Chinese teacher-scholars are eager to engage in such efforts.

References

Bean, J. C. (2011). *Engaging ideas: The professor's guide to integrating writing, critical thinking, and active learning in the classroom*. John Wiley & Sons.

Dewey, J. (1910). *How we think*. D.C. Heath.

Dong, Y. (2015). Critical thinking education with Chinese characteristics. In M. Davies & R. Barnett (Eds.), *The Palgrave handbook of critical thinking in higher education* (pp. 351–368). Springer.

Emig, J. (1977). Writing as a mode of learning. *College Composition and Communication, 28*(2), 122–128.

Ennis, R. H. (1964). A definition of critical thinking. *The Reading Teacher, 17*(8), 599–612.

Graff, G. & Birkenstein, C. (2017). *They Say/I Say: The moves that matter in academic writing*. W.W. Norton.

Hobson, E. H. & Schafermeyer, K. W. (1994). Writing and critical thinking: Writing-to-learn in large classes. *American Journal of Pharmaceutical Education, 58*(4), 423–426.

Lloyd, G. E. R. (1996). *Adversaries and authorities: Investigations into ancient Greek and Chinese Science*. Cambridge University Press.

McLeod, S. H., Miraglia, E., Soven, M. & Thaiss, C. (2001). *WAC for the new millennium: Strategies for continuing writing-across-the-curriculum programs*. National Council of Teachers of English.

Ochsner, R. & Fowler, J. (2004). Playing devil's advocate: Evaluating the literature of the WAC/WID movement. *Review of Educational Research, 74*(2), 117–140.

Palmquist, M. (2018, December 4). *WAC and critical thinking: Exploring productive relationships* [Keynote address]. 2nd International Conference on English Across the Curriculum, Hong Kong.

Paul, R. (1994). Teaching critical thinking in the strong sense. In K. Walters (Ed.), *Re-Thinking reason: New perspectives in critical thinking* (pp. 181–198). SUNY Press.

Paul, R. & Elder, L. (2002). *Critical thinking: Tools for taking charge of your professional and personal life*. Pearson Press.

Rademaekers, J. (2018). Getting specific about critical thinking: Implications for writing across the curriculum. *The WAC Journal, 29*, 119. https://doi.org/10.37514/WAC-J.2018.29.1.06.

Stapleton, P. (2001). Assessing critical thinking in the writing of Japanese university students: Insights about assumptions and content familiarity. *Written Communication, 18*(4), 506–548.

Townsend, M. & Zawacki, T. (2013). Conversations in process: An observational report on WAC in China. *The WAC Journal, 24*, 95–109. https://doi.org/10.37514/WAC-J.2013.24.1.06.

Wu, D. (2012). *Introducing writing across the curriculum into China: Feasibility and adaptation*. Springer.

Yoshino, A. (2004, July 16). Well-intentioned ignorance characterises British attitudes to foreign students. *The Times Higher Education Supplement*.

Zhang, T. (2016). Why do Chinese postgraduates struggle with critical thinking? Some clues from the higher education curriculum in China. *Journal of Further and Higher Education*, 1–15. https://doi.org/10.1080/0309877X.2016.1206857.

Zhao, Y. (2014, November 1). *Fooling the emperor: How is creativity misapplied in China?* Yong Zhao. http://zhaolearning.com/2014/11/01/fooling-the-emperor-how-is-creativity-misapplied-in-china/.

13 Using the Onion Model to Scaffold the Case Analysis Genre in Information Systems

Maria Pia Gomez-Laich, Thomas D. Mitchell, Silvia Pessoa, and Michael Maune
CARNEGIE MELLON UNIVERSITY QATAR

Abstract: Previous studies in systemic functional linguistics (SLF)-based genre pedagogy have shown the value of explicit instruction in enhancing student writing. However, most of these studies have been carried out in primary and secondary school contexts (e.g., Brisk, 2014; Humphrey & Macnaught, 2016), with significantly less research in higher education contexts (Dreyfus et al., 2016). The study we present in this chapter addresses the need for more research in higher education contexts and continues the tradition of the SLATE Project (Dreyfus et al., 2016) by providing an example of scaffolding student writing at the university level through an interdisciplinary collaboration. We present our approach to scaffolding a key disciplinary genre in information systems (IS)—the case analysis—which requires analytical argumentative writing. Specifically, we show how we modeled writing processes for case analysis, from the pre-writing process of analysis, to the pre-writing process of integrating analysis as support for claims, to the process of incorporating valued language resources in the written product. While our focus here is on one genre in one discipline, our approach to scaffolding analytical argumentative writing could be useful in support of a wide range of writing in the disciplines (WID) contexts.

Keywords: collaboration, disciplinary writing, genre-based pedagogy, analytical argumentative writing, explicit instruction

The information systems (IS) discipline focuses on how information technology (IT) systems are developed and how individuals, groups, organizations, and markets interact with IT (Sidorova et al., 2008). Writing is an important component of professional IS work, as written communication is the skill most often explicitly requested by employers, according to Michelle Liu and Diane Murphy (2012). Reflecting this demand in the workplace, the *IS 2010 Curriculum Guidelines for Undergraduate Degree Programs in Information Systems* (Topi et al., 2010) make explicit that "IS professionals should be able to communicate effectively with excellent oral, written, and listening skills" (p. 21). While previous research has recommended that IS courses promote the development of students' written communication skills (Merhout & Etter, 2005), a gap still exists between employers' expectations and the average written communication skills of IS graduates (Liu & Murphy, 2012). This gap is likely driven by at least two factors. Firstly, while faculty across the disciplines may recognize the need for their students' communication skills to improve, their understanding of what they value in student writing is often largely tacit. As a result, they sometimes articulate that understanding in ways that may be confusing to students (e.g., "be critical, but not judgmental"; Lancaster, 2014). Another factor is that learning disciplinary ways of thinking and writing new genres is very challenging for students, particularly in an English as an additional language (EAL) context (Dreyfus et al., 2016). Given this gap, it is vital for IS students to learn to write effective disciplinary texts, and one way to help them accomplish this is through explicit writing instruction.

For the past two years, we have been supporting academic literacy development in an IS program at a branch campus of an American university in the Middle East, where most of the students have English as an additional language. Taking an approach grounded in systemic functional linguistics' (SFL) genre-based pedagogy (Martin & Rose, 2007; Rothery, 1996), we have collaborated with IS faculty to revise assignment guidelines and make explicit the expected purpose, parts, and language resources of the discipline's genres (for an overview of our collaborative process in one class, see Pessoa et al., 2019). In this chapter, we present our approach to scaffolding a key disciplinary genre in IS—the case analysis—which requires analytical argumentative writing. Specifically, we show how we modeled three stages of the case analysis writing process: (1) the pre-writing process of analysis, (2) the pre-writing process of integrating analysis as support for claims, and (3) the process of incorporating valued language resources in the written product. While our focus here is limited to one specific disciplinary genre, our approach to scaffolding analytical argumentative writing can be useful in support of a wide range of writing in the disciplines (WID) contexts.

Previous studies in SFL-based genre pedagogy have shown the value of explicit instruction in enhancing student writing (Brisk & Zisselsberger, 2011; Gebhard et al., 2011). Explicit instruction can help students understand the various rhetorical moves that are expected within their specific discourse community (Mitchell & Pessoa, 2017; Pessoa et al., 2018). However, most research on the effects of explicit instruction has been conducted in primary and secondary school contexts (e.g., Brisk, 2014; Humphrey & Macnaught, 2016), with significantly less research in higher education contexts (Dreyfus et al., 2016). The research we present in this chapter addresses this need and continues the tradition of the SLATE Project (Dreyfus et al., 2016) by providing an example of an interdisciplinary collaboration aimed at scaffolding student writing at the university level.

The Case Analysis Genre: Expectations and Challenges

As noted above, one of the most common writing assignments in IS courses is the case analysis. Although little research has investigated the case analysis genre in IS (however, see Miller & Pessoa, 2016), this genre has been studied extensively in the fields of business and business communication. The case analysis follows the Harvard case method (Leenders & Erskine, 1989), providing students with a case and asking them to write an analysis and a solution to the problems presented in the case. Louise Mauffette-Leenders et al. (1997) describe a case as a "description of an actual situation, commonly involving a decision, a challenge, an opportunity, a problem or an issue faced by a person (or persons) in an organization" (p. 2). A case analysis, then, is a "written case response in which writers analyze a case and identify key factors influencing events and actions in the case or influencing possible recommendations and decision-making" (Nathan, 2013, p. 59). In a business case analysis, writers apply business concepts, theory, and knowledge to the analysis of business problems and business decision-making processes (Zhu, 2004). The IS case analysis is similar, but the concepts, problems, and solutions often have a technological component.

The practice of writing a case analysis has a wide range of targeted learning outcomes. It may allow students to develop an understanding of theoretical concepts; connect theory with application; develop analytical, problem-solving, decision-making, and higher-order reasoning skills through the integration of multiple concepts; apply disciplinary models to business problems in order to bring real-world issues and dilemmas into the classroom; and participate in experiential learning (Forman & Rymer, 1999; Hackney et al., 2003; Mauffette-Leenders et al., 1997).

The case analysis genre is challenging for students for two important reasons. The first major challenge stems from the fact that expectations for its organization are not consistent across courses (Miller & Pessoa, 2016; Pessoa et al., 2019); some professors provide a set of questions to be answered discretely, while others expect a mock-professional document (and even among these there may be variation based on the rhetorical demands of the case). Although the organization of instances of the genre vary, case analyses often follow a problem-solution structure which includes an analysis and evaluation of the case using concepts from the discipline (i.e., business or IS) and recommendations for the company/organization to enhance its practice based on the preceding analysis (Gardner & Nesi, 2012). Thus, to effectively meet the rhetorical demands of this problem-solution structure, the case analysis genre involves analytical argumentative writing, which is the second reason why this genre presents challenges for students, particularly second-language learners.

Even as students gain familiarity with the genre, it is challenging for them to know when to report on the case and when they need to analyze and make well-supported claims about the case (Miller & Pessoa, 2016). In other words, students can misinterpret the assignment to be asking for knowledge display when the professor actually expects knowledge transformation (cf. Scardamalia & Bereiter, 1987; Young & Leinhardt, 1998). Therefore, without explicit instruction, students may only demonstrate an understanding of the details of the case. However, professors expect students to engage in higher-level skills of applying disciplinary concepts analytically in support of evaluative claims about the company's problems and potential solutions to solve them. To make such distinctions explicit for students, we have found the Onion Model (Humphrey & Economou, 2015) to be a useful scaffolding tool.

SFL-Based Genre Pedagogy and the Onion Model for Scaffolding Disciplinary Writing

In this section, we provide a brief overview of SFL-based genre pedagogy (Martin & Rose, 2007) and the Onion Model (Humphrey & Economou, 2015). SFL genre pedagogy consists of three main phases of instruction: deconstruction, joint construction, and independent construction. Students analyze (deconstruct) a model text with a teacher, then jointly compose a text in the same genre, and finally compose a text in the same genre independently. In our collaboration with IS faculty supporting writing of the case analysis, we focus primarily on strategies for the deconstruction and independent construction phases of instruction (we do not engage in joint construction of texts because of time constraints).

To scaffold student writing of the case analysis, we draw on Sally Humphrey and Dorothy Economou's (2015) Onion Model, a model of academic language which sees the discourse patterns of description, analysis, and argument as layered (hence the name) and interdependent. The Onion Model can aid in unpacking the language expectations of genres across the disciplines and help students move beyond knowledge display by drawing their attention to the differences between the three discourse patterns and how analysis requires description, and argument requires analysis.

According to the Onion Model, description involves "reproduc[ing] knowledge usually by summarizing" and is organized by time or by entities (Humphrey and Economou, 2015, p. 40). In other words, it refers to when writers use description to represent agreed-upon information from the discipline or ideas from sources without re-organizing them. Such representations can be organized with a focus on entities (i.e., people, things, and qualities) or events (as a narrative that unfolds in time). For example, a student attempting a case analysis might think it is only necessary to demonstrate an understanding of the case and simply describe the problems the company faced with chronological organization: *In the early 1980s, the company first started to experience problems. In 1985.* . . .

Analysis is characterized by "re-organisation by the writer of information from the field, or one or more sources, in some original way for the purposes of the text" (Humphrey and Economou, 2015, p. 42). This often involves applying a disciplinary framework to a case, an example, or data of some kind. A disciplinary framework may be thought of as a discipline's agreed-upon classificatory and compositional schemes, or, in other words, its analytical lenses. Analytical writing is organized by the elements of the disciplinary framework—that is, sentences and paragraphs are often grouped together based on the relevant components of the framework. For example, a student writing a case analysis might be asked to apply the disciplinary framework of innovation to the details of the case. This framework is composed of five different elements: incremental, radical, product, process, and complementary innovation. After using the framework to consider the details of the case, the student might decide that only two elements are relevant and productive for analysis, and assert, *The LEGO company implemented two types of innovation: incremental and complementary.* Then, the student would need to demonstrate the accuracy of the analysis by providing some details of the case: *LEGO implemented incremental innovation when it changed the materials used to make its bricks. Having suffered some setbacks, LEGO switched from metal to plastic and increased the affordability of the product.* The student provides details from the case with description, but in support of the analysis; the case provided the information about the change in materials, but the student had to identify this as incremental innovation and use this information for the purposes of their text. While description alone is usually not sufficient for meeting the expectations of university writing, it is often necessary when used purposefully to further analysis.

Finally, with the discourse pattern of argument, the writer "develops and argues for an explicit evaluation of, or claim about" ideas or perspectives within a field of study (Humphrey & Economou, 2015, p. 44). Whereas analysis is organized by the disciplinary framework, argument is organized by a claims-reasons framework that the writer generates for the purpose of the text. The writer takes a position and provides reasons to support it, maintaining a consistent evaluative stance throughout and using interpersonal resources to reference outside voices and to guide the reader towards the position. Analysis is often embedded within this claims-reasons framework in support of the writer's position. For example, a student might write, *LEGO implemented innovation with mixed success. It was very successful in implementing incremental innovation, but mostly unsuccessful in its implementation of radical innovation.* With these two sentences, the student has created a claims-reasons framework that will use the analysis based on the disciplinary framework to support the overall argument.

Given the known challenge students at our university faced with the IS case analysis—reporting the details of the case at the expense of more valued analytical and argumentative writing—the Onion Model has proven to be a useful tool for the analysis of model texts and materials we generated to scaffold their independent construction.

Context and Data Sources: Scaffolding Writing in an Information Systems Course

In this section, we explain how we scaffolded case analysis writing in an introductory IS course at a branch campus of an American university in the Middle East. All courses at this institution are taught in English, and the curriculum largely follows that of the main campus in the US. Through collaboration with information systems faculty and analyses of assignments and student writing, we developed several strategies to better scaffold the case analysis genre.

To scaffold the writing of the case analysis, we first collaborated with the IS professors to revise assignment instructions to better reflect the expected language patterns—description, analysis, and/or argument—of the assignment (for a detailed overview of the revisions to an assignment, see Pessoa et al., 2019). Once the assignments had been redesigned, we conducted a series of in-class writing workshops to scaffold student writing of the case analysis. In the first of these workshops, which is the focus of this chapter, we began with a brief overview of the Onion Model. We explained that we were discussing the Onion Model because we had learned from analyzing the writing of students in prior iterations of the course that students did not generally meet expectations for analysis, but rather just re-presented details from the case. We explained to the students the need to explicitly distinguish between this type of descriptive writing and the analytical and argumentative writing that they were expected to do. We were careful to point out that some description would be necessary in their case analysis, but that their writing should not primarily be about showing that they had read and understood the case. Rather, they would need to analyze the case and then provide and support an argument in response to the assignment prompt (_How successful was the company's implementation of innovation?_).

To walk students through the pre-writing process of analysis, we provided a visualization (see Figure 13.1) to help them understand what it means to analyze. This visual representation of the process of analysis is not specific to the case analysis genre, but rather shows what any student must do to analyze using a particular disciplinary framework. In this visualization, we show how, for case analysis, students need to consider the assignment questions and source texts about the case provided by the professor in light of information about the discipline they have learned in class and from their own research about a company. The information from the course includes the disciplinary framework, which the students must relate to the details of the case (the "data") that they gather from the source texts and their research. For this assignment, the disciplinary framework students had to use was _innovation_, which comprises different elements: product (innovating new products), process (innovating new ways of making products), radical (introducing something new and different to the market), incremental (making small changes to existing products), and complementary (finding new ways to market existing products).

The visualization shows how to break down a case into its constituent parts and group details according to _relevant_ elements of a disciplinary framework; while there may be many elements that constitute a disciplinary framework, the student might find that certain elements do not relate to the details of the case. Once the relevant parts of the framework have been applied, the student needs to evaluate the overall case according to the prompt. Thus, for a prompt asking about the company's success in implementing innovation, the student would: (1) analyze the details of the case considering each element of the disciplinary framework, (2) decide which elements are relevant to the events of the case, (3) evaluate the company's success in implementing each relevant type of innovation, and (4) use these evaluations to make an overall evaluation about (the degree of) the company's success.

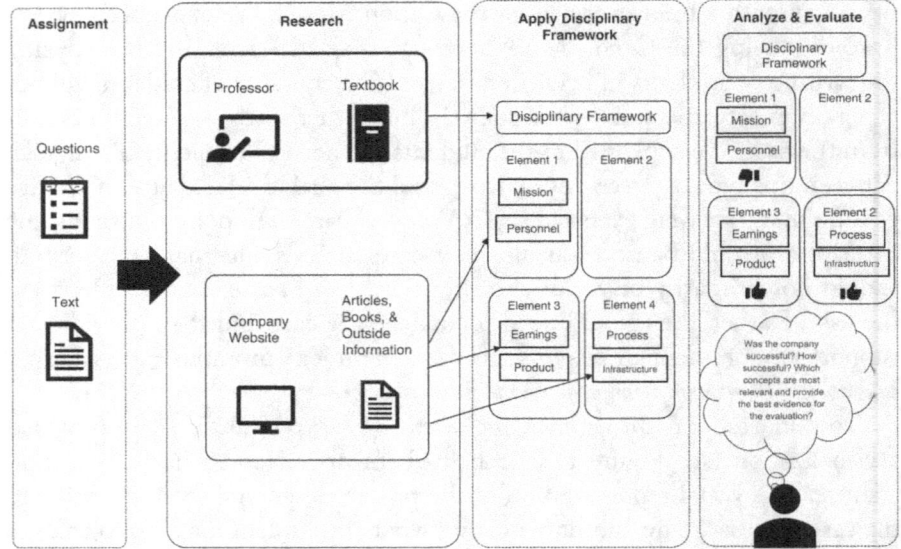

Figure 13.1. Visual representation of the pre-writing analytical process.

As we discussed this process with the students, we related it explicitly to the Onion Model. In order to encourage students to use purposeful description, we told them to collect pieces of information from the case that would support their analysis and evaluations. We also reinforced the idea of this being an analytical process that could apply to other assignments or other courses *and* that this same case could be analyzed using a different disciplinary framework from IS or another discipline. In other words, we tried to get the students to see how they were applying a particular analytical lens so that they did not think we were just giving them step-by-step instructions for a single assignment.

To get the students to see how their pre-writing analysis could be used in support of an argument, we provided a visual representation of the process for writing a case analysis (see Figure 13.2) whereby we showed how the discrete evaluations produced from the analysis could be used in support of an overall evaluation in response to the prompt. If the analysis showed that the company was successful in, for example, the implementation of two types of innovation, then this analysis could be used to make an overall evaluative claim about the company's success. Thus, we emphasized the need to take a step back from the analysis and consider what it means as a whole in relation to the prompt.

The visual representation highlights the fact that students need to create and organize their text with a claim-reasons framework that integrates the disciplinary framework-based analysis as support for an evaluation. To do

Using the Onion Model

so, they need to front an evaluative claim (e.g., LEGO *was <u>successful</u> in its approach to innovation, particularly in its use of <u>complementary and incremental innovation</u>*) and provide reasons for this claim (e.g., *LEGO's use of complementary innovation was successful <u>because it led to an increase in profits and to the growth of the company's customer base</u>*). To achieve this, students need to engage in analysis that involves breaking down the case into its smaller parts and showing how its parts fit into the elements of the disciplinary framework of innovation. As Humphrey and Economou (2015) argue, it is the students' analysis that "determines the choice of entities (elements of the disciplinary framework) to be included" in the text (p. 45).

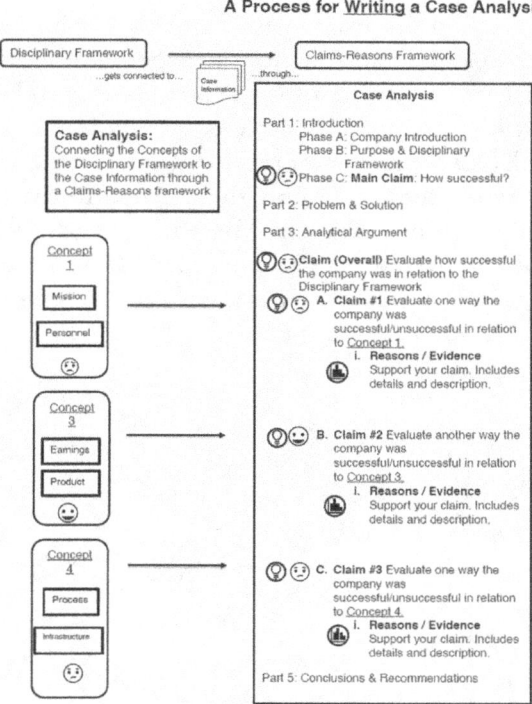

Figure 13.2. *Visual representation of process to use analytical pre-writing to write a case analysis.*

Analysis of Student Writing

In what follows, we show how one student who participated in our writing workshops filled out the visual representation of the analytical process before writing the case analysis.

247

Given that this student was taking an introductory IS course, the case analysis assignment was based on two short texts that narrated problems encountered by the LEGO company and the solutions the company implemented (Basulto, 2014). Basically, the aim of the assignment was to have students analyze the strategies that the LEGO company implemented to overcome its decline in sales in the early 2000s and the extent to which LEGO was successful in the implementation of these strategies. In order to achieve this, students first needed to describe the case in their own words (i.e., summarize and synthesize the problems that the company faced and the solutions it implemented), and then analyze and evaluate the extent to which LEGO's strategies were successful in overcoming their problems. Students were to rely on the disciplinary framework of innovation (as explicated in the course) and refer to the various types of innovation introduced (e.g., incremental vs. radical innovation, process vs. product innovation). Figure 13.3 shows how before writing the case analysis, the student analyzed the case of the LEGO company by breaking its important details into parts, grouping them, and determining how they related to the elements of the disciplinary framework of innovation. Based on the analysis, the student then determined the overall evaluation (i.e., *LEGO was unsuccessful in its implementation of incremental innovation, but was successful in its implementation of complementary innovation*).

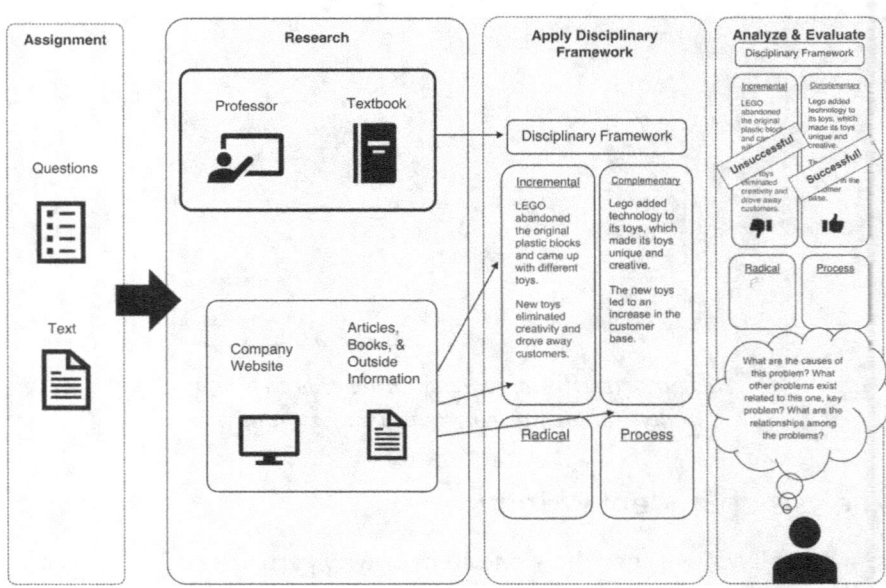

Figure 13.3. Analysis graphic organizer with content from student paper.

Using the Onion Model

The annotated analytical argument section of the case analysis assignment produced by the same student is shown in Figures 13.4 and 13.5. In the introductory paragraph of the analysis/argument section, the student uses the disciplinary framework of innovation, and labels and defines the kinds of innovation that are the focus of the analysis: incremental and complementary innovation. The student succeeds in making explicit evaluations (e.g., *In LEGO's case, this approach was unsuccessful*), and in providing a claims-reasons framework to support the asserted evaluations of LEGO's performance. For example, in the second paragraph, the student signals their overall evaluation of LEGO's success and their intention to apply one of the specific elements of the disciplinary framework (i.e., complementary innovation). The student then contextualizes the analysis by accurately defining this element of the disciplinary framework according to established knowledge of the field. Then, the student shows how complementary innovation was implemented by LEGO, thus demonstrating an understanding of this element of the disciplinary framework by applying it to information from the case.

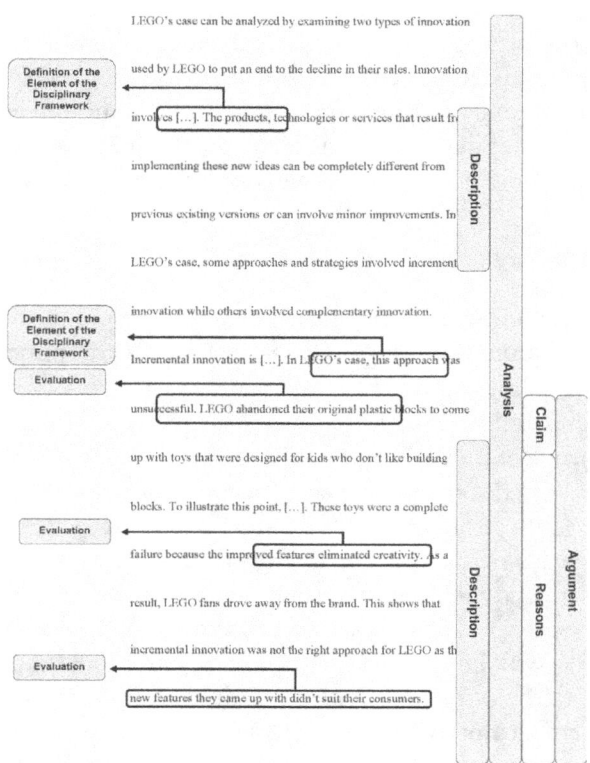

Figure 13.4. Student's analytical argument section of the case analysis assignment.

The student uses description (e.g., *LEGO used technology, LEGO transformed*) in service of their analysis that technology was the "something" that LEGO associated with its original product. The student moves from this analysis to supporting their asserted evaluation (*this approach was successful*). The student condenses their analysis of LEGO's use of complementary innovation into a single phrase (*this approach*), and then proceeds to give three reasons for the evaluation, namely that the use of technology had unique aspects, it allowed for creativity, and it was engaging to adults as well as children.

Within each element of the framework, the student provides a claim and reason for LEGO's success (e.g., *In addition to uniqueness, this approach allows more creativity; the technology merged with LEGO's new toys allows more space for hacking, tinkering and finding new ways of creating*), provides details from the case to support that reason, and establishes a causal link between these details and an increase in sales (e.g., *These features are great selling points, so they helped in increasing sales for LEGO*). With these causal links, the student effectively uses technical language from the definition of complementary innovation to remind the reader that they are illustrating the company's successful implementation of this strategy. Overall, this student is very effective in weaving together analytical and argumentative writing to meet genre expectations. The student combines analysis using the disciplinary framework—the received taxonomy of innovation—with argument using their own claims-reasons framework to support the asserted evaluation of LEGO's success/failure.

Discussion

Student writing at university varies greatly depending on context and discipline. For English for Academic Purposes (EAP) instructors, this presents challenges in terms of establishing expectations and scaffolding learning for student writing, especially regarding analytical and argumentative writing. In WID contexts, the challenge of the variety of writing genres across the disciplines can be successfully addressed through language-focused scaffolding, such as the application of SFL genre pedagogy and the Onion Model of academic language.

In this chapter, we have shown a variety of strategies for scaffolding student learning in disciplinary writing that can be adapted to other disciplines. This is evident in our own work, as we have recently extended the lessons learned from our collaboration with information systems to organizational behavior. Through this approach, EAP instructors can help scaffold disciplinary literacy and help students succeed in composing convincing analytical arguments across the curriculum. This approach can be useful in contexts where EAP is challenged by moving students from knowledge display to knowledge transformation.

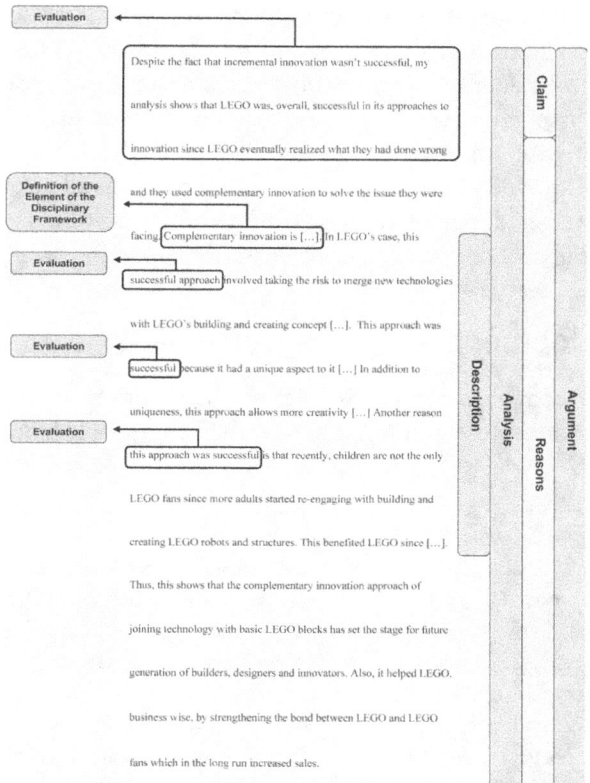

Figure 13.5. Student's analytical argument section of the case analysis assignment continued.

Our approach to scaffolding the case analysis genre was made possible by having an invested IS professor who was interested in addressing student needs through a focus on language. He helped us learn the disciplinary knowledge and worked with us to make our materials accessible to students. His willingness to engage in recurrent reflection about the effectiveness of the scaffolding materials and experiment with adjustments were instrumental for the positive outcomes of this collaboration. The small size of the university (around 400 total students housed in a single building) also facilitated regular interactions with the disciplinary instructor.

Our ongoing research focuses on how students take up our scaffolding materials, and how disciplinary faculty merge language knowledge with content knowledge in their teaching and feedback. Our preliminary analysis suggests that students are taking up the instruction in their writing through improved argumentation and analysis. Even low-graded assignments show signs of our scaffolding, such as a pervasive use of a claims-reasons framework with a clear evaluation in the thesis and topic sentence positions. We have seen evidence of benefits to the faculty as well. The instructor in the introductory IS course who teaches the case assignment has become very adept at identifying the discourse patterns of description, analysis, and argument, and draws on this knowledge in his lectures and written feedback. Our research provides further evidence of how productive interdisciplinary collaboration between writing and content faculty can be in supporting student learning.

Acknowledgement

This research study was made possible by NPRP grant # 8-1815-5-293 from the Qatar National Research Fund (a member of Qatar Foundation).

References

Basulto, D. (2014). Why LEGO is the most innovative toy company in the world. *Washington Post*. https://www.washingtonpost.com/news/innovations/wp/2014/02/13/why-lego-is-the-most-innovative-toy-company-in-the-world/.

Brisk, M. E. (2014). *Engaging students in academic literacies: Genre-based pedagogy for K–5 classrooms*. Routledge.

Brisk, M. E. & Zisselsberger, M. (2011). We've let them in on the secret: Using SFL theory to improve the teaching of writing to bilingual learners. In T. Lucas (Ed.), *Teacher preparation for linguistically diverse classrooms: A resource for teacher educators* (pp. 111–126). Routledge.

Dreyfus, S., Humphrey, S., Mahboob, A. & Martin, J. M. (2016). *Genre pedagogy in higher education: The SLATE Project*. Palgrave Macmillan.

Forman, J. & Rymer, J. (1999). Defining the genre of the "case write-up." *Journal of Business Communication, 36*, 103–133.

Gardner, S. & Nesi, H. (2012). A classification of genre families in university student writing. *Applied Linguistics, 34*(1), 25–52.

Gebhard, M., Willet, J., Jimenez, J. P. & Piedra, A. (2011). Systemic functional linguistics, teachers' professional development, and ELLs' academic literacy practices. In T. Lucas (Ed.), *Teacher preparation for linguistically diverse classrooms: A resource for teacher educators* (pp. 91–110). Routledge.

Hackney, R. A., McMaster, T. & Harris, A. (2003). Using cases as a teaching tool in IS education. *Journal of Information Systems Education, 14*, 229–234.

Humphrey, S. & Economou, D. (2015). Peeling the onion—A textual model of critical analysis. *Journal of English for Academic Purposes, 17*, 37–50.

Humphrey, S. & Macnaught, L. (2016). Functional language instruction and the writing growth of English language learners in the middle years. *TESOL Quarterly, 50*, 792–816.

Lancaster, Z. (2014). Making stance explicit for second language writers in the disciplines: What faculty need to know about the language of stance-taking. In T. M. Zawacki & M. Cox (Eds.), *WAC and second language writers: Research towards linguistically and culturally inclusive programs and practices* (pp. 269–298). The WAC Clearinghouse; Parlor Press. https://doi.org/10.37514/PER-B.2014.0551.2.11.

Leenders, M. R. & Erskine, J. A. (1989). *Case research: The case writing process*. University of Western Ontario.

Liu, M. X. & Murphy, D. (2012). Fusing communication and writing skills in the 21st century's IT/IS curricula. *Information Systems Education Journal, 10*, 48–54.

Martin, J. R. & Rose, D. (2007). *Working with discourse: Meaning beyond the clause* (2nd ed.). Continuum International Publishing Group.

Mauffette-Leenders, L. A., Erskine, J. A. & Leenders, M. R. (1997). *Learning with cases*. University of Western Ontario.

Merhout, J. W. & Etter, S. J. (2005). Integrating writing into IT/MIS courses. *International Journal of Information and Communication Technology Education, 1*, 74–84.

Miller, R. T. & Pessoa, S. (2016). Role and genre expectations in undergraduate case analysis in information systems. *English for Specific Purposes, 44*, 43–56.

Mitchell, T. D & Pessoa, S. (2017). Scaffolding the writing development of the argument genre in history: The case of two novice writers. *Journal of English for Academic Purposes, 30*, 26–37.

Nathan, P. (2013). Academic writing in the business school: The genre of the business case report. *Journal of English for Academic Purposes, 12*, 57–68.

Pessoa, S., Gomez-Laich, M. P., Liginlal, D. & Mitchell, T. D. (2019). Scaffolding case analysis writing: A collaboration between IS and writing faculty. *Journal of Information Systems Education, 30*, 42–56.

Pessoa, S., Mitchell, T. D. & Miller, R. T. (2018). Scaffolding the argument genre in a multilingual university history classroom: Tracking the writing development of novice and experienced writers. *English for Specific Purposes, 50*, 81–96.

Rothery, J. (1996). Making changes: Developing an educational linguistics. In R. Hasan & G. Williams (Eds.), *Literacy in society* (pp. 86–123). Longman.

Scardamalia, M. & Bereiter, C. (1987). Knowledge telling and knowledge transforming in written composition. In S. Rosenberg (Ed.), *Advances in applied linguistics: Reading, writing, and language*. Cambridge University Press.

Sidorova, A., Evangelopoulos, N., Valacich, J. S. & Ramakrishnan, T. (2008). Uncovering the intellectual core of the information systems discipline. *MIS Quarterly: Management Information Systems, 32*, 467–482.

Topi, H., Valacich, J. S., Wright, R. T., Kaiser, K., Nunamaker, J. F., Jr., Sipior, J. C. & de Vreede, G. J. (2010). IS 2010: Curriculum guidelines for undergraduate degree programs in information systems. *Communications of the Association for Information Systems, 26*. Article 18.

Young, K. M. & Leinhardt, G. (1998). Writing from primary documents: A way of knowing in history. *Written Communication, 15*, 25–68.

Zhu, W. (2004). Writing in business courses: An analysis of assignment types, their characteristics, and required skills. *English for Specific Purposes, 23*, 111–135.

14 Beyond "Coping" to Natural Language Work: A Case Study at a Transnational Campus

Jay Jordan
University of Utah

> Abstract: Literature in second language writing often describes as "coping" a range of student activities, from creative attempts to clarify assignment prompts to relying on native/home languages to resisting teachers' demands altogether. While "coping" has provided valuable insights into the students' creativity that may be overlooked by their putative language differences, the term risks re-inscribing deficit-based thinking that students' creativity perhaps only appears in the face of intransigent faculty expectations. This chapter presents data from a case study of an undergraduate student at the Korean branch of a US-based transnational university. It argues that the student's nuanced academic work was consistently informed by her implicit desire to connect that work with other language acquisition in the complex ecology of the campus.
>
> Keywords: second language writing, rhetoric, transnational, writing across the curriculum (WAC), Korea

Literature in second language writing points to a range of ways to theorize what Ilona Leki (1995) refers to as "coping strategies." Leki's qualitative analysis of interviews, observations, and assignment-based and research journal-based writing revealed student responses to writing tasks ranging from clarifying the demands of assignments to relying on their native/home languages to resisting teachers' demands altogether. In perhaps the most telling reported comment in Leki's study, her student "Ling" demonstrated her awareness of cultural/linguistic difference and her simultaneous desire to employ such difference productively:

> [T]he strategy that Ling used most effectively was taking advantage of first language/culture by relying on her special

status as an international student. As the semester went on, she attempted to incorporate something about China or Taiwan into every piece of writing she did, saying, "I am Chinese. I take advantage." Thus, her term paper in Behavioral Geography became a comparison of Taiwanese and U.S. shopping habits. Her term paper in World History became a comparison of ancient Chinese and Greek education and this despite her history professor's direct request that she not focus yet again on China. In this case she used a combined strategy of resisting the professor's request and of reliance on her special status as a Chinese person, and it worked. (Leki, 1995, p. 242)

As Leki's term has circulated in scholarship since, the concept of "coping strategies" has provided valuable insight into the creative ways students can exceed predefined limits imposed on them because of their putative language limitations. In Pat Currie's (1998) often-cited case study, her student, Diana, employed textual borrowing as a creative survival strategy, copying and pasting terms from a course text into her own writing as a way to satisfy her professor's and teaching assistant's goal of helping her adopt and adapt field-specific vocabulary. As Diana related to Currie in an interview,

> Usually I stick to the book because they give you a better expression of what you're supposed to say. Usually you would say "department" but in the book they say "unit" and that will give you another terminology, so you won't just stay with certain areas. You try to expand your knowledge of what actually in society the people are using the term. (Currie, 1998, p. 10)

But while "coping" through imitation seems more positive and less academically or ethically fraught than "copying," I argue that the term risks re-inscribing deficit-laden implications that second language writers act with agency primarily, if not exclusively, in the face of intransigent faculty demands and rigid academic and disciplinary expectations. In other words, the term suggests not only that students can perhaps *only* "cope," but also that instructors and faculty members can *only* create inflexible assignments and evaluation/assessment mechanisms that necessitate students' coping.

My three-and-a-half-year longitudinal study of students and their instructors at a transnational campus (hereafter referred to as the "Asia Campus") suggests that students can and do act with considerably variable competence, and it also suggests that the ground for that competence is extremely nuanced and capacious. Despite assumptions that Korean students demonstrate monolithic characteristics (including filial and social conservatism as well as a lack of spontaneous procedural knowledge of English), I have encountered students whose backgrounds, experiences, goals, and implicit awareness of the transnational campus' unique material and rhetorical affordances and constraints demonstrate surprising diversity. I have also encountered faculty informants who creatively negotiate their expectations, balancing a clear desire to support students' understanding of disciplinary expectations on the one hand with an awareness of how those expectations are under pressure in a transnational context on the other. In this chapter, I want to focus on one student's instances of "coping" that show not only her adaptive responses to writing/speaking tasks but that also hint at broader entanglements of assigning and doing writing, especially in a transnational setting. Overall, I argue, this student's work shows her development of more "natural" responses to the complex language ecology of her campus of a transnational university.

Sensitizing to "Coping"

I refer to "sensitizing concepts" here following Herbert Blumer (1954) and Kathy Charmaz (2003), who define them, respectively, as ideas that provide "reference and guidance in approaching empirical instances" (Blumer, 1954, p. 7) and as "starting points for building analysis. . . . points of departure from which to study the data" (Charmaz, 2003, p. 259) rather than stable theory machines into which we feed data for predictable results. Previous research has certainly sensitized me to the emergence of students' coping and to other evidence of their creative agency. In detailing Diana's strategies, for instance, Currie (1998) noted that Diana deployed textual borrowing in the absence of direct instruction about or scaffolding of writing in her management course. But beyond Diana's uses of textual borrowing to approach tacit generic and stylistic demands, Currie argued that Diana's strategy more broadly provided evidence of ongoing natural language acquisition and allowed her to "enact . . . the role of competent [organizational behavior] student" (p. 11), appropriating language to identify herself as an emerging member of an academic and professional community. She sought assistance from and invited knowledge sharing among peer students, modified sentence and paragraph structures to emulate explicit models she found, and—tellingly—strategically *avoided* textual borrowing when a low-stakes assignment made doing so unnecessary. For Currie, this last action of Diana's highlighted her awareness of a need to manage cognitive load, but it also showed that Diana did not simply default to copying out of a lack of competence. Congjun Mu and Suzanne Carrington (2007) discussed their Chinese student participants' similar management strategies: while their students read extensively in their fields for conceptual knowledge, they also clearly read to collect choice idiomatic expressions they could then paraphrase and repurpose in their own writing.

In studying South Korean high school and university students, Kyoung Rang Lee and Rebecca Oxford (2008) noted even more elaborate and, crucially, adaptive strategies. Where their high school student informants memorized and/or dictated expressions they encountered in relevant language learning materials, university students apparently felt freer to use more entertaining content, such as music, film, and magazines, and in some cases, they imitated favorite English-speaking actors or attempted to predict upcoming lines of dramatic dialogue. Underlying such adaptation and creative use of academic and entertainment material is what Xiao Lei (2008), following Leo van Lier (2004), described as an approach to ongoing language learning that "potentially involves the whole world" (Lei, 2008, p. 219). One of Lei's student informants, Henry, described his tendency to "extract some beautiful sentences and words from literary works, keep them in [his] notebook, review, recite, and remember them," using them selectively in his own writing. He went on to relate that sometimes the expressions "pop[ped] up in [his] mind" as he wrote (p. 224). As Henry and Lei's other informant, Jenny, reported, they could feel "temporarily immersed in an English environment while living in a Chinese-speaking society" (p. 225) as a result of such language work—an environment that Lei argued afforded them opportunities to feel like more "natural" composers of English.

The transnational campus where I have conducted research is a rich site where natural and artificial ideas about place, nationality, and conditions for education are in flux. US-based assumptions about higher education—ranging from the role of general education to faculty informality with students to the idea that "participation" in class can and should mean "individual speech" —interact daily with Korean assumptions about educational specialization and about wide distances between faculty and students. The mix is sensible on a daily basis, and it has required creative adaptation. Again, as I argue, students' own complex adaptation is apparent—and not merely "coping."

Campus Ecologies and "Natural" Language Work: The Case of Alice

"Alice" is a South Korean national in her late 20s who majored in communication from her enrollment at the Asia Campus in 2014 until her 2018 graduation. She attended Korean primary and secondary schools throughout her education and traveled briefly to Canada during high school. She has been and remains active on social media—especially Instagram and YouTube, where videos and images show evidence of her interests in travel, food, and differences in the ways Koreans and Americans interact. Like many of her peers, Alice found the dual adjustment from high school English courses (which emphasized grammar and speaking exercises over writing) into the required first-year writing courses at the Asia Campus—and *then* from those courses into gateway news and magazine writing courses in the communication major—highly challenging. An additional course on public speaking prompted further anxiety among many of the students, even though relatively formal speaking contests are a staple of Korean middle and high schools. In the following excerpt, Alice relates her response to a speech assignment that shows clear evidence of what Leki and other scholars might well call "coping":

> Jay[1]: How do you feel like, well, do you feel like the way you write has changed since you've been here? You're in your fourth semester now, and, if so, how do you feel like it has changed as a result of being here?
>
> Alice: So, compared to my work during the first semester, I think it improved a lot actually. Yeah, because my English skills actually improved throughout the semesters and listening to professors' lectures, I guess-
>
> Jay: Listening to lectures helps
>
> Alice: Mm hmm, and actually reading a lot helps too.
>
> Jay: Can you be specific about how you've improved? Are there particular things that you've noticed that you feel more confident about?
>
> Alice: So it's only about writing, right?
>
> Jay: Writing or speaking, I mean, they are related. So, if you feel like one has gotten better than the other, or things like that, that would be interesting to know.
>
> Alice: Yeah, ever since I took the public speaking class, it was Professor W.'s class, that one was a tough one. Cause he wouldn't give us an A if we tried to read from the paper. So

---

1   All transcriptions use minimal markup provided by the professional transcriber. Deletion of end punctuation indicates at least some overlap with the next utterance. Ellipsis on an otherwise blank line indicates the exclusion of at least one line of quoted transcripted speech.

I have to memorize the whole speech. I had to. To get an A. So I did it for every speech.

Jay: Wow.

Alice: Like, which was about five to eight minutes.

Jay: So you were writing these speeches?

Alice: Yeah, I wrote the script and memorized the thing

Jay: Each time

Alice: Word by word. Yeah, each time, and I think that helped me a lot.

... Jay: memorizing, how did you go about memorizing the presentation? The speech you had to give.

Alice: The last presentation I gave was kind of huge because there was a speech competition. He [Professor W.] made a speech competition, like [Asia Campus] students, [another university's] students, yes, and I had to go there to just get an A. And for that, it was also long, it was an eight-minute speech. So what I did was I wrote the whole script and then I read it several times and then without script, I started giving a speech with my, what, recorder? And I, of course I would make mistakes. Whenever I would do it, I stopped that, and I'd listen to what I say and I'd do it again and again and again and finally I memorized the whole thing. I think it's also because I hear a lot what I'm talking about. Myself.

Jay: So you say the speech into the recording, you listen to it, and then you

Alice: Yeah

Jay: Okay, that was pretty fascinating actually.

Alice: So I don't think, cause even Professor W. didn't know that I memorize the whole thing.

Considering that the instructor had asked students to speak extemporaneously—not reading or memorizing—Alice's memorization appears similar to the kind of resistance Leki's student, Ling, showed. To be sure, Alice is highly motivated by assignment and course grades, and her perfect GPA at graduation was a clear symbol of her desire to, as Leki's student, Ling, put it, "take advantage." Here, though, like Leki's student, Henry, Alice also shows complex awareness of and adaptation to other, less obvious considerations. Her listening to lectures, for instance, gave her a guide that could, like the expressions that "popped up" into Henry's mind, be available for later occasions, such as her speech.

Indeed, Alice's awareness of the importance of "natural"-seeming comfort with English even in academic or professional environments inflected her tacit definition of "research," a term that may have arisen in my student and faculty interviews more than any other single word:

> Alice: I think that writing well is, for students who are using their second language, I think research skill is actually different. So when I try to write my paper, I try to read it, just read news stories that are, even though, I mean . . . that are related to or not related to the topic I'm about to write. So that I can be prepared with my writing. And I think that's, that's research. No? Because it's really hard for us to create our own expressions. Cause it won't be natural.
>
> Jay: OK. You mean written expressions.
>
> Alice: No matter how we try, yeah.
>
> Jay: Why do you think, you said that research is especially important for students who speak English as a second language. Why is it especially important for students like you?
>
> Alice: Because without research skills, um, you won't achieve the, you won't be able to write what you want to write. I think whenever I try to write something, I try to find similar writings. I mean, similar expressions.
>
> Jay: So similar to the type of writing you want to do?
>
> Alice: Not even though when the writings are not related to my topic, at all, there might be similar expressions that I want to write.
>
> Jay: You're reading the sources that you feel you need to read in order to do the research. But then you also read other things.
>
> Alice: Other things too.

> Jay: And how do you find those other things if they're not related to the topic?
>
> Alice: Just random things.
>
> Jay: Just random things.
>
> Alice: Yeah, I would, might be, I would maybe read textbooks or magazines. I don't know, and like, I just um skim through it and if I find similar expressions, that I want to write, I use that and after I do it like once or twice, it kind of, I can kind of memorize it so that I can use it again. It's not much problem later.

Alice here relates her adoption of an autodidactic method that foreign language teachers have long advocated—that is, reading whatever you can get your hands on in the target language. Interestingly, she shows (as a university student) some of the material selection techniques of *both* Lee and Oxford's (2008) high school *and* university students: among the "random things" at hand are secondary sources for class research, class texts themselves, websites, and quite likely, other textual and not-so-textual sources from social media, given her habits and interests. The combination of those interests and relevant media plus Alice's motivation to learn and rehearse course content for the A grades she felt she needed generated a storehouse for her expressions—and one that I believe is available to her in ways that are not strictly a function of memorization. Alice's hedging around how she "kind of" memorizes is telling: while individual expressions may themselves be important as task-based demonstrations of language competence (much as creating real or virtual decks of flashcards can help language learners expand vocabulary), Alice's browsing practices suggest routines and habits in line with her affective orientation to ongoing English learning.

In a very different assignment, Alice balances "natural" expression, formal writing, and a similarly broad implicit definition of "research" that to my reading demonstrates her negotiation of a need to be credible and creative within complex course- and institution-based expectations. As with "memorization," Alice's approach to "research" in this instance also points to an expansion of that concept's definition:

> Alice: So uh, for the abnormal psychology paper [in a course with the same title], I focused on defining the actual and true meaning of sexual masochism and sadism disorder.
>
> Jay: Okay.

Alice: Cause if it's going to be called a disorder,

Jay: Mm hmm

Alice: It has to have like some characteristics, 'cause um, not all the sadists, sadistic and masochistic behaviors are disorders. And the textbook defined what it was,

Jay: Yeah.

Alice: Shortly. So I kind of wanted to define it with more examples-

Jay: Okay.

Alice: From, I decided to use news articles, because I thought it was going to be easy for me to use real examples, like incidents that happened, with sexual harassment-

Jay: Yeah?

Alice: Yeah. Things like that. For the articles. So I, I did use news articles, two news articles for the paper and one, one scholarly article for the paper

. . . Alice: I chose it because I thought it would be fun, but actually it wasn't because it was harder for me to find like sources, scholarly sources, that was written about that. I mean, there were a lot of sources about that, but not many that I could actually use for the paper.

Jay: Why's that?

Alice: I don't remember exactly, but I think it was because it was too specific. And the textbook only defined the meaning, so to match with the textbook, I had to, yeah, I think that's why it was so hard, there wasn't a lot of sources.

Jay: So you thought it was going to be easy, it was not as easy as you thought it was going to be, how did it turn out? Like, how successful was it?

Alice: So, at first, I thought it was going to be easy, but then I realized that it wasn't too easy. But when I was using news articles, when I decided to use news articles, it became better.

Jay: Okay.

> Alice: Because my idea was to first talk about the subject, sadists, sadistic disorder. The sadistic disorder, I define it first, and then um, sadistic disorder and sadistic behavior are two different things, and then I thought, what is actual incident that is a disorder? If it's on the news, and the person was caught by the police, that's going to be a disorder.
>
> Jay: Yeah, sure.
>
> Alice: So yeah, that's how it became more easy.
>
> Jay: I understand, because if you're seeing, if you're seeing examples in the news, those are very clearly very bad examples-
>
> Alice: Yeah, criminal that has disorder, mostly, yeah.

For Alice, the textbook definitions and descriptions of specific disorders, while technically useful, did not provide enough descriptive range to motivate her writing. While she read her professor's insistence on APA formatting as a clear *formal* requirement, she also detected significant topical and evidentiary affordances beyond that documentation style, and she turned to news articles covering sexual assault to provide compelling heuristic detail. While her easy equation, "if it's on the news, that's going to be a disorder," is highly questionable, her strategy responds to the assignment's content flexibility, rehearses her copious approach to identifying and repurposing diverse source material, and specifically uses examples of newswriting—a collection of genres with which she had become familiar through other coursework and which she was motivated to learn to produce herself, owing in part to her already growing proficiency with and interest in social media.

Reflecting on interactions with faculty members, Alice relates her attempts to cultivate relationships that in turn afforded her not only additional opportunities to understand assignment and course expectations more explicitly but also to develop more "natural" language abilities. During an interview in her third year at the campus, Alice recalled a shift in her approach to reading that suggested an advantage of the small size of the campus:

> Alice: Before, I think, I think writing took more time for me to finish. Cause, I don't think I knew exactly what professors wanted. And, I was focused on understanding all of the materials I had, but I, as time went by, I realized it's not about understanding everything, so I started using some tactics that I could write things faster, and for, to be able to like, satisfy professor's needs, I think.

Jay: Okay, what kinds of tactics, you talked about tactics?

Alice: For example, like I told you um, if I was, if it was my first semester in language and culture class [introductory linguistics course], I think I would have tried to understand all the things in the articles.

Jay: If you had taken it during your first semester, yeah, okay.

Alice: Yeah, and I would have cried or something, every day. But I knew that the professor didn't want me to do that. I mean, he would want me to do that, but he knew that it was difficult, and what he mainly wanted was for us to focus on more important things that he taught during classes. Yeah, it's not, not um, it's not. Important things don't mean difficult things. I tried to, I kind of started understanding order, main things I have to focus.

Jay: So you were getting better at figuring out what the important things were.

Alice: Yeah, what to focus, and what to not use too much energy for.

Jay: Okay, okay, okay, how did you decide, do you think? What was difficult, and what was actually important?

Alice: Mm, first, I looked at abstract, and-

Jay: Okay, so the article, as you're reading the articles.

Alice: I mean, I read the articles, and I think I should understand everything, so I try to understand everything about abstract only, and then-

Jay: Okay.

Alice: Maybe a little bit about the conclusion, read the conclusion, and then I keep my, choose what to use from the body. Is if it's about articles, using articles, yeah. That's what I do.

Jay: Okay, okay, okay, yeah, are there other tactics that you've used? It sounds like the tactic there is that you've learned to read, like if you're looking at really difficult articles, you read them, you choose what to read, you're being selective about what you read, rather than trying to like start at the beginning and go all of the way through?

Alice: I talk to professors. And I focus on what they say, because I think, if they're giving us what to write, like, assignments, they want something, I think. And I think the most important thing to focus on is to that, what they want. What they want to try to teach us, through the whole classes. Um, yeah, I try to think about that, and then I try to listen to what they say, and I try to talk to them personally, if I can. I could all the time, because it's a small campus here. That was really helpful, for me to understand what they wanted.

Alice's general approach is easy to characterize in terms she, herself, provides: give the professor what they want—an approach that underlies many coping strategies. Beneath that superficial description, though, lies a more complex response rooted in Alice's ongoing language learning and socialization. Granted, even as an introductory course, the language and culture class Alice remembers typically includes at least some examples of scholarly literature, which can overwhelm students with jargon and give rise to the kind of survival impulse ("understand all the things in the articles") Alice mentions.[2] Again, on the surface, Alice's habit of regularly meeting faculty members in office hours appears to be a ploy to determine what they really want. But the motivations surrounding Alice's interactions with faculty members are nuanced—as are faculty members' own motivations for meeting Alice and other students. While Alice relates, for instance, that the instructor for her language and culture course may ideally have wanted her to learn "all the things in the articles," she suggests that his more pragmatic attitude was that "important things don't mean difficult things." It is not clear from Alice's comments whether that phrase came word for word from her instructor or whether it represents her pithy summary of what she was learning as she developed time/load management strategies through the language and culture course. However, her comment provides evidence of at least implicit negotiation of expectations between student and faculty, and it also points to a range of both academic and social rationales for individual

---

2   That impulse to "understand all the things" was visible one of the first days of my first semester at the campus, when I walked into the classroom to which I was assigned to find the whiteboard covered with math terminology. I asked one of the students why it was all there, and she told me several students had been in the room late the night before writing and memorizing the terms for their online math course.

meetings. Alice repeats her goal of learning more and more about "what they [faculty members] want," but she also expresses that she consistently tries to listen to them—in class and one on one. Read in a wider context of Alice's desire for more natural English language ability, that emphasis on listening reflects the specific goal of listening for evidence of assignment/course criteria, but it also reflects a broader goal of listening for acquisition more broadly.

Discussion: Language Work in Transnationally Nested Eco-Systems

Writing teaching and learning at the Asia Campus inevitably interanimate with other activities and phenomena, exemplifying what Urie Bronfenbrenner (1979) in the context of human development termed "a system of nested eco-systems" subject to perturbing or ripple effects from one scale to another. Thus, Alice's "coping" is more appropriately understood as a range of actions that account for ecological complexity, and teachers' expectations are more appropriately understood as negotiations within the ecosystems that nest and overlap at the Asia Campus.

To be sure, Alice's language acquisition continued throughout her time in her major. But as van Lier (2004) argues, language learning is emergent: it arises from a collection of elements in ways that, even if the elements can be counted, exceed that sum. Using the metaphor of young children learning the game of soccer/football, van Lier notes that basic rules eventually give way to young athletes' development of a "feel for the game" in which "the game reorganizes itself from 'running after the ball wherever it rolls' to 'moving the ball around collaboratively in strategic ways'" (p. 81). Elsewhere, van Lier argues that "teaching does not cause learning" (p. 196) any more than rules "cause" the game. While the "rules" of the "game" remain consistent, the ways players orient themselves certainly evolve as play continues so that knowing the rules however well does not directly translate to effective play. As Christine Casanave (2009) argues in describing the "language games" of graduate students in her study, the game metaphor, while seeming to be an unserious way to describe the importance of language work in multinational/transnational settings, accurately captures the tenuous balance of rules, boundaries, and creativity inherent to language acquisition. Indeed, Diane Larsen-Freeman (2015) presses on the term "acquisition" itself and argues for a shift in applied linguists' thinking from *acquisition* to language *development* because she understands the former term to be inaccurate. Acquisition for Larsen-Freeman implies that there is a stage at/beyond which a person developing language competencies may "have" the language, while development suggests precisely the kind of emergence "through use in real time," evolution, and synergy that is more typical of ecologies (p. 494; also see Marshall & Marr, 2018; Marshall & Moore, 2013).

If the contexts in which Alice and her faculty members/instructors teach, learn, and work are nested eco-systems, it is perhaps no surprise that "natural" emerges as a way to describe desirable language development. Lei (2008) argued that the students in her study "felt that they could write real English, that is, create a natural English flavor" (p. 225) in a predominately Chinese-speaking context to the extent they had access to English-language media and literary models. Lei analyzed students' work, following tenets of activity theory (Engeström, 1987, 1999; Prior, 1998; Russell, 1995, 1997; Villamil & de Guerrero, 1996), as "mediated actions which are consciously taken to facilitate writers' practices in communities" (p. 220), and it seems clear that Alice's work responds to a very wide set of community considerations. Alice's memorization-for-extemporaneity approach to composing and delivering a public speaking assignment was strategic, and even resistant. Her academically purposeful research and frequent office visits were clearly also socially inflected opportunities to habituate to what she considered natural expression and interaction.

Reconceptualizing students' coping as a range of "natural" adaptations to a nested ecosystem should prompt greater awareness for teachers, students, and researchers. The "linguistic environment immediately increases in complexity when we envisage a learner physically, socially, and mentally moving around a multidimensional semiotic space" (van Lier, 2004, p. 93). So, the shift from seeing "coping" to detecting "natural" language work is a way to recast multilingual composers in terms that foreground their agency and also the agency and adaptability of instructors.

However, given the complexity of this transnational educational experiment, it is important to note that students' agency may lead to outcomes many educators may not prefer or may critically question. In Alice's case, for instance, her experiences in major coursework, as a teaching assistant, as a social media user, and as a media intern led her to an initial career choice as a so-called "star teacher" in Korea. Korea's overheated English education market makes such a choice indeed seem to be a natural one: the most famous teachers in after-hours "cram schools" (called *hagwons* in Korea) and/or on television can earn millions of dollars annually (Fifield, 2014). Thus, Alice's own awareness of Korea's educational ecology prompted her to act in a way responsive to available resources not only within her transnational campus but also within the whole transnational educational and social scene she inhabits.

Just as there is no way to disentangle the educational experiment from the nested university, national, and neoliberal/international ecologies that inform transnational education, there is no way to disentangle students' and instructors' interactions and reflections from the affordances and constraints that enable and help direct them.

References

Blumer, H. (1954). What is wrong with social theory? *American Sociological Review, 19*(1), 3.

Bronfenbrenner, U. (1979). *The ecology of human development: Experiments by nature and design.* Harvard University Press.

Casanave, C. P. (2009). *Writing games: Multicultural case studies of academic literacy practices in higher education.* Routledge.

Charmaz, K. (2003). Grounded theory: Objectivist and constructivist methods. In N. K. Denzin & Y. S. Lincoln (Eds.), *Strategies for qualitative inquiry* (2nd ed., pp. 249–291). Sage.

Currie, P. (1998). Staying out of trouble: Apparent plagiarism and academic survival. *Journal of Second Language Writing, 7*(1), 1–18.

Engeström, Y. (1987). *Learning by expanding: An activity-theoretical approach to developmental research.* Orienta-Konsultit.

Engeström, Y. (1999). Activity theory and individual and social transformation. In Y. Engeström, R. Miettinen & R.-L. Punamäki (Eds.), *Perspectives on activity theory* (pp. 19–38). Cambridge University Press.

Fifield, A. (2014, December 30). In education-crazy South Korea, top teachers become multimillionaires. *Washington Post.* https://www.washingtonpost.com/world/asia_pacific/in-education-crazy-south-korea-top-teachers-become-multi millionaires/2014/12/29/1bf7e7ae-849b-11e4-abcf-5a3d7b3b20b8_story.html.

Larsen-Freeman, D. (2015). Saying what we mean: Making a case for "language acquisition" to become "language development." *Language Teaching, 48*(4), 491–505.

Lee, K. R. & Oxford, R. (2008). Understanding EFL learners' strategy use and strategy awareness. *Asian EFL Journal, 10*(1), 7–32.

Lei, X. (2008). Exploring a sociocultural approach to writing strategy research: Mediated actions in writing activities. *Journal of Second Language Writing, 17*(4), 217–236.

Leki, I. (1995). Coping strategies of ESL students in writing tasks across the curriculum. *TESOL Quarterly, 29*(2), 235.

Marshall, S. & Marr, J. W. (2018). Teaching multilingual learners in Canadian writing-intensive classrooms: Pedagogy, binaries, and conflicting identities. *Journal of Second Language Writing, 40,* 32–43.

Marshall, S. & Moore, D. (2013). 2B or not 2B plurilingual? Navigating languages, literacies, and plurilingual competence in postsecondary education in Canada. *TESOL Quarterly, 47*(3), 472–499.

Mu, C. & Carrington, S. (2007). An investigation of three Chinese students' English writing strategies. *TESL-EJ, 11*(1), 1–23.

Prior, P. (1998). *Writing/disciplinarity: A sociohistoric account of literate activity in the academy*. Erlbaum.

Russell, D. R. (1995). Activity theory and its implications for writing instruction. In J. Petraglia (Ed.), *Reconceiving writing, rethinking writing instruction* (pp. 51–77). Erlbaum.

Russell, D. R. (1997). Rethinking genre in school and society: An activity theory analysis. *Written Communication, 14*(4), 504–554.

van Lier, L. (2004). *The ecology and semiotics of language learning*. Kluwer Academic.

Villamil, O. S. & de Guerrero, M. C. M. (1996). Peer revision in the L2 classroom: Social-cognitive activities, mediating strategies, and aspects of social behavior. *Journal of Second Language Writing, 5*(1), 51–75.

15 Correctness Revisited: How Students (Mis)Identify and Comment on Error in Peers' Drafts

Chris M. Anson
NORTH CAROLINA STATE UNIVERSITY

Abstract: Because teachers continue to feel conflicted about the role of error in writing instruction, it is important to understand students' existing capacities for identifying and avoiding error. Student peer review offers a unique way to study how students identify and discuss error in their peers' drafts, thereby informing intervention both in foundational courses and in courses across the curriculum. This chapter describes a study of student error identification in L1 writing courses in the United States. Students in two sections of a foundational university writing course commented on each other's drafts using an oral screencast program. Drafts were coded for the 20 most commonly identified errors from a previous corpus study. The 58 screencasts were transcribed and coded for every error (mis)identified by students. Results showed that students identified approximately one-tenth of the errors made by their peers, while approximately one in four errors identified were not actually errors. A comparison of results from the two sections (taught by different instructors) also revealed stark differences in the focus and nature of students' comments on error. Because both sections of the course were taught to the same outcomes, the results point to the influence of instructional ideology and genre of the writing on students' constructs of the role of error in peer review.

Keywords: error, grammar, peer review, correctness, instructional ideology

In the field of writing studies, the subject of error detection has historically played a vexed role. For several decades, the literature on teacher response in first-language (L1) instruction eschewed a focus on "surface" details in favor of advocating for broader structural, rhetorical, and meaning-based concerns (e.g., Hillocks, 1986; Hunter & Wallace, 1995; McQuade, 1980).[1] This orientation has also characterized writing-across-the-curriculum programs as well as writing centers, whose missions often overtly explain that tutors will work with students on all aspects of their writing, avoiding a central focus on grammar and correctness (Burchett, 2019).

Although writing researchers have long been interested in the nature, causes, and detection of error (Anson, 2000; Bartholomae, 1980; Hartwell, 1985; Kroll & Shafer, 1978; Noguchi, 1991; Shaughnessy, 1977; Weaver, 1996), error still often exists, but at the margins of instructional attention in writing programs, writing across the curriculum/writing in the disciplines (WAC/WID) programs, and writing centers, with commentary that "systematic instruction in grammar, usage, mechanics, and punctuation is on the wane . . . " (Sloan, 1990, p. 299). Uncontested, long-standing research from meta-analyses supports such an order of priorities. George Hillocks (1984) remarked that "the study of traditional school grammar (i.e., the definition of parts of speech, the parsing of sentences, etc.) has no effect on the quality of student writing" (p. 160), echoing the conclusion of Richard Braddock et al. (1963) twenty years earlier that "the teaching of formal grammar has a negligible or . . . even a harmful effect on the improvement of writing" (pp. 37–38). More recently, a meta-analysis of studies focusing on elementary and high school instruction found a statistically significant negative effect for grammar instruction across all ability levels, "indicating that traditional grammar instruction is unlikely to help improve the quality of students' writing" (Graham & Perin, 2007, n.p.).

At the same time, few educators recommend entirely ignoring surface error. And in spite of the conclusive results of the research on grammar, teachers from the early grades through graduate education continue to identify error, admonish students to study it, and recommend a variety of resources to help them avoid it. If educators in foundational writing courses as well as in discipline-based (WAC/WID) courses are to develop theoretically informed methods to help writers identify and avoid error—since it will never disappear as a concern—they need to know more about the role of error in students' writing. This includes understanding students' constructs of error, what errors they identify or mis-identify in their own and each other's writing, what explanations, if any, they offer, and whether those explanations are

---

1   In L2 instruction, focus on surface correctness is justifiably stronger because of the need for students to learn grammatical, lexical, and other aspects of the language, and the challenge is to interweave such instruction into broader rhetorical concerns.

accurate. Students' identification of error may come from external sources (such as rules taught to them explicitly in previous instruction, or accurate or erroneous feedback from digital grammar tools), or from their difficulties processing a text (sensing that "something is wrong" and simply guessing that an error is creating the difficulty). In addition, both explicit and tacit rules that students bring to peer review can lead to the incorrect identification of error, the imposition of a rule where none is needed, or the overgeneralization of a learned rule to cases where it should not apply.

Knowing more about these aspects of students' knowledge and abilities is crucial for the design of effective programs for faculty development across other courses and disciplines, as well as responsible, theoretically informed ways to integrate the detection, learning, and repair of error into writing instruction. A number of methods can be employed to investigate such questions; for example, case studies using discourse-based interviews (Odell et al., 1983) could be conducted with students about their own drafts or the drafts of their peers to bring prior knowledge about error to the surface. Before unearthing such complexities in students' constructs of error, however, it is important to know more about basic patterns of error identification on a larger scale. How often do students identify error in their peers' drafts?[2] How accurate are they? Which errors do they identify? How do they talk about these errors? It is these questions that the study reported in this chapter sought to investigate.

Initial Explorations of Error in Peer Response

The study of student peer response is often confounded by the effects of data collection. Video or audio recording live peer response groups can affect students' interactions or make them self-conscious. This study employed a screencast program that students used to comment on their peers' rough drafts for an assignment. The screencast method allowed for a naturalistic inquiry of error conceptualization and identification in students' focus on the improvement of their peers' drafts.

First, Institutional Review Board (IRB) approval was obtained for the study, as required in U.S. institutions for the consent of human subjects. Forty-three

---

2   By "error," this study refers to incorrect or garbled grammar and syntax, wrong word usage, incorrect punctuation, incorrect spelling, and other surface features to be described. It does not include aspects of style, such as informal register. The study also ignored cases in which an error (such as a fragment) appeared to be deliberate and in the writer's control.

undergraduates at a large, research-extensive university were recruited to participate. Students were enrolled in two sections of a foundational (L1) writing course taught by two experienced writing instructors. The instructors were familiarized with Jing, a simple screencast program, that allowed for five-minute audio-visual commentaries (Anson, 2018; Anson et al., 2016). In the process used in this study, after reading a peer's draft, a student activated the Jing program and then talked about the paper while scrolling through and optionally highlighting bits of relevant text. The student could pause the recording and continue or discard it and start over. When the five minutes elapsed, the program prompted the user to upload the video to the learning management system associated with the course. After receiving and opening the screencast, the peer could then play and replay the audio-visual recording.

Students were trained in class to provide peer response on each other's drafts using the program. The process was integrated into students' coursework, which maintained authenticity and provided motivation. A brief video and written instructions were also made available, and students tested the program first to ensure functionality.

At the point when students had completed a full rough draft of one of the main (3–5 page) assignments in the course, they sent their draft electronically to the two other members of their peer-response group or their partner in the case of pairs. Students then opened and read a peer's draft, activated Jing, and provided audio-visual commentary. The teachers gave their students peer-response guides that helped to focus their attention on salient issues.

After opt-outs from the study and the removal of incomplete data or poor recordings, 56 screencasts were deemed usable, created by 36 students—18 in each teacher's class. Screencasts were professionally transcribed and cleaned of all non-content-based hesitations ("um," "uh," etc.) and obvious repetitions ("I . . . I read your paper"). The number of words in each transcript and the elapsed time of the screencast were then determined.

Students' drafts were coded for the presence of the most common errors as reported in research by Andrea Lunsford and Karen Lunsford (2008), which replicated an earlier study by Robert Connors and Andrea Lunsford (1988). In Connors and Lunsford's study, over 21,000 papers graded and commented on by 300 teachers in their first-year composition courses across the United States were collected. Trained assistants coded the papers for all errors present in the papers and all those identified by the instructors. Statistical analysis revealed the top 20 most often committed errors along with rates of instructor identification.

Because the original study was conducted before most students had access to word processors, Lunsford and Lunsford (2008) replicated the study to see if the patterns had changed over the previous 20 years. New IRB requirements severely restricted access to student work, yielding a smaller set of 1,826 graded papers from first-year writing courses at institutions across the United States. In a random stratified sample, Lunsford and Lunsford found interesting differences in the top 20 most often identified errors. Some of these differences appeared to be the result of word processing corrections or substitutions. For example, incorrect spelling moved down the ranks, while wrong word, faulty capitalization, and faulty hyphen use moved up.

Because it was important to study the extent to which students discussed errors that teachers are most concerned about, the list of the most often identified errors in the Lunsford and Lunsford corpus was used as the basis of analysis (see appendix). In addition to these, a 21st category, "other," captured seven further errors that were present in a number of papers but not cataloged in Lunsford and Lunsford's study. These errors are included in the appendix.

Students' drafts were read and coded for the presence of the errors. Fifteen percent of the drafts in the corpus were randomly selected for second-pass coding; agreement was .92. Next, transcripts of the screencasts were coded for every error students identified in their peers' papers. Only surface-level features such as grammar, punctuation, spelling, reference format, and usage or lexis (such as wrong word) were coded, in parallel with the errors previously identified in the drafts. Sub-coding captured whether any explanations were accurate or inaccurate. The following examples illustrate the codes and sub-codes.

Error correctly identified

Original sentence: Respondents were asked to make public post.

Peer's comment: "Post" should be plural.

Correctly explained

Original sentence: This articles exemplifies uses for soybean protein. . . .

Peer's comment: I think you can take the "s" off of "articles" right here, to make it singular so that it reads "This article. . . ."

Incorrectly explained (errors not explained correctly or explained in an ambiguous or misleading way)

Original sentence: "The same low status car was used, except was spray-painted to avoid recognition and a passenger was added to increase distractions."

Peer's comment: "Was used, except was." I don't know if this whole sentence . . . I remember when I read it, like I felt like your tense was off or it just . . . you could have changed something.

Error incorrectly identified (non-errors)
Original sentence: Alcohol-related car accidents and injuries are a serious problem in the world today.
Peer's comment: So in here [alcohol-related] you should take out the hyphen.

When transcripts were unclear (such as "I think this should be a comma," where "this" was ambiguous), the screencast was replayed to locate the reference. The vague item was then interpolated into the transcript (e.g., "I think this [semicolon] should be a comma"), and the item was coded.

General Results

Across the corpus of 36 drafts, students made 599 errors, for an average of 16.6 errors per paper. Table 15.1 shows the ordered frequency of the errors; #2–21 are from Lunsford and Lunsford (2008). Because errors could be made disproportionately by specific students, a test of within-writer frequency was conducted. None of the data showed a statistically significant effect that skewed the overall results, suggesting that the errors were distributed relatively evenly across the cohort.

Table 15.1. Rank-ordered errors in students' drafts

Rank order of error	Type of error	Lunsford & Lunsford rank	# of errors
1	Other (seven errors not in Lunsford and Lunsford's top 20)	n/a	127
2	Wrong word	1	102
3	Unnecessary comma	10	64
4	Missing comma in a compound sentence	12	59
5	Vague pronoun reference	8	51
6	Missing comma after introductory element	5	34
7	Missing or unnecessary hyphen	20	33
8	Missing word	6	24
9	Faulty sentence structure	13	22

Table 15.1. Rank-ordered errors in students' drafts (continued)

10	Mechanical error with a quotation	4	20
11	Unnecessary shift in verb tense	11	13
12	Unnecessary or missing apostrophe	9	13
13	Comma splice	14	13
14	Unnecessary or missing capitalization	7	10
15	Incomplete or missing documentation	3	9
16	Missing comma with a nonrestrictive element	16	6
17	Poorly integrated quotation	19	3
18	Sentence fragment	17	3
19	Lack of pronoun/antecedent agreement	15	2
20	Incorrect spelling	2	1
21	Fused (run-on) sentence	18	0

Several interesting observations arise from these results. First, of the errors categorized in Lunsford and Lunsford (2008), lexical errors (wrong word) were also the most frequent, and nearly double the next most frequent error (the use of an unnecessary comma). The following excerpt demonstrates a wrong-word error (the use of "that" for "who"):[3]

> Texting during class harms the student's learning capability and students *that* text during class are more likely to receive lower grades.... [italics added]

Second, while some errors generally matched the frequency of those in the Lunsford and Lunsford corpus, others did not, suggesting that the subjects did not always commit errors that teachers most often marked in the national sample. For example, spelling was the fifth most common error in Lunsford and Lunsford's study (dropping from first place in the earlier study), but came in almost last, with only one case in the entire corpus. Third, of 599 identified errors, 21 percent were not included in Lunsford and Lunsford's list, suggesting that in spite of their lower identification by teachers, these are still errors that students often commit.

As shown in Table 15.2, coding of screencasts revealed that students pointed to 105 (14%) of the 599 identified errors. Of those, 72 were correctly explained

---

3   The distinction between "that" and "who" for inanimate objects vs. humans is rapidly blurring in casual speech and may eventually disappear. In this study, "trailing edge" errors—those increasingly accepted but not usually in formal prose—were counted as errors, whereas those that have almost entirely disappeared, such as split infinitives, were not.

and 23 were incorrectly explained, with the balance (10) simply noted but not explained. Students also identified 36 non-errors as errors, meaning that on average one out of every four errors was not an error.

Table 15.2. Error counts

Total errors in drafts	599
Number identified	105
Correctly explained	72
Incorrectly explained	23
Noted, not explained	10
Non-errors as errors	36

To this point, the data show that students do identify legitimate errors in their peers' drafts, but not much more than one in ten of all the errors present. It is not clear whether they are selective about which errors they identify or are unaware of the errors they overlook. Their explanations of the errors they do identify are correct about 75 percent of the time; but many are also incorrect or ambiguous, suggesting that they sometimes intuitively and correctly pick up on surface problems in their peers' drafts but do not know the explicit rules behind what they identify. Finally, they point to a small but not insignificant number of non-errors.

Distinctions Between Instructor's Classes

In addition to the overall results, some significant differences appeared in the two instructors' classes (they will be referred to pseudonymously as "Corrine" and "Emily"). Because students were all provided the same orientation to screencasting and were in sections of the same general course taught to the same learning outcomes, these differences were intriguing. For the purposes of this chapter, a comparison of the data from the classes of the two instructors will serve as the remaining focus of analysis.

First, in the two instructors' classes, both the number of words spoken and the elapsed time of the recordings differed significantly ($p < .01$). In Corrine's class, students' screencasts averaged 322 words (153 seconds of elapsed time), while in Emily's class, students' screencasts averaged 520 words (231 seconds of elapsed time). Many of the students in Emily's class used most or all of the five minutes provided in the Jing app, while many of Corrine's students used only half that amount. Second, further comparisons revealed that Corrine's students spoke more about surface aspects of the writing, while Emily's students focused more on broader rhetorical and content-related concerns. As a result, Corrine's students had a higher error identification rate than Emily's students.

To further study these differences, the transcripts were subjected to an additional corpus analysis. In a previous study (Anson & Anson, 2017; Anson et al., forthcoming), nearly 500 writing teachers and scholars were administered a survey asking them to provide ten terms they associate with expert commentary on student writing and ten terms they associate with novice (student) commentary. Statistically, the most common expert terms were largely broad (global) terms for rhetorical and structural concerns: *audience, purpose, focus, clarity, organization, support,* and the like. The most common novice terms were mostly local, surface-level terms: *grammar, spelling, punctuation, flow, awkward, sentence,* and *comma*.

Applying the most frequently listed expert and novice terms from the survey study to the screencast transcripts yielded stark differences between Corrine and Emily's students, as shown in Figures 15.1 and 15.2. As shown in Figure 15.1, Emily's students far more often used terms associated with broader global issues in writing (*audience, purpose, readers, focus, development,* and *ideas*), suggesting response to the ideational and interpersonal functions of writing (Halliday, 1973). In contrast (Figure 15.2), Corrine's students far more often used terms associated with local, textual functions (*sentence, word, grammar, comma, correct*).

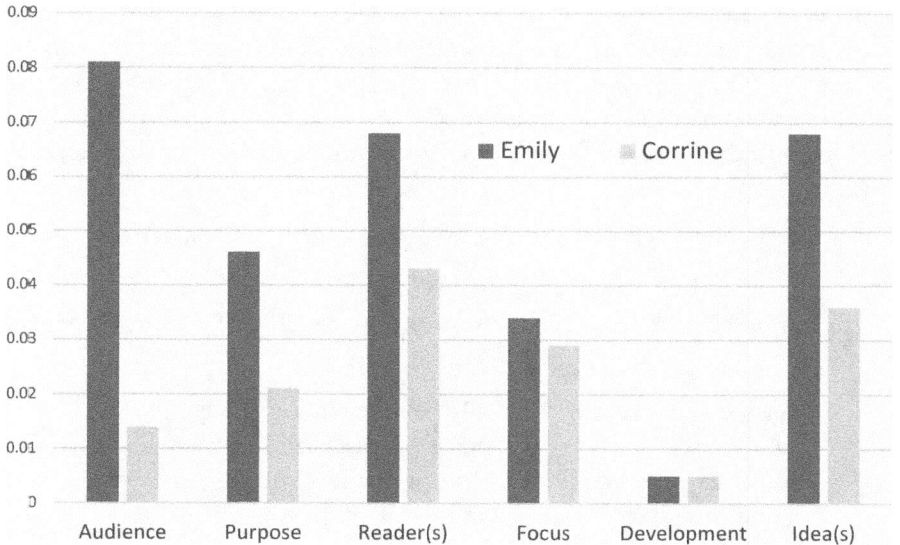

Figure 15.1 Global Terms Used Across the Screencast Corpus

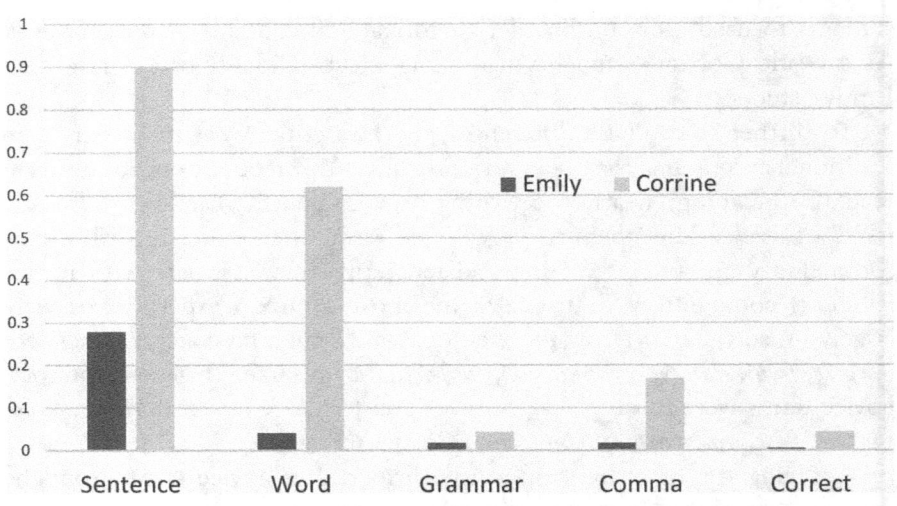

Figure 15.2 Local Terms Used Across the Screencast Corpus

The focus of the students' commentary was also related to the amount of time they spent commenting, with the more content-focused comments in Emily's class taking longer than the more error-focused comments in Corrine's class. In part, the differences in length of commentary can be intuitively explained based on the time it takes to comment on meaning-based issues compared to the identification of error (a possibility that could also explain why teachers are often pulled toward error identification when reading large amounts of student writing). Students focusing predominantly on error can move rapidly through a paper, calling attention to what to "fix," while students relating to the meaning of the paper must elaborate on their responses to their peers' ideas. "Drew," for example, fixed an error in a peer's draft in 15 words:

> Right here where you have "native to native," I think that's supposed to be hyphened.

In comparison, "Kelsey" shared a confusion, which took her far more time to explain:

> As a reader who doesn't really have much knowledge in this multiverse theory, I was kind of confused on like the second rule that you mentioned. The first rule that you state was something like a particle can exist in all possible locations at once. But then, here you kind of like said you were going to recap what we've learned so far, and so I didn't really know

when this recap ended and like when you were going to introduce the next rule.

With the use of a modified constant-comparison method from grounded theory (Glaser & Strauss, 1967), the screencast transcripts were read, re-read, and compared in order to note broad tendencies in students' commentary. Because in most cases each student produced more than one transcript, it was possible to compare those pairs or sets to identify whether they shifted the nature and focus of their response across or between their peers' papers. After no such shifts were found, the descriptions were then refined into three response styles or dispositions that appeared to form the procedural knowledge students brought to the process of reading and commenting on their peers' papers.

The *Proofreader/Editor* focuses predominantly on the surface features of their peers' writing, identifying errors and making corrections. The Proofreader/Editor rarely becomes immersed in the content of the paper; any global comments are usually introductory or conclusory in nature ("Hi, Paul. I read your paper and I found some things to focus on," or "So that's about it. Good luck"). Some Proofreader/Editors are more tentative in their identification of error ("I'm not sure, but I think this should be 'is'"), while others take on the persona of an informed instructor ("So you should fix this apostrophe and make sure you look for dummy subjects").

The two peer responses by "Giselle," one of Corrine's students, offer a clear example of this style. Giselle's responses averaged 283 words (388 and 179), generally matching the average length of screencasts in Corrine's class (322 words). (Giselle found more errors to identify in the first peer's paper than the second, which explains the difference in the length of commentary.) Of the 388 words in Giselle's first peer review, 356 focused on surface errors. The remaining 34 words were introductory: "Hey [peer's name]. So I went through and read your paper and I would, just made some . . . highlighted words and suggestions that I would consider revising." Of the 179 words in Giselle's second peer response, 122 focused on surface errors. The remaining words were, as in her first response, introductory and conclusory ("But other than that, your paper is off to a good start"). Disregarding the opening and closing comments, Giselle spent 100 percent of her commentary making corrections: in the first paper, two tense corrections, two word choice corrections, the placement of a comma, the use of italics, a number needing to be spelled out, the use of quotation marks, and proper citation format (period inside quotation marks); in the second paper, numbers needing to be spelled out, the placement of a comma, and the use of a colon to introduce a series.

Thus, Giselle entirely ignored the content of her peers' papers, in spite of the interesting nature of the articles the peers wrote about (for the first peer, a study showing that students who start drinking alcohol before the age of 19 are more likely to engage in other risky behavior; for the second peer, a study investigating the effects of violent video games on adolescent aggression).

The *Interpreter*, in stark contrast, becomes immersed in the writer's meaning and in the rhetorical and structural ways it is being communicated. Commentary can include direct connections to the reviewer's own experience ("I also wanted a doctoral degree when I was a kid"), suggestions for clarifying a point ("I didn't see a relationship between the exam and the degree"), or questions about material needing clarification or elaboration ("Is there something important that people should know about it, does it affect people in any way, shape, or form?"). For the Interpreter, the surface nature of the text appears at this stage to be unimportant.

Two peer responses by "Erik," one of Emily's students, demonstrate this style of commentary. Erik's responses averaged 555 words (561 and 546), generally matching the average length of screencasts in Emily's class (520 words). Of the 555 words in Erik's first peer response, none focused on surface matters. For example, Erik said this about his first peer's draft, reflecting his reading and interpretation but also implying that the writer could clarify a point:

> In paragraph 2 you talked about a license examination and I have a question about it. I don't understand why you'd have the examination because I didn't see any relation between the exam and the degree.

Like his first peer response, 100 percent of the 546 words in Erik's second peer response focused on the peer's content—asking some questions, relating to the material, and making global suggestions, as in this comment:

> You talked about your personal interest in aerospace engineering or astrophysics but I don't see much personal experience like how a specific program or the discovery of NASA inspired you and excited you or which contribution they made.

Thus, for the Interpreter, the purpose of peer response is primarily to create a kind of readerly transaction with the writer, reacting to meaning and either implying or directly suggesting broad improvements in the content.

The *Comprehensive Reviewer* represents an amalgam of the two previous styles. The reviewer may focus first on meaning-related concerns and then, toward the end of the commentary, shift to smaller, local concerns. Alternatively, the response can move back and forth between global and local matters, especially if the reviewer is working linearly through the draft and does not want to return to previous parts with a change in focus. This style of review is sometimes more preoccupied with providing feedback for revision than connecting personally with the draft, except by way of explaining how particular problems affect the reading process; but the focus on the interpersonal and ideational functions of language are still clear.

Two peer responses by "Chad," one of Emily's students, illustrate the style of the Comprehensive Reviewer. Chad's responses averaged 762 words (797 and 728), exceeding the average for Emily's students (520 words), and far more than for Corrine's students (322 words). Of the 797 words in Chad's first peer response, 255 focused on local surface issues. Chad spent considerable time sharing his reading of the draft, especially what the writer did effectively, as shown in this excerpt:

> The next paragraph, this is what I really learned a lot from, explaining all the little things about being an architect, you know, the long tests, and I think it's really interesting and it's a fun thing to read and I think it's a good way to explain your topic before giving us the argument on what the complaint . . . or, the problem is or the topic.

About two-thirds of the way through the response, Chad shifted his focus to smaller details:

> Just little minor things. I think "objectives" here should be singular. I'm not sure if that's what you intended or you made a mistake somewhere else. But I think the singular "objective" would fit better there. And then, I think you put "though" instead of "through," so that's just another thing I wanted to point out.

Similarly, of the 728 words in his second peer response, Chad spent 128 words pointing out local, surface errors and also made a more general admonition that the peer writer should take time to proofread the entire paper. Like his response to the first peer, he focused on the surface problems at two points during the recording, alternating between global and local concerns.

After the three response styles were created from the corpus, transcripts were placed into one of the three styles based on a predominance of features within each category. (For example, if a transcript overwhelmingly focused on ideational and interpersonal functions of the text but included only a single reference to an error, it was categorized as "Interpreter.") The results in Table 15.3 show the extent to which students of the two instructors fit the styles.

Table 15.3. Number of students fitting response styles, by teacher

Teacher	Proofreader/Editors	Interpreters	Comprehensive Reviewer
Corrine	15	0	3
Emily	1	4	13

Interpreting the Differences: The Role of Genre and Orientation

Because the students in the two courses were demographically similar—almost entirely first-year students entering from high school—and the courses were being taught in the same program to the same outcomes, the differences in the results must originate in something other than group differences. Further analysis of the contexts suggests two possible answers: the teachers' orientation toward peer response, and the assignment genre.

For many high school students, peer response is a new process when they reach a first-year college writing course. Wei Zhu (1995) reviews research that documents the difficulties students experience with peer response arising from a lack of knowledge about writing and how to provide effective response. What teachers do to orient students, therefore, can exert an important influence on how students behave when engaged in the process, a finding reported in Anson and Anson (2017) in the context of a digital peer-review system. Additionally, what students focus on and how they focus on it are shaped by their interpretations of the teachers' instructional ideology, conveyed through stated preferences and course materials. If a teacher frequently references or lectures about surface correctness, takes points off for errors in students' final drafts, or otherwise gives the impression that students must conform to standard edited English, students may behave in ways that avoid or mitigate the teachers' focus on these issues. If a teacher encourages students to connect with their peers' intended meanings or show how they are affected as readers, students may withhold a focus on surface details in favor of such content-related responses. In a study of how writing was used in a physical geography course, for example, Anna Rollins and Kristen Lillivis (2018) found that the inclusion of a vague grammar criterion on a rubric for essay exams was inappropriately influencing instructor response (and in some cases causing them to mis-identify errors), and drawing attention away from what they actually wanted to focus on. With 20 percent of the grade devoted to grammar, students in their study may have been distracted from a focus on demonstrating their knowledge of the material as they tried to avoid error, a conclusion reached in early research on the writing processes of underprepared students (Shaughnessy, 1977).

Artifacts from the teachers' courses show that Corrine was ideologically more focused on surface correctness, while Emily was more focused on rhetorical and meaning-making processes. (Corrine's preoccupation with error was often noted in the screencast comments. For example, one student remarked that "You used 'et al.' throughout your essay and I think [she] said to use 'and others.'") Corrine's peer-response questions included four elements, one being correctness, but even the element of "rhetorical purpose" was defined as "proper heading, etc." In contrast, Emily's materials emphasized meaning construction, the engagement and response of the reader, and rhetorical concepts such as the writer's stance.

In addition to these instructional influences—which permeate all courses where students write—the assignment's genre may have affected their peer responses. Emily's assignment asked students to write a proposal for a research project and explain their personal motivation for the inquiry. Corrine's assignment was an objective summary and analysis of an argument made in a research study of the student's choice. (In a later assignment, the students located an article that posed counterarguments to the first article's findings and put the two studies in dialogue with each other.) Thus, both the writer's and the responders' personal investment in each paper may have differed, with Emily's students drawn to connect with the research topic (as had the authors) and Corrine's students viewing the summary as more detached, therefore focusing more on the quality of the writing than the articles' content. This possible influence on the focus of peer review is important to consider in assignments across the curriculum, some of which leave less room for broader, more readerly interactions than others.

A partial model of the influences on students' peer response process helps to explain the extent to which they focus on error (see Figure 15.3). In this model, influences include writerly elements such as the reviewer's disposition toward peer response, their ability to read and critique others' drafts in progress, and their prior experience; instructional elements such as the teacher's beliefs about writing and the orientation of students to the process; textual elements such as the genre of the assignment and its constraints; and contextual elements (which were not studied here), including student rapport and the general climate of the classroom. Although a small number of students in both Corrine's and Emily's classes did not fit the pattern of the majority, it is likely that some combination of the elements in this model pushed one section more strongly toward error identification and the other away from it. When considered next to the general results of the study's focus on error, it appeared that Corrine's students more problematically focused on error because they did so erratically, without a sufficient fund of knowledge to identify or explain all errors correctly, in some cases helping their peers and in others perhaps confusing or misleading them, all while downplaying the role of meaning construction and interaction with the writer's ideas.

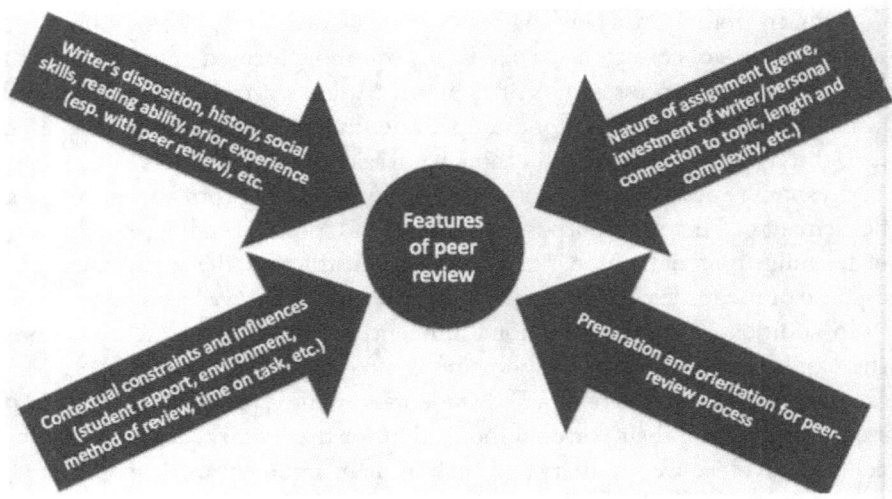

Figure 15.3. A partial model of influence on peer response.

Considered in the context of the three response styles previously described, this model suggests that students may *temporally construct* an approach to peer review depending on the various influences. A student who brings the disposition of a Proofreader/Editor into a writing class where there is a strong emphasis on response to meaning, especially when a writing assignment is designed to engage readers' responses, may lean toward the disposition of an Interpreter—in the same way that a highly skilled writer might respond to a colleague's draft in a proofreading or editing mode when asked to do so. (Otherwise, it would seem unlikely that most of the students in Emily's class brought different "stable" dispositions to the peer-review process than those in Corrine's class.) However, the nature and extent of this kind of flexibility among novice writers has yet to be studied fully. For example, experienced writers may have developed abilities to switch easily among different reading and response orientations depending on the task at hand, while novice writers may be more habituated to a certain orientation (such as Proofreader) from past experience or interpretation of the response task and find it difficult to shift perspectives without intervention and coaching.

Discussion and Implications

Among the issues this study raises, it is clear that the field of writing studies must more strongly confront its conflicts about the role of error in composition instruction and WAC/WID. If students are identifying errors during peer response, what are the effects of their incomplete or erroneous knowledge on their peers' learning and revision? Does recognizing that students do not understand enough about grammar and other surface matters to respond effectively mean that they should be told to ignore all such matters in favor of response to meaning? If so, when and by whom are students' errors pointed out to them, and in what form, and with what advice? Although theoretically, writers learn to avoid error inductively, through exposure to written texts and through the writing process, this does not alleviate all errors, leaving them vulnerable to poor performance in other academic contexts and later embarrassment in their chosen professions.

At the same time, few in the field of writing studies would advocate a return to grammar instruction and a predominant focus on correctness. Some recent scholarship even advocates greater acceptance of nonstandard language or "code-meshing" in students' writing (see Young, 2011). But in the context of the attractiveness of peer response, it would also seem inadvisable to instruct students to provide more meaning-based response while leaving error detection and correction to teachers, because doing so could also subvert students' response to meaning with the message that correctness (the teacher's realm) counts more, and create a double standard. Helping students to become comprehensive reviewers may be one possible solution, but it does not alleviate the challenge of ensuring that students bring adequate linguistic knowledge to the task of responding to error in their peers' drafts.

This study also raises implications for the continued support of students' writing in courses across the curriculum. Instructors in such courses often disproportionately foreground surface error relative to other content-based concerns (Anson, 2015). Yet these same instructors are themselves often apprehensive about grammar, confessing an inability to name and describe it correctly (which they assume is the job of English departments and writing programs). Or they feel unable or untrained to "teach" writing (Plutsky & Wilson, 2001). Many WAC leaders and some educators within the disciplines therefore urge a focus on more general aspects of expression ("If something is garbled, have the student try to rephrase it") or urge instructors to ignore error in favor of engaging with the students' meaning (see, for example, Hansen and Hansen, 1995). But the paradox that faculty believe good writing is "correct writing" while they are also reticent to focus explicitly on correctness needs further inquiry and new approaches to faculty development.

Across the curriculum, more research on peer review is also needed to understand the role of error relative to the learning of course content. In a study comparing students' and teachers' responses and their effects on students' revisions in several disciplinary courses, Larry Beason (1993) found that attention to surface-level revisions was far more prominent than attention to global/meaning revisions. Comparing his results to those of two similar studies, Beason found that all three groups "paid most attention to Surface-level Revisions, least to Global-meaning Revisions" (p. 415), perhaps because it may seem easier to "fix" simple errors than reconsider a complex thought or provide further evidence for an assertion. Eric Paulson et al. (2007) found in an eye-movement study of peer review that students did focus on errors in a student draft, as measured by their eye fixations. But when asked to respond to the writer, they gave general admonitions to avoid error rather than specific advice. As in Beason's study, students also tended to focus much of their attention on surface issues. These results are problematic when in most courses across the disciplines, content-focused comments designed to spur revision are usually considered more important for achieving the learning outcomes.

Finally, the students in this study were L1 speakers of English. Considerable new research in L2 contexts has been emerging but suggests a similar need to study the role of error and correctness. Carrie Chang's (2016) review of 103 studies of student peer review in L2 writing classrooms over two decades reveals a number of gaps in our knowledge, including the effects of training, the role of checklists or rubrics, the timing of feedback, the configuration of peer-review groups, the medium of response, and the effect of peers' comments on subsequent revision, including, in particular, "their improvement in local (e.g., grammar, vocabulary, punctuation) . . . writing areas" (p. 108). Complicating such inquiry is the fact that L1 and L2 learners may feel differently about a focus on grammar and surface correctness, partly because learning a second language in an academic setting usually involves the direct teaching of grammar and the conventions of discourse. Ironically, L2 learners may bring more explicit knowledge of grammatical principles to their peer reviews than L1 learners, although this knowledge may be partial or imperfect. Further research of peer review in courses across the disciplines that have mixed populations of international L2 students and L1 speakers of English (or at universities in non-Anglophone countries where English is the medium of instruction) could reveal such differences.

Acknowledgements

I wish to thank Chen Chen of Winthrop College and Meridith Reed of Brigham Young University for their assistance with this project.

References

Anson, C. M. (2000). Response and the social construction of error. *Assessing Writing, 7,* 5–21.

Anson, C. M. (2015). Crossing thresholds: What's to know about writing across the curriculum? In L. Adler-Kassner & E. Wardle (Eds.), *Naming what we know: Threshold concepts of writing studies* (pp. 203–219). Utah State University Press.

Anson, C. M. (2018). "She really took the time": Students' opinions of screen-capture response to their writing in online courses. In C. Weaver & P. Jackson (Eds.), *Writing in online courses: How the online environment shapes writing practices* (pp. 21–45). Myers Education Press.

Anson, C. M., Anson, I. G. & Andrews, K. (forthcoming). Teachers' beliefs about the language of peer review: Evidence from a key-terms survey. In P. Jackson & C. Weaver (Eds.), *Revisiting peer review: Critical reflections on a pedagogical practice*. Myers Education Press.

Anson, C. M., Dannels, D., Laboy, J. & Carneiro, L. (2016). Students' perceptions of oral screencast responses to their writing: Exploring digitally mediated identities. *Journal of Business and Technical Communication*, *30*(3), 1–34.

Anson, I. G. & Anson, C. M. (2017). Assessing peer and instructor response to writing: A corpus analysis from an expert survey. *Assessing Writing*, *33*, 12–24.

Bartholomae, D. (1980). The study of error. *College Composition and Communication*, *31*(3), 253–269.

Beason, L. (1993). Feedback and revision in writing across the curriculum classes. *Research in the Teaching of English*, *27*(4), 395–422.

Braddock, R. R., Lloyd-Jones, R. & Schoer, L. A. (1963). *Research In written composition*. National Council of Teachers of English.

Burchett, A. M. (2019). *Naming the practice: An examination of writing center mission* [Unpublished master's thesis]. North Carolina State University.

Chang, C. Y. (2016). Two decades of research in L2 peer review. *Journal of Writing Research*, *8*(1), 81–117.

Connors, R. J. & Lunsford, A. A. (1988). Frequency of formal errors in current college writing, or Ma and Pa Kettle do research. *College Composition and Communication*, *39*(4), 395–409.

Glaser, B. G. & Strauss, A. L. (1967). *The discovery of grounded theory: Strategies for qualitative research*. Aldine.

Graham, S. & Perin, D. (2007). *Writing next: Effective strategies to improve writing of adolescents in middle and high schools*. Carnegie Corporation.

Halliday, M. A. K. (1973). *Explorations in the functions of language*. Edward Arnold.

Hansen, R. S. & Hansen, K. H. (1995). Incorporating writing across the curriculum into an introductory marketing course. *Journal of Marketing Education*, *17*(1), 3–12.

Hartwell, P. (1985). Grammar, grammars, and the teaching of grammar. *College English*, *47*(2), 105–127.

Hillocks, G., Jr. (1984). What works in teaching composition: A meta-analysis of experimental treatment studies. *American Journal of Education*, *93*(1), 133–170.

Hillocks, G., Jr. (1986). *Research on written composition: New directions for teaching*. ERIC Clearinghouse on Reading and Communication Skills and National Conference on Research in English.

Hunter, S. & Wallace, R. (Eds.). (1995). *The place of grammar in writing instruction: Past, present, future*. Boynton/Cook.

Kroll, B. M. & Shafer, J. C. (1978). Error analysis and the teaching of composition. *College Composition and Communication*, 29(3), 242–248.

Lunsford, A. A. & Lunsford, K. J. (2008). "Mistakes are a fact of life": A national comparative study. *College Composition and Communication*, 59(4), 781–806.

McQuade, F. (1980). Examining a grammar course. *English Journal*, 69(7), 26–30.

Noguchi, R. R. (1991). *Grammar and the teaching of writing: Limits and possibilities*. National Council of Teachers of English.

Odell, L., Goswami, D. & Herrington, A. (1983). The discourse-based interview: A procedure for exploring the tacit knowledge of writers in nonacademic settings. In P. Mosenthal, L. Tamor & S. A. Walmsley (Eds.), *Research on writing* (pp. 221–236). Longman.

Paulson, E. J., Alexander, J. & Armstrong, S. (2007). Peer review re-viewed: Investigating the juxtaposition of composition students' eye movements and peer-review processes. *Research in the Teaching of English*, 41(3), 304–335.

Plutsky, S. & Wilson, B. A. (2001). Writing across the curriculum in a college of business and economics. *Business and Professional Communication Quarterly*, 64(4), 26–41.

Rollins, A. & Lillivis, K. (2018). When rubrics need revision: A collaboration between STEM faculty and the writing center. *Composition Forum*, 40. https://compositionforum.com/issue/40/rubrics.php.

Shaughnessy, M. P. (1977). *Errors and expectations*. Oxford University Press.

Sloan, G. (1990). Frequency of errors in essays by college freshmen and by professional writers. *College Composition and Communication*, 41(3), 299–308.

Weaver, C. (1996). *Teaching grammar in context*. Heinemann; Boynton/Cook.

Young, V. A. (2011). Should writers use they own English? In L. Greenfield & K. Rowan (Eds.), *Writing centers and the new racism: A call for sustainable dialogue and change* (pp. 61–72). Utah State University Press.

Zhu, W. (1995). Effects of training for peer response on students' comments and interaction. *Written Communication*, 12(4), 492–498.

Appendix: Top 20 Most Often Identified Errors (Lunsford & Lunsford, 2008)

1. Wrong word
2. Incorrect spelling
3. Incomplete or missing documentation
4. Mechanical error with a quotation
5. Missing comma after introductory element
6. Missing word
7. Unnecessary or missing capitalization

8. Vague pronoun reference
9. Unnecessary or missing apostrophe
10. Unnecessary comma
11. Unnecessary shift in verb tense
12. Missing comma in a compound sentence
13. Faulty sentence structure
14. Comma splice
15. Lack of pronoun/antecedent agreement
16. Missing comma with a nonrestrictive element
17. Sentence fragment
18. Fused (run-on) sentence
19. Poorly integrated quotation
20. Missing or unnecessary hyphen

Other errors identified in students' drafts:

- Subject-verb agreement
- Lack of parallelism
- Number spelled out/not spelled out
- Italics for quotation and vice versa (e.g., in titles)
- Dangling modifier
- Adjective/adverb confusion
- Article error

16 The Praxis of Innovation in Writing Programs

Andy Frazee and Rebecca E. Burnett
GEORGIA INSTITUTE OF TECHNOLOGY

Abstract: This chapter describes ways our Georgia Tech Writing and Communication Program fosters innovation and argues that any writing, writing-across-the-curriculum, or English-across-the-curriculum program can nurture similar innovation appropriate for their local institutions and communities. We argue that faculty members who practice innovation transform themselves as well as their environment, benefiting students and, often, their community partners. We begin by presenting background information about our program; we then argue that our two-part programmatic mission—one part focusing largely on our responsibility to faculty and another part on our responsibility to students—creates a space for innovation. We then discuss five characteristics of faculty-centered professional development: professional culture, working conditions, expertise, long-term careers, and an exploratory mindset. The penultimate section discusses five characteristics of teaching and learning: rhetoric, process, multimodality, collaboration, and assessment. The chapter concludes by posing questions for other programs considering ways to stimulate innovation.

Keywords: educational innovation, writing programs, professional development, teaching and learning, rhetoric

In Georgia Tech's Writing and Communication Program, we value innovation. Our students innovate in their work in our first-year composition, business and technical communication, and research classes. Our faculty innovate in their teaching, scholarship, service, and professional development. And our program innovates in the ways our curriculum, pedagogies, and professional development adapt to a changing world. Innovation is important because it provides intellectual excitement and practical value and because it is often transferable "across different disciplinary areas, time periods, and cultures" (Tierney & Lanford, 2016, p. 1), the very thing we want our students to do with their learning and our faculty to do with their scholarship and pedagogy.

What does this innovation look like? On a typical day, in our composition courses, students might build optical toys—kaleidoscopes or zoetropes—to understand media archaeology or develop graphic novels that address mental health issues for community clients. In our upper-level business and technical communication courses, students might create suites of workplace artifacts (e.g., memoranda of understanding (MOUs), white papers, websites, or podcasts). In creating these workplace artifacts, students might be involved with a community-based project to help a neighborhood reduce problems with easy access to healthy food for local residents. Or students might be involved with a campus-based project to create and design poetry machines to be used in public spaces across campus. In hallways and offices, faculty members discuss classroom activities, their aggressive scholarly agendas, and their service and outreach work. Faculty members plan events with speakers such as the University of California-Berkeley linguist who invented Klingon or the Cisco co-founder who supports Jane Austen scholarship. Or they plan curricular innovations—like a Wikipedia Edit-a-Thon—or write grant proposals to be submitted to government agencies. And beyond their classrooms and programmatic work, they prepare for a diverse array of careers, from tenure-track faculty members to user experience analysts at tech companies.

In the following case, we describe ways our program fosters innovation and argue that any writing, writing-across-the-curriculum, or English-across-the-curriculum program can nurture similar innovation appropriate for their local institutions and communities. We begin by presenting background information about our program; we then make our argument about the ways our two-part programmatic mission creates a space for innovation. Then we discuss five characteristics of faculty-centered professional development: professional culture, working conditions, expertise, long-term careers, and an exploratory mindset. In our penultimate section, we discuss five characteristics of teaching and learning: rhetoric, process, multimodality, collaboration, and assessment. We conclude by posing questions for other programs considering ways to stimulate innovation.

Background

Our Writing and Communication Program (WCP) serves 5,000–6,000 undergraduates in approximately 250 class sections per year in courses including learning support, first-year multimodal composition, multimodal business and technical communication, and proposal and thesis writing. WCP has 40 faculty (36 limited-term Brittain Postdoctoral Fellows and four lecturers and/or visiting lecturers, all with Ph.D.s) and a robust leadership team that encourages innovation.

Faculty design courses to address our programmatic outcomes—some set by the State of Georgia Board of Regents and the rest determined by our program. Our outcomes are consistent, our standards are high, our criteria for assessing student work are common across all courses, and faculty determine their course themes based on disciplinary expertise. Our WCP faculty arrive with strong disciplinary knowledge and teaching experience, and they look forward to expanding their pedagogical repertoire.

We encourage faculty to use campus and community resources, which help students understand that multimodal communication extends beyond the classroom. The following are representative examples of our first-year multimodal composition projects:

- Course theme: social justice. Students read U.S. Representative John Lewis' (2013) graphic novel *March* and then hosted Representative Lewis for a Q&A session before creating their own comics.
- Course theme: 18th–19th century literature. Students participated in a workshop in the institute's Paper Museum, learning about broadsides (public announcements common in the period) by making rag paper and learning about changes in literacy practices as they prepared to create their own public broadsides.
- Course theme: environmental activism. Students met with representatives from a local nature preserve, who brought area animals (including opossums, falcons, owls, and snakes) whose habitats are stressed by encroaching urban infrastructure.
- Course theme: Shakespeare. Students partnered with a class of incarcerated men studying the same plays, each group reading and responding to the other's critical essays.

Creating projects such as these requires a professional and pedagogical culture of innovation—one that recognizes and uses local resources and that encourages pushing disciplinary boundaries.

Creating a Space for Innovation

In defining innovation, we agree with Tracy Bridgeford, Karla Kitalong, and Dickie Selfe (2004) that "to *innovate* means to introduce a new idea or to reintroduce an old idea, perhaps in a new way or context" and that "an *innovative approach* is one that introduces, rearticulates, or creatively juxtaposes theories or practices, especially those not currently or commonly used within" a particular context (p. 5). Building on this definition's emphasis on ideas and context, we see innovation as rhetorical, attending and adapting to particular rhetorical situations, each with its own exigencies, affordances, technologies, and available means of persuasion. For us, potentially innovative situations include (but are not limited to) the classroom; the program, unit, or institution; the discipline; and the local and global communities—as well as the myriad micro-situations that constitute these, such as individual discussions with students, committee meetings, hallway chats with other faculty, and conferences. We support the view that faculty members who innovate transform themselves as well as their environment, benefiting students and, often, their community partners (see Boden, 2019).

Figure 16.1 illustrates that our faculty begin with commonly accepted means of persuasion—that is, knowledge of core elements for teaching writing, such as rhetorical situation, process, and conventional genre. They begin with what they know—their disciplinary body of knowledge and their familiarity with the foundations of rhetoric and process. As they move through our program, they learn about additional means of persuasion—what for them become pedagogical and curricular innovations, expanding their knowledge and experience. We encourage and support their curiosity about ways to take advantage of our culture, expectations, and resources. Their curiosity fuels innovation that, as Figure 16.1 shows, moves beyond the boundaries of their entry-level status quo to include attention to multimodality and digital pedagogy.

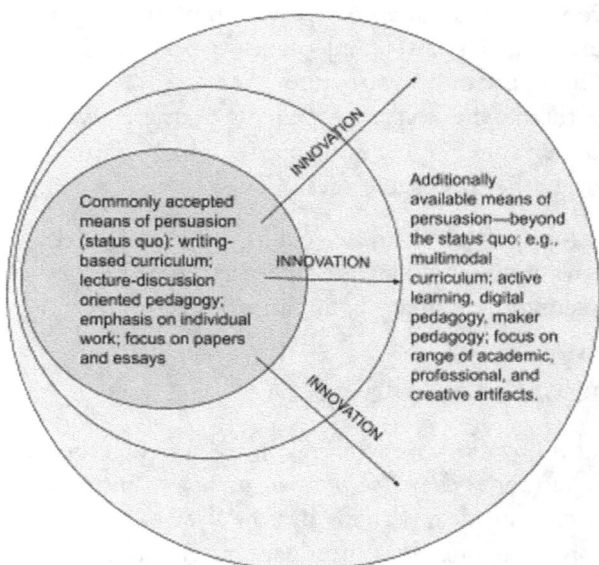

Figure 16.1. Expanding the available means of persuasion in the writing and communication curriculum.

We create a space for innovation through our two-part mission (Figure 16.2), with one part focusing largely on our responsibility to faculty and another part on our responsibility to students. The two parts of our mission support each other synergistically to encourage innovation.

Programmatically, we cultivate and model the interaction between the two parts of our mission to encourage our faculty to push the boundaries of their thinking and doing, prompting them to test, explore, and investigate alternatives. We want faculty to be confident and brave about recognizing the means available to them and taking risks in trying those means. In our program, we are not just preparing students to be global leaders; we are also preparing and supporting our faculty who will themselves be leaders.

> Georgia Tech's **Writing and Communication Program (WCP)** embodies the Institute's motto, "Progress and Service," and enacts the Institute's strategic goal of ensuring that innovation, entrepreneurship, and public service are fundamental characteristics of our graduates and our faculty. The Writing and Communication Program achieves these goals by fostering the interplay between professional development and teaching and learning for the benefit of Georgia Tech students, the state of Georgia, the United States, and the world as a whole.

> **WCP's Faulty-centered Professional Development** — Prepare postdoctoral fellows/lecturers for professional success, whether in higher ed or the broader workplace, by refining professional competencies, extending interests, and developing new strengths.

> **WCP's Student-centered Teaching and Learning** — Provide opportunities for students in composition, research, technical communication, and learning support—grounded in rhetoric, process, multimodality, collaboration, and assessment.

Figure 16.2. Two-part mission of our Writing and Communication Program.

Faculty-Centered Professional Development

As indicated in our mission statement, our program emphasizes *faculty-centered professional development* in order to equip, permit, and encourage faculty to innovate. This development is grounded in five areas: professional culture, academic working conditions, existing and emerging expertise, long-term careers, and exploratory mindset. Within each section below, we discuss professional development practices. While many could certainly benefit from funding, they primarily require time, effort, and a long-term commitment to creating a supportive professional culture. That these actions do not necessarily require extensive funding is important; it means that they are adaptable and usable in a broad number of institutions that have limited financial resources.

The following extended examples illustrate ways two faculty members developed over their time in our program. These examples highlight ways in which professional development opportunities and teaching and learning opportunities work together to spark innovation.

In the first example, a faculty member expanded her perspective about her career path, shifting from a tenure-track academic career to an industry career. The faculty member (a Brittain Fellow with a Ph.D. in media studies) used her experience and expertise along with opportunities and support available in our program to secure a position as a user experience (UX) researcher, first for a national company dealing with data analysis and later with a company engaged in market research. Despite success in teaching and publishing, the faculty member decided she did not want to continue as an academic. She explored new career paths, developed new competencies, and rebranded herself in language familiar to the corporate workplace:

- The Brittain Fellow met with WCP leadership to discuss resources about using her Ph.D. experience and expertise for careers outside the academy. She received assurance that seeking an alternative career was a responsible decision and then engaged in conversations during professional development meetings to explore career alternatives.
- WCP leadership supported the Brittain Fellow in considering ways to re-label her skills; for example, her educator role as "classroom facilitator" who manages 15 teams in three classes, working on 15 different projects, is akin to the workplace role of "project manager" responsible for personnel, schedule, task assignment, resource allocation, problem resolution, assessment, and so on.
- The Brittain Fellow applied for workplace internships and training sessions that coordinated with her teaching and other professional responsibilities and attended workplace meetups with UX professionals to increase her network.
- WCP leadership and the Brittain Fellow coordinated a plan to offer digital materials, individual consultations, and small-group career transition workshops for other Brittain Fellows.

In the second example, a faculty member used her experience, expertise, and opportunities available in our program to secure a tenure-track assistant professor of technical communication position at a public university in the eastern United States. The faculty member (a Brittain Fellow with a Ph.D. in technical communication) took advantage of programmatic opportunities to reinforce her existing professional competencies and to develop new ones:

- The Brittain Fellow had the opportunity to design and teach linked courses, one connecting an upper-level technical communication course with a first-year multimodal composition course and another connecting upper-level technical communication courses with upper-level computer science courses.
- The Brittain Fellow had the opportunity to coordinate WCP's linked technical communication–computer science capstone courses, leading orientation and new faculty development. As coordinator, she collaborated with faculty in revising the curriculum for this course sequence.
- WCP leadership facilitated a part-time consulting position for the Brittain Fellow with the university's Office of Information Technology to work on campus-wide technical documents, videos, and a website introducing a new learning management system.
- The Brittain Fellow generated conventional academic work—serving as a principal researcher on a project funded by a national professional organization, creating a podcast to highlight her research, co-authoring articles for peer-reviewed journals, and presenting and co-presenting at national conferences.

As these opportunities show, our program is committed to supporting faculty in a professional culture—with positive working conditions, targeted development of teaching and scholarly expertise, long-term career guidance, and an exploratory, creative approach to work. These opportunities, in combination with the teaching and learning practices discussed below, enable faculty to innovate in their teaching, research, service, community outreach, and careers.

Development of Professional Culture

For us, developing a professional culture involves developing the professional identities of individual faculty as well as the collective identity of our programmatic community. Creating and maintaining a professional culture provides a basis for faculty development and collegial support for innovation. For innovation to be possible, faculty should understand the status quo and the leading edge in the disciplines in which they are teaching and creating; they should understand the nature of institutional, programmatic, and community cultures; and they should feel acknowledged and accepted by the local community as having expert knowledge and experience. Attending to professional identity results in discernible benefits:

- Faculty who are respected, supported, and recognized feel more confident in their ability to innovate pedagogically.

- Faculty who are knowledgeable about institutional processes and politics are better able to function within the institution and use its resources to aid student learning and their own professional development.
- Faculty who are a part of a community have a range of people and resources to turn to when developing new pedagogical opportunities or facing pedagogical challenges.
- Faculty who have opportunities for curriculum development, policy development, programmatic assessment, and other forms of programmatic decision-making are more likely to be motivated to innovate in their classrooms and to build curriculum/programs.

The ways teachers feel about and identify themselves are critical to their professional success. These benefits are supported by "psychological processes . . . involved in the development of a teacher identity: a sense of appreciation, a sense of connectedness, a sense of competence, a sense of commitment, and imagining a future career trajectory" (van Lankveld et al., 2017, p. 325). Our program's attention to professional culture reinforces these research-based conclusions.

Development of Academic Working Conditions

Experience has taught us that faculty input about the conditions in which they work is foundational to supporting faculty, student, and programmatic innovation. This input includes topics such as the design of classrooms, the availability of office space and technology, and equitable pay and benefits. This input ensures that faculty expertise in teaching and research is reflected in the educational environment and that faculty have input in selecting the resources they need to teach, research, and innovate. Attending to working conditions—and involving faculty in efforts to improve their working conditions—results in discernible benefits:

- Faculty who are well-supported with adequate space, technology, and other material conditions are likely to be more creative and innovative in their pedagogy.
- Faculty often know about successful teaching practices that can influence the design of learning environments and resources.
- Faculty can design courses that make innovative use of spaces and resources.
- Faculty are aware—through transparent, formative evaluation and feedback—of areas for growth and experimentation in their teaching.

Access to and support for digital technology is one aspect of working conditions we prioritize. While writing and communication can be taught with traditional technologies (e.g., paper and pencils), global communities and workplaces expect college graduates to demonstrate competence in using digital technology. Likewise, colleges and universities in the US increasingly expect faculty to use and teach digital technology. Samantha Adams Becker and her colleagues (2018) summarize trends, challenges, and developments in educational technology that "are likely to impact teaching, learning, and creative inquiry in higher education" (p. 2). One of the long-term trends they identify is "advancing cultures of innovation" (p. 2). We agree with Becker and her colleagues that organizations need to "remove barriers that limit the development of new ideas" (p. 8). For us, that means making sure that faculty have access to and training in digital technology and that they have good working conditions (e.g., safe, clean, and well-equipped workspaces and classrooms; reasonable workloads and class sizes; adequate compensation; and access to professional and pedagogical resources). Good working conditions also include encouragement and support for engaging in innovative activities.

Development of Existing and Emerging Expertise

We value and support both faculty members' previous experience and their existing disciplinary expertise in a range of areas (e.g., digital humanities, multimodal composition, rhetoric, business and technical communication). We also support their emerging expertise and provide mentorship and career guidance. For example, we provide opportunities for them to innovate at the intersection of scholarship and teaching. Encouraging faculty to extend their own interests and expertise results in discernible benefits:

- Faculty members have intellectual interests that provide a rich site for innovation, pushing them to see the synergy between their scholarship and their pedagogy.
- Faculty members develop expertise that enables them to create courses that push students to think and communicate about complex concepts and difficult questions and to pose innovative solutions to world problems.
- Faculty members' broad, interdisciplinary perspectives (especially at a STEM university) reinforce their credibility as scholars and their authority in the classroom.
- Faculty members have expertise as writers, speakers, designers, and collaborators that enables them to create innovative strategies in a variety of modes and media.

In thinking about expertise, we agree with Elizabeth Wardle and J. Blake Scott's (2015) argument about the necessity for faculty to have (following Collins and Evans, 2007) at least "interactional expertise." This form of expertise engages disciplinary knowledge and conversations related to teaching writing courses—even as those faculty may not have a degree, or even coursework, within the relevant domains (e.g., rhetoric and composition, technical communication, writing center studies). Finally, we believe in the importance of supporting faculty in developing expertise outside of either their disciplinary expertise or their pedagogical expertise—expertise that, as we discuss in the next section, supports their long-term career plans.

Development of Long-Term Careers

We believe in supporting faculty members in their search for stable, fair, long-term employment, even in the face of a job market in the United States that has more qualified professionals than available positions. This approach reinforces foundational practices of developing a professional culture and productive working conditions. It also supports faculty members in using their intellectual curiosity to expand their interests and expertise in order to innovate. Supporting faculty in their long-term career plans results in discernible benefits:

- Faculty members create a professional narrative that explains the ways in which their divergent and varied interests signal an innovative career path.
- Faculty members identify aspects of their graduate training that apply to a broad array of professional possibilities in and outside the academy.
- Faculty members see their long-term career trajectory as one that enables them to be change agents—that is, disciplinary innovators who influence the direction not only of students but also of disciplines, organizations, and institutions.
- Faculty members are encouraged to learn new technologies and other skills applicable to a range of career paths.

Long-term career development for faculty members involves attention both to scholarship and to pedagogy. We believe a number of strategies identified by Laura F. Huenneke and her colleagues (2017) as ways to increase research capacity of faculty members throughout their careers apply equally well to long-term career development. We have found that four of the strategies they described are especially fruitful: ongoing attention to professional development and career planning, involving faculty in programmatic and institutional culture and operations, facilitating opportunities through partnerships or collaborations with other units, and providing early support for their workable innovations (particularly in teaching, scholarship, service, and professional development).

Development of an Exploratory Mindset

We encourage exploration, experimentation, and creativity in thinking about teaching, scholarship, service, community and professional involvement, and professional development. We emphasize bravery, taking risks, and a growth mindset. Following from D. E. Berlyne's classic studies (1950, 1960, 1966), we consider an exploratory mindset as based on curiosity and the search for novelty. An exploratory mindset aligns strongly with a rhetorical understanding of innovation as leveraging novel means of persuasion within complex situations—like the classroom or the academic job market. Supporting faculty in developing an exploratory mindset results in discernible benefits:

- Faculty members work in a culture of exploration, experimentation, and creativity that acknowledges and supports innovation (e.g., awards for innovative pedagogy, newsletter stories about innovative research or service).
- Faculty members work in a culture that provides a safety net for experimentation.
- Faculty members are provided with peer and programmatic examples on which to build.
- Faculty members are provided resources for experimentation (e.g., professional encouragement, maker spaces, and networking suggestions).

An exploratory mindset encourages educators to update their competencies and strategies as well as re-think their pedagogical paradigms so they can envision policy changes, design transnational frameworks, tackle digital revolutions, and engage in self-assessment—all as part of their transformative powers (Caena & Redecker, 2019). In our program, an exploratory mindset forms the basis for pedagogical innovation as faculty experiment with new modes of teaching and learning.

Teaching and Learning for Students

As our professional development mission equips and supports faculty for innovation, our student-centered teaching and learning mission provides the concepts, tools, and practices that instantiate innovation in the classroom and elsewhere. Scholars investigating innovation are clear that diversity, intrinsic motivation, and autonomy "almost invariably impact innovation in a positive manner" (Tierney & Lanford, 2016, p. 23). We encourage these factors so faculty can innovate through rhetoric, process, multimodality, collaboration, and assessment—the core concepts of our teaching and learning mission.

The following extended example about the Ivan Allen Digital Archive highlights ways in which professional development opportunities as well as teaching and learning opportunities work together to spark innovation. Our institution's cultural history features social justice, environmental sustainability, and urban development appropriate for our work with this archive.

- As part of a university grant, some of our faculty helped digitize the Ivan Allen Digital Archive, a collection of mayoral documents from the period Ivan Allen Jr. was mayor of the city of Atlanta (1962 to 1970), an extraordinarily contentious period of racial tension and urban development in the United States.
- As part of another university grant, some of our faculty used the Ivan Allen Digital Archive to develop innovative assignments for undergraduate classes, applicable to many course themes (from social justice to urban transit, from architecture to sports, from unemployment to white flight) and available to all our program's faculty.
- Our students can work with documents in the Ivan Allen Digital Archive (including letters, memos, city committee reports, photos, and newspaper articles), creating multimodal projects about issues related to social justice, environmental sustainability, and urban development. Students use archival materials from the city where they are studying to connect them to current issues.
- The students' innovative archival projects have been featured at public exhibitions on campus; photos and videos of their work have been featured on our program's website and on social media.
- As part of their scholarly productivity, our faculty use their pedagogical experiences to prepare and deliver professional conference presentations and to write articles for publication. The presentations and publications draw attention to historical documents with current sociopolitical concerns.

As this extended example shows, we are committed to professional practices that enable faculty to approach teaching and learning—addressed in our program via rhetoric, process, multimodality, collaboration, and assessment—in innovative ways.

Rhetoric

All writing programs need a strong, explicit theoretical grounding; it is part of what makes the knowledge generalizable to other situations and part of what differentiates the art and the craft of writing. For us, that grounding is rhetoric. Students attend to available means of persuasion, discovering unexpected perspectives as rhetorical elements—context, audience, purpose, role, argument, organization, design, visuals, and conventions of language and images—work together in new ways. Asking questions about new means of persuasion provokes critical thinking, helping students to gain an understanding of social and cultural texts and contexts in ways that support productive communication and interaction.

In our program, the classic elements of rhetoric form the structure that enables innovative thinking, melding traditional logic and appeals with new technologies. Students use rhetoric as the basis for their work, creating *logos* in arguments, attending to *ethos* in the context, adapting *pathos* for the audience. In doing so, they select and organize persuasive evidence, consider the affordances of various modes and media, develop an appealing and usable design, and respect professional conventions and style in language and images. Students in a first-year multimodal composition class, for example, used rhetoric to analyze the expectations of an audience wanting to learn about the passage of the 1964 Civil Rights Act. As part of their work, students visited the nearby Center for Civil and Human Rights to gain further contextual background. They then designed a website to explain the historical event, mining a historical archive for pithy examples (in this case, the Ivan Allen Digital Archive).

Process

Programmatically, we expect faculty to help students broaden their understanding of ways to draft and revise their artifacts, since learning productive processes is as important as creating products. Students learn that processes for communication—for example, creating, planning, drafting, designing, rehearsing, revising, presenting, publishing, and disseminating—are recursive, not linear. They also learn that processes are seldom isolated and individual but, instead, take place in environments that involve interacting with others (both in face-to-face and in virtual interaction) at every stage of the process. We also encourage a nuanced perspective about reflection, an essential part of our process(es). Because reflection is not an intuitive behavior for students, our faculty teach it, model it, provide a rationale for it, and build in time to do it regularly (expecting students to reflect on one or more aspects of each assignment during and immediately following the assignment), not just at the end of the course.

In our program, process provides the *how to* of innovation, emphasizing translation, transformation, and transference. These three processes receive special attention because they are critical in academic, community, and workplace communication (Burnett & Cooper, 2019):

- *Translation.* Adapting information for new audiences (e.g., translating an argument from an academic essay to a public blog post, translating information in a medical journal to a mass market newspaper, and translating an aerospace engineering drawing for non-experts watching CNN)
- *Transformation.* Changing and reshaping ideas or information—for example, changing *genre* (print to web), *scale* (thumbnail to poster), *medium* (live demo to video), *mode* (written to oral), *scope* (instruction manual to tip sheet), or *color palette* (four-color to black and white)
- *Transference.* Applying communication strategies from one context or situation to another (e.g., transferring appropriate use of metaphors from academic to workplace situations)

Multimodality

Multimodality informs all the examples of innovative student, faculty, and programmatic work we have discussed in this chapter. We call our curriculum WOVEN, for communication in written, oral, visual, electronic, and nonverbal modes. The WOVEN components work synergistically, though faculty may choose to emphasize one mode over another from project to project. The emphasis depends on the rhetorical situation and the affordances of the modes and media. We support the principles presented in "On Multimodality: A Manifesto" (Wysocki et al., 2019). We agree that while students need to develop technological competence, they also need to analyze media critically, recognize the "inseparable natures of thinking, acting, making, and doing" (Wysocki et al., 2019, p. 19), and respond to the affordances of technologies. Our multimodal emphasis enables students to see that what they are learning in their classrooms connects to the world around them. They are encouraged to innovate—to translate, transform, and transfer—in ways that respond to their developing needs to present arguments to public audiences so that their work has power and influence.

Collaboration

While the initial purpose of a collaboration may not be innovative, collaboration increases the likelihood of generating multiple means of addressing a problem—and the multiple means increase the likelihood that the resulting solution will be innovative. This attention to innovation matters because "organizations are increasingly relying upon the diverse perspectives and expertise of teams to produce novel, innovative solutions" (Thayer et al., 2018, p. 363). The same benefits occur in the classroom, giving students alternative ways to approach assignments. So what do students need to learn about collaboration in order for it to serve as a means to innovation? Researchers note that strong collaborations require both cognitive and social strategies (Thayer et al., 2018). Even though our students have been engaged in collaborative work since kindergarten, few of them have specific skills and strategies for engaging in productive collaboration, so WCP faculty explicitly teach collaborative strategies. These strategies include attention to factors such as cultural context, models in interaction, leadership, team demographics, equitable contributions, time management, and conflict resolution.

Assessment and Evaluation

What we have elsewhere called our "ecology of assessment" (Burnett et al., 2014) includes five categories of formative assessment and summative evaluation: self-assessment, peer assessment, instructor assessment, client assessment, and, finally, programmatic assessment (based on analysis of reflective portfolios). Particularly important is that we use the same criteria, regardless of the categories of assessment or evaluation. For example, the questions faculty teach students to ask themselves about argument or design in their self-assessments are much the same questions the program asks of itself.

How do we use the same categories and criteria for all formative assessment and summative evaluation? Two specific tools are particularly important: First, our *programmatic feedback chart* provides rhetorical categories and assessment criteria unconnected to grades and, instead, connected to feedback. The categories and criteria in the feedback chart are used for all kinds of formative assessment and summative evaluation, modifiable for particular assignments and projects. Second, our programmatic assessment is based on faculty review of selected *cumulative reflective portfolios*, applying the same criteria used for all formative assessment and summative evaluation across the program. Assessment provides students, faculty, and the program with ways to identify processes and concepts that are successful and those that need work. In addition, assessment helps faculty, students, and the program identify processes and concepts that are innovative—that is, what is new to their own processes and products, what risks they have taken, and what strategies they can carry with them.

Conclusion

This case study explains ways our faculty are empowered and supported to use rhetoric, process, multimodality, collaboration, and assessment to create new learning experiences for and with students—innovative courses and assignments, like those discussed in our introduction. Moreover, as the interplay between our program's professional development and teaching/learning missions evolves, faculty model (and students practice) innovation as a constant, critical adaptation to the changing world. The result of this interplay is a culture in which instances of innovation are common, for faculty, students, and the program administrators alike. As with all case studies, though, the generalizability of the culture we describe is, at best, limited. The innovations in our program at Georgia Tech have emerged for a number of reasons tied to our local situation, not the least of which is that our institution is consistently funded, its culture rewards and expects innovation, the leadership strongly advocates for faculty development and curricular rigor and innovation, and our program has been lucky in finding allies in administration who believe in creating stable, secure positions for non-tenure-track and contingent faculty. At the same time, we believe that our argument about the need for writing programs to innovate *is* generalizable and *is* something for all writing program administrators to consider.

What innovation looks like—the problems and opportunities it responds to, the experiments it inspires, and the solutions it prompts—is necessarily different in different situations. We do not argue that a multimodal curriculum or robust technological infrastructure, for example, is required for innovation in writing programs or that innovation is defined by its disruptive nature. Ultimately, innovation in writing and communication programs occurs one step at a time over the long term. As programs consider ways to encourage innovation, they should consider the following questions:

Goals

- What are the goals of the program? How do these goals serve the educational mission of the program and institution? How do these goals advance teaching and learning for students and/or professional development for faculty?
- How does innovation fit into the goals of the program? How does innovation serve the educational mission of the program and institution?

How does innovation advance teaching and learning for students and/or professional development for faculty?
- In what ways can the program lay the foundations for innovation, through curriculum development, improved working conditions, new faculty development efforts, or otherwise?

Arguments

- What are the available means of persuasion?
- How can available resources, technologies, concepts, or allies be integrated?
- What relationships can be built? What arguments can be made?

Collaboration

- How can collaboration with faculty, staff, and students be used in considering and implementing innovation?
- How can collaboration be used with community partners?

Support

- What small steps can be taken, even in the absence of funding? For example, what changes can be made related to programmatic processes, access to information, or the involvement of various stakeholders?
- How can the program strengthen the agency of faculty to explore, experiment, and create? How can the program provide methods of formative evaluation and feedback that support faculty innovation?

More broadly, we hope that writing program, writing-across-the-curriculum, and English-across-the-curriculum administrators and faculty see the urgent necessity for innovating within programs, institutions, and disciplines. We hope to innovate not for the sake of originality, disruption, or public relations. We hope to innovate not just to adapt to the various "new normals," from the precarization of working conditions to the ubiquity of social media. Ultimately, we hope to innovate in order to prompt and support ways of thinking and communicating about the world as it changes and, hopefully, to help it change for the better.

References

Becker, S. A., Brown, M., Dahlstrom, E., Davis, A., DePaul, K., Diaz, V. & Pomerantz, J. (2018). *NMC horizon report: 2018 higher education edition*. EDUCAUSE.

Berlyne, D. E. (1950). Novelty and curiosity as determinants of exploratory behaviour. *Journal of Psychology, 41*(1), 68–80.

Berlyne, D. E. (1960). *Conflict, arousal, and curiosity.* McGraw-Hill.
Berlyne, D. E. (1966). Curiosity and exploration. *Science, 153*(3731), 25–33.
Boden, K. E. (2019). Pedagogical innovation among university faculty. *Creative Education, 10*, 848–861.
Bridgeford, T., Kitalong, K. & Selfe, D. (2004). Introduction. In T. Bridgeford, K. Kitalong & D. Selfe (Eds.), *Innovative approaches to teaching technical communication* (pp. 1–11). Utah State University Press.
Burnett, R. E. & Cooper, L. A. (2019). The synergy of modes and media in academic and professional communication. In A. Braziller, E. Kleinfeld & Georgia Tech Writing and Communication Program (Eds.), *WOVENText: Georgia Tech's Bedford book of genres* (pp. 52–91). Bedford/St. Martin's.
Burnett, R. E., Frazee, A., Hanggi, K. & Madden, A. (2014). A programmatic ecology of assessment: Using a common rubric to evaluate multimodal processes and artifacts. *Computers & Composition, 31*, 53–66.
Caena, F. & Redecker, C. (2019). Aligning teacher competence frameworks to 21st century challenges: The case for the European Digital Competence Framework for Educators. *European Journal of Education: Research, Development, and Policy, 54*(3), 356–369.
Collins, H. & Evans, R. (2007). *Rethinking expertise.* University of Chicago Press.
Huenneke, L. F., Stearns, D. M., Martinez, J. D. & Laurila, K. (2017). Key strategies for building research capacity of university faculty members. *Innovative Higher Education, 42*(5–6), 421–435.
Lewis, J., Aydin, A. & Powell, N. (2013). *March (Book 1).* Top Shelf Productions.
Thayer, A. L., Petruzzelli, A. & McClurg, C. E. (2018). Addressing the paradox of the team innovation process: A review and practical consideration. *American Psychologist, 73*(4), 363–375.
Tierney, W. G. & Lanford, M. (2016). Conceptualizing innovation in higher education. In M. B. Paulsen (Ed.), *Higher education: Handbook of theory and research.* Springer International.
van Lankveld, T., Schoonenboom, J., Volman, M., Croiset, G. & Beishuizen, J. (2017). Developing a teacher identity in the university context: A systematic review of the literature. *Higher Education Research & Development, 36*(2), 325–342.
Wardle, E. & Scott, J. B. (2015). Defining and developing expertise in a writing and rhetoric department. *WPA: Writing Program Administration, 39*(1), 72–93.
Wysocki, R., Udelson, J., Ray, C. E., Newman, J. S. B., Matravers, L. S., Kumari, A., Gordon, L. M. P., Scott, K. L., Day, M., Baumann, M., Alvarez, S. P. & DeVoss, D. N. (2019). On multimodality: A manifesto. In S. Khadka & J. C. Lee (Eds.), *Bridging the multimodal gap: From theory to practice* (pp. 17–29). Utah State University Press.

17 The (Transnational) Past, Present, and Future of the Writing Across the Curriculum Movement

Martha A. Townsend
UNIVERSITY OF MISSOURI

Terry Myers Zawacki
GEORGE MASON UNIVERSITY

Mike Palmquist
COLORADO STATE UNIVERSITY

Julia Chen
THE HONG KONG POLYTECHNIC UNIVERSITY

Abstract: This chapter summarizes and expands on the closing plenary session delivered at the 2018 English Across the Curriculum conference hosted by The Hong Kong Polytechnic University. The first three authors, all second-generation U.S. writing-across-the-curriculum (WAC) scholars, all with transnational WAC experience, discussed the WAC movement's history, current status, and potential futures. The fourth author, a pioneer in the English-across-the-curriculum (EAC) movement, closed the session by sharing her perspective on the past, present, and hoped-for future of EAC in Hong Kong and the wider Asia-Pacific region.

Keywords: writing and learning, writing across the curriculum, English across the curriculum, language across the curriculum, educational reform movements

In December 2015, The Hong Kong Polytechnic University hosted the first international English Across the Curriculum (EAC) conference, attracting more than 300 participants from 13 different countries, along with those from the Chinese mainland and Macau. The inter-institutional conference organizing team, comprising members from four institutions, planned the conference with two major goals in mind: one, to announce that writing across

DOI: https://doi.org/10.37514/INT-B.2021.1220.2.17   311 the curriculum (WAC) is once again emerging in Hong Kong, this time in an adaptation that focuses on both writing and speaking in English across the curriculum in Hong Kong's complicated trilingual context; and, two, to provide a platform for transnational exchange of scholarship, research, and professional development in writing in English in linguistically complex academic environments.

That second goal, along with the successful implementation of many of the planned EAC initiatives, provided a strong motivation for the second international EAC conference, a celebration that included more than one hundred concurrent sessions and plenary talks by Content Language Integrated Learning (CLIL) and WAC scholars from Hong Kong, Europe, Asia, Australia, New Zealand, Africa, the Middle East, and the United States. As presenters in the closing plenary session, the three U.S. authors—all second-generation leaders in the WAC movement and all with transnational WAC experience—offered a three-part roundtable discussion to introduce the history, current status, and potential future of WAC to our largely Asian Pacific audience whom we assumed would have only limited knowledge of the significant role WAC has played as an educational reform movement in the US. In turn, to honor Julia Chen's pioneering EAC role in Hong Kong, we invited her to close the session by sharing her perspective on the future of EAC, including her goal of developing an Asia-Pacific EAC network. This chapter captures the essence of our remarks while also offering an overview of some of the WAC literature and current changes, expansions, and innovations.[1]

Given the somewhat parallel paths that WAC and CLIL have followed and the ways in which these are being joined and adapted in the EAC initiative, we begin our chapter, as we did our plenary panel, by tracing the foundations of WAC from its international roots in the United Kingdom's language across the curriculum movement in the 1960s and 1970s to the principles and programmatic features that strongly structure U.S. WAC today. We continue with a discussion of the recent formation of the Association for Writing Across the Curriculum, a key step in the transformation of the WAC movement from one supported by an informal network of scholars/practitioners into a movement supported by a formal organization with bylaws, committees, and affiliated groups. We follow this discussion with a look into the future and the changes reflected in the growth of international writing-focused conferences and publications, expanded opportunities for sharing scholarly work, and new

---

[1]   In the plenary session, Townsend spoke first, Zawacki second, Palmquist third, and Chen fourth. In this chapter, we write with a collective voice, rather than as individual panelists.

types of research initiatives and networks. We conclude with a discussion of the past, present, and hoped-for future of the EAC movement.

WAC: Foundations, Principles, Practices

Sometimes it is helpful to begin defining a concept by saying what it is *not*. WAC is not about correct spelling, grammar, punctuation, or the many other generic skills of written prose. Nor is it a stand-alone writing course. While WAC practitioners avow those aspects of written communication as necessary, they fall far short of creating "good writing."

WAC is a pedagogical reform movement dating from the late 1960s and early 1970s, with roots in both the US and the UK. Historian of writing across the curriculum David Russell (2002) describes WAC as "the most widespread and sustained reform movement in cross-curricular writing instruction" in U.S. higher education (p. 272). WAC's origins as a distinct movement in the US can be traced to a three-week seminar in 1966 held at Dartmouth College in Hanover, New Hampshire. Forty-seven participants from the US, UK, and Canada, along with 21 consultants from selected non-English disciplines (psychology, theater, speech, education, and linguistics) assembled with the express goal of defining English and outlining the ways it might best be taught. Christiane Donahue (2016), reflecting on the 50th anniversary of the conference, observed:

> *Very quickly, the actual discussions focused in on language and writing; most of the concrete results of the Seminar were about teaching and learning writing, in relation to language, technology, and speech.* (original italics)

A similar movement in the UK, known as language across the curriculum (LAC), had developed earlier in the decade and would prove to be a key contributor to the U.S. WAC movement. A bottom-up movement led by classroom teachers, LAC focused largely on helping students in K–12 settings address the challenges associated with discrimination based on dialect. Among the many scholars whose work shaped and was shaped by the LAC movement, University of London education professor James Britton and his colleagues, working and researching primarily at the pre-collegiate level, produced groundbreaking texts that strongly influenced their U.S. counterparts. Britton's *Language and Learning* (1970) has become a classic exploration of how children use language to shape their individual visions of the world. Similarly, *The Development of Writing Abilities (11–18)* (Britton et al., 1975) strongly influenced—and continues to influence—work in WAC. Although both U.K. and U.S. scholars were reading the same theorists—Bruner, Jakobson, Luria, Moffett, Piaget, Polanyi, Vygotsky—regrettably, LAC was not as sustained in the UK as was WAC in the US.

Despite the diminished presence of LAC in the UK, European and Hong Kong audiences will recognize the somewhat parallel movement of Content and Language Integrated Learning (CLIL), a pedagogy primarily employed in Europe and Hong Kong at the primary and secondary levels with some rather limited application at the tertiary level. As the participants of the 2018 EAC conference surely noticed, all of these language and literacy-related movements—LAC, WAC, CLIL, EAC—share influences and similarities, if not direct overlays (or levels of educational application) in their principles and practices. Indeed, one of the many benefits of the EAC conferences is the bringing together of our respective language and literacy academic professionals, so that we may be reminded of our shared work and explore ways to further our transnational interests on behalf of our students. On a related note, the U.S. WAC movement's biennial conference declared itself in 2006 to be the International Writing Across the Curriculum conference, and members actively seek to share research and pedagogies with transnational colleagues (Townsend, 2019).

In its most general sense, WAC refers to the idea that writing should be an integral part of the learning process throughout a student's education, not merely in required writing courses, but across the entire curriculum (International Network, 2014). As John Bean, one of WAC's early and influential advocates, points out, the relationship between writing and *thinking* is central to the WAC movement (1996, 2011). Specifically, Bean (and many others, including the authors of this chapter) directs our attention to how writing can be used to enhance students' thinking about the content of the material they are studying in ways that deepen their learning.

Inasmuch as most scholars/practitioners understand WAC to be focused on student *learning* first and foremost (as opposed to the reductive nuts and bolts definition of writing one might draw from what WAC is *not*), the following four principles comprise the backbone of writing used in courses throughout the curriculum (International Network, 2014):

1. Writing as rhetorical. Analyzing *purpose* and *audience* is essential to composing or understanding any text.
2. Writing as a process. High-stakes writing (writing that will be graded, for example) involves a complex process of idea formation, drafting, reader feedback, revision, and understanding the rhetorical situation.

3. Writing as a mode of learning. Writing *about* a subject helps the student *learn* about that subject (for example, see Emig, 1977).
4. Learning to write. To be effective, writers must learn to adapt to a variety of rhetorical situations, audiences, and purposes.

WAC Program Variety and Operation

Because WAC is an educational reform movement, as opposed to a prescriptive agenda for teaching students "how to write," WAC takes different shapes at different institutions. As Christopher Thaiss (2001) has observed, "WAC theorists and program leaders have encouraged almost unlimited variety in terms of what counts as writing and how it is evaluated" (p. 308). Moreover, many WAC programs feature a concomitant emphasis on reading and speaking. Some U.S. institutions house WAC programming in their departments of English, in stand-alone programs, and still others within teaching and learning centers or in writing centers, with a variety of administrative structures. There is no unilaterally agreed upon place for situating WAC in higher education (Smith, 1988). In fact, to be effective, all WAC initiatives must be determined by each institution's exigencies: size, institutional type, institutional mission, administrative configuration, fiscal resources, linguistic characteristics of student population, current and former writing requirements, and so on (Townsend, 2012).

Some institutions have a curricular WAC requirement that all students must satisfy in order to graduate, in which case, specific writing-based courses may be flagged as meeting this requirement. For example, it is common to list courses as satisfying a "writing-intensive" or "writing-enriched curriculum" requirement. A wide variety of procedures exist whereby institutions certify and monitor their WAC courses. The more effective programs ensure that WAC program policy and oversight reside under the purview of faculty and that ample resources are available to support faculty in the disciplines who offer WAC courses (Townsend, 2001).

Some institutions differentiate between WAC and WID, or writing in the disciplines (Carter, 2012). In general, WID refers to how professionals in disciplines conduct and teach their writing practices. WID courses typically address questions about how members of particular disciplines, such as history and microbiology, write and think, and how best to help their students learn to write within that discipline. Writing assignments in WID courses often interrogate a discipline's principal genres and explore the typical audiences for the discipline's writing. While we question the distinction between WAC and WID, which equates WAC with writing to learn and WID with writing to communicate within disciplines, it is not an uncommon distinction. It seems more useful to view writing to learn and writing in the disciplines as two ends of a spectrum of WAC emphases (see Palmquist, this collection).

Characteristics of WAC Programs and Courses

For those institutions where WAC programs flag individual courses, examples of writing-intensive course characteristics include low student-to-teacher ratios, restricting teaching to experienced faculty (as opposed to graduate teaching assistants), requiring a stated number of pages or papers with opportunities for revision, distributing writing across the semester, and factoring writing into the course grade (Farris & Smith, 1992).

Instead of flagging individual courses, some institutions flag entire academic units, as is done at the University of Minnesota, where the writing-enriched curriculum (WEC) model was developed (Flash, 2016). In this model, academic units (typically a department) work in partnership with a WEC team of writing specialists to design undergraduate "writing plans" (https://wec.umn.edu/about) that apply to that department's student population. Faculty members in the WEC unit, in consultation with WEC specialists, create, implement, and assess the writing plan they deem appropriate for their students.

Whatever approach they adopt, virtually all WAC programs espouse *critical thinking* as a primary goal for student writing. Each program defines that concept in its own disciplinary framework, often with an emphasis on active as opposed to passive learning. Nearly all WAC programs also share some combination of the following characteristics in the writing students are assigned:

- explicit directions, often designating a specific audience, purpose, and genre;
- a focus on process in addition to product (the steps that must be taken to complete the assignment);
- shorter, more frequent (low stakes) writing, instead of longer, less frequent (high stakes) term papers;
- peer review or other collaboration with students;
- revision based on teacher- and peer-feedback to achieve an improved outcome; and
- explicit grading criteria.

Often a distinction is made between "writing-to-learn" and "learning-to-write," with the former using writing as a means of achieving better understanding of course content, while the latter implies stronger attention to achieving control over a discipline's standards and may employ more stringent grading.

Sustaining WAC Programs

WAC programs are notoriously vulnerable. The WAC literature is replete with cautionary stories of programs disappearing. As Russell (1991) has noted, "The WAC movement, unlike most of its predecessors, attempts to reform pedagogy more than curriculum. . . . [O]n an *institutional* basis, WAC exists in a structure that fundamentally resists it" (p. 295). Some of the obstacles WAC programs face include inadequate support from top-level administrators, assigning leadership to an unprepared director, not providing programmatic support, lack of alignment among elements of a program, failing to ensure *faculty* oversight of the curriculum and program, not undergoing periodic review of courses and the program, and expecting that "improvement" in student writing can be "proven" through pre- and post-testing in flagged courses (Townsend, 2012).

By far the most problematic difficulty in maintaining robust WAC programs, however, is lack of reward for teaching. WAC courses, of whatever type, inevitably require faculty to rethink their teaching methods. Faculty need time to reflect, and plan, and learn new methods, especially if they are steeped in traditional pedagogies. Shifting from faculty-centered to student-centered instruction requires patience, willingness, and support from knowledgeable colleagues and peers, which can detract from research and publication. Russell (1991), again, observes,

> If WAC is to become more than a marginal activity, criteria for promotion, tenure or merit pay must measure and value the kinds of teaching and learning that WAC promotes, though this, like measuring and valuing writing itself, is far more difficult than looking only at more easily quantifiable "outcomes." (p. 296)

The question, of course, is why institutions—and faculty who understand the complications associated with creating and sustaining a WAC program—would invest in WAC. The answer lies in the contributions it makes to student learning while students are taking courses and to their ability to think critically and write effectively once they have graduated. Indeed, in the US, WAC (under the label "writing-intensive courses") has been identified as one of the original high-impact educational practices (Kuh, 2008). Additionally, Andy

Frazee and Rebecca Burnett (this volume) show how WAC supports student and faculty innovation and connection to the community and workplace.

WAC: Current Status

It is evident from even a quick browse of the WAC Clearinghouse website (https://wac.colostate.edu) that ample scholarship and resources are available on building and sustaining WAC programs at the local level in the US. At the national level, however, it seems that only scant attention has been paid to how many new programs are being developed and how many languish or die. The most recent information we have on the numbers of U.S. WAC programs comes from the "International WAC/WID Mapping Project," with numbers based on a survey undertaken from 2006–2008 (http://mappingproject.ucdavis.edu). While numbers on the growth and demise of programs are notoriously hard to track, as the Mapping Project and earlier efforts (Miraglia & McLeod, 1997) have indicated, we know, as Townsend (2012) explains in "WAC Program Vulnerability and What to Do About It," that WAC programs are most vulnerable when funding is cut, if they are not deeply informed by WAC principles, and/or if they are not led by writing-knowledgeable faculty committed to the hard work of program building and strategic in adapting to the local context.

This point leads us to a series of pressing questions that serve as the focus of this section: How can WAC, EAC, CLIL or other such educational reform movements be sustained as fields and as legitimate foci of our scholarship? How can we best introduce and mentor new academics into the field? In what ways might we prepare new and experienced writing studies academics to lead and sustain our increasingly demanding programs? To answer these questions, at least in part, we briefly trace the early difficulty in defining WAC in the US as a practice and a program given the enormous variability of programs across institutions, as we noted earlier. We then contrast this with recent efforts to establish a more formal structure and articulation of what the field comprises—efforts that led to the formation of the Association for Writing Across the Curriculum (AWAC) in 2018.

The Past Leading to the Present

In 1981, following the first decade of WAC initiatives in the US, Christopher Thaiss established what was then called the National Network of Writing Across the Curriculum Programs. In 2004, it would change its name to the International Network of WAC Programs (or INWAC). From the outset, the Network's Board of Consultants (https://wac.colostate.edu/network/), of which Townsend and Zawacki were early members, acted in many ways as the voice of WAC, taking on the role of encouraging, advising, and supporting newcomers and sharing best practices. As Zawacki and Paul Rogers (2001) made clear, however, the Network's role was "not to make policy statements or to define 'WAC,' but rather to help others interested in starting programs . . . that would mirror local institutional cultures and exigencies rather than conform to larger national trends" (p. 6). The most visible manifestations of WAC at the national level were—and continue to be—the International Writing Across the Curriculum (IWAC) conference and the WAC Clearinghouse, a publishing collaborative that has provided a platform for representing the component parts of WAC as a field. The Clearinghouse has become a rich set of scholarly and pedagogical resources for scholars, program administrators, teachers, and writers across disciplines who share an interest in using writing to support teaching and learning.

As WAC programs proliferated and younger scholars joined the Network, they argued for a stronger, more coherent organization, beginning with the need to articulate shared principles and practices to guide the field as well as to establish WAC as a recognized field of study with an increasingly large body of scholarship, including scholarship on program building and administration, often not valued in tenure and promotion decisions.[2]

In 2014, a small ad hoc group of Network members drafted the Statement of WAC Principles and Practices (https://wac.colostate.edu/principles/) as a first step in describing and codifying what we value as a WAC community. The statement included sections addressing the leadership of successful and sustainable WAC programs, a suggested timeline for program development, principles and practices for WAC pedagogy and program assessment, and a rich list of resources and references. The formal articulation of these principles and practices can be seen as the starting point for the steps that were subsequently undertaken, beginning in 2016 at the IWAC conference, to form the Association for Writing Across the Curriculum (AWAC) (https://www.wacassociation.org), which was formally launched in fall 2018.

In the relatively short time since it was established, AWAC's executive board and committees have accomplished a number of goals, including formalizing connections among various WAC and writing-related organizations, promoting the publication of scholarly work on WAC, and providing mentorship opportunities. Among the key organizations with which AWAC has established relationships is the WAC Graduate Organization (WAC-GO)

---

2   For evidence of the need for the latter, see, for example, Townsend (2020).

(https://wac.colostate.edu/go/), which has played an important role in bringing new scholars into the WAC field. WAC-GO was created by graduate students in 2016, well before AWAC was formed, and it continues to be led by graduate students who are advised by a board of experienced WAC professionals. Now under the umbrella of AWAC, WAC-GO sends out a newsletter, offers research support and scholarships to attend the IWAC conference and the WAC summer institute (described below), and, perhaps most importantly, offers a cross-institutional mentoring project that pairs graduate students who do not have access to WAC mentors or courses at their own institutions with established WAC scholars elsewhere for one-to-one mentorship (https://wac.colostate.edu/go/cross-institutional-mentoring-project).

Like WAC-GO, planning for a WAC summer institute (WAC SI) was motivated by a need to mentor and advise those new to WAC, especially new and prospective program leaders. A secondary motivation was the desire to support more experienced directors who faced new challenges or who wished to expand, update, or revitalize their programs. Online registration for the June 2019 institute at the University of Denver opened in early fall; the 30 available slots filled within minutes, with more than double that number on the waiting list, a clear sign of the need for the systematic and sustained support offered by the three-day format. Developed around the theme of building sustainable, high-impact programs, the institute included lectures, workshops, individual consultations, and small group meetings intended to provide opportunities for mentoring and networking. While initially planned as a biennial event, the competition for slots and the subsequent high level of satisfaction expressed by the participants in the first WAC SI laid the groundwork for an annual institute with one in summer 2020 and another in 2021.

Expanding WAC's Focus to Graduate Writing

While U.S. WAC has traditionally focused on undergraduate student writers and writing across the disciplines, alarm in recent years about attrition and extended time to degree in graduate programs has led to questions about the role writing might play in students' choosing to leave their programs or to delay completion, particularly at the doctoral level. This increased attention to writing has resulted, in turn, in calls for more support for graduate student writers and more research on their specific needs (see Rogers et al., 2016, for example). The Consortium on Graduate Communication (CGC) (https://www.gradconsortium.org) was founded in 2014 by WAC, writing center, and Teaching English to Speakers of Other Languages TESOL scholars-practitioners to provide for systematic conversations around best practices for working with English first- and second-language graduate students on written, oral, and multimodal communication.

The CGC holds an annual summer symposium and offers a website that provides curricular resources, scholarly work and research reports, and models for graduate communication courses, retreats, writing groups, and tutorial practices. In addition, and in line with the organization's research and resource goals, a growing body of scholarship on writers at the graduate level has been developed, with publications focused on the cross-curricular writing support needs of domestic and international second-language (L2) English graduate students across the disciplines (see, for example, Simpson et al., 2016 and Lawrence & Zawacki, 2019). As a final point on WAC in the present, we note WAC's increasing engagement with the field of English L2 writing (see, for example, Zawacki & Cox, 2014) as well as its turn to and support for international cross-disciplinary writing research and program building.

WAC: Futures

The 2019–20 academic year marked the 50th year of the first known WAC faculty seminar, a year-long project led by Barbara Walvoord at Central College in Iowa. While that offers an opportunity for celebration for what Russell (2002) has characterized as one of the most enduring movements in U.S. higher education, it also serves as a point for reflection and critique. The theme of the IWAC 2020 conference—*Celebrating Successes, Recognizing Challenges, Inviting Critique and Innovation*—embraces this opportunity, as does this chapter. Looking forward, we anticipate that work will take place on several fronts. The formation of AWAC will lead to increased professional recognition for the field as well as a growth in research, scholarship, and publication opportunities, accompanied by awards and other forms of distinction. We also expect to see growth in the size and diversity of the WAC community. And, certainly, we see continued internationalization of WAC as a movement and a field, affording increased opportunities for sharing scholarly work and collaborating on global research initiatives.

Growth in Scholarship, Professional Recognition, Diversity

We expect to see growth in the amount of research and other forms of scholarship published on WAC and related areas. This growth will be based in part on the growing internationalization of the field. It will also be based on a broadened understanding of the kind of scholarly work that is relevant to

WAC. We are seeing, for example, increased interest in connections between WAC and writing analytics (and the larger field of learning analytics). This connection reflects both the field's longstanding interests in assessment and pedagogical improvements. It also reflects increasing methodological capacity for exploring key questions, such as improvements in the ease of use of corpus analytic tools, tools associated with content analysis, and tools associated with the analysis of big data.

This growth will also be fueled by a growing interest in connections among WAC, second-language learning, and generation 1.5 (immigrant) populations. Similarly, we will also likely see growing scholarly attention to social and labor issues, such as the increasing reliance on contingent faculty labor in the US and the increasing oversight of higher education by government. These areas of interest promise to expand the amount of work taking place under the broader umbrella of WAC.

To accommodate this expanded work—and, to some extent, to encourage it—we expect to see increased opportunities for sharing scholarly work. In the past few years, we have seen the founding of new academic journals, including *Double Helix* (https://wac.colostate.edu/double-helix) and *The Journal of Writing Analytics* (https://wac.colostate.edu/jwa). In response to the large number of high-quality submissions for special issues published by the journal *Across the Disciplines* (https://wac.colostate.edu/atd), the journal editors founded the Across the Disciplines Books series, which recently published its third volume. We are also seeing new conferences that focus on WAC and the related areas of critical thinking and speaking, including Quinnipiac University's biennial Critical Thinking and Writing conference and the EAC conference series. Finally, we are seeing strong representation of scholarship on WAC and related areas in existing national and international conferences, such as the Conference on College Composition and Communication (CCCC), the Council of Writing Program Administrators National Conference, the Writing Research Across Borders conference, the conference of the Special Interest Group of the European Association for Research on Learning and Instruction, and the conference of the European Association for the Teaching of Academic Writing.

In fall 2019, the WAC Clearinghouse editorial board and the AWAC executive committee approved the development of awards to honor professional contributions, both nationally and internationally, to the WAC community. These awards will include recognition for scholarly publication, advancement of WAC principles and practices, excellence in WAC program design and administration, and distinguished contributions to the field. The awards will also serve as a further means of establishing WAC as a distinctive area of study and are likely to increase the number of scholars who see work in WAC and related fields as an area within which to make their disciplinary home.

Recently, editorial board members of the WAC Clearinghouse proposed a new research center, the Bazerman-McLeod Institute for Writing Studies, to serve as a platform for collaborative research across institutions, with a focus on research that involves multiple types of institutions, both nationally and internationally. We expect this kind of initiative to provide a useful foundation for the development of new research instruments and methods relevant to WAC and related fields. The goal of the institute is to support long-term studies in which scholars contribute differentially over time and in consideration of the local conditions within which they work. As a collaboration between the WAC Clearinghouse and AWAC, it is hoped that the institute will serve as a model for similar efforts in the larger field of writing studies in the US and potentially in other countries.

An Increasingly Internationalized Movement

It will not surprise those who attended the Second International Conference on English Across the Curriculum in Hong Kong that we see significant growth ahead in WAC, CAC, ECAC, English for Academic Purposes (EAP), English Across the Curriculum (EAC), Content and Language Integrated Learning (CLIL), and related areas. While WAC is a movement that was launched in the US, it is becoming increasingly internationalized. This is reflected in recent surveys of WAC and writing programs, such as that conducted by Thaiss et al. (2012), as well as the increasing internationalization of our professional organizations as noted above. Since its founding in 1997, the membership of the WAC Clearinghouse publishing collaborative has grown steadily more reflective of the internationalization of the field. More than 30 members of the Clearinghouse editorial board, publications review board, and series editors are from outside the US. This number is larger if international members of the editorial boards of the journals supported by the Clearinghouse are counted.

The internationalization of the field is also reflected in the book proposals and article submissions received by the book series and journals supported by the Clearinghouse. To give just one example, the book series *International Exchanges on the Study of Writing* (https://wac.colostate.edu/books/international/) has been expanded to include a Latin American section featuring books in Spanish, Portuguese, and English. The series will likely expand further in the coming years to include other international sections and publications in languages other than English.

And, finally, one need only look at the growing number of international attendees at the past several IWAC conferences, including a prominent cohort of scholars from Hong Kong who have been attending to learn from and about U.S. WAC at the same time that we are learning from them about the many ways that the principles and practices of writing across the curriculum are being adapted to fit the trilingual contexts of Hong Kong higher education.

English Across the Curriculum: Foundations, Current Status, Futures

Our introduction noted that one goal of the 2015 English Across the Curriculum conference was to announce that WAC was "once again" developing in Hong Kong, so this section begins with a brief description of two past efforts, one in the mid-2000s and another in the early 2010s, to introduce WAC in two universities in Hong Kong. Neither of these efforts was sustained; the first was discontinued after the leader retired (see Braine & McNaught, 2007) and the second when the leader stepped down when project funding ended (Cheng et al., 2014).

Given subsequent educational developments, however, it was clear that a cross-curricular WAC-like program was needed in Hong Kong. As Chen (2019) points out, two top-down education policies—a shift in schools from English medium of instruction (EMI) to Chinese medium of instruction and a lengthening of the undergraduate curriculum from three to four years—that were introduced after the 1997 return of Hong Kong sovereignty to China meant that students needed English writing and speaking support more than ever for their academic pursuits in Hong Kong's EMI universities.

This need could not be met by stand-alone English courses alone because universities are able to allocate curricular space for only two, or perhaps three, credit-bearing undergraduate English courses. Often these courses are included in the freshman and sophomore years, and they tend to be generic academic English (EGAP) in nature. Research shows, however, that it is doubtful students are able to remember and transfer their generic academic English writing and speaking knowledge when preparing for their discipline course assignments—unless there has been reinforcement in their disciplinary courses (Yiu, 2014). The lack of reinforcement and the obvious gap in development of students' discipline-specific writing and speaking skills are reflected in an employer survey on the performance of first-degree graduates. The 2016 employer survey results at one university show that on a 1–5 scale (from disagree to agree), employers ranked the importance of "language proficiency" and "analytical and problem-solving abilities" at 4.17 and 4.19, whereas they ranked graduates' performance in these two areas at 3.75 and 3.57 respectively (Chen et al., forthcoming).

In 2013, an opportunity arose for developing a writing and speaking across disciplines initiative when the Hong Kong University Grants Committee offered start-up funds for the establishment of communities of practice (CoPs). The Hong Kong Polytechnic University (PolyU) established a CoP on enhancing students' English abilities outside of regular EGAP and English for specific purposes (ESP) courses, and called it "English Across the Curriculum" (EAC) to differentiate it from Chinese, the other official language in Hong Kong, and to avoid misunderstanding that the initiative focused on writing skills only. Without teaching assistants and having limited teaching release for staff, the EAC team worked with faculty to develop learning modules that aligned with three of the four WAC principles stated earlier in this chapter: understanding the purpose and audience of the writing/speaking, learning about the discipline through writing about it, and adapting writing to the rhetorical situation and purpose. In view of the relatively low proficiency level of students (a substantial number of students scored around 6 on the International English Language Testing System (IELTS), or equivalent), the EAC learning packages provide grammar handouts, focusing on topics such as the correct use of tense and reporting verbs in the literature review section of an academic text.

In 2014, this one-university CoP grew to a four-university project team that received a government grant of one million Hong Kong dollars to promote EAC staff development. In 2017, the EAC "scheme," as it is referred to in Hong Kong, expanded to a five-university project team that received 7.8 million dollars of government funding to develop (for the digital native generation) a discipline-specific mobile app on capstone/final-year project writing and speaking for presentations.

Despite the progress of the last half-decade, EAC faces numerous challenges in Hong Kong as elsewhere. In an effort to institutionalize and sustain EAC, a 2016 discussion paper proposed establishing an EAC committee comprising academic staff and English language teachers at PolyU, the lead university on the collaborative EAC projects. The University Senate, however, rejected the proposal due to concern that EAC would become a compulsory element in the undergraduate curriculum. Another significant sustainability challenge involves financial resources, just as is the case for WAC in the US. Currently, the EAC team is funded by two government project grants, running out in 2020 and 2021 respectively, and PolyU has yet to commit any financial support to the initiative. To convince university management that EAC is worthy of support, EAC leaders have demonstrated: (1) EAC's economic scalability by extending its reach to different faculties (colleges), departments, and staff; (2) EAC's impact on student assessment performance; and (3) substantial interest in the EAC/WAC/CLIL movements from around the world, as evidenced by international participation in the 2015 and 2018 EAC conferences. A third conference is planned for May 2021. EAC's demonstrated scalability, impact, and international interest indicate its potential for becoming a niche area for PolyU, and, in turn, for other Hong Kong tertiary institutions.

Looking Forward

Within the broader framework that WAC and EAC as pedagogical innovations provide, we have seen a great deal of diversity in pedagogical methods and program design. We expect this to continue. The writing enriched curriculum approach that is becoming widely used in the US (Flash, 2016), for example, has strong application to writing instruction in international settings. We have also seen WAC implemented in ways that take advantage of other high impact practices found in U.S. universities, such as learning communities, service learning, and undergraduate research (Kuh, 2008).

Indications of the willingness of international scholars and writing program leaders to adopt leading practices in their local contexts have already been seen in the institutions profiled in Thaiss and colleagues' (2012) landmark study, *Writing Programs Worldwide*. It seems highly likely that the use of these practices will lead to new approaches that will, in turn, enrich the larger WAC, EAC, and CLIL communities. Indeed, the English Across the Curriculum initiatives that gave rise to the second EAC conference are an excellent example of the innovation and scholarship we can expect to emerge as we apply approaches used in one context to the pedagogical needs of students and teachers in another.

With the power of innovation in mind—and the recognition that the members of the WAC, EAC, and CLIL communities will continue to seek new ways to improve and support the teaching of writing and speaking—we expect that institutional leaders will continue to see writing as increasingly central to the success of teaching and learning in higher education.

References

Bean, J. C. (1996). *Engaging ideas: The professor's guide to integrating writing, critical thinking, and active learning in the classroom.* Jossey-Bass.

Bean, J. C. (2011). *Engaging ideas: The professor's guide to integrating writing, critical thinking, and active learning in the classroom* (2nd. ed.). Jossey-Bass.

Braine, G. & McNaught, C. (2007). Adaptation of the "writing across curriculum" model to the Hong Kong context. In J. Liu (Ed.), *English language leaching in China: New approaches, perspectives and standards* (pp. 311–328). Continuum International Publishing.

Britton, J. (1970). *Language and learning.* Boynton/Cook.

Britton, J., Burgess, T., Martin, N. McLeod, A. & Rosen, H. (1975). *The development of writing abilities (11–18).* Macmillan.

Carter, M. (2012). Ways of knowing, doing, and writing in the disciplines. In T. M. Zawacki & P. M. Rogers (Eds.), *Writing across the curriculum: A critical sourcebook* (pp. 212–238). Bedford/St. Martin's.

Chen, J. (2019). EAP in Hong Kong. In H. Terauchi, J. Noguchi & A. Tajino (Eds.), *Towards a new paradigm for English language teaching: English for specific purposes perspectives in Asia and beyond* (pp. 115–126). Routledge.

Chen, J., Chan, C. & Ng, A. (2020). English across the curriculum: Four journeys of synergy across disciplines and universities. In B. Spolsky & H. Lee (Eds.), *Localizing global English: Asian perspectives and practices* (pp. 84–103). Routledge.

Cheng, W., Chan, M., Chiu, H., Kwok, A., Lam, K. H., Lam, K. M. K., Lim, G. & Wright, R. (2014). *Enhancing students' professional competence and generic qualities through writing in English across the curriculum.* The Hong Kong Polytechnic University.

Donahue, C. (2016). *A brief history (from the U.S. perspective).* 50th anniversary Dartmouth institute and conference. https://dartmouthwritinginstitute.wordpress.com/1966-seminar/a-brief-history/.

Emig, J. (1977). Writing as a mode of learning. *College Composition and Communication, 28*(2), 122–128. https://www.jstor.org/stable/356095.

Farris, C. & Smith, R. (2000). Writing-intensive courses: Tools for curricular change. In S. McLeod & M. Soven (Eds.), *Writing across the curriculum: A guide to developing programs* (pp. 52–62). The WAC Clearinghouse. https://wac.colostate.edu/books/landmarks/mcleod-soven/ (Original work published 1992 by Sage Publications)

Flash, P. (2016). From apprised to revised: Faculty in the disciplines change what they never knew they knew. In K. B. Yancey (Ed.), *A rhetoric of reflection* (pp. 227–249). Utah State University Press.

International Network of Writing Across the Curriculum Programs. (2014). *Statement of WAC principles and practices.* https://wac.colostate.edu/principles/.

Kuh, G. D. (2008). *High-impact educational practices: What they are, who has access to them, and why they matter.* Association of American Colleges & Universities.

Lawrence, S. & Zawacki, T. M. (Eds.) (2019). *Re/Writing the center: Approaches to supporting graduate students in the writing center.* Utah State University Press.

Miriglia, E. & McLeod, S. H. (1997). Whither WAC? Interpreting the stories/histories of enduring WAC programs. *Writing Program Administration, 20*(3), 46–65. http://associationdatabase.co/archives/20n3/20n3miraglia.pdf.

Rogers, P., Zawacki, T. M. & Baker, S. E. (2016). Uncovering challenges and pedagogical complications in dissertation writing and supervisory practices: Findings from a multi-method study of doctoral students and advisers. In S. Simpson, N. Caplan, M. Cox & T. Phillips (Eds.), *Supporting graduate student writers: Research, curriculum, and program design* (pp. 52–77). University of Michigan Press. https://doi.org/10.3998/mpub.8772400.

Russell, D. R. (1991). *Writing in the academic disciplines, 1870–1990: A curricular history*. Southern Illinois University Press.

Russell, D. R. (2002). *Writing in the academic disciplines: A curricular history*. Southern Illinois University Press.

Simpson, S., Caplan, N., Cox, M. & Phillips, T. (Eds.). (2016). *Supporting graduate student writers: Research, curriculum, and program design*. University of Michigan Press. https://doi.org/10.3998/mpub.8772400.

Smith, L. Z. (1988). Why English departments should "house" writing across the curriculum. *College English, 50*(4), 390–395. https://www.jstor.org/stable/377611.

Thaiss, C. (2001). Theory in WAC: Where have we been? Where are we going? In S. H. McLeod, E. Miraglia, M. Soven & C. Thaiss (Eds.), *WAC for the new millennium: Strategies for continuing WAC programs* (pp. 299–325). National Council of Teachers of English. https://wac.colostate.edu/books/landmarks/millennium/.

Thaiss, C., Bräuer, G., Carlino, P., Ganobcsik-Williams, L. & Sinha, A. (Eds.). (2012). *Writing programs worldwide: Profiles of academic writing in many places*. The WAC Clearinghouse; Parlor Press. https://doi.org/10.37514/PER-B.2012.0346.

Townsend, M. A. (2001). Writing intensive courses and WAC. In S. H. McLeod, E. Miraglia, M. Soven & C. Thaiss (Eds.), *WAC for the new millennium: Strategies for continuing WAC programs* (pp. 233–257). National Council of Teachers of English. https://wac.colostate.edu/books/landmarks/millennium/.

Townsend, M. A. (2012). WAC program vulnerability and what to do about it: An update and brief bibliographic essay. In T. M. Zawacki & P. M. Rogers (Eds.), *Writing across the curriculum: A critical sourcebook* (pp. 543–556). Bedford/St. Martin's.

Townsend, M. A. (2019). A personal history of WAC and IWAC conferences, 1991–2020. In L. E. Bartlett, S. L. Tarabochia, A. R. Olinger & M. J. Marshall (Eds.), *Diverse approaches to teaching, learning, and writing across the curriculum: IWAC at 25* (pp. 21–32). The WAC Clearinghouse; University Press of Colorado. https://doi.org/10.37514/PER-B.2020.0360.

Townsend, M. A. (2020). Valuing new approaches for tenure and promotion for WAC WPAs: Advice for higher education and the writing studies community. In N. Elliot & A. Horning (Eds.), *Talking back: Senior scholars deliberate the past, present, and future of writing studies* (pp. 326–336 and, with M. Rifenburg, 339–342). Utah State University Press.

Yiu, R. (2014). A case study of Hong Kong undergraduates undertaking their disciplinary writing tasks and its implications for EAP pedagogy. In X. Deng & R. Seow (Eds.), *The 4th CELC Symposium Proceedings* (pp.107–115). National University of Singapore. http://www.nus.edu.sg/celc/symposium/4thsymposium.html.

Zawacki, T. M. & Cox, M. (Eds.). (2014). *WAC and second language writers: Research towards linguistically and culturally inclusive programs and practices.* The WAC Clearinghouse; Parlor Press. https://doi.org/10.37514/PER-B.2014.0551.

Zawacki, T. M. & Rogers, P. M. (Eds.). (2001). Introduction. In T. M. Zawacki & P. M. Rogers (Eds.), *Writing across the curriculum: A critical sourcebook* (pp. 1–10). Bedford/St. Martin's.

§ Contributors

Chris M. Anson is Distinguished University Professor, Alumni Association Distinguished Graduate Professor, and Director of the Campus Writing and Speaking Program at North Carolina State University. He has published eighteen books and 140 articles and book chapters focusing on writing and has spoken widely in the United States and thirty-four other countries. His professional summary is available at www.ansonica.net.

John Blake is Associate Professor in the Center for Language Research at the University of Aizu. His current research focus is on creating practical online tools that help people learn English. His research draws on corpus linguistics to analyze texts and computational linguistics to create rule-based and probabilistic-based pattern-searching tools or pipelines.

Rebecca E. Burnett is Professor Emerita in Georgia Institute of Technology's School of Literature, Media, and Communication as well as Professor Emerita in the Department of English, Iowa State University. She has recently taught technical communication, technical narrative, photography, and visual rhetoric. Her research and consulting continue, focusing on assessment, digital pedagogy, multimodality, leadership, risk communication, technical communication, and visual rhetoric.

Yammy Chak is a Teaching Fellow in the Department of Applied Social Sciences, The Hong Kong Polytechnic University. She has taught courses in leadership, service learning, social work practice, and counseling. Yammy also has extensive front-line experience in individual counseling as well as training of teachers and social workers. Her research interests include positive youth development, training, and program evaluation.

Christy Chan is Senior Tutor in the English Language Centre, City University of Hong Kong. She manages English language support services and self-funded projects. Her funded research focuses on entrepreneurship education, mobile English support, and professional development for university English teachers in Hong Kong. Her professional interests include English across the curriculum, quality assurance in higher education, and discourse analysis.

Julia Chen is Director of the Educational Development Centre at The Hong Kong Polytechnic University and courtesy Associate Professor at the Department of English. She was the chief organizer of the 2015 and 2018 international conferences on English Across the Curriculum (EAC) and the principal investigator of several large-scale government-funded inter-university projects on EAC and using technology for academic literacy development.

Contributors

Sinh Ngoc Dang is a Lecturer of English and Economics at the Faculty of Linguistics and Cultures of English-speaking Countries, University of Languages and International Studies—Vietnam National University in Hanoi, Vietnam, where he teaches English, macroeconomics, American economic history, and international economics.

Felicia Fang is a Language Instructor in the English Language Centre, The Hong Kong Polytechnic University. Felicia has taught academic and professional English courses. Her research interests lie in the areas of language assessment and EAC. Felicia has collaborated with researchers in language assessment and EAC projects.

Andy Frazee is a Senior Academic Professional in Georgia Institute of Technology's School of Literature, Media, and Communication, where he serves as the Associate Director of the Writing and Communication Program. He teaches multimodal composition, postmodern literature, and business communication. He is an award-winning poet who also does research about assessment, digital pedagogy, multimodality, contingent labor practices, and professional development.

Jeffrey Hugh Gamble is Assistant Professor in the Department of Foreign Languages at National Chiayi University in Taiwan. His teaching emphasizes English teaching pre-service teacher training and in-service English teacher training. His research interests include educational policy for language learning, innovative instructional design, adaptive language instruction, and the role of technology in teaching and learning.

Maria Pia Gomez-Laich is Assistant Teaching Professor of English at Carnegie Mellon University in Qatar, where she teaches courses in academic reading and writing and digital humanities. She earned her Ph.D. in Second Language Acquisition from Carnegie Mellon University. Her research areas include academic writing development, second language writing, task-based language teaching and learning, and intercultural pragmatics. Her research has appeared in international journals such as *The Modern Language Journal*, *Linguistics and Education*, and *Foreign Language Annals*.

Ivan Wang-Hei Ho is Assistant Professor at The Hong Kong Polytechnic University. He received his Ph.D. degree in electrical and electronic engineering from Imperial College London. He teaches courses and supervises research projects on mobile application development, the internet of things, wireless communications, and vehicular networking. He is an associate editor for *IEEE Access* and *Transactions on Circuits and Systems II*.

William R. Holden III is Professor in the Global Communication Center at the Japan Advanced Institute of Science and Technology. He is a research writing specialist with many years of experience. His professional interests include English for Specific Purposes (ESP), learning strategies, and vocabulary acquisition. His personal interests include music, film, literature, and travel.

Jay Jordan is Associate Professor of Writing & Rhetoric Studies at the University of Utah. His research focuses on intersections between second-language (L2) writing and rhetoric and composition. He is finishing a longitudinal, transnational writing across the curriculum (WAC) research project and is working on a monograph exploring histories and theories of rhetoric in multilingual composition. He teaches courses in composition theory and pedagogy, stylistics, and English as an international language.

Hannah Y. Lai is an English-language Instructor at The Hong Kong Polytechnic University, where she teaches Workplace English for Business Students and Workplace English for Social Science Students. Her research interests include English across the curriculum, STEM vocabulary, internationalization, and persuasive communication.

Grace Yuk Wan Lim is a Teaching Fellow in the English Language Centre of The Hong Kong Polytechnic University. She received her Ph.D. and M.A. in Applied Linguistics from universities in Hong Kong and UK. She is working on university-funded projects featuring the use of English in discipline subjects. Her research interests include English across the curriculum, discourse analysis, and mobile teaching.

Linda Lin, who holds a Ph.D. in applied linguistics, works as program coordinator for the English Language Centre of the Hong Kong Polytechnic University. She has extensive experience in L2 language learning and teaching, L2 language writing analysis, and pedagogic development. Her research interests include academic writing, vocabulary learning, corpus analysis, and applications of concordancing in teaching and learning.

Vicky Man is a Senior Lecturer in the Language Centre, Hong Kong Baptist University (HKBU) and a recipient of the General Education Teaching Award. She is the coordinator of several credit-bearing courses including HKBU's core academic English course and a general education course on World Englishes. Her professional interests include writing and speaking across the curriculum, pronunciation pedagogy, and World Englishes.

Michael Maune is a Lecturer for the Writing, Rhetoric, and Professional Communication (WRAP) program at MIT. His teaching focus is on developing writing pedagogy applications informed by rhetoric and applied linguistics. He earned his Ph.D. in English Education from Purdue University. His research interests include applied corpus linguistics for writing instruction, experimental and applied functional linguistics, and analysis of knowledge practices through Legitimation Code Theory.

Contributors

Thomas D. Mitchell is Associate Teaching Professor of English at Carnegie Mellon University in Qatar, where he teaches courses in academic reading and writing, style, professional writing, and discourse studies. He earned his Ph.D. in Rhetoric from Carnegie Mellon University. His research has appeared in international journals such as the *Journal of Second Language Writing*, *Linguistics and Education*, *Journal of English for Academic Purposes*, and *English for Specific Purposes*.

Bruce Morrison is the former Director of the English Language Centre of The Hong Kong Polytechnic University. His research focus has primarily been on the tertiary English language experience for non-native speaking students, the language-related challenges they face, and the various strategies they employ to overcome these. His other research interests include independent language learning and the impact of computer-mediated teaching for tertiary English language teachers. He has published journal articles, book chapters, and edited books in these and other areas.

Matthew Overstreet is Assistant Professor of English at Khalifa University in Abu Dhabi. He has a Ph.D. from the University of Pittsburgh and has taught writing and writing pedagogy all over the world. His research interests include writing and cognitive development and the various ways technology shapes how we think, write, read, and relate.

Mike Palmquist is Professor of English and University Distinguished Teaching Scholar at Colorado State University. His scholarly interests include writing across the curriculum, the effects of computer and network technologies on writing instruction, and new approaches to scholarly publishing. He is the founding editor and publisher of the WAC Clearinghouse (https://wac.colostate.edu).

King-Wah Pang is Associate Professor in Logistics and Operations Management in the Department of Logistics and Maritime Studies, The Hong Kong Polytechnic University. His research interests range from logistics to operations management and optimization. His research work appears in highly-ranked international journals including *IIE Transactions*, *Transportation Research Part B*, and *International Journal of Production Economics*.

Silvia Pessoa is Associate Teaching Professor of English at Carnegie Mellon University in Qatar, where she teaches courses in academic reading and writing and sociolinguistics. She earned her Ph.D. in Second Language Acquisition from Carnegie Mellon University. Her research areas include academic writing development, second language writing, sociolinguistics, bilingualism, and immigration studies. Her research has been funded by the Qatar National Research Fund and has appeared in international journals such as the *Journal of Second Language Writing*, *Linguistics and Education*, and the *Journal of English for Academic Purposes*.

Barbara WY Siu is a Senior Teaching Fellow in the Department of Civil and Environmental Engineering at The Hong Kong Polytechnic University. Her primary areas of teaching are transportation engineering, planning, operations, and management. Dr Siu is actively engaged in language enhancement initiatives for technical students. Dr Siu received the Faculty Award for Outstanding Performance in Teaching in 2017.

Alan Thompson has a Ph.D. from the University of Toronto and teaches at the Faculty of Foreign Languages, Gifu Shotoku Gakuen University, in central Japan. His main research interests are in language contact and change, theatre, translation, and English language teaching.

Martha (Marty) Townsend is Professor Emerita of English at the University of Missouri, where she directed the *Conference on College Composition and Communication* (CCCC)'s award-winning Campus Writing Program. Her publications have played a central role in the conceptualization and development of WAC programs in the United States and abroad. She is a former literacy consultant to The Ford Foundation and consults widely on WAC program implementation, development, and assessment. She holds a B.A. (1983) and M.A. (1985) in English from the University of Utah and a Ph.D. (1991) in English from Arizona State University.

Elza Tsang is a Senior Lecturer at the Centre for Language Education, Hong Kong University of Science and Technology. She is overseeing the development of the English curriculum for senior science students, including English courses for teaching capstone report/final-year project writing and science communication. She has been involved in several funded projects related to English teaching. Her academic interests include English for Academic Purposes (EAP) genres, eLearning, and reflective teaching.

Alan Urmston is an independent educator and consultant based in Hong Kong. He was formerly Assistant Professor in the English Language Centre at The Hong Kong Polytechnic University, where he was coordinator of assessments and Director of the English Language Testing Unit. He teaches courses at the masters and doctorate level, consults for universities, government and commercial assessment providers, and is actively involved in the field of language assessment as a researcher, reviewer, editor, and developer. In one of his current projects, he is helping the Polytechnic University to assist colleagues across the university in the development of rubrics for the assessment of writing and speaking across the disciplines.

Ai Chun Yen is Associate Professor in the Department of English, National Dong Hwa University, Taiwan. Her research concerns theories of constructivist learning environments and technological applications. Her recent specific research interests are bilingual education, strategic teaching and learning, and literature in language education.

Terry Myers Zawacki, Emerita Professor at George Mason University, has published books and articles on writing in the disciplines, writing centers, writing assessment, and the internationalization of writing studies. Her books include *Engaged Writers and Dynamic Disciplines*, *WAC: A Critical Sourcebook*, and *WAC and Second Language Writers*. She is an editor of the WAC Clearinghouse series *International Exchanges on the Study of Writing* and serves on a number of editorial boards in the US and transnationally.

www.ingramcontent.com/pod-product-compliance
Lightning Source LLC
Chambersburg PA
CBHW071229070526
44583CB00017B/2104